EASTERN ILLINOIS PANTHERS FOOTBALL

BY DAN VERDUN

NIU PRESS/DEKALB IL

Library of Congress Cataloging-in-Publication Data
Verdun, Dan.
Eastern Illinois Panthers football / Dan Verdun.
    pages cm
Summary: "A sports history of the EIU football team from its origins in 1899 to the present.
Features discussion of players, coaches, and local sports reporters who all figure into the his-
tory of Panther football, as well as EIU football alumni who have achieved national recogni-
tion"-- Provided by publisher.
 Includes bibliographical references.
 ISBN 978-0-87580-483-5 (hardback) -- ISBN (invalid) 978-1-60909-164-4 (electronic)
1. Eastern Illinois University--Football--History. 2. Eastern Illinois Panthers (Football team)-
-History. I. Title.
GV958.E38V47 2014
796.332'630977372--dc23
 2014016273

Dedicated to all those who wore the blue and gray over the years

CONTENTS

THE EARLY YEARS
(1899–World War II)

Illinois Intercollegiate
Athletic Conference;
Charles Lantz; Early
Panthers in the Pros

POSTWAR ERA
(late 1940s–1950s)

Maynard "Pat" O'Brien;
1948 Corn Bowl Team;
Lou Stivers; Ray Fisher

THE 1960s

Rod Butler; Dick
Portee, Ted Schmitz;
Gene Vidoni; Roger
Haberer

THE 1970s

Mike Heimerdinger;
Nate Anderson; Willie
White; Ted Petersen

THE DARRELL MUDRA ERA

(1978–1982)

Darrell Mudra; The Miracle of '78; 1980: The
One That Got Away;
Mike Shanahan; John
Teerlinck; Chris "Poke"
Cobb; James Warring;
Alonzo Lee; Pete Catan;
Scott McGhee; Randy
Melvin; Jeff Gossett;
Donald Pittman; Jeff
Christensen; Kevin
Staple; Jerry Wright;
Robert Williams

EASTERN AIRLINES ERA

(1983–1986)

Al Molde; Sean Payton,
Roy Banks; Evan Arapostathis;
John Jurkovic

APPENDIX

Best Early-Era Teams
(1899–1971); Best All-
Division-II Team (1972–
1980); Best All-I-AA/FCS
Team (1981–2013);
Panthers in the Pros;
Retired Panthers Jerseys

BIBLIOGRAPHY AND RESOURCES

FOREWORD

by Bob Spoo, Eastern Illinois Head Coach, 1987–2011

In 1961, ABC's *Wide World of Sports* premiered with Jim McKay as host. It began with the words "The Thrill of Victory and the Agony of Defeat." Those words aptly describe what athletics—and coaching, in particular—are all about.

Coincidentally, 1961 is the same year I began my coaching career, one that would last for 50 years. I look back now with a great sense of pride and fulfillment in having been a member of that wonderful and honorable profession. For me, it certainly was a labor of love, and my life has been profoundly enriched because of the experiences and relationships I've had throughout the years.

Since this book is about Eastern Illinois Panther football, I would just like to encapsulate my coaching tenure there by reflecting on the words James Mason spoke in the movie *The Verdict*: "You don't get paid to do your best, you get paid to win."

Despite the fact that the first two years and the last two years were losing seasons, let the record show that in total, we won more games than we lost during those 25 years. The thrill of victory surpassed the agony of defeat. I am most proud, however, even more than the wins and losses, of the realization and satisfaction that we did things the right way. We conducted our program honorably, with integrity, with respect for the game and with dignity. If most of the young student-athletes who came through our programs were better men when they left than when they came to us, and I believe that to be true, then we accomplished our mission as coaches. We may have lost some battles but we won the war.

William Arthur Ward once said, "Feeling gratitude and not expressing it, is like wrapping a present and not giving it." In my 25 years at Eastern Illinois University I've had much to be grateful for and many wonderful people to thank for enriching my life and that of my family. It has been an honor and privilege to have served as head football coach at this outstanding University. It has been my life and my home and will continue to be for, hopefully, many years to come.

If I was able to accomplish anything of significance during my tenure, and that is for others to judge, then it could not have been done without the support and dedication of those I so greatly admire and respect.

I thank all the coaches who over the years have displayed their loyalty and commitment to me and to the players they coached with great enthusiasm, respect and professionalism. I am proud of my association with them. They represent the best in the coaching profession, and it has been my good fortune to have worked side by side with those honorable men.

Without players there would not be athletics, teams, games, or any of the other pageantry we associate with sports. Without the players there would be no memories to hold dear, and it is because of the players that I am able to reflect back over the past 25 years with a sense of gratification and fondness. I thank you all for your many sacrifices and perseverance in good times and bad, and for your loyalty to me, my coaches and Eastern Illinois University. You make us all proud. What you have accomplished over the years has been an inspiration to me, and I will forever be grateful.

Thanks must also go out to the Charleston community for their support of all EIU athletics, their acceptance of our program and their generosity through the years. I hope that in some small way we were able to repay your kindness by the manner in which our team represented itself on the field.

To those people behind the scenes—administration, faculty, student body, strength and conditioning staff, athletic trainers, equipment managers and secretaries—you have my heartfelt thanks. We would never have been successful without your contributions.

It's been said that "behind every successful man is a great woman of patience, encouragement and dedication." I would amend that to say behind every successful man are great women of patience, encouragement, dedication and unconditional love. I'm referring to the two most important people in my life, my wife Susan and my daughter Katie, for without their devotion and support, anything I've accomplished in my coaching career would not have been possible. I owe them everything and will never cease to be grateful.

Finally, I would like to thank Dan Verdun, the author of this book, for inviting me to share in a small way in its writing. I appreciate and respect Dan's efforts and countless hours, days, weeks and months in its preparation. Congratulations Dan, and thanks for telling the story of Eastern Illinois Panther football.

ACKNOWLEDGMENTS

As with any project of this magnitude, there are so many people to thank. First and foremost would be my wife, Nancy—also an Eastern Illinois alum—and our children, Tommy and Lauren. I love them all very much.

This book would also not have been possible without the unfailing support and love of my parents, the late Paul and Marion Verdun. Like most of us, I never realized just how much my parents did for me as I was growing up until I began raising my own kids. Thanks also to my brothers Jeff, Don and Ron. Like most siblings, we had our disagreements growing up, but my brothers have always been there for me. May this always be the case.

This book would not have been possible without the efforts of a multitude of people at NIU Press. Starting with the initial contact by Sara Hoerdeman, I have been blessed to have worked with such wonderful and talented people throughout the project. I wish to publicly thank Sara, Shaun Allshouse, Susan Bean, Barbara Berg, Cara Carlson, Kenton Clymer, Mark Heineke, Linda Manning, Eric Miller, Alex Schwartz and Pat Yenerich. The book you are holding in your hands exists because of all the hard work and dedication from the folks at NIU Press.

A huge thank-you goes out to my close friend Barry Bottino for all his advice, guidance and support along the way. Barry and I often talk and text Panther football (and many other less important topics). We're already looking at next season's schedule and following the recruiting rumors.

Other friends have contributed in more ways than they will ever know. So, thanks to Bob Bima, Tom Doran, John Eisenhour, Mike Fitzgerald, Al Lagattolla, Tim Lee, Jeff Long, John Ralph, Mike Ramey, John Ryan, Bryan Sibert and Jeff Strohm.

Huge thanks go out to each former coach, athlete, administrator, band director, dance team, or cheer team sponsor who took time out of their lives to open their memory banks and share them with a complete stranger. This book is about you. Hopefully you will enjoy reading it as much as I did writing it.

Special thanks go to former Eastern head coach Bob Spoo, not just for writing the book's foreword but for being a wonderful human being. Talk to anyone who has ever met Coach Spoo and you will be blown away by what a remarkable man he is.

Much of the information in this book comes from each of the universities involved. Behind all the media reports that hit newspapers, magazines, radio and TV shows, along with Internet sites are the people of the sports information offices and media relations departments. Thus, I would like to thank Dave Kidwell and Rich Moser of Eastern. I have had the pleasure of working for and knowing Dave since my days as an Eastern student. Nearly everyone I talked with for this book had nothing but good things to say about Dave. Rich and his staff went out of their way not only to track down information for me, but also to gather nearly all the photos you find in this book. Thanks also to Sandy King of the athletic department for sending along additional photos. I likewise thank Dr. William Perry, Bob Martin, Steve Rich and Barbara Burke. Valuable contributions were also made by Clint Bays, Coordinator of Equipment & Stadium Facilities.

In addition, Todd Kober and Mike Williams of Illinois State, Mike Korcek of Northern, Jason Clay of Southern and Patrick Osterman of Western were invaluable with their help. The same is true for Sharon Lipe and Kathy Jones at SIU, and Amy Spelman and Susan Welsh at WIU. Additional assistance was provided by

Eric Burdick of Cal Poly, Brad Gust of Auburn University, Marcia Illes of Purdue University, Annabelle Myers of North Carolina State, Heath Nielsen of Baylor University, Michael Oriard of Oregon State University and Kyle Schwartz of the Ohio Valley Conference. Kyle put me in touch with two longtime observers of OVC athletics, Neal Bradley and Karl Park. Thanks to all three for giving me an OVC lens on Eastern Illinois football.

In addition, a huge thank-you goes out to Dr. Robert Hillman, the University Archivist at Eastern. I would also like to thank Jim Erdmann for his time, knowledge, insight and memorabilia. Dorothy Ewald provided me with the photo of Rod Butler, while Susan Stucco, Frank Pitol's daughter, sent the reunion picture of the 1948 Corn Bowl team. Nancy Marlow and Lisa Dallas supplied information about the Pink Panthers. Kudos as well to Clyde Frankie of Casey-Westfield High School for his assistance.

Valuable information was available through Student Publications at EIU. The files of *The Daily Eastern News* and numerous editions of *The Warbler* brought facts and photos.

From the NFL ranks, my thanks go out to Jack Brennan and Danny Katz of the Bengals; Craig Kelley, Vernon Cheek and Pam Humphrey of the Colts; Rich Dalrymple and Jancy Briles of the Cowboys; Rob Crane of the Packers; Michael Pehanich and Maureen Wade of the Redskins; Greg Bensel, Justin Marione, Michael C. Herbert and Sondra Egan of the Saints; and Robbie Bohren of the Titans. From the CFL came help from Jamie Cartmell (BC Lions), Kelly Forsberg (Sask. Rough Riders), and Mitch Bayless and Melenee Mehler (Calgary Stampeders).

Invaluable assistance came from members of the media. Thus, I'd like to recognize and thank the following for their help: Rick Armstrong of the *Aurora Beacon-News*; Bob Asmussen of the *Champaign News-Gazette*; Jack Ashmore and Mike Bradd, the outstanding broadcast voices of Eastern athletics; Taylor Bell, formerly of the *Chicago Sun-Times*; Ken Woodell, iconic voice of Eastern athletics; Terri Cox of the *Journal Gazette & Times-Courier*; Josh Buchanan of *Phil Steele's Football*; Brandon Lawrence of *The Sports Network*; Michael MacCambridge, author of so many landmark sports histories; Dan McCool, formerly of the *Des Moines Register*; Murray McCormick of the *Regina Leader-Post*; Bob McGinn of the *Milwaukee Journal Sentinel*; Brian Nielsen of the *Journal Gazette & Times-Courier*; Anthony Nunez of Houston-gamblers.com; Randy Reinhardt of the *Bloomington Pantagragh*; Carl Walworth of the *Journal Gazette & Times-Courier*; Bill Williamson of espn.com; and Len Ziehm of the *Sun-Times*.

Fellow sports historians and writers Bob Gill, Scott Lacey and John Maxymuk offered not only support and information but also key pieces of advice and insight.

Finally, I would like to thank the Dudes of Douglas Hall. In the fall of 1983 I left home a naïve, awkward 18-year-old and found a new home in Room 205 of Douglas Hall. I cherish the memories of those years at Eastern where I grew in too many ways to even begin to tally. So, thanks to Tom and Alex, Jim and Dale, Timmy Dingo and Brian, Bryan and Eric, Alex and Hutch, Bill and Big Eric, Stine and Ken, Jeff, Tim and Mark, Wayne, Robert and Roy, John and Sean (yes, that Sean). But, most of all to Brad, my roommate for four years, I can honestly say, we never fought about anything. We've both come a long way from watching sports and MTV (back when it actually played music videos) on a 12-inch black-and-white TV in our dorm room when we should have been studying more...

EASTERN ILLINOIS UNIVERSITY PANTHERS

INSTITUTION FOUNDED—1895

LOCATION—Charleston

FOOTBALL ESTABLISHED—1899

COLORS—Blue, Gray & White

WEBSITE—http://www.eiupanthers.com/

MASCOT—Billy Panther

NATIONAL CHAMPIONSHIP—1978 (NCAA Division II)

HIGHEST NFL DRAFT PICK—Jimmy Garoppolo, New England Patriots, 2nd round, 62nd overall pick

FAMOUS ALUMNI IN OTHER SPORTS—Tim Bogar (baseball), John Craft (Olympic track & field), Kevin Duckworth (basketball), Matt Hughes (ultimate fighting), Schellas Hyndman (soccer), Marty Pattin (baseball), Kevin Seitzer (baseball), Dan Steele (2002 Winter Olympic Bobsled Bronze Medalist)

FAMOUS NONSPORT ALUMNI—Joan Allen (actress), Jim Edgar (former Illinois governor), Joan Embrey (animal and environmental advocate), Ted Gregory (Pulitzer Prize–winning reporter), Burl Ives (actor, writer, folksinger), Ben Livingston (actor and screenwriter), John Malkovich (actor), Charlotte Martin (singer-songwriter), Luke Ryan (motion pictures), Larry Smith (former CNN anchor), Jerry Van Dyke (actor)

INTRODUCTION

Eastern Illinois University was founded in 1895. Just four years later, the school fielded its first football team. Over the course of the next 11 decades, the Panthers have captured the hearts and imaginations of a loyal following of students, alums and fans across the state, region and nation.

Eastern football has grabbed headlines thanks to the likes of Mike Shanahan, Sean Payton, Brad Childress, Tony Romo, and Jimmy Garoppolo.

Yet, there are plenty of other spellbinding stories such as these:

- How Darrell Mudra turned a one-win team into national champions in one year

- The World War II veteran–laden team that captured a conference title and a berth in the Corn Bowl

- The former quarterback and Chicago Bears' draft pick who became a Big Ten Conference umpire and worked the Orange Bowl

- The wide receiver who later became a world champion in kickboxing & boxing

- The two-time All-American who battled depression and substance abuse

- The record-setting running back diagnosed with Lou Gehrig's disease

- The lightning-fast wide receiver from Florida who was voted the Outstanding Rookie in the Canadian Football League

- The former Academic All-American offensive lineman who is now an orthopedic surgeon

- The all-conference receiver who started a campus chapter of Mothers Against Drunk Drivers when his girlfriend was killed in a tragic accident

- How New Orleans Saints head coach Sean Payton thrived in the pass-happy offense of head coach Al Molde

- The man who became the first (and long overdue) African-American head coach at a state university in Illinois

- Players who have had their numbers retired by EIU

- Illinois High School Association Hall of Fame members

- Super Bowl winners

- Pro Bowl players

- NFL draft picks

- Those who made their post-football life in the fields of education and business

THERE ARE RECOGNIZABLE NAMES INCLUDING

- Dino Babers
- Pete Catan
- Poke Cobb
- Jim Edgar
- Jimmy Garoppolo
- Jeff Gossett
- John Jurkovic
- Erik Lora
- Randy Melvin
- Al Molde
- Darrell Mudra
- Sean Payton
- Ted Petersen
- Tony Romo

- Mike Shanahan
- Bob Spoo
- John Teerlinck

These individual stories span every decade from the 1940s to the present day. They not only focus on the glory days of college football but also on what occurred before and since those years of eligibility. Many of these men also played professionally. You name a league and an EIU player has been there: the National Football League, Canadian Football League, United States Football League and the many forms of Arena ball. Legendary head coach Bob Spoo was the Most Valuable Player of the long forgotten Tri-State Football League.

The book has been painstakingly researched using newspaper and magazine archives and online sites and databases. Additional information has been supplied via the sports information departments and alumni offices. And to write an extensive and accurate chronicle, personal interviews have been conducted with more than 75 coaches, players, administrators, sports historians and media members. After all, firsthand accounts are generally the most riveting and insightful.

Football remains our nation's most popular sport. The appeal of this book is far-ranging. Not only does it cover the topography of Illinois, but alumni are scattered throughout the country. Moreover, people who never attended EIU will have an interest in discovering or reliving the merits of this fine football program. With the book centering on players and coaches over the past six decades of football history, all age groups will find something to enjoy.

The Internet age has made it easier. An EIU alum now living in Florida can listen to his beloved Panthers online. A fan from California can follow the Panthers via the EIU website year-round. A proud graduate can turn the volume up when Tony Romo declares "Eastern Illinois" during the player introductions of a *Sunday Night Football* telecast. No longer do you have to purchase a media guide; it's available free in downloadable form. Panther wear can be purchased with relative ease from a home computer or electronic device. A search on YouTube nets you Sean Payton as a Chicago Bears' quarterback or singing onstage with pal

Kenny Chesney (the viewer can decide which is more difficult to watch).

So, what qualifies me to write this book (a question more than a few people asked along the way)? For starters, I was once entering a local Charleston establishment when then-Eastern offensive lineman and later NFL-replacement player Chris Geile was checking IDs.

"Hey, your birthday is the day after mine!" bellowed Geile in a nonoffensive lineman statement.

Seriously though, I attended Eastern from 1983 to 1988. I earned undergraduate degrees in history and journalism. While there, I worked for *The Daily Eastern News*, the award-winning campus newspaper. In fact, I served as sports editor and covered a conference champion football team with a quarterback by the name of Payton. I also worked in the university's sports information office under the guidance of Dave Kidwell, the well-known SID who taught me many things about Panther athletics and beyond. I've sat in the stands and seen many of the players and coaches included in this book. I am one of a handful of people who saw the final collegiate games in the careers of Sean Payton, Tony Romo and Jimmy Garoppolo (does that make me a bad luck charm?).

I have taught language arts and social studies for more than a quarter century. Currently, I teach in Naperville District 204. On the side, I have written feature stories for the likes of *The Aurora Beacon-News, Charleston Times-Courier, Lincoln Courier*, <profootballresearchers.org> and <collegehockeynews.com>. My first book was on Northern Illinois Huskies football.

The idea for the book has always been floating around inside my head. It finally took the time to work its way out.

True, I didn't get everyone I wanted for the book. So, when you say, "Hey, where is so-and-so?!" know that I made attempts. Sometimes the game plan works to perfection. More often than not, it has to be altered. And while Erin Andrews wasn't on hand to ask me about halftime adjustments, know that there were plenty along the way.

I was able to interview many of the individuals in the book. If a chapter ends with the

Four-Down Territory sidebar, know that I was able to personally interview that particular coach or player.

This book's purpose is to bring together for the first time a collection of EIU football lore. If you're a graduate, you'll enjoy reading about your alma mater. If you didn't attend EIU, yet are still a fan, there's plenty for you here as well.

Thank you for your time. I truly appreciate it. Hopefully, the journey you are about to embark upon as a reader will be as much fun as it was for me to research and write about.

The first Eastern football team in 1899.

A BRIEF HISTORY OF EIU FOOTBALL

Humphrey Bogart, August Busch Jr., James Cagney, Al Capone, Duke Ellington, Ernest Hemingway, Alfred Hitchcock, Gloria Swanson and E.B. White were all born in 1899. So was Eastern Illinois State Normal School football.

According to the official EIU athletics website, Otis Caldwell—the university's auditor of accounting—was named the first head coach, and the team played its early games on a field located where the current Student Services building resides.

That inaugural Eastern team took on a team from nearby Oakland. Later, Caldwell's team played a game in Effingham against Austin College. Eastern lost both games.

Eastern used a series of volunteer coaches until the 1911 season. That year, Charles Lantz was hired as the school's first athletic/physical education staff member.

During Lantz's first decade at Eastern, two players would lose their lives. In 1915, Paul Root was injured on a hard tackle against Illinois State. Root played one more down, collapsed on the field and later died at the hospital of a broken neck.

Another Eastern player from the same era, Corporal Martin Schahrer, was killed in action during World War I on October 3, 1918. Schahrer had been Eastern's captain in 1916 and class president in 1917.

Lantz coached football for 24 of his 42 years in Charleston. A Gettysburg College graduate, he won 95 games while leading Eastern. His 1928 team was the last undefeated football squad in Eastern history. The team earned a share of the Little 19 Conference championship that year.

Lantz's 1930 team became known as the "uncrossed goal line club" for its defensive prowess. Eastern posted a 6-1-1 record and did not allow any opponent to score a touchdown the entire season. Eastern's lone loss came against Southern Illinois University on a safety. The team also tied Bradley University 0-0.

Howard Ballard lost his life serving during World War II. Ballard, a multisport star, attended Eastern from 1931 to 1935. He was posthumously inducted into Eastern's Hall of Fame in 1996.

Charles Hall, an African-American, enrolled at Eastern in 1938. Hall participated in both football and track for the Panthers before withdrawing in 1941 to enlist in the Army. After being commissioned as a "Tuskegee Airman," Hall became the first African-American fighter pilot to shoot down an enemy aircraft.

Quarterback Bill Glenn launched a different sort of aerial attack. Glenn became the first Panther to earn All-American status. Glenn, a native of St. Louis, led Eastern to a 6-1-1 record in 1940. Named second-team Little All-American, he completed a then-school-record 65.1% of his passes. Glenn later played two years with the Chicago Bears and their Newark, New Jersey farm team.

Following World War II, a large number of veterans returned the Panthers to glory on the gridiron. Under the direction of head coach Maynard "Pat" O'Brien, Eastern won the Illinois Intercollegiate Athletic Conference title and a berth in the Corn Bowl, an annual event held on Thanksgiving in Bloomington. Eastern defeated rivals Northern Illinois, Illinois State and Southern Illinois that season.

Despite the success of the 1948 team, Eastern

Darrell Mudra and his staff turned around the fortunes of Eastern football by winning the 1978 NCAA Division-II national championship. From left to right, the coaches were Jeff Gardner, Felix Lobdell, Jerry Brown, Harvey Willis, John Teerlinck, Gale Wilson, Joe Taylor and Mike Shanahan. Mudra is kneeling in front.

football struggled mightily for the next three decades. Eastern produced just three winning seasons in that time. Moreover, only one of those (1961) came after 1951.

During that period, Eastern suffered greatly when many Illinois schools began offering scholarships while the Panthers did not. Ray Fisher, a multisport star in the 1950s, played professionally for Pittsburgh and the original Dallas Cowboys.

By the end of the 1960s, the IIAC had disbanded. In the meantime, Eastern moved into a renovated Lincoln Field and began offering scholarships for the first time. Though the Panthers still continued producing losing records, Eastern's fortunes began to change with stars such as All-American running back Nate Anderson, wide receiver Willie White and offensive lineman Ted Petersen. Anderson became the first back in EIU history to rush for more than 1,200 yards in consecutive seasons.

Meanwhile, a movement to drop Eastern's football program drew strong support. University president Gilbert Fite, however, withstood the pressure and decided to allow one more coach the opportunity to salvage the Panther program.

Athletic director Mike Mullally convinced Darrell Mudra to return to football after a two-year retirement. Mudra hired former Eastern quarterback Mike Shanahan and former Western Illinois defensive lineman John Teerlinck

as his coordinators. Molding the returning core of players and some junior college transfers into one solid unit, the new coaching staff convinced the team it could win. The Panthers responded with a miracle turnaround from a 1-10 record in 1977 to the NCAA Division II national championship in 1978.

The Mudra years would be the finest in Eastern history. In his five years at the Panther helm, Mudra would post a remarkable 47-15-1 record. In addition to the '78 national championship, Mudra's Panthers occupied the No. 1 national ranking position for the 1980 regular season. Though Eastern would lose the '80 national championship game to Cal Poly, Mudra's legacy would endure.

A number of outstanding players donned the Panther blue and gray during Mudra's time, including the school's all-time leading rusher, Chris "Poke" Cobb, defensive stars Pete Catan, Randy Melvin and Robert Williams and quarterback Jeff Christensen.

After two national championship game appearances, Eastern left the Division II ranks to join the NCAA I-AA level in 1981. The Panthers were joined by their Mid-Continent Conference foes in the move up in competition and status.

Eastern quickly established itself as a I-AA power. In 1982, the Panthers climbed to No. 5 in the national ratings. Spearheaded by a stout defense and a balanced offense, Eastern advanced to the quarterfinals of the I-AA playoffs.

Though Mudra resigned to accept the head coaching position at conference rival Northern Iowa at the end of the 1982 season, Eastern continued its winning ways under head coach Al Molde.

After making the playoffs again in 1983, the Panthers became a charter member in the newly formed Gateway Conference in 1985. Eastern also played its first night home games in '85 thanks to the "Brighten O'Brien" project. A year later, Molde's Panthers won the conference title and advanced to the I-AA quarterfinals. Sean Payton led the potent, pass-oriented Panther offense. Payton threw for more than 10,000 yards in his Eastern career.

One of the biggest highlights of that 1986 season occurred when Rich Ehmke kicked a school-record 58-yard field goal on the final play of a 31-30 Homecoming victory over rival Northern Iowa.

When Molde left for Division I-A Western Michigan following the '86 season, former Purdue quarterback and assistant coach Bob Spoo took over the Eastern program. Twenty-five years later, Spoo left as Eastern Illinois' all-time leader in coaching victories, earned nine playoff appearances and produced numerous All-Americans. With a philosophy based on a solid running game and dependable special teams, Spoo's program churned out 1,000-yard rushers like clockwork.

The Panthers continued to send players to the National Football League. Defensive line-man John Jurkovic, defensive back Chris Watson and Pro Bowl quarterback Tony Romo led the way.

The Panthers left the Gateway in 1996 to join the Ohio Valley Conference. Romo excelled by capturing three straight OVC Conference Player of the Year Awards (2000–2002). He capped his collegiate career by winning the coveted Walter Payton Award as the top player in I-AA football.

Linebackers Nick Ricks, Clint Sellers and Donald Thomas each were honored as OVC Defenders of the Year. Running back Vincent Webb was the OVC Offensive Player of the Year in 2006.

From 1999 to 2009, Eastern won five OVC championships, qualified for seven FCS play-off appearances and posted more victories than any other OVC program since 2000.

Following Spoo's retirement, former Eastern assistant Dino Babers took over as Panthers' head coach. Babers brought a fastbreak offense from Baylor, where he served as an assistant coach for four seasons. While the offense re-wrote the Eastern record book, the Panthers won back-to-back OVC championships under Babers in 2012 and 2013.

Babers' 2013 team won in a dynamic and explosive fashion that netted the Panthers national attention and a No. 2 national rank-ing. Quarterback Jimmy Garoppolo joined Romo as Panthers who have won the Walter Payton Award, the annual honor for the most outstanding offensive player in the FCS. Only seven other schools have had two recipients of the award.

Eastern Illinois has appeared in the I-AA/FCS playoffs 15 times. The Panthers won two conference championships (1986, 1995) as members of the Gateway Conference. After joining the OVC in 1996, Eastern has been crowned champions seven times (2001, 2002, 2005, 2006, 2009, 2012, 2013).

Tony Romo was a three-time Ohio Valley Conference Offensive Player of the Year.

THE EARLY YEARS
(1899–WORLD WAR II)

Action from Eastern's 6-0 victory over rival Millikin University in 1913.

ILLINOIS INTERCOLLEGIATE ATHLETIC CONFERENCE

It's been more than 40 years since the Illinois Intercollegiate Athletic Conference (IIAC) last crowned a championship football team. Yet, for those who competed, the memories are as fresh as the smell of cut grass on the first day of fall practice.

"It was great," said Bob Heimerdinger, the 1951 conference Most Valuable Player from Northern Illinois University. "It was made up of the people you knew from high school, and you saw them every year."

Heimerdinger, the father of former NFL offensive coordinator and Eastern Illinois graduate Mike Heimerdinger, added that the IIAC's strength was the men who ran it.

"They were the whole ball of wax," he said. "In those days, those men were everything. They coached the sports, and they ran the PE departments."

Those men included Heimerdinger's coach George "Chick" Evans. Others were Charles Lantz and Maynard "Pat" O'Brien of Eastern, Ray "Rock" Hanson and Vince DiFrancesca of Western and Ed Struck of ISU. Southern was coached by the likes of Glenn "Abe" Martin (1939–1949), Bill Waller (1950–1951) and William O'Brien (1952–1954).

"It was just those five state schools when I played," said 1947 conference MVP Red Miller of Western, who later coached the Denver Broncos in the Super Bowl.

"Northern and Southern were the biggest schools, ISU was in the middle and Western and Eastern stayed about the same size," said Lou Stivers, captain of Eastern's 1948 conference champions.

"(The IIAC) was every bit as tough as the Mid-American Conference," said Jack Pheanis, who played with Heimerdinger and later coached under both Evans and Howard Fletcher at NIU. "The Mid-American was better at publicizing themselves. They also had a number of people on all the (NCAA) committees."

One of the attractions of the IIAC was its wide-open play.

"The Big Ten was known for its running game," said Pheanis, who began his playing career at the University of Illinois. "We (the IIAC) were a passing league."

Tom Beck, named all-conference on both offense and defense in 1961, enjoyed playing in the IIAC. Today he is enshrined in the College Football Hall of Fame for his coaching exploits.

"It was a great time," Beck said. "I loved going on the trips and being with the guys. We traveled by bus to the games. We did take the train down to Carbondale to play Southern. We took a bus to Kankakee and then boarded the train."

Jack Dean played halfback for NIU's 1963 national championship team and later served as the head coach at Eastern.

"(The IIAC) was special because people don't realize how many great players came out of that league," Dean said. "You look at Western. They had guys like (future AFL star) Booker Edgerson and (first-round NFL draft pick) Leroy Jackson. You went down to Southern and they were always loaded.

"Eastern Michigan had Hayes Jones, who was an Olympic hurdler (who won gold in the 110-meter hurdles in the 1964 Games). Central Michigan was just so tough in football."

When asked just how strong the IIAC was, Dean used an analogy.

"I consider it very close to what the Mid-American Conference is today," he replied.

According to a 1970 article in *The NCAA News*, the league claimed most of the Illinois institutions of higher education. It was nicknamed the "Little Nineteen," though in 1928 it had a membership of 23 schools.

Former Illinois State track coach Joe Cogdal noted that the IIAC had roots dating back to the 1870s, when a number of schools banded together for oratorical contests. Cogdal was associated with the conference for 43 of its 62 years of existence.

The first intercollegiate football game was played in 1881 between ISU and Knox College. By 1894, a football association was established.

The conference was officially formed in April 1908 with eight charter members—Illinois State, Illinois Wesleyan, Bradley, Millikin, Monmouth, Knox, Lombard College and Illinois College.

The first track meet was held May 22, 1908.

The league expanded rapidly. Eastern and Western joined the league in 1912 and 1915, respectively.

In 1920, the name "Illinois Intercollegiate Athletic Conference" was adopted. Conference membership reached a peak of 23 schools in 1928, when virtually all of the small colleges of Illinois were included.

Scott Lacey, a 1991 Illinois State graduate, created an IIAC website as well as posting information on wikipedia.com. One of the main obstacles for Lacey and other researchers has been the sketchy information about the conference.

"I have seen so many seasons during those early years that there was no clear decision from the conference (about) who was the champion," Lacey said in an e-mail. "It didn't help that so many teams played different numbers of conference games and often didn't play each other."

An interesting footnote is that Eastern's 1928 conference championship roster included future actor, writer and folksinger Burl Ives as a lineman.

Private schools withdrew during the 1930s, until in 1942 only Eastern, Northern, Southern, Western and Illinois State remained.

In 1950, the league became the "Interstate Intercollegiate Athletic Conference" when Central Michigan and Eastern Michigan joined, upping membership to seven schools.

Carver Shannon, an African-American from Mississippi, came north to star in the Southern Illinois backfield during the '50s.

"I used to have these dreams that I'd be running the ball through and around everybody," said Shannon, who later played for the Los Angeles Rams. "I'd wake up and those dreams were pretty much coming true in the real games."

Shannon also realized that any running back's success is dependent on his line.

"So, I started recruiting for us," he said. "I went to places like Memphis and got players like Houston Antwine and Willie Brown."

Antwine became an NAIA wrestling champion at SIU and later earned All-Pro honors six straight seasons in the American Football League. Brown, a guard, managed to be selected as the Interstate Intercollegiate Athletic Conference Most Valuable Player in 1959.

"Things really took off," said Shannon, now living in California. "Sometimes they would have to put seats in the end zone to get everybody in."

Shannon was one of the main reasons. As a sophomore in 1956, he ran the ball for seven yards per carry en route to being named IIAC MVP. By 1958, Shannon's senior season, the Salukis had hit full stride. SIU posted its best record in more than a decade with a 7-2 mark. Teammate Cecil Hart took home conference MVP honors.

Meanwhile, Western Illinois won back-to-back conference championships in 1958 and 1959 under head coach Lou Saban. The '59 Leathernecks posted an undefeated season in which they outscored opponents by a 303-104 margin. WIU shut out its final two opponents.

"Lou Saban was all business," said tackle Wayne Lunak. "He was more like the legendary Paul Brown. He was the hammer. I remember one of our running backs came out of his office and said Lou just kicked me out of school. I told him that the football coach can kick you off the team, but not out of school. It didn't matter; the running back left (school)."

Miller, a Macomb native, returned to his alma mater and served as one of Saban's assistants along with Joe Collier, Art Duffelmeier and Guy Ricci.

"That was a special group of players through and through," said the 82-year-old Miller from his home in suburban Denver.

When Saban left WIU for the Boston Patriots of the newly founded American Football League, the Leathernecks took a hit.

"Lou needed coaches he could trust so he took Joe Collier and Red Miller with him," Leatherneck star Booker Edgerson said. "Of course, that hurt us."

Northern Illinois won three straight IIAC championships from 1963 to 1965. In fact, the Huskies captured the '63 NCAA College Division national championship under head coach Howard Fletcher. NIU featured a shotgun-spread passing attack that took college football by storm.

Sports Illustrated featured quarterback George Bork in a three-page feature titled "A Big Man in Any League." Bork and his Northern teammates found their way into *Time* magazine. CBS aired game highlights nationally. Bork was interviewed on NBC Radio. Pro scouts from the likes of the Green Bay Packers, Dallas Cowboys and San Francisco 49ers came to see him play.

"That 1963 season is my greatest memory (of my career)," said Bork, a College Football Hall of Fame member.

The IIAC began to change in 1961 when Eastern Michigan and Southern Illinois withdrew. Northern Illinois followed suit in 1966.

The conference officially disbanded at the end of the 1969–1970 academic year. Thus, Western Illinois was the last IIAC champion, winning the conference title in the fall of 1969 under College Football Hall of Fame coach Darrell Mudra.

"We kicked people all over the field pretty good when I was at Western," Mudra said from his retirement home in Florida.

Mike Wagner, who later won four Super Bowls with the Pittsburgh Steelers, earned NAIA All-American honors that championship season for the Leathernecks.

"It was a big thing for a small program at the time," Wagner said from his home in Pennsylvania.

"Mike Wagner was the All-American boy," said former WIU assistant coach Pete Rodriquez. "He was blond-haired and blue-eyed. He had all the attributes to be a fine player. You don't find someone like him at Western Illinois usually. He got overlooked by a lot of people and bigger schools. He really blossomed at Western."

While Northern became a Division I football program in 1969, the rest of the Illinois schools played at the NCAA College Division and then Division II levels through the 1970s.

Eastern, under Mudra, won the 1978 Division II national championship. Mudra's coaching staff included Mike Shanahan as offensive coordinator and John Teerlinck as defensive coordinator.

Shanahan, who won consecutive Super Bowls as the Broncos' head coach, returned to the NFL to coach the Washington Redskins in 2010. Teerlinck, the defensive line coach for the Indianapolis Colts, has been part of four Super Bowl coaching staffs.

With NIU continuing to play at the Division I-A level, the four remaining schools all transitioned from Division II into I-AA (now called the Football Championship Subdivision) football in the early 1980s. Interestingly, Southern Illinois played as a Division I independent from 1973 to 1976, while Illinois State played at the I-A level from 1978 to 1981 before moving to I-AA status.

When the Gateway Conference was formed in 1985, Eastern, Southern, Western and ISU became charter members. Eastern left the league in 1996 to join the Ohio Valley Conference in all sports.

"You wonder, where is the rivalry?" said Eastern quarterback Roger Haberer, who played in the 1960s. "Today when Eastern plays Eastern Kentucky, it just isn't the same. Maybe it will be someday, but there was more rivalry in those days (of the IIAC)."

Southern, Western and ISU remain together in the Missouri Valley Conference (the Gateway officially changed its name in 2009).

"When you look back now it would be nice from the traveling and financial aspect (to still be together)," said Stivers.

ILLINOIS INTERCOLLEGIATE ATHLETIC CONFERENCE FOOTBALL CHAMPIONS

- 1910—Illinois Wesleyan
- 1911—Millikin
- 1912—William & Vashti College
- 1913—Disputed **Eastern Illinois**, William & Vashti
- 1914—**Eastern Illinois**, William & Vashti
- 1915—Illinois College
- 1916—Millikin
- 1917—Lombard College
- 1918—No Champion
- 1919—Millikin
- 1920—Millikin, North Central, Wheaton
- 1921—Lombard College
- 1922—Lombard College
- 1923—Lombard College, Mt. Morris
- 1924—Knox College, Lombard
- 1925—Bradley, Monmouth
- 1926—Bradley, Monmouth
- 1927—Bradley
- 1928—**Eastern Illinois**, Millikin

- 1929—Knox, Lombard
- 1930—Millikin, Mt. Morris, Southern Illinois
- 1931—Monmouth
- 1932—Illinois Wesleyan, McKendree
- 1933—Illinois Wesleyan
- 1934—Augustana, Millikin
- 1935—Millikin, Monmouth
- 1936—Illinois Wesleyan, St. Viator
- 1937—Bradley, Illinois College, Illinois State
- 1938—Northern Illinois
- 1939—Illinois State, Western Illinois
- 1940—Carthage (WI), Illinois State
- 1941—Illinois State, Northern Illinois
- 1942—Western Illinois
- 1943—No Champion
- 1944—Northern Illinois
- 1945—Illinois State
- 1946—Northern Illinois
- 1947—Southern Illinois
- 1948—**Eastern Illinois**
- 1949—Western Illinois

INTERSTATE INTERCOLLEGIATE ATHLETIC CONFERENCE FOOTBALL CHAMPIONS

1950 Illinois State
1951 Northern Illinois
1952 Central Michigan
1953 Central Michigan
1954 Central Michigan, Eastern Michigan
1955 Central Michigan, Eastern Michigan
1956 Central Michigan
1957 Eastern Michigan
1958 Western Illinois
1959 Western Illinois
1960 Southern Illinois
1961 Southern Illinois
1962 Central Michigan
1963 Northern Illinois
1964 Northern Illinois, Western Illinois
1965 Northern Illinois
1966 Central Michigan
1967 Central Michigan, Illinois State
1968 Central Michigan, Illinois State
1969 Western Illinois

Source: Illinois Intercollegiate Athletic Conference http://slacey19690.jimdo.com/

CHARLES LANTZ

To many, Charles Lantz is Eastern Illinois athletics.

Lantz's Eastern Hall of Fame biography calls him "a pioneer in the field of physical education." It further adds that his name is "a byword in Midwest collegiate athletic circles during the first half of the 20th Century."

Lantz was born in Harrisburg, Pennsylvania in 1884. He attended Harrisburg High School and Gettysburg Academy. He was a 1908 graduate of Gettysburg College. While there, Lantz competed all four years in football, basketball and baseball. Upon graduation he coached and taught chemistry for three years at the Harrisburg Academy.

Lantz arrived at Eastern in 1911. He served as the school's first athletic director until his retirement in 1952. In addition, he coached football, basketball and baseball. In 1935, Lantz relinquished his football and basketball duties but continued coaching baseball. He directed sports and physical education for men without assistance until 1932.

During his tenure Lantz posted 14 winning football seasons. He coached 170 football games, 373 basketball games and more than 400 baseball contests. Lantz's football teams were undefeated at home during his first eight seasons, including a 104-0 rout of Pana.

Lantz's football success began immediately. His 1911 team posted a 4-2 record. A year later, his 1912 team was 6-1. Lantz's winning ways continued in 1913 (6-2) and 1914 (8-0-1 including a 3-3 tie with conference rival Millikin).

An early edition of the *Warbler*, Eastern's yearbook, lauded Lantz and his football exploits:

"Mr. Lantz's powerful machine romped through their schedule to the conference championship, clinching their claim for the high honors each year by defeating the chesty Millikin eleven on the Decatur gridiron," proclaimed the 1913 *Warbler*.

The annual also noted that three Eastern players made the "all-star team of secondary schools (selected) by Coach (James N.) Ashmore of James Millikin University."

The honored Eastern trio was Sumner Wilson, Bruce Corzine and Herman Cooper.

According to the *Warbler*, Ashmore said, "Wilson flitted around over the field like a cockroach on a billiard table."

After mediocre records in 1915 and 1916, Eastern returned to form under Lantz with a 4-1-1 season for 1917. However, World War I intervened, forcing the cancellation of the 1918 season. Lantz's team then struggled to regain its winning ways in the three years following the war.

Yet, good fortune would soon return to Eastern football. The *Warbler* declared, "A ray of hope flickered persistently in the fall of '21 when enough real men came back to school to reinforce 'the knee pants brigade' to assemble a machine of considerable potential strength."

The yearbook further asked the question, "Have you seen any big fellows enrolling?" The *Warbler* then made reference to a "strapping 210-pound man."

Lantz's 1922 football team began a string of winning seasons by finishing the year with a 4-0-2 record.

It was Lantz himself who highlighted the return to glory in the *Warbler*.

"(Forrest) Greathouse," Lantz wrote, "was a real star in 1922."

Lantz further wrote that Greathouse of nearby Toledo was fast and often used on both end runs as well as "hitting the line." The coach also noted Greathouse was a "sure tackler" and "one of the best in catching forward passes."

According to the *Warbler*, Greathouse "kicked the goal from placement that beat Lincoln College in the last second of the last game." Thus, "the Lantzmen were an undefeated team."

The *Warbler* heralded the 1922 team as "The Best Eleven since 1913."

While Greathouse scored four touchdowns that season, quarterback Mack "Gilly" Gilbert led the team with five TDs. According to the *Warbler*, Gilbert's touchdown to upset Rose Poly was the highlight of the season.

Other stars of the '22 season the *Warbler* chronicled were George Sumner Anderson and William James Creamer. Anderson reportedly weighed 230 pounds and "brought up the average weight of the team considerably." Creamer, a Hoopeston native, was lauded for "his tackling (that) was a crowd's delight."

Charles Lantz served Eastern in numerous capacities.

Lantz's 1928 team became the last undefeated squad in school history with a 7-0-1 record. The team earned a share of the Little 19 Conference title. Burl Ives of Jasper County was a two-way lineman of that championship team. In 1959, Ives won an Oscar for Best Actor in a Supporting Role.

Lantz's 1930 team was one of the best defensive units in school history. They became known as the "uncrossed goal line club." Eastern was 6-1-1 that season and did not allow an opponent to score a touchdown the entire season. The team's only loss came against Southern Illinois University. SIU won the game 2-0 when Eastern's punter stepped on the end zone line. Eastern also tied Bradley University 0-0 that fall.

In all, Lantz coached football for 25 years at Eastern (1911–1934, 1944). His career record was 95-65-13. Lantz finished with a .589 winning percentage.

During Eastern's long affiliation with the Illinois Intercollegiate Athletic Conference (later the Interstate Illinois Intercollegiate Athletic Conference), Lantz served as league president eight times.

"He was here when I arrived (in 1948)," said Eastern Hall of Fame basketball player Tom Katsimpalis from his retirement home in Alabama. "They called him Potsy, which he didn't like very much. Mr. Lantz was a likable gentleman. He was the figurehead of Eastern Illinois athletics. Everyone was fond of him."

Following his retirement, Lantz was selected for the National Association of Intercollegiate

Athletics (NAIA) Hall of Fame. In 1982, he was inducted into the Eastern Hall of Fame.

EARLY PANTHERS IN THE PROS

While contemporary Eastern fans regularly follow the fortunes of former Panther quarterback Tony Romo and head coaches Mike Shanahan and Sean Payton, many aren't aware of the early Panthers who prowled the National Football League.

Shortly after the original founders of what turned out to be the NFL gathered in the showroom of a Canton, Ohio, automobile dealership, Lenny High became the first former Eastern player to land on a pro roster.

Quarterback Bill Glenn was the first Panther drafted by an NFL team.

High, a native of Bement, Illinois, appeared in one game for the Decatur Staleys in 1920. The Staleys, coached by George Halas, later relocated and became the Chicago Bears.

High, an end, was listed as 5-foot-11 and 195 pounds. Ironically, High was born in 1895, the year that Eastern Illinois State Teachers College opened its doors. He passed away in 1975.

Joe "Punkin" Snyder earned Little All-America status in 1939. The two-time all-conference center and middle linebacker also threw the shot and discus at Eastern. After dropping out of school, Snyder worked in a steel mill but also played with the Calumet Indians of the minor league American Football League.

Snyder was drafted into the armed forces and served from 1941 to 1954. He was injured in the Battle of the Bulge and received the Purple Heart and the Silver Star.

Snyder later returned to Eastern and finished his degree in 1957. He taught in the Charleston school system and ultimately was elected as Charleston's mayor. Among his political accomplishments were initiating Route 16, setting aside several new parking areas and updating Eastern's sewage system.

Snyder passed away in 1977 and was inducted into Eastern's Hall of Fame in 1998.

Meanwhile, quarterback Bill Glenn became the first Eastern player ever drafted by an NFL team. The Chicago Bears chose Glenn in the 19th round of the 1941 NFL Draft as the 159th overall pick.

Glenn, a native of St. Louis, was a second-team Little All-American quarterback in 1940. Glenn led Eastern to a 6-1-1 record his senior year. He completed a then-school-record 65.1% of his passes.

According to football historian John Maxymuk, the 6-foot, 157-pound Glenn saw playing time with the Bears.

"Bill Glenn appeared in two games for the Bears when Sid Luckman left for the Merchant Marines in 1944," Maxymuk wrote in an e-mail. "Glenn played against the Redskins and Rams in October. Before that, he had quarterbacked the Bears' farm team, the Newark Bears, along with Colgate's Johnny Long, who also joined the big club in 1944."

In those two NFL games, Glenn completed one pass in four attempts for 22 yards. He also rushed for one yard on one attempt.

Clyde Biggers coached Eastern football from 1965 to 1971. Prior to that, however, Biggers was a 24th-round draft pick by the Green Bay Packers out of Catawba College. While the 6-foot-5, 255-pound tackle failed to make the Green Bay roster, Biggers joined the Richmond Rebels of the minor league American Football League in 1948. Biggers, nicknamed "Red," played one game with Richmond before being released. The Bethlehem Bulldogs then signed Biggers.

Eastern quarterback Ed Soergel signed with the Cleveland Browns in 1951, but later starred in the Canadian Football League. Center Lou Stivers was property of the Detroit Lions the same year.

Another Eastern star, Ray Fisher, played tackle for two seasons with the Pittsburgh Steelers (1958–1959). In 1960, Fisher played defensive tackle as a member of the original Dallas Cowboys.

In the interim, many former Panthers played in the still-thriving minor league football system.

"In the 1960s, the United Football League, the Pro Football League of America and the Continental Football League all had teams representing Chicago, and the PFLA also had other teams in the general vicinity," said minor league football historian and author Bob Gill. "Dozens of players from Eastern, Western, Southern and Northern Illinois played for those teams."

According to Gill, those former EIU players included LeRoy Blackful, Bob Cook, Bob Fulk, Jim Lynch and John Puff.

"I'm sure many more players from Illinois schools played in the Central States League (successor to the Tri-States League, which changed its name in the early 1960s), since its teams were concentrated around the Great Lakes, but I don't have rosters for that league. It was a lower level, with teams in smaller towns and players making less money, but was still interesting—something like the Carolina League in baseball today. In that analogy, the Continental League or the Atlantic Coast League would be the equivalent of the International League or the Pacific Coast League," said Gill, author of two books on minor league and independent football.

POSTWAR ERA
(LATE 1940s–1950s)

MAYNARD "PAT" O'BRIEN

Upon entering O'Brien Field many have asked the question, "Who was O'Brien?"

The short answer to that can be found on the Eastern athletics website or in a media guide.

According to his EIU Hall of Fame biography, O'Brien's track and field credentials "will rival anyone in the nation."

O'Brien grew up in Canton and attended Lombard College and Illinois Wesleyan. He earned 11 letters in football, basketball and track. He later received his master's and doctorate from the University of Illinois.

During World War II, O'Brien served 42 months in the Navy. In addition, he worked with the University of Minnesota's famed football coach Bernie Bierman at the Iowa preflight program. O'Brien commanded a regiment of 1,200 cadets at the Memphis Air Station and served as flight desk officer and athletic officer aboard the USS *Bunker Hill*.

Following the war, O'Brien became an Eastern staff member. He served the university's physical education and athletic programs in numerous capacities.

O'Brien held the position of head football coach during his first nine seasons at Eastern. His 1948 Panthers won the Illinois Intercollegiate Athletic Conference title and earned the first postseason bowl appearance in school history.

"He was my contact at Eastern," said Panther Hall of Fame basketball player Tom Katsimpalis. "He came to Gary, Indiana where I lived and helped recruit me to Eastern."

In later years, when Katsimpalis was Eastern's Director of Athletics, O'Brien was his neighbor.

"He lived right behind me," Katsimpalis said. "Pat was very knowledgeable about track, cross-country and football. Anyone who played for him would give their arm for him."

Though he initiated the school's wrestling program in the early 1950s, O'Brien is best known for his being Eastern's head track coach for 27 years. He guided the Panthers to the 1974 NCAA Division II national co-championship in his final season. O'Brien was selected as the Division II Coach of the Year that season.

Maynard "Pat" O'Brien coached football, track, cross country and wrestling at Eastern.

O'Brien was also the head cross-country coach for 18 seasons, winning back-to-back Division II national championships in 1968 and 1969.

During the late 1960s, O'Brien served as the head of the men's physical education department and chaired the building committees that planned the construction of both the Lantz building and football stadium. In 1971, the university cited his outstanding service to the campus community by presenting him a "Distinguished Faculty Award."

Upon his retirement in 1974, the university rededicated the football stadium in his name.

O'Brien served as meet director for both the NAIA and NCAA national track meets. He coached 26 All-Americans and two Olympians (John Craft and Sandy Osei-Agyeman).

"Pat O'Brien spent a lot of time with those two, especially John," Katsimpalis said. "All that work certainly paid off."

Craft said, "Dr. O'Brien was a very unique individual. He was quite demanding in his expectations. But I found him to be quite fair. The day before a competition Dr. O'Brien would gather everyone in a circle and go around that circle and tell everyone his expectations for you. After the competition he would again go around the circle. If you didn't perform up to expectations he wanted to know why. Some people didn't like that, but I didn't mind it. I like honesty. I respond best to openness. You either liked Dr. O'Brien or you did not like him. There was no gray area."

Craft wrote his master's thesis on O'Brien and his contributions to Eastern in 1974. Johnie H. Meisner later used it as a reference for his 1976 book *Coach Maynard "Pat" O'Brien (Take Your Mark)*.

When Craft came to Eastern in 1965 from Momence High School, he walked onto O'Brien's track team. As a prep athlete, Craft had competed in the long jump, high jump, sprint events and relays. O'Brien immediately made Craft a triple jumper.

"I had no idea what that even was," Craft said. "Dr. O'Brien was a big Irishman. He was probably around 6-foot-1 or 2 and 260 pounds, maybe closer to 300 by that time. He smoked a pipe all the time. When he told you something, you did it. I didn't even think of questioning it."

O'Brien was also a member of the U.S. Olympic Committee as well as president of both the NCAA and NAIA national coaches associations in track and cross-country.

Like his Eastern predecessor Charles Lantz, O'Brien was inducted into the Eastern Hall of Fame in 1982. He also is enshrined in the NAIA Hall of Fame.

Longtime sports information director Dave Kidwell began his association with Eastern back in the 1960s as a student.

"Dr. O'Brien was a mover and shaker in Panther athletic history over four decades as a coach, teacher and administrator," Kidwell said. "He was one of the most well-respected track and field coaches in the nation, and left his mark on the international scene by developing John Craft into an Olympic triple jumper.

"As the chair of physical education, Dr. O'Brien oversaw the design and construction of the Lantz Building, which included a fieldhouse. At the time it was constructed, I would definitely contend the fieldhouse was a unique indoor facility in this state. Let's be honest, the fact that Dr. O'Brien was also the track coach was certainly the reason we have a fieldhouse. He took care of his program. But the rest of the university ultimately benefited with an indoor facility that other outdoor sports, plus physical education classes and recreation programs could utilize during inclement weather. Because of his physical size and sometimes gruff nature, he could be very intimidating to students, but when you could approach him in a downtime, he had a very relaxed manner so his proverbial 'bark was worse than his bite.'"

1948 CORN BOWL TEAM

While few good things come from war, World War II played a key role in Eastern's lone bowl appearance.

The year was 1948, and the Panthers claimed the Illinois Intercollegiate Athletic Conference crown and earned a bid to the Corn Bowl in Bloomington.

"About all of us were back from the service," said Lou Stivers, the captain of those bowl-bound Panthers. "Only about one or two starters weren't veterans. Several were married."

Even Panther head coach Maynard "Pat" O'Brien was a veteran.

Stivers had served for three years during the war. As was the custom of the day, the Olney native played both ways.

"I played center and middle linebacker," Stivers said. "When the ball went over to the other team, you hit instead of getting hit. I guess it was retaliation in some ways."

The Panthers did plenty of hitting that season. Eastern yielded just 13 points to conference opponents.

"We were the first ones to beat every state school except Illinois, of course," he said.

Eastern knocked off Western, Northern, Illinois State and Southern en route to its first conference title since 1928.

Thus, the Panthers were invited to face off against Illinois Wesleyan in the second annual Corn Bowl.

The game was played on the Titans' home field in hopes of raising attendance from the disappointing inaugural event that drew around 5,500 fans.

The change in venue worked. According to the Dec. 1, 1948 issue of *The Argus*, Wesleyan's student newspaper, "Over 8,500 Thanksgiving Day football enthusiasts delayed their turkey dinners for two hours."

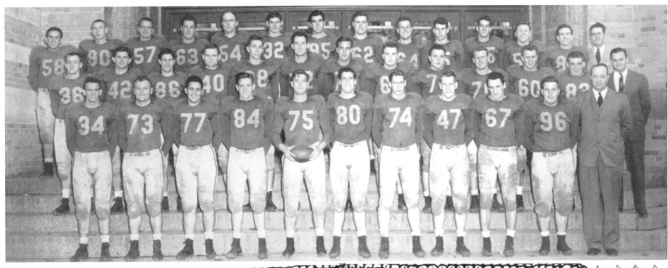

Wesleyan's fans went home to that turkey dinner with smiles on their faces as the Titans prevailed 6-0. The Titans' defense held Eastern to just 91 total yards.

On offense, Wesleyan switched from running its traditional single wing formation in favor of the T formation. The Titans appeared to take a first-half lead when Hank Bennett ran in from the 12-yard line. However, the touchdown was nullified when Wesleyan was whistled for a penalty. Eastern then held on downs.

Later in the first half, Wesleyan's Byron Willhoite came up just short on a 34-yard field goal attempt. After Eastern failed to move the ball, John Lopinsky punted the ball to what *The Argus* called "the coffin corner."

A few plays later, Wesleyan hit on a big play. Titan quarterback Gib Baechler completed a pass to Don Larson who "zig-zagged his way through the Panther secondary and into the open, but was pulled down from behind by Don Johnson after a 50-yard jaunt."

The Argus pointed out that Johnson ran the 100-yard dash in under 10 seconds.

After Wesleyan failed to move the ball, Eastern threatened to break the deadlock. The Pan-

thers drove to the Wesleyan two-yard line, but were unable to score.

"In the back of my mind it seems we had a touchdown called back," Frank Pitol, a Panther end and guard, told Brian Nielsen of the *Charleston Times-Courier* in a 1993 story.

Pitol's memory was correct.

The Argus reported, "The IIAC champs ran off a play after the half had been officially declared over, and there was a dispute by the EI team, for they had scored on that play; but the official won out, as he always does."

Wesleyan capitalized on an Eastern turnover in the second half. Titan captain Curt Brown intercepted an Eastern pass that led to the game's lone score. Wesleyan strung together a mix of passes and runs to move to the Eastern three-yard line. From there, Baechler "took the pigskin and sneaked through center to score standing up."

In its recap of the game, *The Argus* lauded several Eastern players.

"Eastern followers can be proud of John Lopinsky, who punted into the Titan coffin corner many times. If it hadn't been for the fine work of this artist, the score may have

Members of the 1948 Illinois Intercollegiate Athletic Conference champions and Corn Bowl participants.

been different. Russ Ghere and Chuck Gross played brilliant defensive games for the Panthers. These boys seemed to be in on every tackle. The Titans also found out why the Eastern squad elected Lou Stivers as its captain this year, for he played a magnificent game at the center spot," read the Wesleyan newspaper's account.

Stivers remembered the postgame as well as the Corn Bowl itself.

"There was a banquet after the game for both teams. It was a lot of fun," he said.

Stivers remained friends with many of his teammates following their days at Eastern.

"Most of us went into education," he said.

Among those friends were Bill Snapp, Howard Barnes, Pitol and Ghere. The latter three, like Stivers and O'Brien, are all members of Eastern's Hall of Fame.

Barnes, nicknamed "Slug," started every game at left guard all four years. He averaged 17 solo tackles a game his senior season and was voted as the Panthers' Most Valuable Player in '48. In addition to being a first-team all-conference selection, Barnes was the IIAC MVP. He was inducted into the Illinois Coaches Hall of Fame for football in 1990. He coached for 29 years in the Wheaton school system and compiled a 115-38-6 coaching record.

Pitol was a multisport standout for Eastern, lettering in three sports—football, basketball and track. He was twice named all-conference as a guard and end. In basketball Pitol played center; he competed in the discus and javelin in track. Following graduation, Pitol taught, coached and served as athletic director at Collinsville High School. Pitol was inducted into the Illinois Basketball Coaches Hall of Fame. He also was recognized as the IHSA Athletic Director of the Year in 1987 and 1990.

"Frank and I were great friends," said Stivers. "Back when the St. Louis Cardinals played football Frank worked for them. His job was to sit on a chair and stay between the crowd and the Cardinal cheerleaders. He was sort of a security guard. He called it the greatest job in the world."

Ghere lettered five times in football and track for the Panthers. He earned honorable mention All-IIAC in 1948. As a prep coach, Ghere registered a 123-102-11 record in a 34-year career at Villa Grove and Bridgeport. His teams won or shared seven conference championships with two undefeated seasons. In 1982, the Villa Grove football facility was named in his honor. In 1984, Ghere was inducted into the IHSA Football Coaches Hall of Fame.

Don Johnson was another of the team's standouts. Johnson, a Charleston High School graduate, had attended the University of Illinois for a year on a football scholarship prior to entering the Navy. He served as a sonar and radar operator in the Pacific theater.

Following the war, Johnson attended Eastern, where he became one of the Panthers' best all-around athletes of the 1940s. He lettered three years in football and was a unanimous all-conference selection. Johnson led the team in scoring for the 1948 season. He lettered four years in track. Johnson once ran the 100 in 10 seconds flat and set a then-school-record 22.4 in the 220.

Johnson later taught 36 years at Carlsbad (California) High School. He was nominated for the California High School Teacher of the Year in 1972.

War shaped all these men.

"I think the Army was tougher (than football)," Ghere told Nielsen. "You were away from family and friends. I think it helped me a lot. The experience wasn't enjoyable but I think it helped me."

It also helped make Eastern football history.

LOU STIVERS

Perhaps it should come as no surprise that a member of what journalist Tom Brokaw dubbed The Greatest Generation would be a history buff.

"I've always loved history, still do to this day," said 85-year-old Lou Stivers, the captain of Eastern's 1948 Illinois Intercollegiate Athletic Conference champions.

Not only did Stivers love history, he also made it. Following an unbeaten regular season, he and his Panther teammates represented the IIAC in the short-lived Corn Bowl.

"(The bowl game) was put together by a civic group in Bloomington as a fund-raiser,"

Stivers recalled. "They figured if they put together two teams they could make some quick money for their cause."

Eastern lost the Corn Bowl, 6-0, to Illinois Wesleyan, yet that doesn't nag at Stivers over 60 years later.

"We had a good time and enjoyed ourselves," said the two-time all-conference selection as linebacker and center.

Stivers grew up in Olney, Illinois where he learned the value of hard work and determination.

"While I was in high school I worked as a roughneck in the oil fields on Friday and Saturday nights," he said. "After our game Friday night a crew would come by and pick us up."

Stivers and the crew then worked from midnight until seven or eight the next morning.

"I made $1 an hour and $16 for the weekend," Stivers recalled. "Being in high school, that was pretty good."

He added that his coaches didn't really like it.

"They were afraid we'd get hurt," he said.

Like many of his generation, Stivers joined the war effort right after his high school graduation.

"We had 15 days to settle our affairs, and then we went into the service," he said.

For Stivers that meant the Air Force, where he trained Chinese and English bomber crews.

Once the war was over, Stivers enrolled at Eastern with Neil Hudson, a friend from high school.

"Neil had been in the Rangers in the service," Stivers said. "He played basketball and football. He first went to Illinois, but decided not to stay. On his way back to Olney, he stopped (at Eastern) and wound up enrolling."

About two-thirds of Eastern's football team consisted of ex-servicemen going to college on the GI Bill.

"Most of us lived in GI trailers," he said. "Those trailers were where Taylor and Lincoln Halls are today. They went over to where the football field is.

"They weren't luxurious by any standard, but they served the purpose," he said.

Many of the players were married; some had children. Stivers married the second year he played football.

Members of the 1948 Corn Bowl reunited at a reunion in 2008. Front row: Lou Stivers, Morris Tschannen, Bill Crum, Eugene Scruggs, Paul Arnold

Back row: Frank Pitol, EIU President William Perry, Bill Pennybacker, Vern Wagner

(Photo courtesy of Susan Stucco)

The 1948 Panthers were coached by Maynard "Pat" O'Brien, the man whose name Eastern's football field bears.

"He was a typical veteran," Stivers said. "He understood the veteran problems."

O'Brien also helped Stivers upon the player's graduation from Eastern.

"He was from Carlinville, and O'Brien helped me get a job there," said Stivers.

Before accepting the teaching and coaching position at Carlinville High School, Stivers had an offer to weigh from the Detroit Lions of the National Football League. However, the NFL in those days was a far cry from the multibillion dollar business it has become.

"Detroit's offer was for $4,500," Stivers said. "I kept those contracts around. My boys had no concept of the money. They said that I must not have been very good."

Stivers turned down the Detroit offer to take the job in Carlinville.

"My wife June and I were expecting our first son (Mike)," Stivers said. "I wanted to be in education, so I figured I may as well get started."

Stivers taught a full load of American history, coached three sports and directed the school play—all for a $3,000 salary.

"Some guys get that for one sport today," Stivers quipped.

Still, money wasn't everything. Stivers worked in the Carlinville school system for 41 years, first as a teacher and coach, then as an administrator.

"Anybody who coaches for the money must be a class idiot," Stivers said. "Seeing the students and players succeed, that's your payback."

Stivers saw several of his athletes wind up with scholarships over the years.

"They played everywhere from Michigan to the state schools, and I was thrilled for every one of them," he said.

Stivers coached several basketball, football and track teams to league titles. In addition, two of his girls' basketball teams advanced to the state tournament.

Stivers and his wife also raised their two boys during his career. Mike recently retired from his job as assistant superintendent in Bethalto. Phil is in the restaurant business in Cincinnati.

Thus, Stivers and his wife moved back to Charleston when he retired in the early 1990s.

"It's a good place to be," Stivers said. "We like it here. It also puts us between the St. Louis area and Cincinnati for our sons."

The move also put him back in touch with Eastern athletics. Stivers helped with the high school state track meet, which is annually held at O'Brien Field.

It also allowed him to attend reunions for the Corn Bowl team. The most recent was held in 2008, 60 years after Eastern history was made. However, as national statistics indicate, the Greatest Generation is quickly dwindling.

"I hesitated about even going because so many of the fellows have passed on or weren't able to make it," Stivers said. "But (former Eastern sports information director) Dave Kidwell talked me into going. I'm so glad that I went."

Stivers added, "About six or seven of our group were there. A couple of them had Alzheimer's so bad that their wives just chauffeured them around."

Being back in Charleston has also allowed Stivers, the former two-way star, to follow Eastern football closely again.

"The quarterback now, this Christensen kid, his dad played here too," he noted in a 2009 interview.

Spoken like a true history buff. The Greatest indeed.

FOUR-DOWN TERRITORY

Favorite Football Movie: I really don't have one, sorry.

First Car: My wife and I bought a little used Ford in 1947 for $300.

Worst Summer Job: That job working as a roughneck in the oil fields was the hardest.

Favorite Subject in School: History.

RAY FISHER

Ray Fisher's athletic resume may seem hard to believe in today's collegiate sporting world: He earned 11 letters and top conference honors in three different sports.

"I would like to have been a better football player, but everyone has his limitations," said a modest Fisher from his Fairfield home.

Fisher is considered one of Eastern's most versatile athletes of all time. Playing at a time when sports were becoming more specialized, he didn't just participate. Ray Fisher excelled.

As a four-year letterman in football, Fisher was chosen all-conference in his final two seasons as a defensive lineman. He was also the Illinois Intercollegiate Athletic Conference heavyweight wrestling champion in 1954 and '55. As if that weren't enough, Fisher also captured the conference title in the shot put at the 1955 IIAC outdoor track meet.

Fisher was born south of Mattoon. His family moved to Charleston when he entered grade school.

"Eastern was a teachers' college back then," he said. "All of the student teachers got to try out their methods on us."

He attended Eastern State High School, which was located on the university campus.

"It was on the second floor of Old Main," Fisher said. "Down below was the grade school."

Fisher was active in prep sports, advancing to the state finals as a shot-putter. After high school graduation, he saw only one choice for college.

"I didn't even think about any other schools. It was Eastern," he said. "I was familiar with the campus. Most of the people I already knew were going there. It was just a natural choice."

Fisher quickly found his niche in Panther sports. Hall of Fame coach Maynard "Pat" O'Brien was the face of Eastern athletics in those halcyon days. Best known for his credentials in track and field, O'Brien also coached football and started the Panther wrestling program a few years prior to Fisher's arrival.

"He was my original football coach," Fisher said. "We appeared to have a real nice little team going into my senior year. For reasons I've either forgotten or never knew, they brought in a new coach (Keith Smith in 1956 and then Ralph Kohl in '57).

"I don't want to talk badly about anyone, but things went from good to bad to worse. I don't even know if we won a game that last year."

The Panthers didn't. They were winless in eight games that 1957 season.

Fisher cited injuries to key players and a switch to the two-platoon system as being factors in the Panthers' lackluster season.

"I sat on the bench about half the time," he said. "I was used to playing 60 minutes."

With his college days in the rearview mirror, Fisher joined the Marine Corps.

"It was a two-year enlistment, same as if you were drafted," he said. "I had heard that San

After playing for the Pittsburgh Steelers for two seasons, Ray Fisher was a member of the inaugural Dallas Cowboys team in 1960.

Diego had a really nice football team."

San Diego is exactly where Fisher landed. He played on a team that included future pro players: Hank Smith (San Francisco 49ers), Darryl Rogers (Los Angeles Rams) and Ted Karras (Chicago Bears).

"Rogers, of course, later was the head coach of the Detroit Lions," Fisher said. "Karras wasn't as famous as his brother, Alex, but was a pretty darn good player."

As was the rest of the team Fisher joined. In fact, the San Diego–based club won the mythical All-Service Championship in 1958.

"I got to be on a winning team, which was nice," Fisher said. "We played the likes of San Diego State and Fresno State. It seems like we may have played Arizona State. We went over to Hawaii and played the university and other service teams for a couple of games."

When his Marine stint ended, Fisher followed Karras to the Pittsburgh Steelers. There, he played for two seasons under the direction of head coach Buddy Parker. Fisher, listed at 6-foot, 230 pounds, saw action on both sides of the line.

"I started out as a nose guard but learned my lesson pretty quickly that wasn't for me," he said. "They switched me to offensive tackle."

Fisher often had problems with Parker.

"He used his players like tools," Fisher said. "I remember one time Ted (Karras) was in the back end of the plane throwing up. Ted was on loan from the Bears if I remember right. Anyway, Parker turns around from the front of the plane and said, 'Practice that growl some more because you're going back to the Bears.'"

Fisher became a starter in Pittsburgh for the 1959 season. Despite being in a position to protect quarterback Bobby Layne, the lineman and the signal-caller were often at odds.

"We didn't always get along so well," Fisher said of Layne, the well-known late-night carouser on the downside of his Hall of Fame pro career. "Maybe it was because I had just come out of the Marines and was tired of taking orders, but Layne and me never did see eye-to-eye."

A knee injury ended his playing days in Pittsburgh. The Steelers left him unprotected when an expansion draft was held to stock the rosters of the newly formed Dallas Cowboys and Minnesota Vikings for the 1960 NFL season.

The Cowboys, under the direction of former New York Giants defensive coordinator Tom Landry, grabbed Fisher despite his injured status.

"Tom Landry was a gentleman," Fisher said.

The Cowboys managed only a tie in their 12-game inaugural season. Landry kept Fisher on the roster for the entire year.

"He gave me every chance to come back (from injury)," Fisher said. "They really didn't rehabilitate injuries back then like they do now. I didn't realize how much leg strength I had lost until the next year."

Fisher was clearly a broken football player.

"I knew it was the end," Fisher said. "Even though he had to cut me, Landry was a class act."

Fisher said the most he ever made in football was "around $9,000."

"In those days the good quarterbacks and running backs made something like $15,000 to $20,000," he noted. "Things didn't really take off until the AFL came along and raised player salaries."

Fisher went back to school and became a fishery biologist for the state of Illinois.

"I can truly say I enjoyed it every day for 30 years," Fisher said. "I couldn't have found a job I liked better."

Fisher presided over a block of "eight to ten counties in the southeastern portion of the state." He even passed up chances to be moved into the state office in Springfield.

"I loved being outdoors. A desk job wasn't for me," Fisher said.

Fisher's son, Vince, played football at Indiana University before a knee injury ended his career. After college, Vince became an Illinois state police officer.

Fisher's daughter, Elizabeth, lives near Springfield and has four children.

Fisher was inducted into Eastern's Hall of Fame in 1983.

After taking early retirement in 1992, Fisher spent time enjoying his five grandchildren as well as hunting and fishing.

"I have about a three-acre vineyard," he said. "I'm a hobby winemaker. I don't sell it, but do give some away to family and friends."

While he still enjoys being active, Fisher isn't one who longs for his days on the football field.

"I'm the type of guy who would rather be outside doing something rather than sitting in the house watching games on TV," Fisher said.

If you know Ray Fisher's past, that statement wouldn't surprise you.

FOUR-DOWN TERRITORY

Favorite Football Movie: I can't say that I really have one. *The Blind Side* was pretty good, but I wouldn't even say that was my favorite.

First Car: It was a 1931 or '32 Model-A Ford. I drove in from the country when I went to school in Charleston. It got me in some trouble there. One time it wound up in the president's flower bed as part of a prank. Somebody pushed it in there. Another time it ended up on the top steps, that little porch, over at Lantz Gym (today called McAfee Gym).

Worst Summer Job: I rode in an open truck to Montana with a friend. He had a contract to bail hay out there. We worked from daylight to dark. It was tough work. I was probably 16 or 17 at the time.

Favorite Subjects in School: I'd have to say the biological sciences were my favorite.

THE 1960s

ROD BUTLER

Rod Butler's memories don't include game-winning passes as a quarterback or key interceptions from his position in the defensive secondary.

"I have the warped sense of a coach (because) I just remember the things we did attempting to win rather than the actual playing itself," Butler said. "I guess all those years I later coached make me look at things differently."

Butler's perception was shaped by a number of factors. He grew up in the small town of Lovington playing what he called "the American four" sports (football, basketball, baseball and track).

A 1960 graduate of Lovington High School, Butler narrowed his college choices to Eastern and Illinois State Teachers College in Normal.

"I guess I picked Eastern for a couple of reasons," he said. "My high school coach was a graduate from there. My sister went there. Eastern was only about 40 miles from Lovington so it just seemed like a natural fit."

Once at Eastern, Butler quickly acclimated himself to campus life. He enrolled as a physical education major and began to work on his teaching degree.

"Why did I choose PE over say, business? I guess the registration line must have been shorter," Butler joked.

Butler quickly set off on the task of becoming a seven-time letterman in three different sports. In football, he played both ways—quarterback on offense and defensive back on defense. He played guard on the basketball team and threw the javelin in track.

"I was officially 0-for-2 in baseball too," Butler pointed out. "If I remember correctly, I struck out and grounded out. We were way ahead of Greenville (College), something like 18-2. All the regulars were told to practice some more and the subs were sent in to finish up. After the game, it was off to spring (football) practice for me."

Butler honed his future coaching craft under the likes of Ralph Kohl in football and Maynard "Pat" O'Brien in track and field.

"Coach Kohl played on those great University of Michigan teams after World War II," Butler said. "He was a high-quality man. He attempted to dress up a kid from Lovington, and there was a lot of dressing up that was needed."

What about O'Brien, the man whose name the football and track facility bears?

"I was afraid of him," Butler said. "He was a very powerful presence. He told me I would be throwing the javelin. I didn't question him. You just did what you were told. One time I overslept for a track meet. It was one of those meets up at Northern (Illinois University) where we left very early in the morning. Those were the worst 24 hours of my life, waiting to go over to see Coach O'Brien on Sunday morning. How do you explain that you are an idiot? He was a World War II veteran who had seen a great deal in his time. You know how Tom Brokaw wrote that book *The Greatest Generation*?

After his playing days at Eastern, Rod Butler enjoyed a stellar coaching career that included a state championship in 1988.

Those truly were a different breed of men."

Butler not only respected O'Brien, he also saw a softer side in his coach.

"Looking back, his bark was worse than his bite," he said.

Butler finished fourth in the javelin in the Illinois Intercollegiate Athletic Conference meet as a junior and runner-up as a senior.

In football, Butler twice earned All-IIAC recognition and was named an honorable mention All-American in 1963.

Fresh off the 1963 NFL championship, the Chicago Bears selected Butler in the 16th round of the draft.

"In those days the NFL Draft was held in December," Butler recalled. "I was student-teaching down at Sullivan at the time."

However, Butler instead signed as a free agent with the Denver Broncos of the rival American Football League.

"I figured that I would have a better chance of making the team there," Butler said.

Yet, he soon realized just how competitive the world of professional football was.

"There were 13 people fighting for two positions and a spot on the taxi squad (as defensive backs)," he said.

Butler reported to the Broncos' training camp on July 12.

"I was home by the first week of August," he said. "I made it through the first round of cuts, but then got cut myself. You could say I was there for a cup of coffee, that's all. Hey, I just

wasn't good enough to play pro ball."

Consequently, Butler began his teaching and coaching career at Peoria Richwoods High School. He served as an assistant football coach before being hired at Princeton High School in 1966.

By the end of the 1960s, Butler returned to college football. Though he had picked Eastern over Illinois State as a student-athlete, Butler accepted an assistant coaching position with the Redbirds in 1969.

"Your loyalties change when someone is writing you a paycheck," Butler joked.

Butler spent nine seasons at Illinois State before taking a job at Morehead State in Kentucky. He served as the school's defensive co-ordinator.

"I was there about a year and a half," he said. "We weren't winning with Phil Simms as quarterback so I knew it was time to move on."

Butler returned to Peoria Richwoods in 1978, following in the footsteps of the highly successful Tom Peeler.

"I was there the last 16 years before I retired," Butler said. "You could say that I completed the circle by finishing where I started."

Butler did far more than simply finish out his 35-year teaching career.

"Coach Butler was 90-15 in nine years at Peoria Richwoods, including 69-6 from 1985 through 1990," pointed out longtime *Chicago Sun-Times* prep writer Taylor Bell.

Butler told Bell, "I like structure and discipline . . . no earrings, no long hair, say yes not yeah, don't come into my office without permission and don't forget to knock. Most kids respond to it. I don't want them to come back to their 10th reunion and say how soft the coach was."

Eddie Sutter would never say that. Sutter, now a financial adviser for Smith-Barney in Peoria, starred for Richwoods in the 1980s, later played at Northwestern and spent seven years in the NFL. Sutter played for Bill Belichick while a member of the Cleveland Browns.

According to Bell, Sutter said that Butler was every bit as intense as Belichick.

"The fundamentals I learned at Richwoods, the teaching that Butler gave me, I carried with me throughout my career. That's why I was able to play so many years," Sutter told Bell.

Butler's teams qualified for the state playoffs nine straight years. In 1987, Butler's team finished as the Class 5A runner-up. A year later, Richwoods completed a 14-0 season by capturing the 5A title.

While Butler credited Peeler with much of his own success, Bell isn't buying it.

"Butler is too modest," Bell said. "He didn't spend as much time coaching football at Peoria Richwoods as Tom Peeler, his mentor, but he was his own man, high on discipline and long on fundamentals. Peoria may be best known as a basketball town, but coaches such as Peeler and Butler and Merv Haycock and Ken Hinrichs and Bob Smith gave it a strong football identity too."

The same year that Butler's team won a state championship he was also inducted into Eastern's Hall of Fame.

"I really didn't do anything really well," Butler understated. "I feel like I owe a lot of others who helped me along the way, whether it be linemen or coaches or whoever."

Butler spends his retirement days playing golf and helping with his grandchildren. He also continues to follow Eastern.

"My wife and both my daughters went to Eastern," he said. "I still feel a connection. Bob Spoo had a great run there."

When further prodded for memories of his playing days as a Panther, Butler was able to recall a few games.

"We only had one winning season when I was there (1961)," he said. "I do remember a big win against Central Michigan when I was a sophomore. We tied Northern Illinois when they had (future College Football Hall of Famers) George Bork and Tom Beck (in 1961). We missed an extra point. Otherwise, we would have beaten them."

Butler also remembered a fight that broke out in a game against Southern Illinois in Carbondale.

"It was the biggest fight I've ever seen," Butler said. "They called off the last minute of the first half. I don't even know how it started, but it was a mass stampede. It was Southern's Homecoming game, and people were coming out of the stands."

Order was somehow restored and Eastern escaped to the visiting locker room. Butler said his teammate Bob White's jersey was torn in the brawl.

"In those days you could only dress and bring something like 38 players on the road for conference games," Butler said. "Jack Kaley, who was the baseball coach and an assistant for football, summed it up best. In his best Don Adams' *Get Smart* voice he said, 'Guys, it's 38 against 10,000 out there.'"

Though a half century has passed since he last played collegiately, Butler still recalls his formative years at Eastern.

"My mother always said that I thought the world was flat and dropped off at Bethany," he said. "But I learned some valuable things (at Eastern) that helped me down the road. There were things I learned about line play and such, but there were things I learned about life that still hold true today."

FOUR-DOWN TERRITORY

Favorite Football Movie: That Denzel Washington one, *Remember the Titans*. I always wanted to take a team to a graveyard like he did.

First Car: A 1949 Ford. My brother-in-law junked it. I went and got it and bought two used tires, one for $2 and another for $1. It also needed a battery. I could only drive it up to about 40 miles an hour and then it would begin to shimmy. I drove that back and forth from Lovington to Eastern. I didn't get there very fast either way.

Worst Summer Job: Painting the outside of buildings.

Favorite Subject in School: History. It was my minor in college. Again, that's probably because the (registration) line was the shortest.

DICK PORTEE

Dick Portee hadn't planned on going to college, let alone playing football at Eastern.

"My (high school) counselor didn't have me on that track," said Portee, "but my high school coach John Alexander pushed me in that direction."

It was Alexander who brought his star running back on visits to Eastern and Western Illinois University after his 1960 graduation from Decatur Eisenhower High School.

At the time, WIU was a powerhouse under head coach Lou Saban, who later coached the Boston Patriots and Buffalo Bills. The Leathernecks had just completed an unbeaten 1 959 season.

"(Saban) was very nice to me and Mr. Alexander, but Western wasn't very friendly (in terms of recruiting me)," Portee said. "I wasn't very big, only about 5-(foot)-6 and 155 pounds."

In contrast, Eastern was a struggling program, then coached by Ralph Kohl and assisted by Jack Kaley.

"Our high school team had played at Charleston during the 1959 season," Portee said. "I ran for 120 yards on 10 carries against them. Ralph Kohl was there to see it, and that game was still in his mind."

Thus, Portee committed to Eastern.

"There weren't any scholarships in those days," he said.

Instead, Portee attended Eastern under an education program in which he would pay back his costs by teaching in the state's public educational system upon graduation.

"I also had a couple of jobs," he said. "I worked in the student union for a time. I also worked in the athletic laundry."

Portee remembers Kohl as "a beautiful guy. He was an All-American at Michigan. I really enjoyed playing for him."

Meanwhile, Kaley, who also served as Eastern's baseball coach, "cut me two years in a row."

Dick Portee has coached for nearly 50 years (Photo courtesy of North Carolina State University Athletics).

Portee got the message.

"I gave up after that," laughed Portee.

During the early 1960s, very few African-Americans attended Eastern.

"It was very limited, there were maybe 12 athletes and there were 10 or 12 African-American women at that time," Portee recalled.

The experience was quite different from his days at Eisenhower.

"Decatur was pretty integrated at that time," Portee said. "(Eastern) was a lot different."

Portee didn't view himself as a pioneer or trailblazer.

"I never thought about it," he said. "I was just happy to get an opportunity. I was blessed.

I was a survivor. There was a lot happening (culturally) in those years. Looking back, maybe it was really something, but I never thought about it back in those days."

Moreover, Portee enjoyed his time at Eastern.

"It was all good," he said. "It was a learning experience. There was only one black family in Charleston. But, no, I didn't really encounter any racism. If I did, I was naïve to it. We made it work."

Though he could have lived on campus, Portee and other African-Americans chose to be housed off-campus by Ona Norton. Beginning in the 1950s, Kohl asked Mrs. Norton and her husband, Kenneth, to assist in housing black athletes.

"My wife and I stopped by Charleston in the summer (of 2010)," he said. "I tried to find the house, but couldn't locate it."

Though he spent most of his time away from the classroom and football field with other African-Americans, Portee mentioned white teammate Gene Vidoni.

"We had an intramural basketball team," Portee said. "Gene was the only white guy on our team. I asked him if he wanted to play with us. He was a good friend."

During Portee's time at Eastern, the Panthers struggled on the field.

"We weren't real good in football," Portee said, "but we played hard."

After playing as a wingback his freshman year, Portee switched to the defensive backfield as a sophomore. While he played in an era when most teams still favored the running game, Portee faced innovative coach Howard Fletcher's pass-happy Northern Illinois offense.

"They had George Bork at quarterback, and he could really throw the ball," Portee said. "They threw it all around."

NIU won the 1963 Mineral Water Bowl and was declared NCAA College Division national champions. Bork, who played in the Canadian Football League, was later enshrined in the College Football Hall of Fame.

Portee also remembered the assassination of President John F. Kennedy. Unlike the NFL, Eastern cancelled its game the weekend after Kennedy's death.

Rod Butler was one of Portee's Panther teammates.

"He was an outstanding football player," Portee said. "He grew up in Lovington, which is about 13 miles from Decatur. We didn't know each other in high school, but we later coached together at Illinois State."

Portee made second team All-Interstate Intercollegiate Athletic Conference in 1964, his senior season.

Upon graduation, he returned to his alma mater. Portee spent five years at Decatur Eisenhower, where he taught physical education and driver's education. Portee coached football, basketball and tennis.

In 1969, Portee moved to the collegiate level when he accepted a position at Illinois State University.

"I was one of the first two African-American coaches hired there," he said.

While at ISU, Portee earned his master's degree in Health and Physical Education. Portee coached defensive and offensive backs for the Redbirds through the 1976 season. In 1977, he became the recruiting coordinator and defensive backs coach at Cornell University of the Ivy League.

The University of Maryland was his next coaching destination. He spent time coaching outside linebackers and wide receivers for the Terrapins from 1982 to 1989.

"We won three Atlantic Coast Conference championships under (head coach) Bobby Ross," he said.

While at Maryland, Portee was part of one of the biggest comebacks in NCAA football history. Future NFL quarterback Frank Reich rallied the Terrapins from a 31-point deficit to a victory over Miami in 1984.

"That game still gives me goose bumps," Portee said.

When Al Molde left Eastern after the 1986 season, Portee applied for the Panthers' head coaching position.

"I never got an interview," he said.

Instead, Eastern hired Bob Spoo, the former Purdue assistant who would coach the Panthers through the 2011 season.

Meanwhile, Portee became a running backs coach at North Carolina State in 1990. He spent nine years with the Wolfpack before joining Chris Palmer's Cleveland Browns staff for one season.

"It was the Browns' first year back in the NFL as an expansion team," he said. "There was a lot of history there. I cherish that year in the pros."

Portee returned to North Carolina State in 2000 under head coach Chuck Amato. Future San Diego Charger Philip Rivers quarterbacked the Wolfpack during that era.

"He threw the ball real funny," said Portee of Rivers' unorthodox mechanics. "He still does, but now he's making millions of dollars."

Portee lost his job when Amato was fired in 2006. Portee landed assistant coaching jobs at North Carolina Central University and Fayetteville State after departing NC State.

Though at one time he would have liked the

chance to become a head coach, Portee is satisfied as an assistant.

"I've enjoyed the process," he said. "Those days (of becoming a head coach) are past. I've enjoyed being a coordinator. I want the kids to be good on the field and successful off it.

"I've been coaching football for 45 years. It's been quite a career."

FOUR-DOWN TERRITORY

Favorite Football Movie: *Brian's Song* because of the nature of the movie. It's a very moving film. It's an emotional movie.

First Car: A 1954 Chevy. I bought it used. I paid $15 a month for a couple of years. I put a Hurst shifter in the floor.

Worst Summer Job: I worked at Wagner's Casting in Decatur. It was a foundry. My father worked there. I worked there for two summers. That was tough work.

Favorite Subject in School: I was all athletics. You have to understand that I was one of the few who went to college from my high school. I enjoyed PE. I loved (the game) bombardment on Fridays.

TED SCHMITZ

Ted Schmitz could have played at any one of the state universities in Illinois, but only Eastern offered him the chance to play two sports.

"I visited all the schools," Schmitz said. "Northern, Southern, Western, Illinois State. Even Monmouth was somehow in the picture. But only Eastern said I could play two sports, no ifs, ands or buts."

Those two sports were football and baseball. Hence, Schmitz agreed to join the Panthers following his graduation from Streator High School in 1962. Ironically, Northern Illinois was coached by the legendary Howard Fletcher, a Streator native, at the time.

"The funny thing is that my first game at Eastern was against Northern," Schmitz said. "I remember that I broke a tooth in the game."

Playing at 5-foot-10 and 180 pounds,

Schmitz began his Panther career as a center and linebacker under head coach Ralph Kohl.

"It was a good bunch of guys to play with in that era," Schmitz said. "We didn't win many games. We had no speed. One year we started with a couple of wins, and then we lost (wide receiver) Tad Heiminger to an injury on a kickoff. We had no depth. I'm not sure we won another game."

Clyde Biggers took over as Eastern head coach in 1965, Schmitz's senior season. Though he liked Kohl, Schmitz immediately noticed a difference with Biggers.

"He was a big man, something like 6-7 and 260 pounds," he said. "He would school you. He would quiz you on things like down and distance. He was so thorough. I learned things from him that I have used to this day."

According to Schmitz, Biggers was also innovative.

"He would have pictures taken from the press box or roof," Schmitz said. "Those pictures would be in our locker room at halftime for us to review. He was doing this back in 1965. The next year they outlawed it."

Schmitz, one of the team's captains, was also able to concentrate solely on defense under Biggers.

"It was the beginning of platoon football. I didn't have to play both ways anymore. I never felt so rested," Schmitz said. "It was like a treat."

As for baseball, Schmitz joined football teammates Gene Vidoni and Roger Haberer on the Panther roster. For Schmitz, playing in the 1964 NAIA World Series proved to be the ultimate baseball memory.

"That was the most thrilling thing," he said. "It was in St. Joseph, Missouri. Seeing all those great players, the scouts on hand and the big crowds was so much fun."

The Panthers, coached by Bill McCabe, lost a pair of one-run decisions in the Series. The first came when Fred Beene of defending champion Sam Houston State outdueled Charleston native Marty Pattin of Eastern, 2-1. Both pitchers would play in the major leagues.

Schmitz had to catch the second game because regular Gene Vidoni's hand was too swollen from Pattin's fastball in the Series opener.

"Otherwise I might not have played," Schmitz said.

Schmitz began his coaching career as a graduate assistant under Biggers. He and Ben Newcomb coached the freshmen. Schmitz spent every weekend scouting the next Panther opponent.

"In those days you got in your car and drove to see them play," he said. "You came back and wrote up your report and got it ready to share with the team."

After coaching for two years at East Peoria High School, Schmitz joined Newcomb's staff at Augustana College in Rock Island. Future NFL star Ken Anderson quarterbacked the Vikings.

"He was something else," Schmitz said.

In 1972, Schmitz landed a job on Gerry Hart's staff at Illinois State. He was joined there by former Panther teammates Rod Butler and Dick Portee. Schmitz remained at ISU through the 1980 season.

Schmitz was reunited with Hart in 1981 in the Canadian Football League. The pair coached with the Saskatchewan Roughriders for two seasons. In 1983, Schmitz joined the Hamilton Tiger-Cats as their defensive coordinator.

"We were quite successful," Schmitz said. "In eight years, we played in four Grey Cups."

In 1986, Hamilton won the Grey Cup. A year later, Schmitz took over the team as interim head coach when head coach Al Bruno suffered a heart attack.

Former Panther teammate Roger Haberer wasn't surprised by Schmitz's success.

"For his size, Ted was pretty darn tough (as a player)," Haberer said. "But, as you can tell by his career as a coach, he was pretty smart on the field as well."

After his days in the CFL ended, Schmitz coached in the Arena 2 Football League. In 2005, he started the Bloomington Extreme of the United Football League. Today, the franchise is known as the Edge.

"We built it from scratch," he said. "We started the team in December, went to camp in March and played our first game in April.

"Three years later we were in the championship game."

Schmitz, the team's director of player personnel, signed former Tuscola High School

Ted Schmitz is the personnel director for the Bloomington Edge of the Indoor Football League (Photo courtesy of the *Bloomington Extreme*).

and Illinois State star quarterback Dusty Burk.

"He's the reason why we played for the championship," Schmitz said.

Burk, the head football coach at Normal University High School, later became the Edge offensive coordinator.

"Our game (the IFL) is better (than Arena 2)," Schmitz said. "We play with four defensive backs, not three like they do. We have no nets. In Arena 2, there's no real coaching, no real strategy. I hated it."

According to Schmitz, much of the Edge success is in part because of his alma mater.

"The No. 1 success we have is Eastern Illinois," Schmitz said. "Roc (Bellantoni) and I have worked together to bring (former Panther) players here."

Among the former Eastern players to have suited up for the Edge are B.J. Brown, Andre Raymond, Anthony Rubican, Ke'Andre Sams and Jeff Sobol.

In addition to his duties with the Edge, Schmitz has worked as the color analyst on ISU Redbird football broadcasts since 2000.

"I love it," he said. "Calling the game from the press box is like coaching. This makes football year-round for me. When ISU ends its season, it's time for the Extreme. When we end our season, it's time for ISU again."

Each season, ISU and Eastern renew their "Prairie State Rivalry."

"It's really fun," Schmitz said. "I am close to both coaching staffs. I love the players on both teams."

So, who does he root for?

"I'm working for ISU, but a little bit of my heart is with Eastern."

After all, 50 years ago, the Panthers made Ted Schmitz an offer he couldn't refuse.

FOUR-DOWN TERRITORY

Favorite Football Movie: I'd probably pick *Rudy*. As far as the emotions go, it's hard to beat. You can almost picture yourself in his shoes. It's one of the few movies I can watch over and over.

First Car: A 1941 Plymouth. It had three gears and running boards. We had a lot of fun in that car. There were things like panty raids in those days. I gave my paycheck for it, which was about $100.

Worst Summer Job: I worked for Streator Drain Tile. I was 16 years old. I had to carry around these 109-pound tiles all day long. It just wiped me out.

Favorite Subject in School: I wasn't any good in English . . . I like math.

GENE VIDONI

One might be tempted to give Gene Vidoni's name a quick glance and move down the 1964 Little All-American list. Then, someone mentions that Vidoni didn't start his collegiate football career *until his junior year.*

"Ralph Kohl was the football coach back then," said Vidoni. "He liked my aggressiveness on the baseball field. He asked me to come and play football."

Vidoni had played both sports at Pekin High School. He arrived at Eastern via a baseball scholarship.

"I played in the *Peoria Journal-Star* Sunday League," Vidoni said. "It was a pretty competitive league back in the '60s and '70s. There were five or six other guys from the Peoria area (who played at Eastern)."

Vidoni soon took over catching duties for Jack Kaley's Panthers. Vidoni's scholarship covered only a portion of his tuition.

"In those days (Eastern athletes) had their tuition and what was called a state job," Vidoni explained. "My spring job was to maintain

home plate and the mound. It paid something like $60 a month. It was pretty minimal."

Thus, when Kohl offered a scholarship to cover more of his tuition, Vidoni accepted the football coach's offer.

Vidoni lived with another Eastern football player, running back Rod Butler.

"We lived at 207 Lincoln," he said. "Now it's a parking lot."

The very trait that attracted Kohl's attention made Vidoni a standout at defensive end. Vidoni earned not only the honorable mention Little All-American honors, but also took home Interstate Intercollegiate Athletic Association first team and EIU Most Valuable Player accolades.

"I just went out and played as hard as I could play," Vidoni said. "My dad always told me to do things the best you can do them, so I carried that over into whatever came along."

Meanwhile, Eastern football was in the midst of a slide that saw the Panthers not post a winning record until the national championship year of 1978.

"Our defensive line averaged about 195 pounds," Vidoni said. "That wouldn't even make us defensive backs today."

No matter their size, the Panthers' defensive line was anchored by Vidoni.

"Gene was a 175-pound defensive end. I don't think people today could imagine anyone his size playing that position," said quarterback Roger Haberer, who was cocaptain along with Vidoni. "He was the toughest, hardest-hitting player we had in my four years at Eastern. He never took a play off and was always going 100%."

Ted Schmitz, who played linebacker for the Panthers, said there wasn't a tougher player than Vidoni.

"Nobody wanted to go against Vidoni in practice," Schmitz said.

Vidoni said, "We didn't win a lot of games, but we had some outstanding players."

He cited Butler, Haberer, Schmitz, Wayne Stingley and Ben Ward. Four of the five are members of the Eastern Hall of Fame.

"We didn't really have a weight room. There was no training table. We had an old block building for a locker room. We were still the smallest state school at that time," he said.

Vidoni pointed out that many of Eastern's athletes participated in two sports.

"We didn't have just guys who showed up for football," he said. "Yet of the 40 or 50 guys we had on the (football) team, about 25 ended up becoming football coaches."

Vidoni, of course, was one such example. He played on the 1964 Eastern baseball team that qualified for the NAIA World Series. Vidoni vividly remembers the Panthers losing the Series opener 2-1 to Sam Houston State. The game was a matchup of future major league pitchers Marty Pattin for Eastern and Fred Beene for Sam Houston State.

"Marty struck out 17 and he couldn't throw a curveball that night," Vidoni said. "He was bouncing it all over the place. He called me out to the mound and said, 'Just sit back and I'm bringing the fastball.' He was probably throwing in the low 90s that night. He struck out 17 with just his fastball."

And what a fastball it was. Vidoni had to place his hand in an ice bucket between innings.

"I couldn't play the next game because my hand was so swollen," he said.

A season later, Vidoni was named the team's MVP and all-conference catcher. He next played in the San Francisco Giants' minor-league system. Though he never played higher than the Double-A level, Vidoni relished his time in pro baseball.

"I was fortunate to be on the same field with some of the (San Francisco) greats in spring training," he said. "I was catching. Juan Marichal was pitching. Big (Willie) McCovey was batting. Willie Mays was in center. Mays and (Orlando) Cepeda, neither of those guys were as big as you thought they'd be, but boy could they play."

Vidoni spent time in the minors with future Giants Al Gallagher and Bobby Bonds.

"I used to buy Barry Bonds ice cream cones," Vidoni said. "He was only about two or three at the time. Bobby Bonds had three kids under the age of five. Bobby was dirt poor. And look what happened, he and his son both made it big in baseball. They wound up with more than enough money for ice cream cones."

Vidoni's baseball career came to an end when he was drafted into the Army in 1966.

"If it weren't for getting drafted, I have to think that Gene would have made it (to the major leagues)," said Schmitz. "(Former Eastern player) Bart Zeller made it (for one game with the St. Louis Cardinals in 1970). Gene was better than Bart Zeller."

When he was discharged from military service in 1968, Vidoni returned to school and finished his degree.

In 1969 he was hired by the Casey, Illinois school district. He coached football, basketball and track.

In 1971, Vidoni started the school's baseball and intramural basketball programs. He coached baseball until 1999 and was inducted into the Illinois High School Baseball Coaches Association Hall of Fame.

During that same stretch, Vidoni served as an assistant football coach. Casey won the 1985 state championship and finished as the runner-up in 1982 under head coach Keith Sinclair, also an Eastern graduate.

Along the way, Vidoni influenced numerous individuals, and not all of them Casey students.

"Coach Gene Vidoni was first and foremost a teacher," said Jeff Strohm, who student-taught under Vidoni in 1988.

Gene Vidoni played in the San Francisco Giants' farm system prior to becoming a successful prep coach at Casey-Westfield High School (Photo courtesy of Terri Cox).

Strohm had competed against Vidoni-coached teams as an athlete at rival Marshall High School. Strohm, a fellow EIU graduate, later served as an assistant basketball coach for two Final Four teams.

"He taught his students and those around him every day about life, relationships, and about whatever sports or activity they were undertaking," Strohm said. "He was the epitome of tough love. He cared and touched people's lives, not by telling them what they wanted to hear, but by telling them what they needed to hear.

"The greatest thing you can say about him and really any teacher/coach is he helped prepare, those who were fortunate to be around him and those who were taught by him, for the rest of their lives. He instilled the values of work ethic, commitment, loyalty, perseverance and honesty to all he touched. His humility and candidness was a rarity in his profession. His legacy is that many people's lives are a success because of what he taught them."

Vidoni retired in 2000 and moved to Louisiana for a brief time.

"Mr. Sinclair kept in touch with me every Friday," Vidoni said.

When Casey wasn't happy with the direction its football program was going in, Sinclair and Vidoni were coaxed out of retirement to rekindle the Warriors' pride. The duo agreed to return.

So did the Casey program. Starting in 2003, the Warriors made deep runs in the Illinois High School Association playoffs. In 2008 and 2011, Casey finished as the Class 2A runner-up.

The Warriors' home field was named Sinclair-Vidoni Field.

"That's quite an honor," Vidoni said. "We joke they probably put it up with Velcro."

In 2001, Vidoni was enshrined into the Eastern Hall of Fame. A six-time letterman, Vidoni fondly recalls his days on the gridiron.

"I cherish those two years I played football at Eastern," he said.

FOUR-DOWN TERRITORY

Favorite Football Movie: I've seen a lot of them. My favorites are probably *Rudy* and *The Blind Side*. I liked *Rudy* because of the human aspect, the heart of the individual. He made something out of nothing. *The Blind Side* shows that if someone gets a chance, anything can happen.

First Car: It was a '56 MG Roadster, a two-seater. I bought it up in Naperville. I didn't know if it would make it home. Once I got home I did a lot of work on it.

Worst Summer Job: I didn't have any bad ones. In those days if you had a summer job and you could make a little money, you were lucky.

Favorite Subject in School: Physical education, of course. I liked algebra, but didn't do very well in what came afterward.

ROGER HABERER

Football can be viewed from a number of different perspectives. The players on the field and the coaches on the sideline might see things one way. The fans in the stands and the media in the press box might see another. There's also a group of individuals who must see it all with the most objective of eyes. Roger Haberer is one such man.

Haberer was an official. More specifically, he was an umpire on a crew that refereed for the Big Ten Conference.

"I worked some big games over the years," said Haberer. "But, I always looked at any game that I worked as being special."

It didn't start out this way. Roger Haberer wasn't born in the stripes and cap of a game official. In fact, Haberer was quite an athlete in his own right.

He grew up in Pocahontas, Illinois, a small town in southern Illinois.

"The town was around 715 people when I grew up, but it has really grown since then. It's up to around 800 now," joked Haberer of the town that also spawned country music singer Gretchen Wilson.

"There were basically three things to do there," Haberer said. "Hunt, fish and play baseball."

In high school Haberer expanded his list to include basketball and football. That caught the attention of former Eastern football player turned assistant coach Jim Erdmann.

"He brought Dave Sibert, a friend of mine, and me up to Charleston in the spring of 1962 during the baseball season," Haberer said.

Haberer committed to Eastern where he would excel at both football and baseball.

"I played for Ralph Kohl," Haberer said. "We were less than mediocre. We didn't have any spring football. There were only about 40 guys on the traveling squad."

Still, Haberer won the starting quarterback job early in his collegiate career.

"I actually started the last two games my freshman year," he said. "My sophomore year I started the season at quarterback, but was out with a busted shoulder.

"We had this play where I would fake the screen one way and then turn and throw it to the other side. Well, the play took so long to develop that I took quite a shot."

Yet, in 1964, Haberer established himself as a Panthers standout. The junior passed for a career-high 1,443 yards and 13 touchdowns. Yet, it was a victory over conference power Central Michigan that stands out in his mind.

"We upset them here," Haberer said. "We had lost pretty one-sided up there the year before (35-15). So to win 17-14 my junior year was a pretty big deal."

Haberer turned out to be a pretty big deal himself. Finishing his career with 3,647 passing yards, he was a two-time All-IIAC selection and earned honorable mention status as a Little All-American quarterback.

On the baseball diamond, Haberer started as a first baseman/catcher on the Panthers' 1964 NAIA World Series team that sported future major league pitcher Marty Pattin.

Haberer led the 1966 team with a .371 average. He earned all-conference honors and was chosen as Eastern's Most Valuable Player. He was also the recipient of the Charles Lantz Award that honored a senior for academic and athletic achievement.

Despite his baseball prowess, it was football that gave him a shot at the professional game. The Chicago Bears selected Haberer in the 19th round of the NFL draft.

"In those days there weren't any mini-camps," he said. "It was a 10-day camp. It was eye-opening. I realized I didn't know how to

prepare for it. I threw and threw beforehand (to try and get ready)."

The Bears' camp was held at Soldier Field and featured the likes of Gale Sayers, Dick Butkus and Doug Buffone.

"What quickness they had," Haberer said. "There was a play I was to spin left and hand the ball off to Sayers. He was so fast that he was past me before I knew it. I couldn't make the handoff."

Though he was cut by Chicago, Haberer still views those 10 days positively.

"It would have been nice to have made it, but sometimes things just don't work out," he said. "George Halas treated me well. I still have a football he sent me. In fact, I'm looking at it right here on the shelf."

With pro football no longer in the picture, Haberer began his teaching career. He started out in Tinley Park.

"I taught there four years, but then my wife (Barbara) and I were looking to get back

Panther head coach Clyde Biggers (left) and quarterback Roger Haberer.

downstate to raise our children," he said.

Thus, Haberer landed a job in the Casey school district, not far from the town where he earned eight collegiate letters.

"We settled in Charleston," Haberer said. "We lived there from 1970 until 2006. Then, we moved to Mattoon."

At Casey, Haberer taught math, coached briefly, and served as both a counselor and athletic director.

"We do a little bit of everything in a school like Casey," Haberer noted. "You help out wherever you can."

At Casey, Haberer was reunited with former Eastern teammate Gene Vidoni.

"We worked together for 15 years," Haberer said. "Gene is still at it. He's coaching football even after he retired. And he, along with Keith Sinclair, is still going strong."

During his time at Casey, Haberer began his career as a football official.

"I was already umpiring baseball and refereeing basketball," he said. "One summer I was up at Baker Field in Charleston with my two kids. A friend of mine came up to me and asked if I'd ever thought about officiating football. He said I ought to try it."

After dismissing the idea at first, Haberer soon joined the four-man crew. He began at the high school level.

"We were doing South 7 (Conference) games in places like Champaign and Springfield," he said.

By his second year, Haberer found himself also officiating collegiate games.

"Herm Rohrig, who was with the Big Ten, got me some work at Illinois State and Western Illinois," Haberer said. "Some guys have to wait 10 or 12 years for something like that. I was very fortunate."

He credits friend and fellow official J.W. Sanders with his growth as an official.

"He was very instrumental in my career," Haberer said. "He basically lived around the corner from me. He was very particular on how a game should be officiated. He worked really hard at it."

Haberer also recalls working as many as three scrimmages in a single day with Charleston native and future NFL official Ken Baker (son of Eastern Hall of Famer Merv Baker).

"We'd drive to DeKalb and work at Northern and then head back down to Terre Haute for a scrimmage at Indiana State. Then it was back to Charleston to work at Eastern," Haberer said. "All for little to nothing in terms of pay."

Yet, the experience paid off. By 1991, Haberer was working Big Ten Conference games, something he would do for 15 years. He retired as an official in 2005.

"It was a great experience," he said.

Haberer worked as an umpire, the official who lines up approximately five yards off the line of scrimmage on the defensive side of the ball.

"The position, of course, that makes it fairly dangerous," Haberer said. "You're between the linebackers with players behind you. It's the only position with players behind you.

"When you get hit, you get hit from the blind side. A good umpire can control the players on the line of scrimmage."

Despite the umpire's vulnerability to danger, Haberer was only injured once during his time in the Big Ten.

"I missed a total of 10 minutes in 15 years," he said. "I pulled my calf muscle. It was a cold day and I slipped. The Michigan State trainer taped me up and put something in my shoe to raise my heel to take the stress off it. I made it to the fourth quarter but reaggravated it and finally had to come out."

Haberer also recalled a time when his past mixed with his present.

"I was working a game up at Michigan," he said. "We had just gotten dressed and were getting ready for the game. They had these really big pictures up on the wall of their former All-Americans. I looked up and there was my old coach Ralph Kohl. His big ole head was smiling down on me. Sure, he was younger in the picture, but it was him. Ralph had first played for Bear Bryant at Kentucky but then transferred to Michigan after the war. He was an All-American at Michigan. That's just a funny little story I remember."

Haberer worked 12 bowl games during his career. He twice officiated the Orange Bowl. Yet, the Big Ten sticks with him.

"They really duke it out," Haberer said. "I had the Michigan–Ohio State game five times. I had the game the year Michigan won the national championship (1997). I also had the game when Ohio State won the national championship in 2002. You get on the field and realize those two really don't like each other. Michigan and Michigan State could also be pretty heated."

When asked if certain Big Ten coaches were rougher on officials than others, Haberer replied, "Sure, but I don't want to get into that."

However, Haberer did offer that "some of the ones you think would be really tough were actually pretty good guys."

Haberer cited former Michigan head coach Lloyd Carr as an example.

"I'd take him over a lot of coaches. He'd scream at you and then go back to coaching his team," he said.

Haberer also mentioned three coaches as "real gentlemen." That trio included Joe Paterno of Penn State, Randy Walker of Northwestern and Bill Mallory of Indiana.

"One time I made a heck of a mistake (against Mallory's Hoosiers)," Haberer recalled. "He didn't like it, but he just went on with the game."

In 1989, Eastern honored Haberer by inducting the former two-sport star into its Hall of Fame.

"It gives you a little pride to know that people recognize what you've accomplished," Haberer said. "However, I would have given up (the induction) for a few more wins in the fall."

No matter the number of wins Haberer helped bring home during his Panther football career, his success will easily stand the test of time.

FOUR-DOWN TERRITORY

Favorite Football Movie: I really don't have one. Some of them are very unrealistic. I guess maybe I look at them too seriously. Having said that, I love *Major League*.

First Car: It was a 1954 Ford. My dad got it for me my sophomore year. It had a huge steering wheel. It used more oil than gas.

Worst Summer Job: I always worked construction back home. I guess it was pouring a pier in a creek down in Bond County. I had to vibrate that concrete down. It was over 90 degrees. We weren't at it for too many days, but it does stand out in my memory.

Favorite Subject in School: Math. I still enjoy math.

THE 1970s

MIKE HEIMERDINGER

It seems only natural that Mike Heimerdinger became a coach.

"When I was probably about six or so I remember being at my dad's practices and games," said Heimerdinger, then the offensive coordinator for the Tennessee Titans, in 2009.

Heimerdinger's father Bob was no ordinary high school coach. The senior Heimerdinger had been a Little All-America quarterback for the Northern Illinois Huskies in the early 1950s.

"A friend of mine's dad worked for the (DeKalb) *Chronicle* and we were at a Northern Illinois football game," Heimerdinger recalled. "I must have been in seventh grade or so. They were honoring All-Americans from Northern Illinois. I remember seeing my dad on the field. I said, 'What's he doing out there? He never played football.'"

Heimerdinger's friend's father then took him into the university's field house and showed him Bob Heimerdinger's retired jersey.

"It was the only one that was retired at the time," Mike Heimerdinger said. "(He never said a word about it), that was my father."

Heimerdinger grew up with sports all around. As a youngster he served as the manager for all his father's high school teams.

"I picked up towels, I moved starting blocks, I chased down loose basketballs," he said. "I went to a Catholic grade school about three blocks from the high school. I was over at practice every day."

Weekends meant NIU home football games.

"That's what we did every Saturday," Heimerdinger said.

When Heimerdinger reached high school he played football, basketball and baseball.

"You went one to the other with maybe a day's break in between," Heimerdinger said. "You learned to make decisions in other sports by playing more than one. That's something missing today, but that's what you have to do to play (today)."

Yet, his father didn't coach him in high school. Instead, the senior Heimerdinger became the freshmen football coach at NIU under Howard Fletcher and later Richard Urich.

"Mike was in high school at that time, (and) Mike was a good athlete," Bob Heimerdinger said. "Everyone says he can't wait to coach his own kid. I was not that way."

Heimerdinger explained that he had learned firsthand just how difficult it was to coach a son from seeing his friends and colleagues go through it.

When his prep career ended, Mike Heimerdinger had just two offers. One came from Augustana College. The other came from a familiar face, Jack Dean, the head coach at Eastern.

"I grew up watching Jack play," Heimerdinger said.

In fact, Dean had played for Heimerdinger's father at DeKalb High School and then as a halfback at NIU under head coach Howard Fletcher.

"Jack was undersized but nobody could catch him," Heimerdinger said. "My dad and I watched him play in Canada (in the Canadian Football League) on TV. Today, he'd be a slot receiver and a return man on punts and kickoffs."

Thus, Heimerdinger enrolled at Eastern to play football under Dean and baseball under Bill McCabe. There, Heimerdinger roomed with a quarterback from Oak Park named Mike Shanahan.

Shanahan's collegiate career ended when one of his kidneys had to be removed following an injury in the Panthers' spring game.

"He was real close to death," Heimerdinger said. "I remember sitting in the hospital and the priest came in to give him last rites. When you're young you never think anybody is going to die. That really put it into perspective."

While Shanahan was forced to give up his football playing career, Heimerdinger chose to concentrate on baseball solely.

"I figured that I had a chance to play (baseball) on the professional level," he said.

Heimerdinger played center field and became an integral part of the Eastern offense. He still holds the Panther career record for stolen bases with 51.

"Most people don't believe that when they look at me now," Heimerdinger laughed. "I took a lot of pitches to get on base. I could run."

So why has his record held up for over four decades?

"Metal bats may have changed things," Heimerdinger speculated. "There are more doubles and triples these days."

Heimerdinger and his Panther teammates qualified for the 1974 Division II World Series under head coach J.W. Sanders.

"We got to go all the way to Springfield," Heimerdinger quipped. "Seriously, it was a great experience. It rained all week. We were ahead and our pitcher was shutting them down. They couldn't touch him, but after a rain delay, he cooled down and they got to him."

Eastern lost the game and settled for a fourth-place finish at the World Series.

In hopes of getting an offer to play professional baseball, Heimerdinger stayed on to assist Sanders for a season.

"That offer never came," he said.

Heimerdinger then took a job coaching and teaching at Johnsburg High School. After he spent two years in the prep ranks, an offer came from an old friend, Mike Shanahan.

"I had gone and visited Mike every year (as Shanahan moved up the college coaching ranks). Mike was at the University of Florida, and they had an opening for a graduate assistant," Heimerdinger said. "I jumped at it. That got me into college football."

Heimerdinger became part of a revitalized Gator program that earned a bowl berth.

"We had Cris Collinsworth at receiver," Heimerdinger said. "We ran the run-and-shoot (offense). Only about four teams were doing that then. We went from 1-10 to the Tangerine Bowl."

The following year Heimerdinger moved to his first official assistant coach job at the Air Force Academy. From there he progressed through a series of jobs that took him from the likes of North Texas State to Cal State Fullerton to Rice to Duke.

Then in 1995, Shanahan again called him with an offer. Heimerdinger's former Eastern teammate hired him as receivers coach with the Denver Broncos.

"I was at Mike's house when his Super Bowl ring from the 49ers came," Heimerdinger said. "I said, 'Oh, I'd like to get one of those.' Mike said, 'We'll get one. We'll get more than one.'"

Shanahan's prediction was fulfilled when the Broncos won consecutive Super Bowls in 1997 and '98. Joining Heimerdinger on the Denver staff was John Teerlinck, the former Western Illinois star who served as Eastern's defensive coordinator during the 1978 national championship season.

"Heimerdinger is very well respected," said former Broncos' beat writer Bill Williamson, who now covers the AFC West for espn.com. "He has a nice track record. Quarterbacks have

Mike Heimerdinger served as the offensive coordinator for two NFL teams (Photo courtesy of Tennessee Titans).

flourished under him. (Former Denver wide receiver) Rod Smith loves him. Smith credits Heimerdinger for his career. Smith went from an undrafted free agent to a potential Hall of Fame receiver."

After leaving the Broncos, Heimerdinger served as offensive coordinator with the Tennessee Titans and the New York Jets.

During his time in the NFL, Heimerdinger saw plenty of change.

"People are throwing the ball more than ever," he stated. "It used to be, run the football and play good defense. That's still important (but) a good quarterback always gives you a pretty good chance. Look at what Drew Brees did with New Orleans."

When the topic of becoming a head coach came up, Heimerdinger responded, "I'd like to. It's always been a goal, but for that to happen we'll have to find the right fit with an owner."

Of Heimerdinger's chances of becoming an NFL head coach, Williamson said, "He's been that hot candidate two or three times. His name has been out there. People think a lot of him, but I just don't know if he'll ever get the chance."

Heimerdinger never got that chance. In November 2010 he underwent treatment for cancer. Three months later, the Titans interviewed Heimerdinger twice for their head coaching position when Jeff Fisher resigned. However, Tennessee hired offensive line coach Mike Munchak as Fisher's replacement.

A day later, Munchak fired Heimerdinger, who had a year left on his contact.

"It's never easy to be fired," Heimerdinger said. "(Munchak) has had to do what's good for the Titans. I appreciate my time here, but it's never easy to be fired."

On September 30, 2011, Heimerdinger passed away after his nearly year-long battle with cancer. He was 58.

"It is with a heavy heart, but a trust in God, that we say good-bye to our beloved Dinger who lost his courageous battle with cancer," Heimerdinger's wife, Kathie, said in a statement. "Mike approached cancer with the same vigor and tenacity that he approached any football game—to win. Even in the final minutes he never gave up—that was our Dinger."

FOUR-DOWN TERRITORY

Favorite Football Movie: I really can't think of one. I'll watch them. If something like *Rudy* comes on TV, I'll watch it, but if it's taken me this long to think about it, I guess I don't really have a favorite.

First Car: I got it in 1968. It was a '64 Comet. I had to carry a case of oil around in my trunk. I had to add oil about every week. I never took that car farther than my house. I always figured it would break down if I went too far.

Worst Summer Job: I worked on a Del Monte cleanup crew at midnight. There were all kinds of cleanup jobs that went with it. Cleaning the conveyor belt for peas was probably the worst. You had to use your hands and take off the rotten ones.

Favorite Subject in School: History, by far. That was my major.

NATE ANDERSON

Those who played with Nate Anderson at East St. Louis Lincoln High School may never have expected him to become Eastern's first "big-time" football All-American, especially as a running back.

"I was a defensive back in high school," said Anderson from his home in Belleville. "We were five or six deep at running back."

Anderson also competed in basketball and track during those days.

"Back in my day when you went out for sports, you went out for sports," he said.

When his prep career finished, Anderson didn't receive any scholarship offers. Yet, former high school teammate Victor Brooks, who ran track at Eastern, urged his friend to enroll.

"He told me to give it a try," Anderson said.

Thus, Anderson enrolled at Eastern during the summer after his high school graduation.

"I needed to work on my grades," Anderson said. "I never really did enough in high school. But, I got my act together."

Anderson praised the learning atmosphere at Eastern.

"I had this English professor who helped me

out early on," he said. "I don't even remember her name, but she looked at my first essay and told me to come see her. I got up at eight o'clock in the morning and went over for some help. She really turned me around. She got my confidence together. I got a B out of that class."

Anderson also faced the adjustment to a predominantly white student body.

"I faced some cultural changes," he said. "I came from an all-black high school. But the people at Eastern were great. I enjoyed my time there. It was a nice campus. There were small classes."

He also enjoyed the town of Charleston.

"I got to know people in town," Anderson said. "I wasn't just one of those people who only stuck to campus."

By spring, Anderson decided to walk on to head coach Clyde Biggers' football team.

"I wanted to play," he said. "With my grades in order, it worked out."

Anderson began playing defensive back and "a little tight end."

"They ran me on an end around a few times," Anderson said. "It seems like I'd go for about 25 yards each time."

Biggers and his staff quickly noticed.

"The coaches said, 'Nate, come over here and run the ball.' The defense couldn't get me down."

Anderson entered Eastern as a 6-foot-2, 180-pound freshman. By the time he earned the starting position as a scholarship tailback, Anderson weighed 205 pounds.

"I wasn't a big-time weight lifter," he said. "I was afraid of supplements. So if steroids would have ever been an issue, you didn't have to worry about me. I didn't even want any painkillers. No thank you."

Once in the Panther offensive backfield, Anderson became a star. He was named a College Division Kodak/AFCA First Team All-American in 1972.

"I shocked myself," he said. "I was very surprised. You think about the whole country in Division-II, I thought I'd maybe be honorable mention, but not first team."

Anderson rushed for 1,255 yards that 1972 season. His highlight game came against Southwest Missouri State.

"They had a bunch of guys from East St. Louis," Anderson recalled. "They came over to the ho-

tel we were staying at. They were saying to me, 'You're just a defensive back. You might have all these 100-yard games now, but you ain't all that.'"

Anderson proved to be all that and more as he rushed for 259 yards as Eastern dropped a 41-37 shootout.

"Sure, there was added motivation that day," he said. "The coaches knew that teams were ready for what we had been doing so they put in a new play. It was a sprint draw. I was a cutback runner. We ran a little misdirection, I cut back and was into the clear."

Anderson carried the ball a then-school-record 296 times his senior year for 1,261 yards and 10 touchdowns as a senior. He also ran for a career-best 268 yards against St. Joseph's, a mark that still ranks as the No. 2 single-game high for an Eastern back.

"People were coming to see me run the ball," he said. "It was a lot of fun."

Anderson's junior and senior seasons marked the first time an Eastern back had rushed for more than 1,000 yards in a season. His 2,516 yards in those two seasons made him the Panthers' all-time leading rusher at the time.

Jack Dean took over as Eastern head coach when Biggers resigned in August 1972. Dean fondly remembered the player he called "Nate the Great."

Nate Anderson (44) was the first Panther to rush for more than 1,000 yards in a single season.

"He was the best player I ever coached," said Dean. "He is also one of the best people I have ever known. His personal career overshadows his football, even though he was an All-American.

"Look up his record, he is a legend. When we had him in football, we put him at tailback because he was the biggest and fastest guy we had. He had a great career and was a great ball carrier with pretty good hands and a great blocker. He played behind an offensive line that was usually outmanned, so he got most of his yards on his own. He really took a beating because he ran straight up, like Jim Brown. He was a team and campus leader, although he was sort of quiet and soft-spoken, but (he) carried a big stick."

Dean further marveled at Anderson's athletic ability.

"Nate could have been an All-American at outside linebacker, strong safety or tight end, which probably would have been a better place for him in the pros."

The Washington Redskins chose Anderson in the 14th round of the 1974 NFL Draft. He was also taken by the Chicago Fire of the fledgling World Football League.

"I felt like I had a good camp with the Redskins," he said. "But the last day of cuts, they let me go. (Washington head coach) George Allen wanted to keep older players. There weren't any taxi squads in those days. I had nowhere to go."

Anderson did go to the Fire, but saw no game action behind veteran LeRoy Kelley.

"I went to Jacksonville the next season, but then the league folded," he said.

The NFL wasn't open to welcoming back players from the WFL with open arms.

"(Wide receiver) Paul Warfield was the only one," Anderson said. "That's when I decided it was time to move on with life."

Anderson returned to Eastern and earned his master's degree. He also served as a graduate assistant coach under John Konstantinos for one season.

From there, he began a 34-year career in education. His first job was at Decatur Mac-Arthur High School from 1977 to 1982. He coached track and football.

"I also coached freshman girls' basketball because they didn't have anyone else to do it," he said.

As both a teacher and coach, Anderson stressed respect and responsibility.

"I told them there aren't any stars," he said. "If you want to find athletes you can go down to any park, but it's the off-the-field situations that matter just as much. Use your education as a vehicle."

Anderson carried his mantra in his own life.

"I always try to represent my university well," he said. "It's something for the rest of your life."

Anderson's career also took him to places such as Cairo, Rock Island and his native East St. Louis. His jobs ranged from teacher and coach to counselor and school administrator.

"I got my doctorate," he said. "I started out as a dean of students and also worked as assistant principal and principal."

Dean said, "Nate was a tremendous educator and advocate for kids."

Anderson also served on Eastern's Board of Trustees from 1995 to 2004, including five years as chairman.

"I drove back and forth so many times to Eastern that I felt like I repaid my scholarship," he joked.

Even today in retirement Anderson remains active in education and with Eastern.

"I'm an adjunct professor to Lindenwood University in St. Louis and also for Southeast Missouri State," he said. "I work for the St. Clair County regional (education) office."

Anderson also gets back to Eastern "once or twice a season" for football games, often taking his four grandsons.

"When they come with me, we don't sit up in the (university president's) box because they'd eat everything in sight," he quipped.

His other retirement activities consist of golf and motorcycle riding.

"I have a 1200cc BMW that I take for long weekend trips," he said. "I go to Tennessee or Kentucky, Wisconsin. I'm planning a trip to Texas."

Does his wife worry about him on these road trips?

"No. She says 'I got enough insurance on you now. Go ahead.'"

Eastern fans will be happy to know that Nate Anderson is still racking up yardage after all these years.

FOUR-DOWN TERRITORY

Favorite Football Movie: *Remember the Titans*. If you listened to my story, that movie makes sense. It's a good story about bringing people together regardless of their differences.

I also like *Rudy* and *The Blind Side*. Sandra Bullock carried that one. If she didn't win an Oscar, she never would have.

First Car: A 1962 Chevy. I got it my first year at Eastern for $250. I had it until my last semester there. I was able to work on it myself. I got to know a few mechanics in town and they let me do a little maintenance in their shops. Like I said before, the people of Charleston were very good to me. If I ever see a '62 Chevy, I'm going to buy it. I'll just park it and look at it.

Worst Summer Job: Oh, I liked 'em all. I worked at a steel factory in Charleston during intersession to make a little money before I moved to Decatur. I worked three weeks or a month. It was the night shift. You had to clean up. The guys that worked there said "You aren't going to do the work, you're one of those college students." But, I won them over with my work.

Favorite Subject in School: Science, especially biology.

WILLIE WHITE

Willie White views his time at Eastern as being part of a group of trailblazers.

"Yes, I do," said White in the summer of 2010. "We definitely were trailblazers. We opened things up for the later success. The whole thing started changing with us."

White made reference to playing at a time when Eastern was first beginning to offer full scholarships. Less than a decade later, the Panthers were NCAA Division II national champions.

"The new stadium was built (during my time at Eastern)," White said. "There was better recruiting and better scheduling. It began with guys like (running back) Nate Anderson going to the Washington Redskins and (offensive lineman) Ted Petersen playing for the Pittsburgh Steelers," White said. "People began to look at Eastern as a place to go. More and more people started looking at Eastern Illinois for pro players."

White came to Eastern by way of Gary, Indiana.

"I was born in Chicago, but I grew up in Gary," said White. "I played all the sports that I could."

Willie White was inducted into the Eastern Hall of Fame in 2010.

For White, that meant baseball, basketball, football and track. White's first love was basketball.

"I wouldn't have gotten to Eastern Illinois if I'd have stayed with basketball," White said.

However, the only basketball scholarship offer came from a small school in Tennessee.

"It was a half scholarship," White said. "I needed a full ride. The only way I was going to go to college was on a (full) scholarship. I was pretty much a lost commodity."

The Eastern coaching staff came to Gary looking at other players. However, White's coach at Gary Westside High School showed some film to Panther assistants Dick Vaughan and Jack Dean.

"My coach had only a little bit of film to show them, maybe only one game," White explained. "But I had some good stats."

What little film they saw convinced the Panthers to take a chance with White, and head coach Clyde Biggers offered the Gary teenager a scholarship.

White's biggest adjustment came in the classroom.

"I never really thought I'd go to college," White said. "My parents had a seventh grade education. I wasn't prepared going into Eastern. I chose (to pursue) a business degree. I always had to fight and struggle. I had some

tough times over there at Blair Hall (where many of my classes were held).

"My first two years were so bad that the rest had to be good. But what I had was commitment. I always find a way to get it done."

While he may have struggled early on in the classroom, White flourished in Dean's offensive scheme.

"Jack Dean came in with his experience in the Canadian (Football) League," White said. "He took Eastern to the next level offensively."

First as offensive coordinator and then as head coach starting in 1972, Dean developed the Panther passing game.

"I enjoyed the excitement of being with a team with great passing attacks," White said. "Sometimes I was in the slot, sometimes I was in the split end or flanker role. Mark O'Donnell was our big receiver. He had 55 catches. We completed a lot of passes."

Many of those passes went to the 160-pound White.

"From the waist down, Willie was the same as a 190-pounder," said Dean. "(He had) tremendous strength in his legs and great jumping ability. He was complemented by another great receiver named Mark O'Donnell.

"Willie was a very hard worker, a quiet leader by example on the team and *very* popular on campus. In those days we threw a lot, and a lot to Willie. There were not many teams using motion at that time, and we used Willie a lot out of the slot. We ran his legs off for most of the games in motion. He was a very intelligent young man who could read coverages changing with him in motion, and he would take advantage of it and find the opening."

White found enough openings and caught enough balls to put him among the nation's leading receivers. In 1971, he ranked second in the NCAA College Division with 915 receiving yards.

"It was a new trend of passing and scoring some points," White said.

During that sophomore season of '71, White set the Eastern single-game record with 15 catches in a game against Illinois State.

"It was one of the first times that we played on synthetic turf because Illinois State had one of the few around," White said. "It's just nice to have held that (record) for so long. I remember the next morning someone gave me the newspaper and it had my picture and played up the record."

Yet, White dwelled on the fact that Eastern didn't win the game.

"We wanted victories," he said. "When you didn't win, it wasn't the same. I had the record, but I would rather have won the game."

One game Eastern did win which still stands out in White's memory is the Panthers' Homecoming triumph over Southwest Missouri that same season.

"We had the ball and it was fourth-and-one," White recalled. "I was in the slot. We ran a play action; I ran a curl over the middle. The ball was delivered to me about seven yards down the field, and I ran about another 20 yards down the field. It was a key play for us keeping the possession."

When Anderson emerged as Eastern's first 1,000-yard rusher the following year, White saw fewer passes thrown his way. His catch total dropped from 65 as a sophomore to 49 as a junior. White caught 20 passes his senior season as Anderson became the focal point of the offense with 1,261 rushing yards.

"That was fine with me because we had a more balanced offense," White said. "Nate came in as a safety when he first started. He was converted to halfback because of his size, strength and speed."

When his collegiate career ended in 1973, White stood as Eastern's all-time leading receiver with 164 catches. That record stood until 1986, when Roy Banks moved past him on the list. Yet, as of the 2011 season, White still ranked No. 2 in Eastern history. Today, he is third on the list.

"That's a surprise to me because of all the balls that Sean Payton and Tony Romo were putting in the air," White said.

White's 2,197 career receiving yards still rank sixth in school history, while his 21 career touchdown receptions are tied for seventh.

White points to Dean for much of his success.

"Jack Dean deserves some credit. He doesn't get that (when people look at Eastern history)," White said. "Jack really taught us how to run routes. He really taught us what a passing game should be."

Despite his early struggles in the classroom, White persevered and earned a business degree from Eastern. He spent the first three years out of college working for the City of Chicago.

"It was sort of an urban community job," White said. "From there I worked for Anaconda Wire and Cable. I've been a little bit of everything. I worked as a sales rep for an insurance firm. I worked for a radio station. I did marketing for comedy showcases. I did just about everything."

In 1990, White made a life-altering decision.

"I went back to school and got certified as a teacher," he said.

After a few years in the classroom, White became an assistant principal. In 2007 he was named as the principal of Jordan Community School in Chicago.

Thus, the same Willie White who himself faced adversity in the classroom is now providing educational leadership.

"Our kids need people who like kids," White said. "It's a pretty tough job given the school climate issues of today. Certainly there are things like the budget constraints, the challenges of an inner city school, but we need people who are committed to do what's best for kids. It's been rewarding for me."

Nearly four decades after he last played for Eastern, White was finally rewarded with induction into the university's Hall of Fame in 2010.

"When I was told, it was a great day for me, for my family and for my friends," White said. "It was special for all of us. It's a great honor.

"I thought it had pretty much passed me by. I served on the (EIU) Board of Directors for a time. I was part of the process but never in the conversation. (As others were inducted and I was not) I was fine with that. I had gotten an education and enjoyed my time and playing career at Eastern. (To have finally been inducted) was a true honor."

Dean, his former coach and mentor, was delighted for his former receiver.

"It is a real pleasure to hear that Willie is entering the EIU Hall of Fame," said Dean upon learning the news. "(He is) so deserving. Willie could have probably played anyplace in the country if he were bigger. Of late, the 'big' schools are using receivers with success that are his size, so it is an interesting point. He was a great player and a fine young man."

Thus, after all these years, Willie White is still blazing trails, one of which lead to immortality in the Eastern Hall of Fame.

FOUR-DOWN TERRITORY

Favorite Football Movie: *Remember the Titans* because of its inspiration. Denzel Washington is my favorite actor. It's a movie that I can relate to so well. The message of living, working and succeeding together is one that will always be important.

First Car: It was an Oldsmobile, probably a Delta 88 if I remember right. I paid $450 for it. I worked all summer to earn the money for it between my freshman and sophomore years of college.

Worst Summer Job: I didn't have one because I was fortunate with all the different ones that I had. Well, maybe Trailmobile while I was at Eastern. That was pretty rough.

Favorite Subject in School: Marketing, I enjoyed that the most.

TED PETERSEN

Ted Petersen readily recalls one of the defining moments in his life.

As a prep star at Momence High School, Petersen was first offered a half scholarship by Eastern.

"I was what you might call a young, raw-boned country kid who didn't really see himself going on (to college)," Petersen said. "But there was a Momence connection between (Eastern defensive coordinator) Jesse James and my high school coach Jack Cherry.

"I wasn't the best player on my high school team, but they saw some upside potential in me."

Still, Petersen turned down the partial scholarship. A short time later, Eastern countered with an offer for a full ride.

"It's scary to think of what could have happened if Eastern didn't do that," Petersen said.

As it turned out, the decision worked well for both the Panthers and Petersen. He wound up as a force on the offensive line under first head coach Jack Dean and then later with John Konstantinos.

"Ted Petersen was a 6-foot-5, 185-pound tight end in high school," Dean said. "He didn't have any other offers, but I thought this big,

old, raw-boned farm kid can play. We played him at tight end first, but he didn't have the greatest hands. We moved him to tackle and later he played guard."

Petersen remembered Dean as "a very enthusiastic guy. He had played for the Washington Redskins, which gave him credence. But, for whatever reason, not everyone bought into him and his program."

Whether that was a factor in Eastern's lack of success during Petersen's playing days is debatable.

"The best season we had when I was there turned out to be 5-6 (in 1976)," Petersen said. "We started out 4-0 and were ranked fifth in the country. But, we won only one game the rest of the way."

In his book *The Missing Ring: How Bear Bryant and the 1966 Alabama Crimson Tide Were Denied College Football's Most Elusive Prize*, author Keith Dunnavant makes the analogy that an offensive line is like a car battery, attracting attention only when something goes wrong.

As an offensive lineman, Petersen agreed with the assessment.

"We tend to get most of the blame and little of the credit," he said. "That's okay. They say if you are ever running from the law, become an offensive lineman and they will never find you!"

Yet, like a car battery, if it fails, nothing will move forward.

Petersen's Panthers did enough forward moving his senior season that he garnered All-American honors.

With the end of his collegiate career came the beginning of his professional one. The Pittsburgh Steelers selected Petersen in the fourth round, making him the highest draft choice in Eastern history at that point.

"My bonus was $13,500 and my rookie salary was $27,500," Petersen recalled. "Today, a fourth-round pick gets around $1.5 million, so the money has really changed."

Yet, Petersen knows full well that life is about more than money.

"I wouldn't trade it for anything. It was a special time," he said. "I'm honored to have played with the Steelers during those years. I earned game balls and some recognition along the way, but in the end, it's what you become that counts. It galvanized the person that I am.

It's the friendships I made along the way that really stay with me."

Those solid Steeler friendships included a pair of former collegiate rivals, quarterback Cliff Stoudt of Youngstown State and safety Mike Wagner of Western Illinois.

"When Eastern had its run (to the 1978 NCAA Division II national championship), I made some bets with those guys along the way," Petersen chuckled. "(Eastern quarterback) Steve Turk was throwing up big numbers and so I spotted Wagner 20 points. Now who gives someone 20 points? But, Eastern won big (40-12) and Mike had to pay up."

Petersen also collected from Stoudt when Eastern held off Youngstown State 26-22 in the national semifinals. The Panthers followed up with a 10-9 victory over Delaware in the title game.

"I was so proud of them," said Petersen. "I was so grateful they won the national championship."

Petersen wound up playing 10 years in the NFL. He won two Super Bowl rings with the Steelers along the way before ending his career with Cleveland and Indianapolis.

After his pro career, Petersen first worked in the construction industry.

"After a couple of years, I fell back into what I studied at Eastern," Petersen said.

Thus, Petersen embarked on a 30-year teaching and coaching career in Pennsylvania.

"My last year with the Steelers I made $150,000, and my first year teaching I made $18,500," Petersen noted. "But, it was a wonderful experience. I never loved anything more. To work with high school students and athletes was addictive. It really is rewarding."

During those years, Petersen's younger brother, Mark, played in the offensive line that protected Sean Payton at Eastern.

"Mark had a good career there," said Petersen. "He was bigger and stronger than me, but didn't quite have the athletic ability to play at the next level."

In 1987, Ted Petersen was inducted into Eastern's Hall of Fame along with former Pro Bowl punter Jeff Gossett.

In late 2008, Petersen returned to his Illinois roots. The former Eastern great accepted a job as athletic director and director of physical education at Kankakee Community College near his hometown of Momence.

Ted Petersen twice played on Super Bowl–winning Pittsburgh Steeler teams in the late 1970s.

With sons Teddy and Garrett grown, Petersen wanted his youngest offspring—six-year-old Samuel—to "grow up in a great place like I did," he said.

"Mom and Dad still live on the farm where I grew up," Petersen added.

So, with life seemingly having come full circle, the former lineman reflected on his Eastern days.

"It's a fantastic school," Petersen said. "I got a great education. It allowed me to appear in Super Bowls, to visit the White House. I'm a big fan of Eastern."

FOUR-DOWN TERRITORY

Favorite Football Movie: *The Longest Yard* (the original, of course).

First Car: 1965 Chevy Malibu Super Sport.

Worst Summer Job: None. I've always looked at jobs as an opportunity.

Favorite Subject in School: History.

THE DARRELL MUDRA ERA

(1978–1982)

Darrell Mudra, aka Dr. Victory, is a member of the College Football Hall of Fame.

DARRELL MUDRA

Darrell Mudra doesn't mind his Dr. Victory moniker.

"It didn't bother me at all," said Mudra from his home in Crawfordville, Florida. "I always felt my doctorate was a factor in getting me some of my jobs in football."

While Mudra was referring more to his academic doctorate in psychology, *The Chicago Tribune* labeled him "Dr. Victory" following Eastern's unexpected run to the 1978 NCAA Division II national championship. *The Tribune* cited Mudra's ability to cure a patient that appeared to be terminal.

Eastern's football program certainly qualified for that. Since the Panthers' 1948 appearance in the Corn Bowl, Eastern had only three winning seasons over the next 30 years. Moreover, just one of those winning campaigns came after 1951.

Pressure mounted to the point that noise was being made to drop football from Eastern's athletic department. But Eastern President Gilbert Fite decided one more coach should be given a chance to right the ship. That coach turned out to be Mudra.

Athletic director Mike Mullally convinced Mudra to come out of a two-year hiatus after being fired by Florida State in 1975.

"I still had two years left on my contract," Mudra recalled. "I fished and coached a Pee Wee football team.

"Mullally was the key guy getting me there. If I remember right, my last year at Western we beat Eastern pretty handily (56-13). Mike remembered that."

Mullally also no doubt remembered the success Mudra had at Western. While leading the Leathernecks from 1969 to 1973, Mudra compiled a 39-13 record.

"Darrell was one of the greatest coaches in the history of college football, yet a lot of people don't know about him," said longtime assistant Pete Rodriguez. "Darrell saw the best in people. He didn't get sidetracked with stereotypes. You trusted in Darrell."

At Eastern, Mudra took over a team that had gone 1-10 the previous season under head coach John Konstantinos.

"We had some talented players from that team," said Mudra. "Things weren't as bad as people thought."

Mudra immediately began to build a positive climate toward winning.

"Coach Mudra is an outstanding person," said middle linebacker Alonzo Lee, later head coach at North Carolina A&T. "He dealt with the mind. He created an atmosphere conducive to winning. He promoted positive attitude."

In addition to the positive climate, Mudra added two key figures to the mix on the coaching staff.

"Mullally got me to hire Mike Shanahan," Mudra recalled. "In fact, if he didn't hire me as head coach, something tells me he wanted Shanahan."

Shanahan, just 25 years old at the time, took over as offensive coordinator. The Oak Park, Illinois native had come to play quarterback at Eastern in the early 1970s, only to see his career cut short by injury.

On the defensive side of the ball, Mudra turned to a former player.

"John Teerlinck had played for me at Western," Mudra said. "One of my former assistants, Pete Rodriquez, said I ought to hire John. John had been selling houses and was making good money at it. But one day John was walking along and saw a group of kids playing sandlot football. It really sparked him."

And Teerlinck really sparked Eastern's defense.

"John was the key to that '78 team," Mudra said. "John was more of a factor than Shanahan (in the success of the team). He was inspirational. He was good in the weight room. John really made a difference."

Together, the staff brought in some key junior college players, including quarterback Steve Turk. Mudra and his coaches also convinced the returning players they could win.

"Shanahan did a great job with Turk," Mudra noted. "He had a great year (in '78). The next year Turk was mediocre without Shanahan (who left to take a coaching position at Florida)."

Eastern began the 1978 season with four straight wins. The Panthers then lost consecutive games to Youngstown State and Akron.

Two years earlier, the Panthers had also gotten off to a 4-0 start only to see their season fall apart and finish 5-6. But 1978 would be different. In fact, Eastern wouldn't lose again.

Shanahan's offense kicked into high gear and rolled up 40 or more points in three of its next five wins, over Northern Michigan, Wayne State, Illinois State, Murray State and Western Illinois.

"Our offense was simple," Mudra noted. "We ran two or three things well. We ran off tackle with Poke Cobb out of the I (formation). We ran play action. We ran play action screens to Cobb. We also had a strong-side pass play to some pretty good receivers."

Following its regular season success, Eastern was one of eight schools to receive an invitation to the NCAA Division II playoffs. The Panthers had only been to the postseason one other time, back in 1948.

"We weren't the best team in the country. Youngstown was. But Youngstown decided to make us their road game. So we went out and beat Cal Davis, 35-31, on the road (in the first round)," said Mudra.

The opening-round victory set up a rematch with Youngstown State at O'Brien Field in Charleston. The Panthers were out to avenge their 40-24 loss to the Penguins from earlier in the season.

"It was a windy, rainy day," recalled Mudra. "Playing at home helped. Things went right for us that day."

In a game televised regionally by ABC, the Panthers held on for a 26-22 victory that sent them into the national championship game.

That title game took place in Longview, Texas. The Delaware Blue Hens and their star quarterback Jeff Komlo (who would go on to play in the NFL) were the opposition.

To prepare for the championship game, Mudra called upon a former assistant for help.

"Deek Pollard, who was on my staff at Western and at Florida State, spent 20 years coaching in the NFL. Well, I called up Deek and asked him what we should do to stop Delaware's Wing T offense," Mudra recalled.

"Deek gave us the plan; John Teerlinck executed it. (One of the main points) was not to follow their motion because they had people running all over the place trying to confuse the defense. Ray Jeske, who wasn't that talented of a player, really had a game that day."

The end result was a stunning 10-9 victory by the Panthers. With the win, Eastern had rebounded from a one-win season to a national championship.

"We played a great game against Delaware," said Mudra. "It was exciting. The whole town turned out there to greet us at the airport."

The win also gave Dr. Victory his second national championship. The first was captured in 1962 at the NCAA College Division level when Mudra's Adams State Grizzlies defeated Northern Illinois 23-20 in the Mineral Springs Bowl.

Expectations were high for another championship season in 1979. Eastern was featured by *Sports Illustrated* in its Division II preview. However, after a 5-0 start, the Panthers were upset by rival Western Illinois, 10-7. Eastern then struggled down the stretch, losing three of its final four games to finish 7-4 and miss the playoffs entirely.

"I coached against Dr. Victory back in 1979," said former Akron assistant Larry Kindbom, later the head coach at Washington University in St. Louis. "He was in the press box during the game, as was I. A fight broke out among his players on the sideline in the wake of our 'upset' victory. It was somewhat surreal for me as a young coach to see something like that."

Mudra, however, righted the ship. In 1980, the Panthers found themselves back in the Division II championship game. After they had been ranked No. 1 in the nation all season, the title result didn't turn out Eastern's way. Cal Poly, led by future Pittsburgh Steelers receiver Robbie Martin, downed the Panthers 21-13 in Albuquerque, New Mexico.

"We had a fluke loss against Cal Poly. We fumbled away one score and gave up a touchdown because we were in a bad defense. We allowed their best player (Martin) to beat us. We were a better team than Cal Poly. They were well coached, but we were better. We were better than the team that won (the '78 title)."

Cal Poly head coach Joe Harper said of Mudra, "He was a very smart guy. He had great success. They ran a protype pro attack offense at a time when it just wasn't done much. They did it really well."

Despite the 1980 title game loss, Mudra's Panthers made the jump along with their fellow members of the Mid-Continent Conference to the NCAA I-AA level in 1981.

In 1982, Eastern clawed its way to a 10-1-1 regular season that saw the Panthers rise to No. 5 in the national rankings. Led by quarterback Jeff Christensen, Eastern advanced to the quarterfinals of the I-AA playoffs.

"He (Christensen) was a talent," said Mudra. "(Offensive coordinator) Chuck Dickerson really developed him. It didn't surprise me that Christensen found himself in the pros."

Following a five-year run with a 47-15-1 record, two national championship game appearances and the 1978 title, Mudra left Eastern for the University of Northern Iowa.

"First of all, Northern Iowa was a great school academically," Mudra said of the decision. "Stan Sheriff was the AD there. He was a good friend of mine and got me to come." (Sheriff took over as athletic director after retiring as head football coach.)

"(The move) cost me five years' retirement in Illinois because I most likely would have stayed that long there. My wife taught in Oakland (just outside Charleston). She loved it there, and it was tough to leave."

Former Eastern athletic director R.C. Johnson, ironically a Northern Iowa alum, remembers Mudra leaving.

"We hated to see it happen. However, we were able to get a good replacement (Al Molde). But everyone knew that Darrell liked to move around quite a bit. Remember, we got him from Western Illinois," said Johnson.

Mudra finished out his coaching career at Northern Iowa with 43 wins in five seasons. Remember the Pee Wee football team he coached in Florida before arriving at Eastern?

"The best kid from that team wound up as my quarterback at Northern Iowa (Mike Smith)," Mudra recalled.

When Mudra finally retired from coaching, his track record spoke volumes. Coaching at seven different colleges, Mudra sent 10 teams to bowl or playoff games. In addition, he coached the 1966 Montreal Alouettes into the Canadian Football League playoffs. Mudra won two national championships, coached two undefeated teams, won 12 Coach of the Year awards and produced winning seasons in 22 of 26 years.

Mudra's 200-81-4 record with a winning percentage of .709 ranked him in the Top 25 all-time for collegiate wins, regardless of division.

Mudra found himself being inducted into six halls of fame, including the College Football Hall of Fame in South Bend, Indiana in 2000.

"I didn't expect it," said Mudra. "(Fellow Hall of Famer and former Arizona State legendary head coach) Frank Kush had a big hand in getting me in. I went in with the likes of Marcus Allen, John Elway, Johnny Rodgers, Willie Lanier and Tank Younger. Eddie Robinson introduced Tank. Eddie said that all the players that came back to Grambling always asked him who was the best player ever to play there. Well, Tank never asked."

Today, Mudra spends his days enjoying retirement with his wife, Jean Marie.

"I love to fish, and this is a great place for that," said Mudra.

He still finds time to follow the game he coached for so many years.

"Five of my players have found their way into the NFL. Ron Erhardt was the head coach with the Patriots. There have also been a number that coached in college. The latest are Joe Taylor (Western) at Florida A&M and Alonzo Lee (Eastern) at NC A&T."

Still, Mudra's favorite team to follow is Northern Iowa.

"The current coach, Mark Farley, played for me," Mudra said. "They've done quite well. I follow them on a regular basis. They usually win the conference year in and year out."

Thus, nearly a quarter of a century since he last coached, Mudra still likes a winner. That makes perfect sense for a man they called "Dr. Victory."

FOUR-DOWN TERRITORY

Favorite Football Movie: *The Longest Yard.*

First Car: We bought it for $75, and all I can remember is that it was not reliable.

Worst Summer Job: Hanging bacon as it came off a conveyor belt to be put in the smoking room.

Favorite Subject in School: English literature.

THE MIRACLE OF '78

As the waning seconds of the 1980 U.S. Olympic hockey team's landmark victory over the Soviet Union ticked away, broadcaster Al Michaels asked viewers if they believed in miracles. For Eastern football fans, that response had to be yes. Two years earlier, those fans had witnessed a miracle firsthand.

"It was the biggest turnaround in the history of the NCAA, that's what I've been told," said Mike Mullally, Eastern's athletic director at the time. "It was highly improbable, but not impossible as things turned out."

The basis for that miracle goes all the way back to 1951. In the 26 years before the 1978 season, Eastern had just two winning seasons. Moreover, the Panthers were coming off a 1-10 record. Rumors that Eastern would drop football were making the rounds.

"It was a foregone conclusion in most people's minds," said Mullally. "In fact, there were only two people who believed otherwise, the university president (Gilbert Fite) and me. I had to convince him, but his vote was the only one that counted."

Mullally then made the decision that may very well have saved the Panther program: He hired former Arizona and Florida State coach Darrell Mudra.

"When I was at South Dakota, he was at North Dakota State," Mullally said. "He was still highly regarded in Illinois. He had credibility."

Mudra, nicknamed Dr. Victory for his ability to resurrect football programs on life support, went to work immediately. He brought in a former defensive star from his days at Western Illinois as his defensive coordinator. That man was 27-year-old John Teerlinck.

At Mullally's urging, Mudra also hired a former Eastern quarterback who had seen his playing days end with a ruptured kidney that nearly left him dead on the operating table. With his playing career over, this Illinois native had turned to coaching and became Mudra's offensive coordinator at the tender age of 25. His name? Mike Shanahan.

"I came close to hiring Mike Shanahan (as head coach)," Mullally said. "But, Mike was only 25 or 26 at the time. Truth be told, if Mike

had been a year older, I would have hired him. But I didn't want people to think I was giving up on the program.

"Part of the deal I made with Mudra was that Mike Shanahan had to be the offensive coordinator."

From day one, Mudra preached success to his team. In fact, Eastern received one vote for No. 1 in the NCAA Division-II poll. That vote was cast by Mudra.

"I wouldn't have hired the guy if he didn't believe and say things like that," Mullally pointed out.

In the eyes of the coaching staff, there was no miracle. There was no magic. It was an age-old formula: hard work.

"It was just good, old-fashioned plain hard work," said Teerlinck, who later coached the defensive line for the Super Bowl champion Indianapolis Colts.

Mullally also points to the players.

"People give me credit, they give Mudra credit, they give Shanahan and Teerlinck and the other coaches credit, but the players deserve credit," he said. "The chemistry on that team was unbelievable. Those intangibles might just be as important as talent when it comes to winning."

Mullally also provided the program with as many upgrades as he could.

"I worked out a deal with Eastern Airlines so that we could fly to places like Northern Michigan," he said. "The plane, of course, had Eastern painted across the side. It was in our school colors. The players thought it was our plane. They were proud of it. It also helped us a little bit psychologically against our opponents. We'd show up in this plane and they'd think, 'Hey now, that must be a big-time program.'"

The football upgrades didn't come cheaply. Mullally eliminated the gymnastics, golf and tennis programs.

"If we didn't do that, we'd just be wallowing around," he said. "I was protecting the quality of the programs. The days of NAIA were gone; we were Division-II. People forget how difficult those decisions were."

Those decisions paid dividends on the football field. The long-downtrodden Panthers finished the regular season with a 9-2 record, qualifying for the Division II play-offs. They opened the playoffs with a victory over Cal-Davis. The win then brought a rematch with Youngstown State, a team that had defeated Eastern 40-24 early in the regular season.

This time around, however, the Panthers hosted the Penguins. The day turned out to be cold and rainy. While the weather played a factor in the game's outcome, Eastern also came to play.

"We had them on our home field," Mudra said. "We were ready for them the second time around."

Eastern surprised Youngstown State, 26-22. With the clock ticking off the final few seconds, Panther fans rushed out of the stands to tear down the goalposts.

"One of the state troopers turned to me and said, 'What are you gonna do?'" said Mullally. "I turned and said back to him, 'I don't know, what are *you* gonna do?' The fans deserved it after all those years of losing. I wanted them to enjoy the moment and relish the victory."

The triumph was more than a moment of vengeance for the earlier loss; the victory sent the Panthers to Longview, Texas for the national championship game.

Eastern's opponent would be the mighty Delaware Blue Hens, a team that had long dominated Division II football. In fact, Delaware would win the title in 1979.

Delaware rolled into the title game averaging 33.6 points a game. The Blue Hens had won their semifinal game with a 41-0 shutout. They were led by quarterback, Jeff Komlo, who would go on to a nine-year NFL career.

Delaware was coached by Harold "Tubby" Raymond, a former Michigan quarterback and linebacker who would earn induction into the College Football Hall of Fame in 2003. Under Raymond, the Blue Hens won three national championships and 14 Lambert Cups, the annual award given to signify small-school supremacy for East Coast football.

"The Delaware coaches were Michigan men," Teerlinck said. "Their uniforms were Michigan, complete with the winged helmet.

"We (Eastern) had uniforms like the Dallas Cowboys. We told our players, 'They're college, we're pros.'"

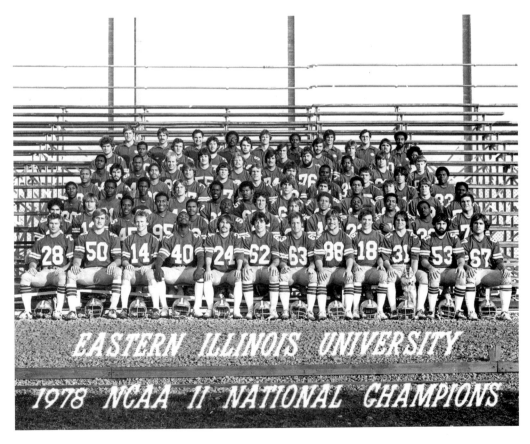

The 1978 NCAA Division-II national champions.

The coaching staffs also had differing views on more than just the way their teams looked on the field.

"(Delaware) had curfews, all their guys wore shirts and ties," recalled Teerlinck. "We had no curfews. We treated our guys like men."

Eastern also felt that the pre-championship focus and hype all settled on Delaware.

"They (NCAA Division II organizers) couldn't have mistreated us more than they did," Mullally said. "But, they also couldn't have done us a bigger favor. The coaching staff and I pointed this out every chance we had to the team."

One of those points came when Eastern discovered that Delaware had already printed T-shirts proclaiming the Blue Hens national champions.

"We found a couple of the shirts," Mullally said. "Our players really got cranked up when they saw those."

Middle linebacker Alonzo Lee, later the head coach at North Carolina A&T, said, "The people who put it on were expecting (Delaware) to win (easily)."

"(Delaware) got put up in a plush hotel where they could eat on site," Lee remembered. "Our hotel was under construction. We had to eat at a Denny's away from the hotel. We were second-class citizens."

Eastern also had to contend with Delaware's vaunted Wing T offense.

"It was an offense that really threw a lot of motion and deception at you," said Mudra.

The offense traced its roots back to the 1950s. Raymond's success was so pronounced that the Wing T became known as the Delaware Wing T. In fact, the offense was so prolific that it was featured in Tim Layden's evolutionary *Blood, Sweat and Chalk: The Ultimate Football Playbook: How the Great Coaches Built Today's Game*.

Yet, Eastern wasn't about to be undone by what Layden called "a truly modern offense, spreading the field, adding straight drop-back passing, and eventually, an option game."

After conferring with former Western Illinois assistant coach Don "Deek" Pollard, Teerlinck devised a plan that revolved around Eastern's defense staying at home and ignoring that motion and deception.

"John and I always had a lot of respect for each other," said Pollard, then an NFL assistant coach. "I always respected John's ability to teach technique. He respected my knowledge of football."

The plan that was hatched relied heavily on Eastern not being fooled by Delaware's motion.

"We had to stay at home," said Lee.

The Panthers would also put pressure on Komlo to make quick decisions. In short, Eastern wanted to get into the Delaware backfield and force the issue.

Teerlinck created huge flashcards to signal in defensive alignments.

"As middle linebacker, I was in charge of that," Lee said.

Teerlinck added, "Alonzo Lee called every defense at the line of scrimmage. He did one helluva job."

Eastern took the opening kickoff and drove to the Delaware 10-yard line. After the drive stalled, Eastern took an early 3-0 lead when Dan DiMartino kicked a 28-yard field goal.

Delaware came back to tie things up when Brandt Kennedy kicked a 19-yard field goal. The Blue Hens then grabbed the lead when Komlo completed an eight-yard touchdown pass to tight end Mike Mills.

However, Kennedy missed the extra point. Thus, Delaware had to settle for a 9-3 halftime lead.

While the offenses had both been riding high coming into the title game, the story quickly became the defenses.

In its summary of the game, *The NCAA News* lauded Eastern's effort in particular.

"The defensive unit, with its continual blitzing, held the potent Delaware offense, ranked No. 2 nationally, to 354 yards—114 yards below its season's average," read *The NCAA News* account.

"We got after their ass," Teerlinck said. "We didn't bite on their motion."

More than 30 years after the game, Teerlinck recalled the play of Lee and defensive stars Pete Catan and Steve Parker.

"Steve Parker came from Triton (College)," the defensive coach said. "We called him Kong because he had such long arms and played like hell."

Teerlinck added that Parker later played with the Colts before dying in a car accident.

Linebacker Ray Jeske registered a then-school-record 21 tackles against Delaware.

Thus, the defense turned the tide for Eastern. Panther safety Kevin Jones recovered a Delaware fumble on the Blue Hens' 19-yard line early in the third quarter.

Working with a short field, Eastern's offense drove to the Delaware one. From there, Chris "Poke" Cobb scored at the 13:08 mark. Cobb, the sixth-leading rusher in Division II that season, would wind up as the Panthers' career rushing leader with 5,042 yards. Tragically, he, like Parker, would later perish in an auto accident.

DiMartino then added the all-important extra point, and Eastern grabbed the 10-9 lead.

From that point, the game settled into a defensive stalemate.

Delaware managed to get into position to win in the game's final seconds. Kennedy, who had kicked a then-team-record 12 field goals during the season, lined up for a potential 45-yarder.

However, his attempt sailed wide right. Thus, Eastern celebrated its national championship.

"We shocked the world," said Lee three decades later.

The Panthers would return to a suddenly football-crazed Coles County.

"The biggest thrill I've ever had was winning the national championship and seeing the reaction of the town of Charleston," said receiver Scott McGhee.

"I've played in the Grey Cup twice, made the USFL playoffs and played on national TV dozens of times, but I don't think I could ever have another experience like that," said McGhee.

Quarterback Steve Turk added, "It really helped put Eastern on the map. All it takes is one thing like that to turn things around. I wouldn't have wanted to have gone anywhere else other than Eastern."

Though Teerlinck went on to a lengthy career as an NFL coach, the memories have not diminished.

"I put it right up there with our Super Bowl win here with Indianapolis," said Teerlinck, who also won consecutive Super Bowls alongside Shanahan in Denver.

"Today, Eastern is the cradle of NFL coaches,"

Pete Catan was a dominant force on the defensive side of the ball.

said Mudra. "The attitudes of faculty and community were changed forever (by our winning the national championship)."

In the aftermath, the university made a highlight film to mark Eastern's moment in history. Chicago Cubs radio announcer Vince Lloyd was the film's narrator.

"I don't remember what we paid him, but he gave us a pretty good rate," recalled longtime Eastern sports information director Dave Kidwell.

"(Lloyd) said it was such a bright spot for the entire state at the time. All of the Chicago teams were really suffering during that era."

But the era proved otherwise for Eastern. And the Panthers and their fans did indeed believe in miracles.

1980: THE ONE THAT GOT AWAY

As Darrell Mudra spends many of his retirement days fishing, he may lament over the one that got away.

Two years after completing its miracle season, Eastern again found itself in the Division II national championship game.

However, this time the tables were turned. Whereas the Panthers upset heavily favored and perennial power Delaware for the 1978 title, the 1980 event featured Eastern as the prohibitive favorite.

After a disappointing 1979 season, Mudra's Panthers had rebounded successfully. Following an opening victory against South Dakota, Eastern dropped consecutive games to Southern Illinois and Indiana State.

Things turned around in the season's fourth game. Eastern routed Northwest Missouri State, 41-7, and hit its stride. The Panthers reeled off eight straight victories to enter the playoffs with a 9-2 record. Moreover, Eastern was ranked No. 1 in the country.

Eastern averaged nearly 32 points per game. The Panthers won their first two playoff games. That set up a showdown with Cal Poly/San Luis Obispo for the national championship.

The title game was played in Albuquerque, New Mexico and was called the Zia Bowl.

"As I recall we did play the underdog role," said Cal Poly coach Joe Harper in the fall of 2009. "(Eastern) was the top dog. They were rolling in the playoffs."

According to Harper, five inches of snow had fallen on the field in the days leading up to the championship showdown.

"After it was cleared of the snow, they brought in helicopters to try and blow it dry," Harper recalled. "It was a muddy field."

The game turned out to be as sloppy as the field conditions. A combination of Eastern's mistakes and Cal Poly's star flanker Robbie Martin determined the result: Mustangs 21, Panthers 13.

"We didn't play very well today and as it worked out, they beat us," Mudra was quoted in the Dec. 14, 1980 special edition of *The Daily Eastern News*. "I still believe we are a better team, but it just wasn't meant to be today."

Eastern—bidding for its second national championship in three seasons—twice fumbled inside the Cal Poly four-yard line.

The first miscue occurred with 1:09 remaining in the first half when running back Rod Slaughter coughed up the ball as he crossed the goal line.

"I was robbed," Slaughter was quoted by *The Daily Eastern News*. "I was laying in the end zone and the ball came loose. Because I was excited about scoring, I let loose of the ball.

"One ref had his hands up in the air (signaling a touchdown) and the other called it

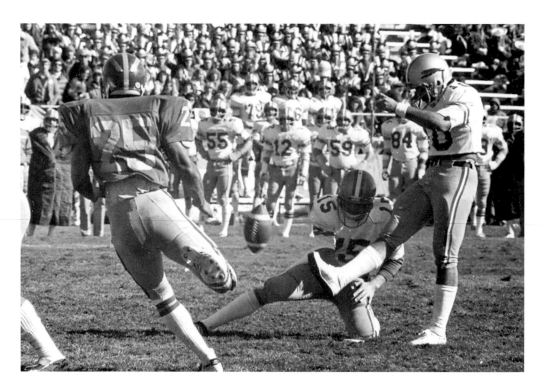

Dan DiMartino kicks a field goal in the 1978 national championship game. Mattoon native Rod Sink (15) is the holder.

a fumble. I could have avoided it if I had just held on to it a little longer."

The other costly fumble came later in the game. Poised on the Cal Poly three-yard line, Eastern freshman running back Ricky Davis lost the ball.

"That was the play that really did us in," said Eastern middle linebacker Alonzo Lee, later the head coach at North Carolina A&T.

Harper added, "Had they gone in and scored, that's a big difference."

Mudra said Davis got the carry because assistant coach Dennis Shaw thought he was more likely to hold on to the ball.

"If we had it to do over, we sure as hell wouldn't put him in there," Mudra said after the game.

Kevin Staple, who had rushed for more than 200 yards combined in the previous two playoff games, was standing on the sideline.

"I don't know what they were thinking," Staple said. "The dude (Davis) never played."

The carry was the only one Davis got in the game.

Meanwhile, Martin was clearly the game's

star. The Kodak All-American scored all three Cal Poly touchdowns.

Martin returned the first punt of the day 42 yards down the left sideline for a touchdown— just 1:58 into the first quarter. He later ran a second punt back for a score, only to have the touchdown nullified by a penalty.

"His first two punt returns set the stage," said Harper, who today runs a group of restaurants with his son.

Martin then caught a pair of touchdown passes from quarterback Craig Johnston in the second half. The first touchdown covered 58 yards while the second was a 33-yarder.

"He was a tough ball player. He had a lot of speed," said Eastern safety Kevin Gray. "On one of them, he made a great catch. On the other, I just screwed up. I got burnt."

Mudra agreed.

"We had the wrong defensive call on," the Panther head coach said of Martin's second TD reception.

The Panthers had set their defense to stop Louis Jackson, the Cal Poly running back who

Junior college transfer Steve Turk thrived in Mike Shanahan's offense.

Chris "Poke" Cobb rushed for 101 yards and the game-winning touchdown in Eastern's 10-9 upset of heavily favored Delaware.

"I'm super elated. This is the hardest game I ever played," Martin said afterward.

Martin would be the 100th player selected in the 1981 NFL draft when Pittsburgh took him in the fourth round.

While Slaughter's fumble did prove costly, the Eastern back ran for 75 yards on 14 carries. He scored the Panthers' two touchdowns in the game. In fact, his second TD put Eastern up, 13-7, at the half.

The second half turned into nothing but frustration for the Panthers. In fact, with the game's fate already sealed late, Eastern allowed itself to put a black eye on the event.

"We lost our cool and poise," Mudra said.

According to *The Daily Eastern News* account, there were "a number of unnecessary and seemingly embarrassing personal foul penalties—after the game was locked up."

In fact, Lee was ejected from the game when his attempts to cause a fumble later in the game were viewed as excessive.

"They (Cal Poly's offensive line) were tackling Alonzo when he'd come in after the quarterback," said Eastern defensive coordinator Chuck Dickerson. "And one of them actually hit Ira (Jefferson) in the mouth. After a while our kids aren't going to tolerate it."

Nevertheless, Eastern did have to tolerate the fact that Cal Poly won the game.

"I guess our luck ran out," said wide receiver

was Division II's leading rusher. Eastern held Jackson to 26 yards on 20 carries.

"They forced us to play left-handed. They played a goal-line defense all over the field," Harper said. "We didn't anticipate that, but they left themselves vulnerable to the pass, which eventually won us the game."

Martin finished the game with seven catches for 164 yards.

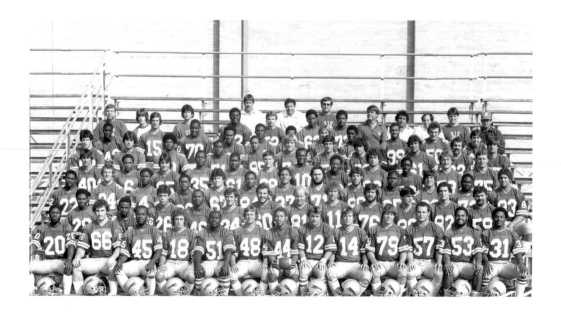

The 1980 NCAA Division-II national runner-ups.

Scott McGhee in the mid-1980s. "Still, I'm proud to have been part of that team as well as the '78 team that won."

MIKE SHANAHAN

The average football fan could tell you Mike Shanahan coached the Denver Broncos to consecutive Super Bowl titles.

Some could even dig a little deeper and remember his tumultuous tenure as head coach of Al Davis' Oakland Raiders. Others might reflect on his offensive coordinator days with the high-flying San Francisco 49ers.

Yet, few would recall the days when the 25-year-old Shanahan piloted Eastern's offense to the 1978 NCAA Division II national championship.

Eastern was familiar territory to Shanahan. He had played there briefly as an undersized quarterback after his prep days at East Leyden High School in Franklin Park, Illinois.

"Eastern Illinois was an easy choice," Shanahan wrote in his 1999 book *Think Like a Champion: Building Success One Victory at a Time*. "It was the only school that offered me a full scholarship."

Shanahan's playing career came to an abrupt end his junior year during the 1974 annual spring game. Speared by a linebacker while running an option play, Shanahan soon found himself in the emergency room. Doctors removed one of his kidneys, which had been ruptured.

A priest was summoned to administer last rites. Shanahan spent five days in critical condition. One doctor later told his father it was the closest he had ever come to losing a patient who actually survived.

Eastern head coach Jack Dean delivered the news that Shanahan's playing days were over. Neither the doctors nor the university would allow him to play again.

"I was crushed," Shanahan said in the book cowritten with Adam Schefter. "I should have been thankful I was alive, but all I could think about was never playing football again."

If playing football again wasn't an option, then Shanahan was intent on doing the next

best thing—coaching football.

"Mike started coaching right away," said roommate Mike Heimerdinger. "He was breaking down film."

After earning his Eastern degree in the spring of 1975, Shanahan worked his way into a position with the University of Oklahoma Sooners, one of the nation's top programs at the time.

"Each day, without invitation," Shanahan wrote, "I would leave the dorm and visit the Oklahoma football office, the locker room, the film room. I would ask the assistant coaches if they needed any odd jobs done, and inevitably they'd have something for me to do."

These tasks ran the gambit. One day Shanahan would drive recruits and coaches to and from the airport. Another day he would help break down game film or chart plays. Eventually, he was accepted into the Sooner fold.

Oklahoma head coach Barry Switzer may not have known his last name, but Shanahan felt "some microscopic part" of the Sooners' 1975 national championship team.

"I was the recruiting coordinator at OU when Mike was a GA for us," longtime coach Jerry

Twenty-five-year old Mike Shanahan was the offensive coordinator for the 1978 national champion Panthers.

Pettibone said in an e-mail. "I was impressed with his work ethic and willingness to learn."

Shanahan left Oklahoma two years later to become a full-time backfield coach at Northern Arizona. It was 1977, and Mike Shanahan was 24 years old.

That same season, his alma mater, the Eastern Illinois Panthers, suffered through a devastating 1-10 season. The Panthers had now strung together 17 consecutive losing seasons. Talk of dropping football was in the air.

Enter Darrell Mudra. The former University of Arizona and Florida State head coach was brought in by Eastern athletic director Mike Mullally.

The Panther AD talked Mudra into hiring the then-25-year-old Shanahan as the team's offensive coordinator.

"Mullally got me to hire Mike Shanahan," Mudra recalled from his retirement home in Florida. "I think he even thought of hiring Shanahan as the head coach for a time."

Shanahan recalled Mudra's first meeting with the team.

"Men," Shanahan remembered Mudra's speech, "you are going to be winners. I've looked at a lot of film and know the talent we have and I know we will get to the (Division II) playoffs with the right plan and the right attitude. There is no reason why we cannot win a national championship."

Mudra's words that day may have seemed hard to believe, but by season's end, they proved to be prophetic.

Under Shanahan's guidance, the offense set 25 school records. It averaged 424.6 yards and 35 points a game. More importantly, Eastern won the national championship.

"(Eastern) didn't have a winning season in 17 years and then to come back and win the national championship made it that much more special," Shanahan told Chad Merda of *The Daily Eastern News* in a 1999 story.

The Division II title also sent Shanahan packing.

"Winning the national championship at Eastern gave me the opportunity to go Division I," Shanahan said in the article.

Shanahan left Eastern to become the offensive coordinator at the University of Minnesota. Following the 1979 season, Shanahan spent four seasons as the offensive coordinator at the University of Florida under head coach Charley Pell.

"At a very young age, I had a few different programs to develop myself with different

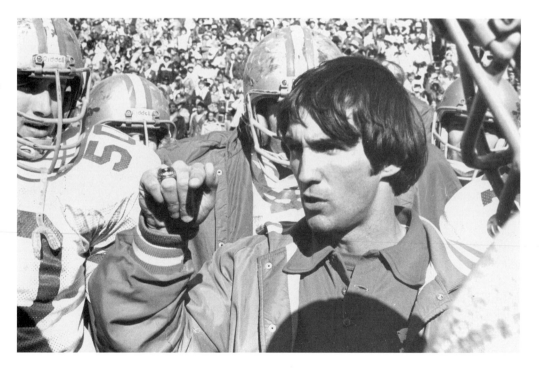

Shanahan. Eastern class of 1974, coached the Denver Broncos to back-to-back Super Bowl titles.

people and different philosophies," Shanahan told Merda.

From there, it was on to the National Football League as Denver's wide receivers coach. Shanahan never returned to the collegiate game again—though there was the possibility of returning to Eastern when Mudra left after the 1982 season.

"When I was at Florida, some scouts asked me if I wanted to coach in the NFL," Shanahan said. "(Before that) I wasn't even thinking about the NFL because I never played pro ball; I didn't think the timing was right in my career (to coach at Eastern)."

Thus, Shanahan removed his name from the list of possible coaches to succeed Mudra. Eastern wound up hiring Al Molde.

The Panthers' loss wound up being pro football's gain. Shanahan won three Super Bowls: one as offensive coordinator with San Francisco in 1994 and two more as the head coach with Denver.

Shanahan first became a pro head coach with the Los Angeles Raiders in 1988.

"Mike was told that he had to keep some of the previous assistant coaches for one year and then he could bring in who he wanted," said special teams coach Pete Rodriquez. "So after one year Mike fired them and was ready to bring in his own guys. Al Davis hired them all back the next day. Everyone knew it was just a matter of time before Mike was fired as well."

The Raiders dismissed Shanahan after just two seasons. It proved to be a decision that would haunt the Raiders. With Denver in their division, the Raiders would face their former coach twice every season. Shanahan posted a 21-7 record against his former employer.

Shanahan was joined by Mike Heimerdinger and John Teerlinck during the Broncos' glory years.

Heimerdinger, Shanahan's former Eastern roommate, served as Denver's wide receivers coach.

Teerlinck, Eastern's defensive coordinator in 1978, served as pass rush specialist with Denver. After moving to the Indianapolis Colts, Teerlinck became one of 23 NFL coaches to win a Super Bowl with more than one team.

As for Shanahan, his run in Denver ended in 2008.

"He spent 14 years as an NFL head coach (in the same city), that's about unheard of nowadays," said former Broncos' beat writer Bill Williamson, now with espn.com. "I think it just got stale for him. It got stale for the players hearing the same message. There were some personnel decisions that caught up with him.

"But the future was always bright with Mike Shanahan. The Broncos were always relevant. They were talked about at the beginning of the season and at the end of the season. The (Denver) defense may have slipped, but his offense was still rolling until the end."

Before working the Broncos beat, Williamson had covered the Minnesota Vikings under head coach Mike Tice.

"Tice had a very loose relationship with the media," Williamson said. "When I came to Denver, I heard horror stories. But I found Shanahan to be easier than I expected. He was very professional. He knew what the media needed. Every day he was available one-on-one for the daily beat writers. That's pretty much unheard of."

After being out of the NFL for two seasons, he signed a five-year, $35 million contract to become the head coach and executive vice president of the Washington Redskins.

"I've got very high standards, just like everybody in this organization," Shanahan said at this introductory press conference. "I can't tell you how long it's going to take. But I can guarantee you: We'll get better every day and hopefully it won't take long to get back to where this organization has been."

Shanahan lasted four seasons in Washington. The Redskins were just 24-40 with one playoff appearance during his tenure.

JOHN TEERLINCK

Have you seen those T-shirts that read "Football is Life"? Those very well could have been custom-made for John Teerlinck.

"All my life I wanted to play pro football," said the Indianapolis Colts' defensive line coach during training camp in the summer of 2009. "Even from a young age, everything I did was geared toward that goal."

Twenty-seven-year-old John Teerlinck ran the defense for the 1978 national champion Panthers.

After Fenwick, Teerlinck arrived at Western Illinois University to play under eventual College Football Hall of Fame head coach Darrell Mudra.

"Darrell was way ahead of his time," Teerlinck said. "He was a great motivator."

Teerlinck earned All-America honors as a cocaptain his senior year. He was the Leathernecks' defensive Most Valuable Player with 122 tackles and 14 sacks his senior season of 1973. He set a single-game record with four sacks.

"John was going to play every down the same way," said former WIU assistant coach Don "Deek" Pollard. "It didn't matter if it was practice or a game. It didn't matter if you were in pads or not. If you were going against John, you'd better strap it on and be ready. He only knew one speed, and it was all-out.

"John Teerlinck was a self-made football player. He didn't have great athletic talent, but he had desire and was self-motivated."

Pete Rodriquez, another WIU assistant, also grew to fully appreciate Teerlinck.

"He's one of my favorite people ever," Rodriquez said. "He needed some discipline in his life. He needed to be steered in the right way. But, John was one of the hardest-working players ever. He beat you out to the practice field. He put in extra time in the weight room. Nobody outworked 'Linck.'"

Dave Tipton, Teerlinck's former linemate at Western, marveled at his friend's drive.

"JT left his pro game at Western," Tipton said. "He always played hurt. John probably should have had surgery along the way, but he didn't want to hurt his chances in the (NFL) draft."

Teerlinck and his Leatherneck teammates flourished under Mudra's leadership. Western posted a 24-8 record during Teerlinck's varsity years (1971–1973).

"At that time, Western was by far the top football school in the state of Illinois," said Teerlinck. "Being Division II, we had 45 scholarships, but we regularly beat teams that were Division-I with 90 scholarships. We beat good programs like Northern Illinois, Central Michigan, Eastern Michigan."

Teerlinck furthered his point that Western indeed was the state's top collegiate program during the era.

Teerlinck reached his goal, playing two years with the San Diego Chargers in the NFL. A knee injury ended his playing career.

Born in Rochester, New York, Teerlinck and his family moved to the Chicago area at a young age. He quickly began working on his dream.

"I played for a Pop Warner League team for the LaGrange YMCA," Teerlinck recalled. "Kids came from all over (Chicagoland) to play for that team. We played all over. We went two years undefeated. The second year, we were unscored upon."

That early success led to further accolades at Fenwick High School. Teerlinck earned All-Chicago Catholic League honors. He was also reunited with many of his teammates from Pop Warner days.

"The *Chicago Tribune* had an all-star team four years (after Pop Warner)," he said. "Half of that Pop Warner team was there."

During his prep days, Teerlinck did anything necessary to perform on the field.

"I had my knee drained and shot up," he recalled. "I was meat on a stick. I have five kids. I wouldn't want any of them to do any of that, but it was a different time then. Those were different days."

"The best barometer by far is the (1974) draft," said Teerlinck. "Take a look at it sometime."

Teerlinck's name appears at the top of the list. He was taken in the fifth round by San Diego, the 105th overall pick.

"Now, that's a third-round pick with 32 (NFL) teams these days," Teerlinck pointed out. "It's also worth about $2 million. I got $15,000 then."

Teerlinck wasn't the lone Western player drafted. Dennis Morgan went in the 10th round to Dallas; Marvin Williams went in the 17th round to New Orleans.

Meanwhile, Northwestern and Illinois would have just two players taken in the 17-round draft (the same number as Northern Illinois). Defensive back Pete Wessel was the Wildcats' first player to go (round six). Tackle Gerry Sullivan was the first Illini player selected. He went in the seventh round.

"The pros don't care where they get their players," Teerlinck said. "They just want guys who can play."

Perhaps no better illustration of that point comes at the top of the '74 draft. Dallas made defensive end Ed "Too Tall" Jones of Tennessee State the No. 1 overall pick.

Mike Wagner, a former WIU defensive back and later an All-Pro safety for the Pittsburgh Steelers, agrees with his former teammate. In fact, Wagner believes that Teerlinck himself is a prime example.

"(John was) outstanding," Wagner said in an e-mail. "He could have played at a Division I school."

Teerlinck wound up starting two games at defensive end for the Chargers in his rookie season. He racked up 7.5 sacks, including three in one game.

Teerlinck followed that up with five starts in the first six games of the 1975 season. Then came the play that ended his career.

"It was October 26, 1975," Teerlinck noted. "I blew out my knee at Oakland."

Though he tried to come back, Teerlinck officially retired in 1977.

"I never intended to coach," he said. "I had sold real estate in San Diego in the offseason. I did pretty well at it, made pretty good money."

But, as luck and fate would have it, Teerlinck spotted some kids playing football in a sandlot one day.

"(Seeing that made me realize) that I didn't know if I could survive without football," Teerlinck said of the memory.

After calls to former Western coaches Mudra and Rodriquez (then at Iowa State), Teerlinck landed his first coaching job at Iowa Lakes Junior College.

"They had nothing there," Teerlinck recalled. "But, through hard work, we turned things around."

That experience would pale in comparison to the turnaround Teerlinck was about to become a key player in. At Rodriquez's urging, Mudra—now at Eastern Illinois—hired Teerlinck as his defensive coordinator.

Mudra had taken the Eastern head coaching position following a 1-10 season by the previous coaching staff. Teerlinck was 27 years old.

"(Being a defensive coordinator at 27) wasn't a big deal," Teerlinck said. "I'd been in pro football."

Teerlinck immediately went to work on his game plan.

"I asked myself who had the No. 1 defense in the country at that time?" he said. "Well, it was Texas A&M. Melvin Roberston was the coach."

Teerlinck called Roberston on the phone and found out the A&M coach would be speaking at a hotel outside Chicago's O'Hare Airport.

"After his speech, he said, 'Meet me in the bar and you're buying,'" Teerlinck said. "A few of us went. Six hours later, I was the only one still there listening to him."

Teerlinck followed up the late night with an invitation to attend A&M's spring practices.

"That spring break the other coaches were talking about going to Panama City or wherever," Teerlinck said. "I was like, bullshit, we're packing up the station wagon and going down to Texas A&M. It's time to get to work. We learned a lot."

Mudra and Teerlinck were joined by a then-25-year-old offensive coordinator named Mike Shanahan.

"We worked the players' asses off," Teerlinck said. "We practiced every day except Christmas and Thanksgiving."

Eastern middle linebacker Alonzo Lee knew Teerlinck was something special almost immediately.

"He was a guy who demanded excellence," Lee said. "I remember him running with us during the summer. I remember him lifting weights with us. He was a crazed dog. He pushed you to the limit. He brought out your best. I believed in him.

"You can't say enough good things about John Teerlinck."

The hard work paid off as the Panthers roared to a 12-2 record and the Division II national championship.

Mudra credited Teerlinck as being the key factor.

"That is very nice of Darrell," said Teerlinck. "We got after it. We had 78 quarterback sacks. We had 78 in '78."

After one more year at Eastern, Teerlinck joined the Illinois staff under Mike White. The Illini had winning seasons in 1981 and '82 and played in their first bowl game since the 1960s.

Teerlinck then returned to pro football, joining legendary coach George Allen with the Chicago Blitz of the upstart United States Football League.

"George Allen taught me so much," Teerlinck said. "I didn't know anything. Pro football is totally different (than college ball). You can't yell and scream. These guys make more money than you do. They can see right through the bullshit right off the bat.

"You've got to know your stuff. You've got to show them things that will help their game. Those things get their attention. When you do that, those guys will run through brick walls for you."

Teerlinck learned well from Allen and others. He coached for three decades on NFL staffs.

"Everywhere we go, we win," Teerlinck said.

His track record speaks for itself. Teerlinck coached in 31 playoff games with five teams. He won three Super Bowls, two with Denver when he was reunited with Shanahan and one with Indianapolis. He coached in five conference championships.

In addition, Teerlinck coached a list of line-men that reads like a Who's Who of the elite in the trenches—Michael Dean Perry, Chris Doleman, John Randle, Neil Smith, Kevin Greene, Bubba Baker, Keith Millard, Robert Mathis and Dwight Freeney.

Through it all he still has strong feelings about Western Illinois. He was inducted into the school's Hall of Fame in 2000.

"It's a great, great honor," he said. "When you think of the few people who get that chance, it's really something special."

He's also proud to be among the great coaches who have called Eastern and Western home.

"Right now people talk about Eastern with Brad Childress with the Vikings and Sean Payton with the Saints and of course, Mike Shanahan, but Western has done pretty well," Teerlinck said. "Think about Lou Saban, Red Miller, Joe Collier . . .

"Forty-eight percent of (NFL) coaches changed last year. Six guys who played for me are now coaches in the league."

One of those is former Eastern star Randy Melvin, who has coached defensive linemen in both college and the pros.

"He (Teerlinck) became my mentor as I got into coaching," Melvin said.

Teerlinck has also had a direct influence on his son Bill, who assisted his father with the Colts' defensive line before returning to the collegiate ranks.

"He coached at Illinois State (under Denver Johnson)," the elder Teerlinck said of his son. "He was there when they had some of their best teams."

Still, Teerlinck's success has come at a cost.

"I've had 14 knee surgeries. I have two artificial knees. I can hardly walk. I can't work out. I've put on weight," he said.

Teerlinck said he has written a book about his experiences.

"It's 44 chapters," Teerlinck explained. "I wrote it for my sons. It will never get published. It's about all the NFL bullshit, and believe me, there's plenty of that. (But) the NFL would never let it come out. And, I want my pension."

Teerlinck certainly deserves that. After all, football is life.

FOUR-DOWN TERRITORY

Favorite Football Movie: *Jim Thorpe, All-American.* I thought I was going to be the next Jim Thorpe when I was a kid.

First Car: It was a 1963 Chevy Malibu. It had a 283 engine in it. My dad got it for $250 around 1968.

Worst Summer Job: I can't say. All the jobs I had I got paid for.

Favorite Subjects in School: Physical education or recess, but I also love history and geography. Those who don't know their history are doomed to repeat the past. History is full of examples. Look at what happens when the defensive team was put on offense; they didn't win. I go to the used bookstore and get 10 or 12 books then take my wife and daughters to Applebees. I spend more money at Applebees. Isn't that something? They're giving knowledge away and food is what we want.

He finished his career in 1979 earning first-team All-America honors by the Associated Press and American Football Coaches Association. Following graduation he would play several years in the Canadian Football League.

The above is Chris "Poke" Cobb's Hall of Fame biography as it appears on Eastern's website. Yet, those mere statistics and accomplishments only begin to tell the legacy of the Panthers' all-time leading rusher.

"The fact he was No. 3 (in career rushing) behind Earl Campbell and Tony Dorsett says a great deal in itself," said former Eastern teammate Alonzo Lee.

When asked to recall the most amazing thing he'd ever seen Cobb do on the field, Lee was at a loss.

"You can't pick one," Lee said. "He did some of the most amazing things you ever saw. It's too tough to pick. He had great runs in every game."

Former teammate Pete Catan agreed.

"He's probably the greatest halfback I've ever

CHRIS "POKE" COBB

Induction Class of 1990 Football

Christopher "Poke" Cobb was inducted posthumously after playing football for the Panthers from 1976 to 1979.

He is considered the greatest running back in EIU history and is a former NCAA rushing record holder with 5,042 career yards. Cobb finished his career holding almost every rushing record at EIU with 1,667 all-purpose yards in a season, 6,077 career all-purpose yards and 49 career touchdowns.

He rushed for more than 200 yards in three games with a career-best 230 yards against Butler in 1976. He had another 13 games in which he rushed for more than 150 yards.

A second-team Associated Press All-American as a junior, he helped lead the Panthers to the 1978 NCAA Division II National Championship in one of the greatest turnarounds in sports history. The previous year's team had posted a 1-10 mark only to finish in the '78 season at 12-2.

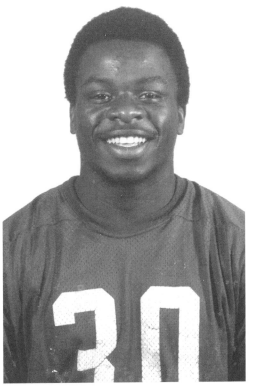

Chris "Poke" Cobb remains the Panthers' all-time career rusher with 5,042 yards.

seen," said Catan, who played professionally in the Canadian Football League and United States Football League.

"Whenever Poke knew it was his time, he would make something happen, regardless of the situation," Catan told Chad Merda of *The Daily Eastern News* in 1999. "Poke would make chicken soup out of chicken pooh."

Mike Mullally, the Eastern athletic director who arrived in Charleston from the University of Oklahoma, called Cobb "as good a ballplayer as I ever saw, and that includes Joe Washington."

Panther All-American wide receiver James Warring said, "If you needed five yards, give the ball to Poke and you've got your five yards."

Cobb still holds the longest touchdown run in school history with a 96-yard score against Tennessee Tech in 1976.

Darrell Mudra, the head coach of Eastern's 1978 national champions, viewed Cobb as a key part of the Panther offense.

"We were able to help out our passing game because every time we faked a handoff to Poke Cobb, the defense had to respect it," Mudra said. "It really opened up the air for us. We got a lot of big yards because of it."

According to Mudra, the '78 champions' offense was fairly simple.

"We had about three things we did well," he said. "Two of those involved Cobb. We ran off tackle out of the I (formation). We ran play action. We also threw screens to him out of the backfield."

In the national semifinal game against Youngstown State, Cobb scored what proved to be the winning touchdown with four minutes remaining.

Against heavily favored Delaware in the national championship game at Longview, Texas, Cobb rushed for 101 yards and scored the Panthers' lone touchdown.

Despite playing such a key role in Eastern's 10-9 victory, Cobb was neither quoted nor photographed in a special edition of *The Daily Eastern News* that commemorated the title.

"He was a very shy guy," Mullally said. "He was so talented, so strong, so quick. He was like a bowling ball when he ran."

Cobb was given his nickname early in life.

"When he was small," his brother Ernest was quoted in *Sports Illustrated* in 1979, "he was kind of slow, crawling around the ground and all, and he was called Porky. When he grew up a little bit, we changed that to Poke."

Like Cobb, fellow Panther Donald Pittman grew up in South Carolina.

"Poke Cobb! What a player!" said Pittman in an e-mail. "(He was) 5-6, 190-200 pounds (that was) all muscle, could cut on a dime with great speed and very, very hard to tackle. Poke went to Clover High School, which was in our region and a part of the York County School District that included Fort Mill, Rock Hill, Clover and York."

After playing the 1980 season for Hamilton in the CFL, Cobb returned to his native South Carolina. There, in 1990, Cobb died in a car accident.

"We would ride home together on occasions and talk about our times back home and all of our great times at Eastern," said Pittman. "I was so grateful I had a chance to spend some time with him a few months before he was killed. That hit me really hard as I am sure it did all the other guys on the team that knew what a special person and athlete he was."

"That was a heartbreaking accident," said Mullally. "I still think about it even all these years later."

JAMES WARRING

The lessons James Warring learned as a wide receiver at Eastern led to his success in both the worlds of kickboxing and boxing.

"When I fought for my first title and lost, I didn't give up," said Warring from his native state of Florida. "I could always look back on that first season at Eastern and know a championship was still possible."

Warring came to Eastern from Miami Killian High School where he excelled in football, basketball and track.

"Our athletic director, Mr. Young, had as much to do with me going to Eastern Illinois as anyone," he said. "We put together some film and sent it up."

The Eastern coaches must have liked what they saw, for soon Warring was part of the 1976 recruiting class that would pay dividends two years later as a key element in a Division II national championship.

First, however, Warring had to endure the infamous 1-10 season under head coach John Konstantinos in 1977.

"They had the right players there, but didn't have the right ideas," Warring said. "We had all these athletes, but they were running the wrong offense."

Warring also had to adjust to the unpredictable weather of the Midwest.

"I remember the first time I saw snow," he said. "I was doing laundry and looked out the window. It was so pretty, so unreal. I couldn't get over it. Then, the next morning when I woke up it looked so dirty."

While Warring said he did adjust to the winter temperatures, he admitted that he gave serious thought to not returning to Eastern after the one-win season.

"I had to make the choice of whether to stay home or come back to school," Warring said. "I prayed about it. Right after I decided to stay, the new coaching staff was hired."

James Warring (85) later won world titles in boxing and kickboxing.

The new coaching staff was led by eventual College Football Hall of Fame head coach Darrell Mudra. Former Panther quarterback Mike Shanahan was the 25-year-old offensive coordinator.

"Those guys made changes right off the bat," Warring said. "They had us running, training, lifting weights. The whole thing was different."

As he would prove years later in the National Football League, Shanahan knew how to use his talent.

"He taught me how to watch tape," Warring said. "It was a discipline. You could look at Coach Shanahan's eyes and know things were right. He knew everything that was going on."

Warring said Shanahan stressed that no matter how good a defense was, every player had predictable habits and made mistakes.

"A good offensive coordinator can do wonders with wide receivers," Warring said. "It showed in our game plan."

As an example, Warring talked about goal-line situations.

"We'd get the ball down there inside the five or so and run those fades," he said. "Everybody runs those now; Mike Shanahan was doing that way back then."

Shanahan also showed the ability to make key adjustments.

"When the defense was all set for the fade, he'd run a play where the receiver stopped and caught the ball on a hook (pattern)," Warring said.

Warring described his strength as a receiver.

"If a ball came close, within two or three feet, it would be a catch," he said. "That's what I did, I made catches."

Warring indeed made catches. During the national championship season, he set school records for receiving yards (980) and touchdown receptions (14). In addition, Warring caught a record four touchdowns in a single game. He earned first-team All-American status.

In the national semifinal game against Youngstown State, Warring was selected as the ABC/Chevrolet Offensive Player of the Game as Eastern avenged an early-season loss to the Penguins.

"It was cold that day," Warring recalled. "This was back in the day when there weren't all these things to keep you warm like now. We had thick pantyhose on underneath our uniforms. We had made our own warmers. But, at the end of the game, it felt like it got warmer. That's what happens when you're on the winning side."

After being lauded by *Sports Illustrated* as one of the favorites for the 1979 Division II

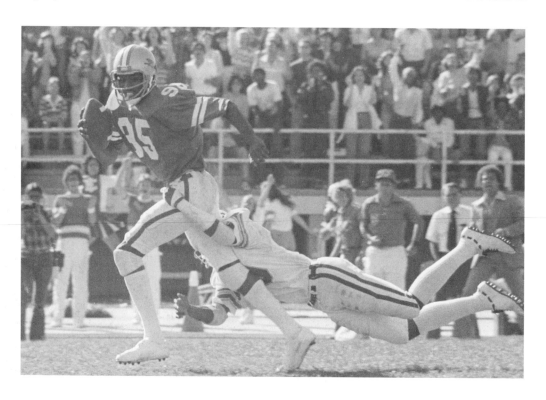

crown, Warring and his teammates didn't even make the playoffs the following year.

"Winning a championship is easy," he said. "The second year is the one that's important. You really have to train and be focused to stay on top."

When his Panther career ended, Warring went to camp with the Oakland Raiders.

"I wasn't there long, but the reason I was there is thanks to everybody from Eastern," he said. "It was a total effort: The coaches, the players, the trainers, everybody."

When his playing days ended, Warring turned his back on football. "I didn't watch it, I didn't follow it," he said. "I just moved on."

Warring moved on to the worlds of kickboxing and boxing. "I had been kickboxing since before I ever went to Eastern," he said.

Warring eventually became a three-time World Kickboxing Association champion. In fact, when he returned to Eastern for a reunion of the '78 title team, he brought his championship belt with him.

So, how and why did Warring get into boxing?

"I needed to learn how to box better (for kickboxing)," he explained. "Kickboxing is much harder because of all that's involved."

He soon fought his way up the boxing ranks.

"I had to pad my record just to get certain fights," he said. "I fought some guys that I really shouldn't have. But, that's the way it was. You can't do that now because of the computer (rankings)."

Warring fought 23 professional bouts. He posted an 18-4 record with one draw. He knocked out opponents 11 times en route to holding the NABF cruiserweight and IBF world cruiserweight titles. In fact, Warring recorded the fastest knockout in history for a world title match when he KO'd James Prichard just 24 seconds into the first round.

"Being the second kickboxer to become a world champion in the sweet science (boxing) turned Warring into a big star," wrote Luca De Franco on thesweetscience.com.

Warring parlayed his ring success into other ventures. He costarred in two movies (*The Opponent* and *Blood Fist II*) and also appeared in the '80s TV series *Miami Vice*.

Later, he became a World Combat Champion in the bare knuckle strikers division.

When his fighting days ended, Warring became a respected boxing referee and judge. He has officiated title bouts for a number of sanctioned boxing organizations. He was later licensed as a referee for the Florida State Athletic Commission in Shin Do Kumate.

In 1995 Warring was enshrined in Eastern's Hall of Fame.

Today, Warring owns and operates his own martial arts business. He has been honored by both the City of Miami and Dade County for his community service work.

"I go out to three or four schools a year for things like Career Day or Black History Day," he said. "I share my story and try to pass on the values of hard work and reaching your goals."

He also has taught those same lessons to his children. His daughter, Joelle, played college volleyball and played for the Jamaican national team. His other daughter studied to become a nurse. His son, Blake, was injured as a high school football player and now attends college.

"I also have two stepsons," he added.

Life has taught Warring much in his 50-plus years.

"To be a champion, sometimes you have to lose and learn from it," he said. "You have to learn to eat, sleep and think only about what you're after. I tell kids all the time that they have so much available to them. These athletes today should take advantage of it. You've got to totally focus on what you are after. Forget about the cell phone. Put aside the texting. Focus on what you want to do and work hard. Go after it."

And perhaps you too can become a success story like James Warring.

FOUR-DOWN TERRITORY

Favorite Football Movie: Sorry, I don't really have one. Not really.

First Car: A '69 Riviera. I drove it to Eastern Illinois. It almost cost me my life. I had never driven on black ice before. I hit a patch somewhere in Georgia or Tennessee, I really can't remember where. Somehow I missed a couple of cars and got hit from behind. But that nice, big bumper on that car absorbed the hit. Nothing happened and nobody got hurt.

Worst Summer Job: I never really had a bad job. I worked one summer at the water plant there in Charleston. I learned so much about the process of water. I also worked for North American Van Lines. That job got me in shape. I was moving pianos from the basement to the upper level. I walked backwards all the time. That really got me ready for my football season.

Favorite Subject in School: It was an athletic training course at Eastern because I use so much of it now at my martial arts business.

ALONZO LEE

The college years are said to be not only the building blocks for one's career, but also a bridge to an individual's destiny. Perhaps a perfect example of that is Alonzo Lee.

"All those things from 1978 I carry with me today," said Lee, the starting middle linebacker on Eastern's national championship team. "They are part of my coaching."

Those parts have led to a coaching career that has spanned more than 30 years. It has

taken him to four different universities, seven Mid-Eastern Athletic Conference (MEAC) titles and the head coaching position at North Carolina A&T.

The genesis to Lee's success in the coaching ranks began in his days at Eastern. After a season at an Iowa community college, Lee found his way to Charleston.

"(Eastern defensive coordinator) John Teerlinck was at Iowa Lakes (Junior College)," Lee recalled. "He noticed me and Kenny Winbush.

"Over Christmas, we came to (Charleston) to visit the place."

Lee was escorted around Eastern's campus by Joe Taylor, the former Western Illinois star who was hired as an assistant coach by Darrell Mudra. The two would cross paths again later in life.

"Joe was a DC guy too," said Lee, a Dunbar Senior High School graduate from the nation's capital.

Lee was sold and transferred to Eastern.

"They brought in 10 to 15 of us from junior colleges. Five of us ended up starters," Lee noted.

Those five combined with the Panthers' returnees to wipe away the disappointment of a one-win 1977 season.

Eastern not only wiped away the disappointment, it rewrote history. The Panthers steamrolled to a 12-2 record and the national championship.

"(We did it) with a lot of hard work and dedication," Lee recalled. "The chemistry built by the coaching staff developed a winning mindset."

The Panthers' march to the championship included a 26-22 home victory over powerful Youngstown State, a team that had soundly defeated Eastern early in the season.

Eastern scored what proved to be the winning touchdown on a three-yard run by Chris "Poke" Cobb with 4:04 remaining.

Youngstown State coach Bill Narduzzu claimed an official "cheated us out of a chance to win" when Panther fans stormed the field in the game's final seconds. Three decades later, Lee would have none of Narduzzu's argument.

"The game was over," he recalled. "There were just a couple of seconds left. They wouldn't have gotten the play off."

Alonzo Lee made all the right calls from his middle linebacker position in the national championship game.

Lee also pointed out that plenty of calls went against Eastern when it lost a road game to Youngstown State, 40-24, in the season's sixth game.

In the national championship game played in Longview, Texas, Eastern's defense keyed the 10-9 win over heavily favored Delaware.

Defensive coordinator Teerlinck praised Lee for his leadership of the Panther defense that day.

"Alonzo Lee made all the right calls from middle linebacker that day," said Teerlinck, later defensive line coach for the Indianapolis Colts.

For Lee, just a sophomore, the game was the pinnacle of his college career.

"We shocked the world," Lee said.

Lee and the Panthers returned to the national championship game two years later. This time around, Eastern was the favorite to win. However, this time around, it was the Panthers who fell victim to the upset at the hands of the Cal Poly Mustangs.

"We had quite a few of the same guys (from '78) on the team," Lee remembered. "But, we fumbled the ball away a couple of times deep in their territory. Sure, they made some big plays . . . we gave up some big punt returns . . . but those fumbles . . .

"That made the difference in the game."

That game marked the end of Lee's college career. He finished as a three-year captain. He led the team in tackles his senior season and wound up an All-American.

Lee graduated with a bachelor's of science degree in therapeutic recreation in 1982 while serving as an assistant coach on Mudra's staff.

"Sean Payton was my quarterback on the JV team," he noted.

Like in his playing career, Lee was a big winner as a coach. He also learned from a big winner: Joe Taylor, the man who had helped bring him to Eastern. Lee and Taylor reunited at Hampton.

"Coach Taylor has taken some of the same (coaching) blueprint to success from those days (under Mudra at Eastern)," Lee said. "I worked for him at two different schools."

Over the years, he developed a reputation for developing championship-caliber defenses. Lee coached at North Carolina A&T, Hampton and Morgan State, all members of the MEAC.

In 1998 and 2001, Lee was honored by the All-America Football Foundation as an Outstanding Assistant Coach. Also in 2001, he was selected as the National Assistant Coach of the Year for NCAA Division I-AA.

"That's really remarkable," said Teerlinck. "The programs he's coached at don't have a lot of resources. Just like when he was a player, Alonzo just works his behind off."

In five of his last 12 years as a defensive co-ordinator, his defenses were tops in the MEAC. In addition, his 2008 Morgan State unit was ranked No. 1 in total defense. A year earlier it had finished second.

Off the field, Lee has also made an impact. During his first stint at North Carolina A&T, Lee started a gospel choir comprised of Aggie football players that performed for church groups and other community organizations in Greensboro.

All this led to his hiring as North Carolina A&T's head coach in January 2009. Lee became the 17th head coach in Aggie football history.

All these years later, lessons he learned under Mudra and Teerlinck have stayed with him.

"I learned a long time ago, leave no stone unturned," Lee said. "Prepare your guys through the week. Work them hard. But on game day, turn 'em loose and have fun."

Those sound like words to build a winning program on.

FOUR-DOWN TERRITORY

Favorite Football Movie: *Remember the Titans.*

First Car: 1958 New Yorker that I bought for $200 while I was at Eastern Illinois.

Worst Summer Job: That was also at Eastern. I worked for Trailmobile. It was over 100 degrees inside those trailers, and you were wearing steel-toed boots.

Favorite Subject in School: Math.

PETE CATAN

John Teerlinck saw Dwight Freeney three decades ago.

Impossible, you say? The four-time Pro Bowl defensive end from the Indianapolis Colts wasn't even born then.

"You know Dwight Freeney? Well, Pete Catan was Dwight Freeney in 1978," said Teerlinck.

And Teerlinck should know. He was an NFL defensive line coach for more than 25 years. He coached in three Super Bowls. He also coached both players.

"Pete's problem was that he was in the wrong place at the wrong time," Teerlinck explained. "Today, he'd play (in the NFL). Back when he left school, everybody played the 3-4 defense. People didn't pass then like they do now.

"Pete wasn't big enough to be an end and wasn't fast enough to be a linebacker. He was a tweener. Like I said, he was in the wrong place at the wrong time."

While his timing didn't work out well for the NFL, Catan came along perfectly for head coach Darrell Mudra's Eastern Illinois Panthers of the late 1970s.

Pete Catan and his famous sledgehammer.

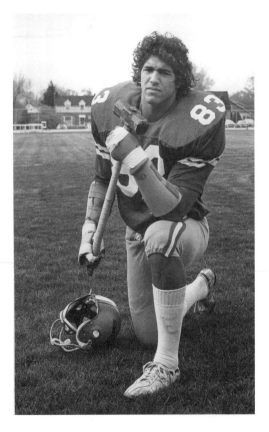

Originally from Penfield, New York, Catan ruled the defensive line at Eastern. A three-year letter winner, Catan led the Panthers to the 1978 NCAA Division-II national championship and a 1980 runner-up finish.

Teerlinck specifically remembers the '78 national semifinal game against Youngstown State, a team that had defeated Eastern during the regular season.

"Catan won that game for us," said Teerlinck, the Panthers' defensive coordinator. "Their quarterback was running the option. Pete broke through, hit him and caused a fumble."

Catan also remembers the play—and what preceded it.

"Their tight end had just missed a pass and he was going back to the (YSU) huddle," Catan recalled in 2012. "For some reason he came really close to our huddle. He took his hands and wiped them on the front and back of my jersey. The next play I came off the line engaging the tackle, the quarterback pitched the ball to the halfback, who fumbled it. I tapped the ball past the halfback and (Eastern linebacker) Ray Jeske came up with the ball."

Catan also played a key role in the national championship game. With Delaware driving for a potential game-winning touchdown in the game's final minutes, Catan and teammate Ira Jefferson took over the line of scrimmage and stopped the Blue Hens' drive.

Thus, Delaware was forced into a 45-yard field goal attempt by Brandt Kennedy. When the kick sailed wide, Eastern's national championship dreams became a reality.

Catan led Eastern in sacks and tackles for loss from 1978 to 1980. He held the school records for sacks in a game (6), season (21) and career (47). He also held the Eastern records for tackles for loss in a game (5), season (19) and career (45).

Catan earned All-American honors all three seasons. He was a first-team selection in 1979 and 1980.

"He was a great team player and leader," said Mudra. "Pete was an amazing player."

Catan will always be remembered as the player who carried a sledgehammer around campus. Or so the legend goes.

"ABC came out to take pictures the day before the Youngstown game," Catan told Chad Medra of *The Daily Eastern News* in a 1999 article. "They had started putting a fence around and the D-line was there. I picked up the sledgehammer, and I walked out."

Catan added that the sledgehammer symbolized the road less traveled. Eastern, known for losing for so many years, was on its way to winning a national championship.

Yet, there were stories that didn't grow into legends; they simply were facts.

"Ole Sledghammer Catan was second to none," said teammate Alonzo Lee, later the head coach at North Carolina A&T. "He put notches into that sledgehammer for each sack."

Lee, the Panthers' middle linebacker, was asked if he had any tales to illustrate Catan's tenacity.

"Lord, have mercy!" Lee said. "There are numerous things. Where do I begin?

"Well, both Pete and I loved to lift those weights. One time it snowed like the dickens. We lived out in those apartments in married housing. We made our way through the wind and snow. When we got to the weight room, it was all locked up. Well, we found a way in. People wondered later what happened to those locks!"

Catan shined more light on the story.

"I took a pair of pliers and undid the fence," he said. "I changed the locks on the doors."

Athletic director Mike Mullally also remembered the incident.

"The campus police called me about someone breaking into the weight room," he said. "I went down to see for myself. The police asked me what should be done. My response was that we need to get 'em a key. That was a change around Eastern, seeing players wanting to use the weight room."

Defensive lineman Randy Melvin, another former teammate, remembers an experience in the days leading up to the '78 championship showdown with Delaware.

"Coach Teerlinck got Pete so fired up that he punched a hole in the wall," Melvin said. "I still remember the look on Coach Teerlinck's face!"

After graduation, Catan signed with the Winnipeg Blue Bombers of the Canadian Football League. He played three seasons in Canada, earning all-league honors in 1982.

Moreover, Catan was selected as the Blue Bombers' defensive MVP that season.

"A Dallas Cowboys scout told me they were going to draft me in the third round, but they wanted me to play outside linebacker. I hadn't played that position in years. Winnipeg wanted me to play defensive end and offered me $15,000, which sounded pretty good to me. It worked out for me. It was meant to be," Catan said.

It was also life-changing. While in Winnipeg, Catan became a born-again Christian, thanks to teammate and CFL Hall of Fame member John Helton.

"John was a true inspiration. I had been raised in church, but it wasn't until John that I came to accept Jesus Christ as my Savior. It gave me definition. It defined who I was."

Catan left the CFL in 1984 to join the Houston Gamblers of the United States Football League. He quickly made his mark with 17.5 sacks, the second highest total in the league.

"His quickness off the ball is what I remember most," said Gambler teammate Joe Bock. "Pete got to the quarterback so fast. He really was only playing at about 240 pounds back in those days.

"(Pro Football Hall of Famer) Bruce Smith is the quickest I ever saw off the ball, but Pete Catan was right up there. He was probably in the top three or four coming off the ball and rushing the quarterback."

"He was just a force," said Anthony Nunez, founder of a website dedicated to the Gamblers. "Pete Catan was just an anchor on the line. He was just brutalizing quarterbacks that season. He was almost unblockable."

Nunez was a teenager during the Gamblers' two-year USFL run. After a career in law enforcement as an adult, Nunez helped organize a team reunion in 2010. In addition to running his website, Nunez collects Gambler memorabilia.

"Catan's was the first Gambler jersey I ever bought," Nunez said. "I paid about $400 for it about two-and-a-half years ago (in 2007). I own three out of four of his jerseys. You have to remember it wasn't like it is today when guys wear a jersey once and then it's sold or auctioned off. (Gamblers') players only had two jerseys for the season in those days, one black and one white."

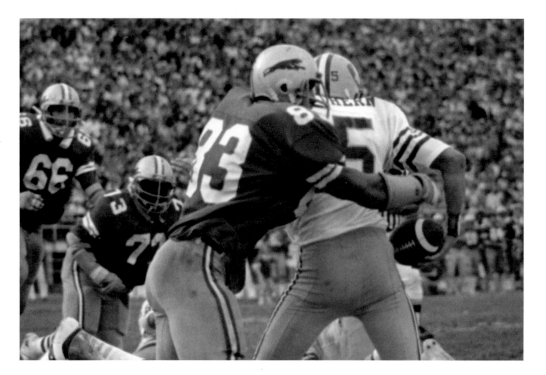

After his Eastern career ended, Pete Catan played in the Canadian Football League and the United States Football League.

Catan was joined in Houston by former Eastern teammate Scott McGhee.

"I joked with Scott that every time I turned around, he was there," Catan said. "We played at Eastern. We played in Canada together briefly, and then we were teammates in Houston."

"Pete and I are still the closest of friends," McGhee said in a 1985 interview with *The Daily Eastern News*. "We really treasured our time at Eastern, and we talk about it often."

Bock grew up in the same area of New York as Catan. Ironically, the two were roommates during the Gamblers' training camp in 1984.

"It's funny that we ended up being put together," said Bock. "Pete was like a brother to me. I really loved that guy. He was such a solid Christian. He was the star while I was more of a fringe player. That didn't matter to Pete. He got me through that whole year."

In a poll of fans, Catan was an honorable mention selection to the all-time USFL team.

When the USFL folded, Catan played briefly for the Tampa Bay Buccaneers and San Diego Chargers as essentially a third-down pass rush specialist.

Following his playing days, Catan worked as a defensive line and strength coach with the Orlando Thunder of the NFL-sponsored World League.

Catan was enshrined in the Eastern Hall of Fame in 1991.

In November 2008, Catan returned to Eastern for the 30th reunion of the 1978 national championship team. Moreover, his daughter was also a student at Eastern.

Panther head coach Bob Spoo invited Catan to address the team before its game against Murray State.

Catan didn't threaten the team with his sledgehammer.

"He was just reassuring us we were brought here to play college football," Eastern center Chris Vacarro told Brian Nielsen of the *Charleston Times-Courier*. "He didn't scream or anything, but he got his point across."

Whether it was a factor in the game's result or not is debatable, but Eastern routed Murray State 34-6 in what Spoo called "our best game of the year."

For nearly two decades, Catan has taught building trades at Woodstock High School in northern Illinois.

"I love what I do," he said. "It's quite an experience to work with these young kids. We use math skills. We build a house from the ground up. We hold an open house, and it goes up for sale. The last one sold in four months."

In the fall of 2009, Catan was placed on the College Football Hall of Fame ballot.

Perhaps John Teerlinck could have seen it coming. After all, he's already seen the future in the past.

FOUR-DOWN TERRITORY

Favorite Football Movie: *Brian's Song.* My best friend from grade school days was Charles Washington, an African-American.

First Car: I bought my parents' Town and Country station wagon in 1980 so that I could go out to my teaching practicum. It was probably 10 years old and had that wood panel siding look. My mom and I had to make hand rests for it because the old ones were worn out. We stuffed some foam in and covered it with denim. It had the same engine you would find in a Sherman tank, a 440 big block.

Worst Summer Job: When I was 14 years old I worked with a brick mason. I made mortar for him in a trough. The guy I worked for was great. He used to say, "Rubber arms, rubber legs, rubber balloons." I didn't know what he meant until the end of the day. Man, were my arms ever burning.

Favorite Subject in School: I tell my kids (students) it was lunch period. I was always hungry, still am.

SCOTT MCGHEE

Scott McGhee has gone from catching passes to snagging talent.

The former Eastern wide receiver and punter today runs McGhee Entertainment in Nashville. He spends his days and nights managing the likes of entertainers Darius Rucker, Chris Cagle and Jypsi.

Before he enrolled at Eastern, McGhee attended Carl Sandburg High School in Orland Park. He lettered in football, wrestling, track and hockey.

An all-state football player, McGhee went undefeated as a high school senior en route to winning a state championship.

McGhee played a key role in 1978 when newly hired head coach Darrell Mudra and 25-year-old coordinator Mike Shanahan took over the offensive reins. Eastern completely turned things around from a one-win 1977 season. The '78 Panthers posted a 12-2 record and won the NCAA Division-II national championship. McGhee caught 41 passes for 878 yards and 10 touchdowns.

McGhee's biggest reception of the year, however, came against heavily favored Delaware in the title game. McGhee caught a 26-yard pass from quarterback Steve Turk that placed the ball on the Delaware one-yard line. McGhee's reception set up Poke Cobb's touchdown that tied the game, 9-9. Dan DiMartino's extra point put Eastern ahead for good. McGhee later helped the Panthers gain valuable field position with a 45-yard catch in the third quarter.

Two years later, McGhee was the team's leading receiver with 44 catches for 763 yards and a then-school-record 16 touchdowns. More importantly, the Panthers returned to the national championship game. However, this time around, Eastern finished as the runner-up when Cal Poly upset the Panthers, 21-13.

McGhee told *The Daily Eastern News* after the championship game loss that "Our luck

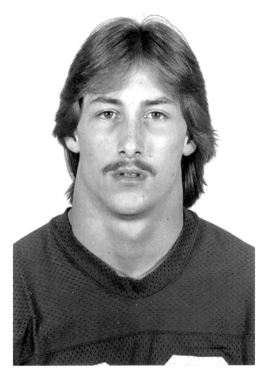

Scott McGhee played on both the 1978 national champions and the 1980 national runner-ups.

was running out. I'm just glad we got there."

McGhee spent time in the Chicago Bears' training camp in the summer of 1981.

"A stop that lasted about as long as half a cup of coffee," McGhee joked.

McGhee next signed with the Toronto Argonauts of the Canadian Football League. He caught 14 passes for 221 yards in seven games for Toronto during the 1982 season. The Argos won the Grey Cup that year.

After he spent the early part of the 1983 season with Hamilton of the CFL, McGhee's pro football career appeared to be over.

However, the fledging United States Football League offered players like McGhee another opportunity. McGhee signed as a free agent with the Houston Gamblers in December 1983.

The 5-foot-9, 172-pound McGhee quickly became a dependable receiver and special teams player in his two seasons with Houston. TV color analyst and former Buffalo Bill Paul Maguire called McGhee "the best possession receiver in the USFL."

Former Gambler teammate Joe Bock said that McGhee was more than just a possession receiver.

"Scotty could make some big plays too. He had a little flash about him," Bock said. "He had excellent hands and speed. He was a high-energy guy. He had a motor that didn't quit."

McGhee was the Gamblers' third-leading receiver with 40 catches in 1984.

"The Gamblers cared about how fast you were as a receiver, not how tall you were," said Anthony Nunez, founder of Houston-gamblers.com and official team historian. "(Offensive coordinator) Mouse Davis chose Scott McGhee for his speed and soft hands. He knew how to catch the ball and how to run."

McGhee became an integral part of the Gamblers' "Run-and-Shoot" Offense that featured future Pro Football Hall of Fame quarterback Jim Kelly as its triggerman.

"You can see a quarterback and set of receivers who were custom-made for that offense," said Nunez. "They were built for the run-and-shoot, and they excelled."

Today, McGhee excels in a different area of entertainment. Most likely it's less painful to promote hits in the music industry than to take them on the playing field.

In 2013, McGhee was inducted into Eastern's Athletic Hall of Fame.

"Scotty's done well for himself," said Bock. "Can't say I'm surprised by that."

RANDY MELVIN

Sometimes football coaches get so caught up in game plans and preparation that they fail to see things around them. Randy Melvin had one such experience.

"It was my most embarrassing (experience)," said Melvin, the former Eastern defensive standout who was then the defensive line coach for the New England Patriots.

The moment came just before the kickoff of Super Bowl XXXVI. The Patriots and St. Louis Rams were lined up for the national anthem. Spirits and emotions were high in a post–September 11 atmosphere.

The attractive young woman who would sing "The Star Spangled Banner" walked out and stood right by Melvin.

"I knew I had seen her before and that she was famous, but I couldn't think of her name," Melvin said. "I asked one of our players, 'Who is she?'"

After shaking his head in disbelief, the player informed Melvin "she" was Mariah Carey.

"It really was embarrassing," he said.

While that may be true, Randy Melvin's career has been as far from embarrassing as one can get.

Melvin was a three-sport standout at Aurora West High School.

"I wrestled up to my senior year," Melvin said. "In track, I threw the shot put and discus."

Yet, it was on the football field where Melvin's star shined brightest. He was set to attend a junior college in California when Eastern contacted him.

"(Assistant coach) Bob Edding started the process," said Melvin. "I figured it was an opportunity to stay in the state. If they were going to offer me a scholarship, I was going to take it."

Thus, Melvin headed off to play for head coach John Konstantinos' Panthers in 1977.

The season proved to be disastrous as Eastern suffered through a 1-10 record.

However, the following year turned out to be one of the biggest turnarounds in football history. New head coach Darrell Mudra replaced Konstantinos. Mudra brought in 27-year-old John Teerlinck and 25-year-old Mike Shanahan as his defensive and offensive coordinators respectively.

"They made an impression, that's for sure," Melvin said. "They cleaned house. They said that if we survived, we'd be a better team."

Eastern was a remarkably better team. The Panthers lost one regular season game. Teerlinck had a direct effect on Melvin.

"He ran 35 or 40 pounds off me," said the defensive lineman.

Teerlinck's memory jibed with the exception of the weight loss.

"He came in at 290 pounds. I ran his ass off and got him down to 240 pounds," said Teerlinck, later a Super Bowl–winning defensive line coach. "He was a beast."

In the NCAA Division II playoffs, Eastern defeated Youngstown State, thus avenging its lone regular season loss.

"That game was such a battle," Melvin said.

Winning the battle moved Eastern into the national championship game against heavily favored Delaware. The Panthers came away with a 10-9 upset of the Blue Hens to cap their historic season.

Twenty-two years later, Melvin again celebrated a championship season when the Patriots upset the favored Rams in the Super Bowl.

"In my mind both are great accomplishments," Melvin said. "It was a thrill at the time I played for Eastern. Nobody could believe we could do it. It was similar with New England.

"There was a commonality. Both teams came together for a common purpose. We still had (separate) groups, but we didn't have cliques."

Melvin's success continued. The following season he was named honorable mention All-American. In 1980, he landed on the All-American second team. The two-time first team all-conference selection was a key player on Eastern's national runner-up that same season.

By the end of his Panther playing days, Melvin held the school record for career fumble

By the end of his Panther playing days, Randy Melvin held the school record for career fumble recoveries and ranked in the top five for career tackles, sacks and tackles for loss.

recoveries and ranked in the top five for career tackles, sacks and tackles for loss.

During his three-year career, the Panthers combined for a 30-9 record with two national championship game appearances.

After his graduation from Eastern, Melvin began his coaching career as an assistant at Urbana High School. He then returned to his alma mater Aurora West. After serving as an assistant for two years, Melvin became the Blackhawks' head coach in 1985. He held the position through 1987.

"I had a chance to go back," Melvin said. "Some of the same teachers and coaches I had were still there. As I look back, they weren't much older than me. It was a good experience."

The following year, Melvin again went back to the future. He left the prep ranks and joined head coach Bob Spoo's staff at Eastern for the 1988 season. Melvin wound up spending the next seven years coaching the Panthers' defensive line.

"Coach Spoo is a great man," Melvin said. "I learned a lot from him. It wasn't just football. I learned to deal with people. I carry that with me today."

When fellow assistant coach Brock Spack left Eastern to join Joe Tiller's staff at Wyoming,

he took Melvin with him. After spending two years together in Laramie, both Spack and Melvin went with Tiller to Purdue.

Melvin again handled the defensive ends. He remained with the Boilermakers for three seasons, before entering into a new phase of his coaching career—professional football.

Melvin was hired to coach the defensive line for head coach Bill Belichick's Patriots. As one would expect, there are differences between coaching at the collegiate level and coaching in the pro ranks.

"The time you spend recruiting at the college level, you spend coaching at the pro level," Melvin explained. "You spend time researching and studying."

The coaching is also markedly different.

"The pros all have the technique down, so you spend time scheming," he said. "You may have to refine or adjust a player's technique, but you scheme most of the time."

Thus, your relationships with the athletes you coach are also different.

"So you spend time with a player like Ted Washington and you talk more about things like your kids learning how to drive (than you do about instructing their technique)," Melvin said.

Since leaving New England after the Super Bowl season, Melvin has bounced back and forth between the college and pro games. He's made stops at Illinois, Temple, the Cleveland Browns and Rutgers. Most recently, Melvin was the defensive line coach for the Tampa Bay Buccaneers.

"I enjoy (coaching) both (levels)," Melvin said. "I love what I do."

Asked if he would someday like to be a head coach, Melvin replied, "Certainly."

However, he was quick to add, "I'm not sure when or if that will happen."

For now, Melvin—a 1995 Eastern Hall of Fame inductee—continues to hone his craft.

"My ego is not such that I need to be here or there," he said.

After all, Randy Melvin isn't normally a guy to overlook the big picture.

FOUR-DOWN TERRITORY

Favorite Football Movie: *Remember the Titans* because of the bonding element. It showed the struggle to become a team. It had a great social element.

First Car: A 1964½ Mustang. It was black with a four-speed.

Worst Summer Job: I worked as a riveter inside a tractor trailer. You had to drive in rivets at the top and bottom of the trailer. It was hotter than blazes. There were a lot of us that worked there. I lasted about two weeks.

Favorite Subject in School: Health. To this day I still enjoy researching and reading about health-related issues.

JEFF GOSSETT

Perhaps it was only inevitable that Jeff Gossett wound up at Eastern. Some things in life are just meant to be.

"My dad (Dutch) coached and taught at Eastern, and my mom (Joan) ran the (university) union," said Gossett from his Dallas area home.

Gossett was born in Charleston in 1957. Shortly thereafter, his family moved to Danville, where his father was a high school swim coach. However, the Gossetts returned to Charleston when Jeff was 12.

"My dad was hired as the assistant swim coach at Eastern and then taught in the PE department," he said.

Thus, Gossett spent his high school years as a three-sport star at Charleston High School.

"I played football, basketball and baseball," he said.

As a wishbone quarterback, Gossett led the Trojans to consecutive 8-1 seasons in both his junior and senior years.

"I wasn't really a wishbone quarterback," he said. "I wasn't much of a runner. With my size and arm, I would have been better off as a drop-back passer."

While he did garner football interest from smaller schools such as Millikin University in Decatur, Gossett drew more offers for his baseball prowess. One such offer came from Eastern.

"I decided to stay," Gossett said. "Eastern offered me a baseball scholarship. My (Charleston) teammate Dennis Conley and I were sort of a package deal. Dennis played second base and I played shortstop. We went as a combination."

Gossett spent his first two seasons on the diamond playing for head coach J.W. Sanders. As an upperclassman, Gossett's coach was Tom McDevitt.

"Playing football wasn't even in my mind at that point," he said.

That all changed when Eastern athletic director Mike Mullally strolled by the university's intramural fields one day.

"I was playing for my fraternity team," Gossett noted. "He saw me punting and wound up talking me into joining the team."

"He was kicking the ball like 60 yards," said Mullally. "He told me that he was just fooling around. I told him that I had a better place for him to fool around."

Mullally took Gossett over to the head football coach John Konstantinos' office.

"John didn't want to give Jeff a chance be-

Jeff Gossett, a Charleston High School star, played in the New York Mets' minor league system before turning to pro football.

cause he hadn't recruited him," Mullally said. "But, I made sure he got a chance to join the team."

Gossett did more than just join the football Panthers, he soon established himself as the team's first-string punter. Moreover, Eastern had roared to a 4-0 start.

"I thought it would be pretty cool to punt for a team that was undefeated," he said. "I finished the season punting for them and wouldn't you know it, we lost every game after that."

The losing streak carried over into the following 1977 season. Eastern was victorious only once, that win coming in the final game of the year.

"I went 16 games (as a Panther) before we won a game," he said.

Still, Gossett led all Division II punters with a then-school-record 43-yard average. His record would stand until Kevin Cook broke it 30 years later.

"(With all that losing), I had a lot of practice punting," he joked.

In the meantime, his success in baseball caught more attention. Gossett was a three-year letterman and earned All-American honors at short. He held both the single-season and career records for triples and ranked in the top 10 for career hits, home runs and RBI. Moreover, the Panthers earned a fifth-place finish in the 1978 College Division World Series.

The New York Mets then took Gossett in the fifth round of baseball's amateur draft. Thus, Gossett found himself playing in the Florida Instructional League rather than punting at O'Brien Field in the fall of 1978.

"Who knew Eastern would turn out to be so good after being 1-10 the year before?" Gossett said.

Apparently, new head football coach Darrell Mudra knew. After casting the lone first-place vote for his team in the national preseason poll, Mudra led the Panthers to their shocking national championship season in one of the greatest turnaround stories in college football history.

"Sure, I would have liked to have been part of it," Gossett said. "In all my years I never won a championship, but my future was in baseball at that time."

Mullally added, "I felt bad for Jeff. I'm sure he still thinks about it today because I do."

Gossett and some friends did drive down to Longview, Texas, to cheer Eastern to victory over Delaware in the national championship game.

While continuing to pursue a baseball career, Gossett returned to the football field for his final year of eligibility in the fall of 1979.

"I told myself, 'I'm not going to miss this national championship thing this time around,'" Gossett said. "We had just about everyone back from the year before."

However, the season didn't turn out the same for Eastern. Ranked No. 1 early on, the Panthers were upset by rival Western Illinois. Eastern then stumbled to a 7-4 finish.

"We didn't even make the playoffs," Gossett said.

Then came the decision that permanently changed his career path. During spring training of 1980, the Mets wanted to convert Gossett into a pitcher.

"I never really pitched growing up," he said. "When I signed to play professional baseball, I set a goal to move up one step at a time."

The Mets' pitching decision meant Gossett would have to go back to Class A ball.

"That decided things," Gossett said. "I decided to pursue football at that point."

Not only did Gossett decide to pursue football, the game pursued him. The day of the 1980 NFL draft, he was working out at O'Brien Field.

"My family lived really close to the field," he said. "My sister came running over and said the (St. Louis) Cardinals and the Dallas Cowboys were on the phone and wanted to talk to me."

Both teams showed interest in signing Gossett to a free agent contract. He decided to go with the Dallas offer.

"Roger Staubach had just retired and Danny White would be their new quarterback," Gossett explained. "Danny didn't want to be their punter anymore."

Thus, Gossett found himself in Cowboys

camp with three other candidates. He also found himself face-to-face with Dallas special teams coach Mike Ditka.

"He was hard nosed and limped around back then," Gossett said of the man who would become a Chicago icon a few years later.

While Gossett punted well in camp, legendary Dallas head coach Tom Landry decided to keep White as both his quarterback and punter to save a roster spot for added team depth.

Thus, Gossett returned to Eastern and finished his student teaching requirement to earn his degree.

Yet, with his baseball career now firmly in the rearview mirror, Gossett wasn't ready to give up on his football dream. In 1981, he began the NFL season with the San Diego Chargers.

"After four games they released me so I moved back to Dallas," Gossett said. "I really liked the city. The weather was great."

Gossett took a job briefly working in a furniture store when a call came from the Kansas City Chiefs.

"Their punter, Bob Grupp, had a separated shoulder so they brought me in," he said. "Frank Ganz was my special teams coach. He was the best one I ever had. He could motivate players and had some of the greatest stories in the world.

"He taught me how to directional punt toward the sidelines. That helped me stay in the NFL for a long time."

Gossett's stay with Kansas City was brief. While he won the punting job in the strike-shortened 1982 season, Gossett was released the following year.

"When the Chiefs fired (head coach) Marv Levy, they brought in John Mackovic. He drafted a punter (Jim Arnold) and you could see what was going to happen," Gossett said.

While he was claimed by the Cleveland Browns, Gossett's next stop came in the upstart United States Football League.

"My old Kansas City coach Marv Levy was with the Chicago Blitz," Gossett said. "They were offering me guaranteed money, which was something a punter didn't get in the NFL."

Gossett easily earned his contract, leading all USFL punters with a 42.5-yard average for the 1984 season.

"I loved playing in Chicago," he said. "A lot of friends and family came to see me play."

Gossett spent the 1985 USFL season with the Portland Breakers. However, the cash-strapped league folded soon thereafter.

"I never did get all my money (from the USFL)," he said.

What Gossett did get, though, was a return to the NFL and the Cleveland Browns. In fact, Cleveland nearly earned its way into the Super Bowl.

"That's as close as I ever came," Gossett said. "'The Drive' took care of that."

"The Drive" Gossett referred to was Denver quarterback John Elway's legendary 98-yard march that forced the AFC Championship game into overtime.

"After they tied it, Denver won the game in overtime on a field goal," Gossett lamented.

The NFL suffered through another labor dispute in 1987. Rather than miss games as they had done five years earlier, NFL owners brought in replacement players.

"After the strike was over, (Browns' head coach) Marty Schottenheimer cut me," Gossett said. "My wife was eight months pregnant at the time."

Gossett landed with the Houston Oilers.

"It worked out well," he said. "I was close enough to Dallas that I was able to be there when our first baby was born. In the NFL you always have Tuesday off, so we induced on that day."

The Oilers drafted punter Greg Montgomery from Michigan State the following spring.

"I could see the handwriting on the wall, but (Houston head coach) Jerry Glanville came and told me that he would work out a trade for me," Gossett said. "He asked me where I wanted to go."

Gossett settled on the Los Angeles Raiders.

"Ray Guy had retired and the weather conditions for punting were ideal," he said.

Thus, Houston sent the 31-year-old Gossett to the West Coast.

"Those were the nine best years of my career," he said. "The coaches had confidence in me."

Gossett also saw a familiar face when he got to Los Angeles. Fellow Eastern Hall of Fame member Mike Shanahan was the Raiders' head coach.

"I had hardly ever talked to Mike," Gossett said. "In the past it was pretty much just a quick handshake. I can tell you that he didn't treat me any differently than the other players."

Gossett worked primarily with Raiders' special teams coach Pete Rodriquez, the former Western Illinois head coach.

"First of all, Jeff was a heck of an athlete," Rodriquez said. "He could throw the ball, he had great hands, which made him a great holder on kicks. He was bright, just a really fine person."

Rodriquez, the coach, also learned from Gossett, the player.

"He actually taught me an awful lot about punting," Rodriquez said. "I was more concerned with kick and punt coverage, blocking schemes, that sort of thing. Jeff really gave me some insight on punting."

Meanwhile, Shanahan's tumultuous tenure with the Raiders lasted only four games into his second season.

"He and (owner) Al Davis just didn't see eye-to-eye," Gossett said. "Al brought (former Raiders' offensive lineman) Art Shell in as coach in 1989."

While Shanahan's time with the Raiders was short, Gossett lasted through the 1996 season.

"Jeff was one of Al Davis' favorite guys," said Rodriquez. "That's a difficult thing to do."

Gossett is considered one of the top NFL punters of the 1980s. He enjoyed his finest season in 1991 when his career-best 44.2 yard average earned him a spot in the Pro Bowl.

Today Gossett works for a company that manufactures scoreboards, a job he began during his playing days.

"I've been at it for 20 years," he said. "When I played, I'd get up early and make calls before I went to practice."

Living in the Dallas metropolitan area, Gossett has also run into his share of Eastern alums.

"Tony Romo and I used to play a lot of golf together when he was a backup," Gossett said. "Now that he's the starter, Tony is just so busy. His dad and I are the same age and have gotten to be good friends. I talk to him about once a week.

"When Sean Payton was an assistant here with the Cowboys, we also talked quite a bit."

Gossett also maintained friendships with Shanahan and Tennessee Titans' offensive co-ordinator Mike Heimerdinger.

"We stay in touch on a pretty regular basis," Gossett said.

Perhaps it was only inevitable. Some things in life are just meant to be.

FOUR-DOWN TERRITORY

Favorite Football Movie: *Brian's Song* I always liked it as a kid. I'm not ashamed to say I cried. *Rudy* is pretty good too. His brothers were great wrestlers at Eastern.

First Car: It was a 1962 or '63 Chevy Impala. My dad paid $500 for that thing. When I was a sophomore I was driving some of the guys to practice. You had to go through this gate. One of the guys yelled something about backing up because there was a fight going on. Well, when I backed up, one of the guys opened the back door and it got caught on the gate. The door never opened after that. I then had a three-door Chevy Impala.

Worst Summer Job: Lifeguarding. It was terrible because you just sat there. I can't sit still for that long.

Favorite Subject in School: History.

DONALD PITTMAN

More than three decades later, Donald Pittman still remembers his recruiting trip to Eastern from his native South Carolina.

"(I was) fretting to get on an airplane for the first time in my life. It was quite an ordeal for a small town Southern boy from Fort Mill, South Carolina, who thought Illinois was on another planet," Pittman wrote in an e-mail.

Yet, Pittman soon realized that other planet would work out just fine.

"From my initial visit and staying with Ted Petersen, I knew Eastern was the place for me," Pittman said.

Petersen, who was often given key recruits by the coaching staff, described Pittman as a "very serious and mature person for his age."

"I am sure he was a joy to coach!" Petersen said.

Much of Pittman's maturity stemmed from his youth.

"Growing up in South Carolina was what I called the simple life," Pittman said. "Even though everybody worked hard, we all played hard as well."

According to Pittman, Fort Mill was a company town, located in the Bible Belt, and specialized in textiles.

"I grew up with the poor and the rich, the black and the white," he said. "I went to school with the grandchildren of (the wealthy) Colonel (Leroy) Springs, but how much money anyone had was never a topic or concern. We were poor and knew it, but we were happy."

Pittman and his family lived off the land as much as they could by farming, fishing and hunting.

"There was a cannery in town so we could can our veggies to use throughout the winters," he said. "I remember at an early age when we would, at times, run out of heating oil, everyone would try to sleep in the same bed to stay warm. The fireplace would only heat the living room and at times we all would huddle by it."

Pittman added that his family "never, never locked our doors when we had a chance to go on vacation to the mountains, two hours away, or the beach, three hours away."

Times were simpler, and Pittman looks back fondly at the memories and early life lessons.

"We would sit on the front porch on many afternoons and talk about anything and everything," he said. "I did not realize how special that was until I got a little older."

Today, all of his family is deceased.

"All were devastating as with any family member. We were all very close," he said.

In addition to working at the local textile mill, Pittman's father farmed. In fact, the plowing was done with a mule. Pittman, today an educator, shares the stories with his students.

"When I tell my students today about my dad using a mule to plow the garden they just shake their heads in disbelief," he said.

The family income was also supplemented by running moonshine.

"The money must have been pretty good for that time," Pittman said. "I can always remember him having an old beat-up car with an awesome engine that could really fly."

Don Pittman had never flown on an airplane until his recruiting trip to Eastern. The South Carolina native finished his career as one of the top defensive backs in school history.

During the summers while in high school, Pittman worked at the textile mill.

"That's when I knew I had to make a better life for myself," he said. "Ninety-plus degrees and breathing cotton lint, and at times working the third shift, was not my idea of a career job."

His family did not have much choice.

"With little education, mill work was the norm in those days," he said. "At the time, that was about all of the jobs that were available. My dad had a fourth-grade education, my mom had a sixth-grade education, and both of my brothers made it through the eighth grade before having to go to work in the mill. I am proud to say I am the only one in my family to finish with a high school diploma."

Today, Pittman has a master's degree and holds a position as principal in his home state.

"I think my parents would have been very proud," he said. "I still have copies of my father's paycheck where he made $34 for a 46-hour work week as a top-paid loom fixer. The day he died in 1979 he was probably making around $8 an hour.

"But they (my parents) did provide for us. Eating wild rabbit with rabbit gravy was a delicacy when you are hungry."

Race was not an issue in Pittman's world until he was in middle school.

"In the early 1970s when integration and busing was the hot topic I was bused to a school called 'George Fish' in an all-black community, in Fort Mill, called 'Paradise.' Likewise, black students were bused to an all-white school across town in an all-white community. I can still remember someone putting up the rebel flag on the flag pole at the all-white school."

Some of the turmoil hit the national headlines and news reports.

"Being young and naïve I still did not know what all the fuss was about," Pittman said. "We were escorted to school by the Fort Mill National Guard. I can remember sitting in science class and a rock, thrown by a black protester, crashed through the window pane onto the floor of our classroom."

Pittman noted there was not much acceptance in either community during those days.

"I often heard that our middle school principal carried a gun during this turbulent time," he said.

According to Pittman, race relations improved during his years at Fort Mill High School. It also played a key role in his future.

"Participating in sports was my salvation," he said. "It kept me in school, and I was fortunate enough to have the athletic ability to get a scholarship, which paid for my college education."

Pittman played football, basketball, track and golf. His father fully supported his coaches.

"My dad told my coach that when I was at school or at practice that he could do whatever he wanted to with me. He told him he could paddle me if I got out of hand or call him and he could whip me with his belt," he said.

At home, Pittman was kept in check by the boot of his father and a switch favored by his mother.

"I can't tell you which one I dreaded the most, boots or switch," he said. "Both methods worked."

When Pittman was a sophomore in high school his mother suffered a stroke and died while at one of her son's football games.

"After losing my mother, I was ready to get away from Fort Mill," Pittman said. "I had South Carolina schools recruiting me, but I wanted to get out of South Carolina to see what other parts of the country were all about."

Thus, Eastern entered the picture. Panther head coach John Konstantinos knew Pittman from his days as an assistant under Lou Holtz at North Carolina State.

"(I had) never heard of Eastern Illinois at that time. I thought that it was somewhere in the northwestern part of the country," Pittman said. "They were interested in a veer quarterback that fit into John's offensive scheme that he wanted to implement at Eastern."

Pittman also heard that Chris "Poke" Cobb, another South Carolina native, had signed with Eastern.

"I knew what caliber of player he was," Pittman said.

Though Clemson and South Carolina offered partial scholarship money, Pittman knew his family needed a full ride in order for him to attend college.

"I was offered full scholarships at I-AA schools Furman and Presbyterian. I was not much of the military type so I ruled The Citadel out early. I actually signed my letter of intent to go to Furman."

However, after slacking off academically his senior year of high school, Pittman was ruled ineligible by Furman.

"That was a blessing in disguise for me," he said.

That blessing came in the form of the 1978 Division II national championship.

"I felt the strength of Darrell Mudra as coach was hiring and surrounding himself with great assistant coaches such as Mike Shanahan and John Teerlinck," Pittman said. "Shanahan and Teerlinck and the other assistants were the field generals that expected greatness each and every day, would not tolerate failure, weakness nor mistakes."

When Eastern upset the University of Delaware in the title game, the moment was even more special for Pittman because December 9 was also his birthday.

"No one gave us much of a chance," he said.

With Eastern clinging to a 10-9 lead, the national championship came down to a 45-yard field goal attempt by Delaware kicker Brandt Kennedy.

"He was nailing them during the pregame warmups at 50-plus yards," Pittman recalled. "I still remember the last play of the game as if it just happened yesterday. I was coming off the defensive left end and all I could think about was blocking his attempt. After seeing him kick in pregame, I thought that was our only chance of winning. After coming off the left end and not (being) able to get a hand on the ball I hit the ground and rolled over to view the kick from behind.

"I knew Delaware's kicker had hit it solid. An awful gut-wrenching pain appeared in my stomach because the kick from my angle was definitely long enough and appeared to be good as it headed right above the upright. When the official signaled no good, which had to be just inches off to the right, the celebration had begun."

Earlier in the week and before the game, Pittman and some of his teammates left the team hotel to enjoy the Texas nightlife at a club down the road.

"We were late for our curfew when Coach Teerlinck walked in looking for us," Pittman said. "Oh, what a sick feeling. He blasted us pretty good and sent us back to the hotel. The ironic thing was that Coach Teerlinck had a couple of black eyes the next day at practice. The word going around was that he got into a tangle with a couple of Texas Rangers. I can see that happening. Coach T was a very intense guy. You don't play in the NFL without being intense."

Pittman was impressed with Teerlinck from their first meeting.

"We had a team meeting to meet our new assistants," Pittman recalled. "John was first to speak. He started yelling in his very intimidating and convincing manner. He said, 'Okay, you bunch of SOBs, we start today, this very second on committing ourselves to winning the national championship.'"

Pittman said Teerlinck immediately grabbed the attention of the team.

"Silence spread throughout the entire room," Pittman said. "From that point on, we all shared a common bond that we could live to fulfill, a common goal that everyone was committed to achieving."

Though recruited as a veer quarterback, Pittman was switched to Teerlinck's defense.

"Shanahan knew I was not happy (in a pro-style offense) and not a great passing quarterback," Pittman said. "He called me into his office and asked how would I feel about playing defense. I jumped at the opportunity and was happy to be giving blows instead of taking them."

The decision worked wonders for Pittman and the Panthers. Pittman earned a defensive backfield spot on the All-Division II era team

for this book. He intercepted five passes, including one he returned for a touchdown, in 1980. Pittman was a key member of the '80 Panthers that spent most of the season ranked No. 1 in the nation before losing the national championship game.

"I know this probably does not make any sense, but the national championship we lost to Cal Poly hurt worse than the one we won against Delaware felt good," Pittman said. "I think we had a better team in regards to talent because we had many experienced players coming back from the '78 team."

However, Pittman noted the losses of Shanahan and Teerlinck as assistant coaches really hurt the team.

"That was the difference in our game planning and preparation," he said.

In addition, the 1980 title game was played on a soggy field in Albuquerque, New Mexico.

"They had a snow-covered field or heavy rains which they tried to dry with helicopters," he said. "That did not work too well. The wet field played into an advantage for Cal Poly. I can remember intercepting a pass in the end zone to stop one of their drives which gave us a chance to win. We drove the ball down to the end zone and fumbled going over the goal line. Boy, that was a frustrating game. Everyone took that loss very hard."

When his days at Eastern came to an end, Pittman realized his playing days were over.

"A few NFL scouts broke my heart after a few workouts by telling me I did not have enough speed to play in the NFL," said Pittman, who ran "probably a true 4.8/4.9 40-yard dash time.

Pittman recalled Shanahan telling him, "Son, only a few make it to the next level and you can't eat a football so you better get your degree."

Though he had a business degree from Eastern, Pittman could not find work in the poor early-1980s economy.

"That's when I was contacted by a superintendent from an area school wanting me to teach and coach," Pittman said. "I coached part-time and went to Winthrop University to get my teaching credentials and as they say, 'The rest is history.'"

That history includes three appearances and two victories in the state championship for girls' softball. Pittman has coached nearly every other sport during his career.

In the mid-1980s, Pittman applied for a graduate assistantship at the University of Florida when Shanahan was a Gator assistant.

"I had my bags packed and ready to go," Pittman said. "Within the next day or two the NCAA hit Florida with a number of rules violations and the head coach (Charlie Pell) and his entire staff were fired. I was going to try again when Coach Shanahan applied for the North Carolina job, which came down between Shanahan and (Mack) Brown."

UNC hired Brown, leading Pittman back to a career in public education.

"The Lord has a plan for us, and I suppose His plan for me was to mentor young people, which has been very rewarding to say the least," said Pittman.

Donald Pittman has come a long way from that first plane ride to Eastern, a ride that isn't just measured in miles.

FOUR-DOWN TERRITORY

Favorite Football Movie: There are some good ones. I think *Remember the Titans* and *Rudy* would be two of my all-time favorites. They both remind me of some of my experiences while playing for the Panthers. *Titans* promotes harmony and togetherness. *Rudy* because it's an awesome motivational underdog story about someone who never gives up on his dreams.

First Car: '65 Ford Mustang (with a) manual transmission with the gears that shifted backwards. (It had a) linkage problem, I think, but don't really know why.

Worst Summer Job: Working the third shift in the cotton mill because it was hot, dry, and dangerous with little pay and cotton lint floating in the air all over the place. Also, I never could get used to sleeping in the day and staying awake all night.

Favorite Subject in School: My favorite subjects were physical education and biology. Physical education because I loved competing, working on my skills and being active. Biology (because) I got a green thumb from my father

when we were on the farm so I loved animals and loved planting things to watch them grow. I continue to have a fairly good size garden to this day.

JEFF CHRISTENSEN

Jeff Christensen has been overlooked before; it's nothing new.

When the subject of great quarterbacks in Eastern history comes up, most immediately mention Sean Payton and Tony Romo. Yet, those who have followed Panther football for generations will also recall a talented kid from just up the road in Gibson City.

"There's no question Jeff doesn't get the credit he deserves," said former Eastern All-American defensive back Robert Williams. "I went against him every day in practice. I know what he could do."

Moreover, Williams remains upset that Christensen has yet to be inducted into Eastern's Hall of Fame.

"That's not right," Williams said. "Jeff doesn't get a lot of credit for whatever reason. He's the best quarterback I ever played with."

Williams isn't alone in his assessment.

Former Southern Illinois defensive back and NFL first-round draft pick Terry Taylor went head-to-head against Christensen in the early 1980s.

"He was good," Taylor said. "He lit us up one time. He had to be, by far in college, the best quarterback I went against. He had a strong arm. He was playing 7-on-7 back there. He and Jerry Wright would hit you for 15, 20 yards. Then they'd try to sneak one behind you."

Wright, who also caught passes from Payton, added, "Jeff was one of the best quarterbacks I've ever played with. He was smart, and he was cocky. Maybe he was cocky because he was smart. Then again, maybe it was the other way around."

Many contend Christensen's absence from Eastern's Hall of Fame has more to do with his personality than his performance on the field.

"Jeff rubbed some people the wrong way," Williams said. "He drove around campus in a white Corvette. He may have gotten into a shouting match with (then Eastern athletic director) R.C. Johnson. All I know is that Jeff Christensen came to play every single day."

Payton played much of his career in a wide-open offense where he averaged throwing the ball more than 40 times a game. The offense Romo played in was also more sophisticated than that of Christensen.

However, Christensen is uncomfortable talking about quarterback comparisons.

"It's impossible to do that in today's era with quarterbacks just as it is with home run hitters and pitchers in baseball," he said. "There is no such thing as the greatest quarterback of all time.

"There are so many different aspects of the game to look at. Brett Favre is the greatest competitor. For athletic ability, it's Roger Staubach. When you look at throwing the deep ball, nobody was better than Steve Bartkowski. When people talk about great footwork, Dan Marino. But, everybody wants to name one guy as the greatest of all time. That's just the reality of it."

As with the pro game, Christensen stops short of naming Eastern's greatest quarterback ever.

"There are a few things I did better than them (Payton and Romo)," he said. "There are three or four things that made me the institution's best. There were a lot of intangibles. I provided leadership off the field. I threw a pretty good deep ball consistently. But, at the same time, there are things that Sean did better. There are things that Tony did better. Heck, there are things that (my son) Jake did better."

In the 1986 movie *The Best of Times*, Kurt Russell played the role of Reno Hightower, a Joe Namath–like figure who starred on the football field yet rankled those off of it. Perhaps that role somehow embodies Jeff Christensen.

"It was about winning, it wasn't about me," he said. "There's a fine line for a great quarterback. You're somehow selfish because you trust yourself to make a play more than you trust anyone else. There's a balance there."

"Jeff always had great expectations for himself," said Darrell Mudra, Christensen's head coach at Eastern. "That was part of the motivation. I never thought of him as being cocky, but he was confident."

Much of that confidence was developed in Christensen's days growing up in Gibson City.

"I saw him as a high school player in the state playoff game that ended Gibson City's season," said Eastern play-by-play man Mike Bradd, who grew up in nearby Colfax. "Jeff was a dominant high school player, especially for a small school like Gibson City. His size (6-foot-3) and throwing ability were far beyond the typical high school quarterback for a school that size. His team was *very* pass-oriented at a time when many small high school teams were run-oriented.

"I remember thinking how hard it was for a high school coach to install a pass defense that could stop a passing offense like that. You simply couldn't consistently cover all of his receivers and he was a good enough passer to find the open man for big gains consistently."

There wasn't a sport in which Christensen didn't excel.

Jeff Christensen led the Panthers to an unbeaten regular season and a berth in the I-AA playoffs in 1982.

"I played basketball, golf, baseball and track," Christensen said.

But, football was the sport that earned him a scholarship to Northwestern under head coach Rick Venturi.

"I won the starting job at Northwestern in the spring (of my freshman year)," Christensen said.

However, when the two-deep roster was posted at the first Wildcat practice the following fall, Christensen's name was No. 2.

"I was upset," he said.

So upset that Christensen took his concerns to NU athletic director John Pont, the former Miami (Ohio) head coach.

"He was a wonderful, wonderful man," Christensen said. "He understood what was going on. He cancelled all his meetings and made 25 personal phone calls to 25 different schools that afternoon on my behalf."

After visiting 15 of those schools, Christensen settled on Eastern.

"They had recruited me back in high school," he said. "Eastern was coming off the national championship and had Steve Turk at quarterback. There's another guy who could play pretty well."

So what led Christensen from the Big Ten to Division-II Eastern?

"I watched two practices," he said. "There was no fluff. I was tired of fluff. They had good players. It was all about winning. Everything they did was about winning."

Ironically, Christensen lost one key component of that winning formula before he ever took a snap as a Panther.

"The day after I made my decision, (offensive coordinator) Mike Shanahan left to go to Minnesota," Christensen said.

With Dennis Shaw in as Shanahan's replacement, Eastern rotated Christensen with senior starter Chuck Wright.

"It was a weird situation," Christensen said.

Weird or not, the Panthers advanced into the 1980 Division II national championship game. Bidding for a second title in three years, Eastern lost a 21-13 decision to Cal Poly.

The next season saw Eastern leave the Division II ranks and move into the world of I-AA football.

"It was different," Christensen said. "It was a big transition year. Two of our key guys got hurt. Then Rob Mehalic, our tight end, got dinged up. That hindered us offensively because we had two freshmen wide receivers."

Eastern struggled through a 6-5 season, but the stage was set for Christensen's senior year of 1982.

Led by Christensen on offense and perhaps the strongest defensive unit in school history, the Panthers plowed through the regular season with a 10-0-1 record.

"I would contend that ('82) team would still go undefeated against these kids today," Christensen said. "We had the 'it' factor."

Christensen enjoyed his finest season, garnering All-American honors. He passed for 2,270 yards and 21 touchdowns. In a 73-0 romp over Kentucky State, Christensen tossed an Eastern-record six touchdown passes.

"A lot of credit goes to (offensive coordinator) Chuck Dickerson," he said. "He was a quasi-head coach."

Eastern, ranked fifth in the last regular season poll, moved into the I-AA playoffs with a legitimate shot to win the national championship. The Panthers won their opening round game, 16-13, over Jackson State in overtime. Christensen threw for 308 yards and one touchdown with an I-AA record 50 attempts.

Eastern then dropped a 20-19 thriller on the road to No. 4 Tennessee State in the quarterfinals.

"You'll always remember the bad things," Christensen said. "I remember that game like it was yesterday."

Christensen completed 26 of 48 passes for 264 yards and three touchdowns in the game.

"We missed two extra points in that game," Christensen said.

The Panthers still almost pulled the game out of the fire. After Christensen threw an interception in the closing minutes, Eastern's vaunted defense got the ball back for one final possession. Christensen got kicker Dave Strauch into range for a 44-yard field goal. However, Tennessee State blocked the attempt and held on for the victory.

Although the loss ended his collegiate career, Christensen continued to shine in the eyes of his teammates.

"Jeff was cool (under pressure)," said Williams. "When we played down at Tennessee State, they had a 100-member band going and people were yelling and carrying on. I've never seen a white boy come to play like that. That was some Brett Favre stuff. Jeff Christensen never flinched."

When his eligibility ended in '82, Christensen held the Eastern career records for total offense, passing yards, touchdown passes, completions and attempts. In addition, he held the Panther single-season marks for those same categories with the exception of TD passes.

As of 2013, Christensen still ranked fifth in total offense (6,185), passing yards (6,282), completions (469) and attempts (925). He was fourth in touchdown passes (51).

The 1983 draft is considered the richest in NFL history for quarterbacks. John Elway, Jim Kelly, Dan Marino, Tony Eason, Todd Blackledge and Ken O'Brien were all taken the first round. Elway, Kelly and Marino are all in the Pro Football Hall of Fame. In 11 of the 16 years following this draft, the AFC was represented in the Super Bowl by a team led by Elway, Marino, Kelly or Eason.

Christensen was selected in the fifth round by the Cincinnati Bengals, the first quarterback drafted since Miami took Marino late in the first round.

"I didn't pay much attention (leading up to the draft), I just worked," Christensen said. "I didn't realize how good I was fundamentally. I was a student of the game. I worked at it really hard."

Ironically, Cincinnati also chose running back Larry Kinnebrew of Tennessee State in the sixth round.

With Ken Anderson's career winding down, Christensen appeared to be in line as the next Cincinnati quarterback.

"The Bengals had three picks in the first round the next year (1984)," Christensen said.

After seeing Cincinnati spend those picks on two defensive players and an offensive tackle, Christensen figured he was safe.

"I went out golfing," he said.

Christensen later found out that Cincinnati drafted Boomer Esiason in the second round. While Esiason become a four-time Pro Bowl

quarterback and 1988 NFL Most Valuable Player, Christensen remained on the bench.

"A lot of things went my way (in college)," Christensen said. "When I got to pro ball, a lot of things went against me."

Christensen would be the final player cut three times by three different NFL teams. It didn't help that NFL teams reduced their rosters to 45 players in the mid-'80s.

"Teams were either keeping three quarterbacks and four running backs or two quarterbacks and five running backs," Christensen noted.

Unfortunately, Christensen's teams—Cincinnati, Philadelphia and Cleveland—all went with the two-quarterback formula.

In Cincinnati, the Bengals kept Turk Schonert over Christensen. In Philadelphia, the Eagles kept promising Randall Cunningham. In Cleveland, it was Mike Pagel.

"I clearly outplayed Pagel," Christensen said. "In the final preseason game I went 11-for-13 with a touchdown. We also got a field goal. That's 10 points in three possessions."

Yet, Cleveland decided to keep Pagel, a player the Browns had traded to get.

At the end of his playing career, Christensen said he made the biggest mistake of his life.

"All I had to do was tell (Cleveland head coach) Marty Schottenheimer that I wanted to coach," Christensen said. "But, I didn't recognize the opportunity when it was there."

Instead, Christensen began a career as a stockbroker.

"I had a two-day-old baby (Jake) at the time," he said. "Things change when you start a family."

Though Christensen continued to work in business, he felt the pull of coaching. Today, he runs a quarterback/receiver academy called Throw It Deep based in the Chicago suburbs.

Why the name Throw It Deep?

"I always threw a good deep ball," he explained. "You have to throw the ball deep effectively to play well and succeed. But, you have to do all the fundamental little things first. It's the feet and legs, not your arm, that start the process. And, it is a process. You don't just start chucking it.

"Any quarterback can throw the ball in the air once. But, can you do it 10 times in a row?

We're teaching how to play quarterback properly."

One of the players Christensen taught properly was his son Jake. The younger Christensen led Lockport High School to a state title. He then earned the starting job at the University of Iowa. However, after losing his job to Ricky Stanzi, Jake Christensen transferred to Eastern for the 2009 season.

"Yeah, it's ironic," his father said. "It was tough, but it was a learning experience for him."

Jake Christensen even donned his father's jersey, No. 11.

So, while Sean Payton and Tony Romo have both been enshrined into Eastern's Hall of Fame, Christensen is still waiting to be called.

"I understand, but I don't understand," he said. "What really matters is what made us great as a team. We had respect for each other. We were only concerned with getting better and winning. We were warriors."

FOUR-DOWN TERRITORY

Favorite Football Movie: Without question, *Brian's Song*.

First Car: A black 1974 Grand Prix with bucket seats.

Worst Summer Job: Walking beans for my father. There weren't a lot of options.

Favorite Subject in School: History.

KEVIN STAPLE

Life can be cruel.

In the midst of a Hall of Fame baseball career, Lou Gehrig was afflicted with amyotrophic lateral sclerosis. Today, the disease is better known as Lou Gehrig's Disease. ALS is an ailment of the nerve calls in the brain and spinal cord that control voluntary muscle movement.

Kevin Staple, twice an All-American running back at Eastern and holder of the Panther single-game rushing record for 19 years, developed ALS at age 49.

Yet, Staple planned to continue his life with the same approach he took as a running back—full speed ahead.

"There's a medication called riluzole. I haven't started my medication yet," he said from the Atlanta area where he taught and coached in the spring of 2010. "For now, it's live a healthy lifestyle. Eat well. Work out regularly."

The diagnosis came in late February 2010.

"I knew about the disease," he said. "It's pretty well documented what it's all about."

Staple first noticed pain in his legs when training with his National Guard unit the previous year.

"It's my belief that I was chosen because I'm so physically strong," he said.

Staple grew up in Markham, a southeast suburb of Chicago. He attended Thornwood High School, where he excelled at both football and track.

"I ran the first leg of the 4x100 relay," he said. "We went down to state four times but never placed."

On the football field, Staple began his career as a linebacker. As a sophomore, he was moved to running back because the coaches liked his speed.

"It was literally the day of a game," he said. "They asked me to play running back because I was so fast. Nobody could catch me. My first carry was a 70-yard touchdown run."

By his senior year, Staple rushed for more than 1,400 yards and 22 touchdowns. He was recruited heavily by Eastern and Western Illinois.

"The ironic part is that the Western coach recruiting me was Mike Williams," Staple said. "He became my running backs coach my junior and senior years at Eastern."

Staple chose Eastern, not because the Panthers were just two years removed from their 1978 Division II national championship season, but rather because he felt he could play earlier.

"Poke Cobb was gone," Staple said. "I figured I'd have a good shot at running back. That was the reason I chose (Eastern)."

When Staple hit fall camp as a true freshman in 1980, there were 21 candidates calling themselves running backs.

"I was third string by the first game," he said. "After two weeks, I was second in the country in kickoff returns."

By season's end, Staple led the Panthers in rushing with 576 yards. He also averaged 22.3 yards per kickoff return, including an 80-yard touchdown against Southern Illinois.

Meanwhile, Eastern appeared on the verge of claiming its second national championship in three seasons.

"I ran for something like 236 yards in the playoffs going into the championship game," Staple said.

However, a snowstorm hit Albuquerque, New Mexico just two days before the title game was played. Helicopters were brought in to dry the field and the grass was painted green.

"It was cold, like 26 degrees or so," Staple remembered.

Despite playing so well leading up to the championship game, Staple carried the ball 16 times for 42 yards against the Cal Poly Mustang defense. Moreover, a key play in the game came when reserve Ricky Davis fumbled near the goal line.

"I still don't know why they took me out and put Davis in," Staple said. "It doesn't make sense even today."

Cal Poly denied Eastern its second national championship, 21-13.

"My sophomore year (1981) we were 6-5," Staple said. "I got hurt in the second game. I separated my shoulder. The negative is that I fumbled seven times that season."

He also managed to rush for a team-leading 700 yards despite missing two games.

The Panthers and Staple bounced back in 1982. With senior quarterback Jeff Christensen at the helm and a rock-solid defense, Eastern roared through the regular season without a loss. Staple led the ground attack with 1,012 yards and 10 touchdowns in the regular season. He also broke loose on a career-best 88-yard run against Youngstown State. In addition, Staple scored five touchdowns in a 73-0 rout of Kentucky State, the highest Panther TD total since 1920.

In the playoffs, Staple added three more touchdowns and led Eastern in scoring. The Panthers advanced to the NCAA I-AA quarterfinals before falling 20-19 in a heartbreaking defeat at Tennessee State.

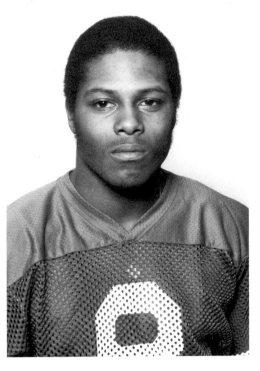

Kevin Staple's single-game rushing record stood for 19 years.

"We got robbed," Staple said. "Doyle Foster intercepted a pass that would have sealed it for us. He was inbounds by a good two feet, but the field had six inches of mud on it by the end. They had straw down and the officials couldn't tell where he was. Tennessee State scored on the very next play. It was a one-handed catch in the back of the end zone."

Despite the poor field conditions, Staple still managed to rush for 112 yards and had six catches out of the backfield.

Staple was named an honorable mention selection on the 1982 Associated Press All-American team.

When the season ended, fifth-year head coach Darrell Mudra announced he was leaving Eastern to accept a position at Northern Iowa.

"We had 21 returnees (for 1983) and Mudra leaves," Staple said. "I was devastated. He asked me to leave and go with him. I told him that I could never do that. I was too into Eastern at that point."

Staple took some measure of pride when Eastern defeated Northern Iowa, 13-0, in '83.

Staple earned Mid-Continent Conference Offensive Player of the Year honors. Yet, his senior season turned into a mixed bag.

"That was the worst year I ever had," he said. "Some of our coaches went with Mudra, some went into the pros (including offensive coordinator Chuck Dickerson)."

There were clashes with new Eastern head coach Al Molde and his staff.

"They ran a super simple system on offense," Staple said.

Yet, the Panthers won nine games during the regular season and again qualified for the playoffs. A week after Eastern lost a 17-14 game against eventual I-AA champion Southern Illinois, Staple rushed for a Panther record 283 yards against Grand Valley State. The previous record of 268 yards had been set by Nate Anderson 10 years earlier.

"I didn't even play the fourth quarter," Staple said.

While that game may have been the highlight of his season, Staple said the lowlight came in a 12-3 victory over Southwest Missouri State in November.

"My parents came down for Parents Weekend," he said. "I only got seven carries in the whole game. I never cried so hard in my life."

Staple's career came to an end two weeks later when Eastern fell to Indiana State, 16-13, in a double-overtime playoff loss.

"I was hurt (for the playoffs)," he said. "I had hurt my ankle playing around in the pool before our last (regular season) game (at Western Kentucky). I played, but wasn't the same player I had been."

Staple, who rushed for 1,008 yards as a senior, finished his career second only to the legendary Cobb on the Eastern rushing list. Staple repeated as Associated Press All-American honorable mention.

Today, Staple holds down sixth place on the career rushing list with 3,296 yards. He has 4,561 all-purpose yards, good for fifth place all-time. Staple is tied for 10th with 25 career touchdowns.

Staple is one of seven Eastern players to have registered consecutive 1,000-yard seasons. Three of those seven—Nate Anderson, Poke Cobb and Willie High—are Eastern Hall of Famers.

In the spring of 2010, Staple was informed that he would also be inducted into the Eastern Hall of Fame.

"This is a dream come true," Staple said upon getting the news.

Staple was accompanied by former Panther teammates and fellow Hall of Fame members Robert Williams and Jerry Wright.

"It was a special day," said Williams, his longtime friend.

After graduating from Eastern, Staple served in the Marines for five years. He also taught at Luther South High School in Chicago. He was the assistant track coach when the Lancers were 1991 and '97 state track champions.

Staple took time away from teaching to try the corporate world.

"I was an analyst at DeVry for a year and an advisor there for three years," he said.

But, the time away from education rekindled his desire to teach and coach.

"I realized that I had a calling to teach," he said.

His mother had moved to Atlanta when Staple was a junior at Eastern.

"I had been shuttling back and forth between Atlanta and Chicago for years," he said. "I had to get away from that snow."

Thus, Staple found himself teaching and coaching in Georgia.

Then came the dire news.

Confronted with a disease with no known cure, Staple soldiered onward.

"I'll just get on living my life and see what happens," he said.

Kevin Staple passed away on May 13, 2012, at age 50 in his home outside Atlanta.

"A truly sad day for all who knew him," said Williams.

himself that would eventually lead to the Pro Football Hall of Fame.

"We'd all check out all the stats in the NCAA's newspaper each week," said Wright from his office at Northern Illinois University. "My senior year we had a big game against Grand Valley State. I go get the paper to see where I ranked nationally. Then I see that he caught *24 balls for 275 yards*. I just threw the paper away. He was like a running back, getting the ball every time."

That *other* Jerry was named Rice and made a national name for himself in the high-powered offense at Mississippi Valley State.

"I wound up meeting him at the (NFL scouting) combine after the season," Wright said.

While it's been said that no one remembers who came in second place, Jerry Wright's story is nonetheless just as remarkable as that of Rice.

Wright grew up on the west side of Chicago. He attended Collins High School, where he played football, baseball and basketball.

"Baseball was supposed to be my ticket out," said the former center fielder/first baseman.

But, a recruiting trip by Eastern assistant Rick Schachner changed that.

"He had come up to see a teammate of mine, Al Jennings, who was a big-time recruit," Wright said. "He saw me on tape playing free safety."

FOUR-DOWN TERRITORY

Favorite Football Movie: *The Program* without a doubt.

First Car: A Fiat Spider four-speed. I got it in the 10th grade and took it with me to Eastern.

Worst Summer Job: I worked at R.R. Donnelly in Mattoon. The Eastern coaches got me that job. I worked third shift and was always tired.

Favorite Subject in School: Social studies. My high school coach Dennis Patowsky from Notre Dame taught many of those classes.

JERRY WRIGHT

While Jerry Wright was setting an Eastern single-season record with 76 receptions in 1984, another Jerry was making a name for

Jerry Wright set Panthers' single-season record of 76 receptions in 1984. It was later broken by Erik Lora.

Soon Schachner and Eastern head coach Darrell Mudra made a trip to Wright's home to meet his mother.

"That really impressed me," Wright said. "I lived in the 'hood. White people didn't come around. Those two guys came to meet my mother one night."

Mudra's Panthers were fresh off a Division II national championship game berth. In fact, Eastern had played in the title game in two of the previous three seasons.

"When I got there, they were loaded at defensive back," Wright said. "I wanted to play as a freshman. I looked at their receiving corps, and it didn't look that good to me."

Eastern's coaches agreed and moved Wright to the offensive side of the ball, a position he had also played in high school. He immediately clicked with quarterback Jeff Christensen.

"Looking back, Jeff Christensen made me a good receiver," Wright said. "He would throw the ball only where I could get it. He'd put the ball on the money and I'd pull it in."

Wright led the Panthers with 29 receptions for 706 yards as a sophomore. Eastern entered the I-AA playoff field with only a tie with Northern Iowa blemishing its record.

In the opening-round playoff game, Wright caught 10 passes for 130 yards as Eastern slipped past Jackson State, 16-13, in overtime.

In the quarterfinals, the Panthers fell, 20-19, at Tennessee State.

"I remember that game like it was yesterday," Wright said. "We grew as a team the whole year. It was an all-mud field that day. That seemed to cause us some problems early. We didn't get untracked right away."

Wright hauled in a six-yard touchdown pass from Christensen midway through the fourth quarter that pulled Eastern within one point. However, an earlier missed extra point and a controversial blocked field goal at the end of the game kept the Panthers from victory.

"There was a roughing the kicker call," Wright said of Dave Strauch's 44-yard attempt in the final seconds. "The officials said it would be assessed on the kickoff. I was like, 'Kickoff, what kickoff?'"

Indeed the rules of the era didn't allow for the penalty to be marked off and then another field goal to be attempted.

With half of his collegiate career over, Wright next had to deal with two major changes at Eastern. First, Christensen was gone, taken by Cincinnati in the fifth round of the 1983 NFL Draft. Then Mudra left to become the head coach at Northern Iowa.

"That was hard for me, not so much for Mudra, but for his coaching staff," Wright said. "The nucleus of that staff did a whole lot for my confidence. When I came to Eastern I was just a ball catcher. They gave me the confidence to grow into a receiver."

In fact, Wright said one of the assistants, Chris Peterson, encouraged him to transfer to a bigger program.

"He said I should be somewhere like the U of I," Wright said. "But all of my friends were here. I was established."

When Al Molde became the next Eastern head coach, Wright and some of his teammates from the Mudra era struggled with the transition.

"I didn't get along with the Molde era," Wright said. "We were a bunch of bandits and renegades. Mudra taught us to have a swagger. If you were producing for Mudra, he took care of you. If you were one of the guys who made it happen on the field, Mudra did all he could for you. Looking back, there was a lot of prima donna in us."

During fall camp there were clashes over things like the hazing of new players.

"We'd make them carry trays, sing songs, tell jokes, things like that," Wright said.

Those who fell short in such duties were sometimes given the penalty of getting their hair cut.

"I was the barber," Wright said. "It wasn't any big deal to the brothers, but the white guys always freaked out."

Things came to a head between the new coaching staff and the holdovers from the Mudra era when the players threatened to boycott a 1983 road game at Western Kentucky. Mudra had promised the players that they would travel by plane rather than by bus to the away game.

"That was a crazy time," Wright said.

Eventually, a settlement was reached. Despite all the difficulties of the transition year, the Panthers again qualified for the playoffs.

Wright again led the team in receptions with 44 catches for 779 yards.

"John Rafferty was the quarterback," Wright said. "I liked Raf, but he was a system quarterback. He was like Trent Dilfer. He was a thinking quarterback. I never thought he was a guy who would throw the ball 40 times in a game."

In fact Rafferty earned the starting job over junior college transfer Gary Scott and a then-unknown named Sean Payton.

"G-Scott threw darts," Wright said. "But he didn't have any savvy. He'd fire the ball at you whether it was a long pass or you were right next to him."

In the final game of the regular season, Payton took over for an injured Rafferty.

"When Sean came into the game I felt differently," Wright said. "This guy knew what was going on. In practice he never threw a spiral, but he was a game player. Some guys are like that. He had a different juice during the game. I was on the Sean Payton bandwagon."

Payton came off the bench to rally Eastern in its playoff game a week later. Though the Panthers fell, 16-13, to Indiana State in double overtime, Wright knew Payton's time had come.

"Sean threw a couple of interceptions in that game, but you saw what he could do," Wright said. "In fact, one of the interceptions was off my arm."

Next up was Wright's record-breaking senior year. While Wright led the team for the third straight season in receptions with his record 76 grabs, fellow receiver Roy Banks set school marks with 1,269 yards and 17 touchdowns.

"It was a natural progression," said teammate Robert Williams. "Jerry Wright's success led to Roy Banks' success."

Wright said it was also a matter of hard work and dedication.

"Roy and Sean were always over at the fieldhouse working on things," Wright said. "I still had a tough time with the coaches so I didn't get myself over there to work out as often as I should have. In retrospect, I should have worked through all that."

Ironically, Wright's record-setting 76 catches came despite nagging injuries.

"I had a stress fracture in my foot for most of the year," he said. "Most of my receptions were read routes that were short and underneath. I couldn't plant my foot like I was used to."

The success of Banks and Wright also opened up opportunities for Calvin Pierce, a former running back who was converted into a slotback/receiver.

"People saw what Roy and I were doing on the outside as the year went along and began to adjust," Wright said. "But Calvin took things to a whole new level on the inside as a wingback or hybrid tight end or whatever you want to call it. He was a Herschel Walker–lookin' cat."

While the Panther offense put up record-breaking numbers, the defense struggled and Eastern finished the season with a 6-5 record.

"I offered to play defensive back but they told me to stay over on offense," Wright said.

Wright enjoyed playing with both Christensen and Payton.

"Those are two similar guys," Wright said. "Jeff was a little more of your prototypical quarterback. He was polished. Jeff came in with high accolades. It's a different feeling when you're the No. 1 guy.

"Sean had to fight his way to the top. He was a renegade. I liked his swagger. Sean was also allowed to run more read options than Jeff ever was."

Following the NFL combine, the undrafted Wright signed with the Tampa Bay Buccaneers as a free agent.

"I should have gone to somewhere like Seattle, but I let my agent make the decision," Wright said. "I got into the best shape of my life. Freddie Solomon of the 49ers lived in the Tampa area. He worked out with us a few times. Anyway, I dropped a few balls. He pulled me aside and said, 'You can't do that. They didn't draft you. There isn't anybody in the front office from Eastern Illinois. You've got to be in midseason form.'"

Tampa Bay released Wright shortly before the season began. The New England Patriots picked him up briefly.

In 1986 Wright gave pro football one more shot. He went to camp with the St. Louis Cardinals, then training on Eastern's campus.

"At that point the realization of life came crashing down on me," Wright said. "I knew it was time to use my degree for something else.

I was disillusioned with pro football. It left a sour taste in my mouth."

After being released Wright decided to pursue a master's degree. Mudra set him up with a graduate assistant coaching job under Bruce Craddock at Western Illinois.

"What I learned from my one year as a college coach was that I didn't want to coach," Wright said. "It's gruesome. Coaches just bury themselves inside, watching film, working crazy hours. I'd tell them that I had to leave for class and they'd ask me what I was talking about. Their classroom was right there in those meeting and film rooms."

Wright also remembers Payton, Banks and Co. routing Western, 37-3, in Macomb that season.

"They just lit us up all day long," he said.

With his master's in hand, Wright took a job with Chicago Youth Centers. From there, he took a position in the counseling center at Northern Illinois University in 1989. Though he worked briefly at other schools, Wright returned to NIU.

He also spent time coaching his son and other youths in the Junior Chicago Bears football program with former Eastern teammates Williams and Roy Ellis.

In 1997, Wright established the football program at Aurora Christian High School, where his son Jason played basketball.

"Don Davidson, the school's athletic director, asked me to get things going," he said. "Starting a program from scratch is hard. There's so much to do. There's equipment to get. There's a field to prepare. There's things you never even think of."

Wright vividly remembers holding his first meeting with the 44 players who turned out for the team.

"I had them write down their football experience on an index card," he said. "Some of them wrote down winning the Tecmo Bowl championship. I asked my son Jason what that was. 'Dad,' he said, 'That's a video game.' I knew we were in trouble then."

Yet, Wright enjoyed the experience.

"It gave me an idea of what coaches go through," he said.

Wright held the job through 2000.

"We played a sophomore schedule that first year and did okay with that, but once we took to playing at the varsity level, it was a whole different story," he said.

When Aurora Christian, under the guidance of former WIU star Don Beebe, reached the 2008 state championship game, Wright couldn't help but feel good.

"That's quite an accomplishment in only 10 years," he said.

Meanwhile, Wright proudly watched from the sidelines as his son earned a basketball scholarship at Eastern.

"We wanted him to play football there too, but (basketball) Coach (Rick) Samuels didn't want to risk him getting hurt," Wright said.

In 2006, Eastern inducted the three-time All-American into its Hall of Fame.

"They had called me up a few years earlier wondering if I had Roy Banks' phone number because they were going to induct him," Wright said. "Your day is comin' though, they told me. I told them I didn't have Banks' number and hung up."

Today, he serves as the Director of Student Support Services at NIU. In addition, Wright serves as the pastor of Rock Christian Church in DeKalb.

"I'm an academic and career counselor," Wright said. "We work with first-generation, low-income students. We show them the right course to take."

Or, perhaps it could be called the "Wright" track.

FOUR-DOWN TERRITORY

Favorite Football Movie: *Remember the Titans.* It reminds me of our story coaching in Chicago.

First Car: It was a Dodge Coronet, a Dukes of Hazzard–looking car my dad bought for me. It was $250. It didn't even have a key ignition. It was a push-button start.

Worst Summer Job: I worked at McDonalds. It was too regimented for me. I was the grill man. But, anytime a burger got folded over or something they told me to throw the food out. Instead of tossing it into the dumpster out back, I had a little stash going in the back of my Coronet.

Favorite Subject in School: The sciences. I liked anatomy, biology. I really enjoyed human physiology when I was at Eastern.

ROBERT WILLIAMS

If fate hadn't intervened, perhaps Robert Williams would have added his name to a long list of Pittsburgh Steelers stalwarts in the secondary.

Williams, a three-time all-conference defensive back at Eastern, saw his pro career derailed by a knee injury in 1985.

"I injured the same knee as last year, on the same exact day, on the same exact kind of play," Williams told *The Daily Eastern News* in October 1985.

A year earlier, Williams spent much of his time recovering from the initial injury after signing with Pittsburgh as a free agent. However, he did manage to recover in time for the playoffs.

In fact, Williams' name identified along with his alma mater came over the airwaves from no less than Dick Enberg when the former Panther made a tackle on special teams in the AFC Championship Game.

"I had made second string by my second year," Williams said in a telephone interview in 2010. "Then came the injury."

The injury occurred late in practice with Williams defending Steelers' tight end Bennie Cunningham.

"It wasn't much at all," Williams said. "I just twisted the wrong way."

However, the injury had long-lasting results.

"Little did I know that depression runs in my family," he said, adding that he had never been injured before pro ball. "I didn't realize it, but I was in the midst of a 24-year bout with depression."

Moreover, both his mother and grandmother had died at young ages. The deaths had been direct results of depression.

"My mom died from a massive heart attack at 46; my grandmother died when she was 52," Williams said.

In addition to his depression, Williams said there were other factors at work.

"I believe that dementia was involved be-

cause of the way I played the game," he said. "I also had substance abuse as a masking agent.

"When I left pro football no one told me how to deal with it."

Williams worked for a time at the Chicago Park District, the Jane Addams Hull House and Corliss High School in Chicago. He joined former Panther teammates Jerry Wright and Roy Ellis in coaching youth football. Williams eventually started his own trucking business.

"The economy went bad and wiped us out," he said. "We still have one truck left over."

With the toxic combination of depression and substance abuse, Williams' situation only grew worse.

Williams said the FBI was soon on his trail.

"It took someone as powerful as the feds for me to listen," he said.

Ultimately, it was the FBI that got Williams the help he needed.

"They put me in therapy for two years," he said. "Not only that, but they paid for my therapy."

Most likely, it saved his life. It definitely turned it around.

"I'm working on a master's degree (in counseling) for higher adult education here (at

Northern Illinois University)," Williams said. "I want to pursue a PhD. My goal is to teach in Leadership Studies."

Williams spends his days going to school full-time and "writing a lot." He has written a collection of poems and thoughts in a book titled *A Journey of Spiritual Restoration*. He has a website called "The Invisible Dragon."

"I've been writing a blog since March 2007," he noted. "I also fancy myself a black-and-white photographer."

All this may seem contrary to Williams' earlier life. He grew up in Chicago and became a football star at Dunbar High School. He also lost his father in those years.

"It was Oct. 31. I was 15 at the time," Williams recalled. "It's ironic because a teammate of mine, Prince Lewis, died at practice that day. I was there. Then I went home and they broke the news to me about my father."

The next day Williams had a game.

"I played," he said.

As his prep career wrapped up, only one school—Coe College in Iowa—pursued Williams.

"That coach called me every day, but I didn't want to go out there," he said.

Then came his break.

"I started in the (summer) all-star game," he said. "There were seven future NFL players in that 1980 all-star game."

There, Williams caught the attention of Eastern assistant coach Rick Schachner.

"I dropped three interceptions that day," Williams said.

But, he held on to the one that counted.

"We were up 12-8 with about a minute left," Williams remembered. "The Catholic League had the ball on our 12-yard line. It was fourth-and-eight. I intercepted a ball in the end zone."

Since college coaches weren't allowed to directly talk to the players, Schachner sent two Eastern players down to the field to talk Williams into enrolling at Eastern.

"Dave Cobb and Wilbert James came down and told me to be at Eastern in two weeks," Williams said.

The transition wasn't easy. Born and raised in Chicago, Williams didn't take to downstate Charleston.

"I wanted to leave for the first two weeks," he said. "I cried to my mom on the phone, but she told me to stay."

Williams was also treated like a lowly walk-on by head coach Darrell Mudra, who had won a national championship just two years earlier.

"They gave me a T-shirt and some black shoes and that was about all," Williams said.

Williams eventually worked his way into some playing time that 1980 season.

"It was spot duties at cornerback and special teams," he said. "I dressed for home games."

When the Panthers played Cal Poly in the national championship game in Albuquerque, New Mexico, Williams did not make the trip.

Over the summer after that first year, his girlfriend's parents tried to talk him into leaving Eastern and taking a job at General Motors.

"Coach Shack told me that if I didn't come back, I'd never know what I could become," Williams said.

He did return to Charleston. By the following spring, Williams was a sophomore starter.

"Coach Shack had a lot of confidence in me," Williams said.

Williams' finest year came as a junior. A team captain, he led Eastern with 59 solo tackles as the Panthers clawed their way to an 11-1-1 record. The team advanced to the I-AA quarterfinals.

"That was the best opportunity to win another national championship," he said.

A look at the record book shows that the '82 Panther defense surrendered only 8.8 points per game during the regular season. Moreover, Eastern recorded three shutouts.

"We always felt that if the offense scored 21 points, we'd win," Williams said.

In the opening round of the playoffs, Eastern slipped past Jackson State, 16-13, in overtime at O'Brien Stadium.

"That was the first time I'd ever seen SWAC football," he said. "It was incredible. That game showed me that we could play with anyone."

In the quarterfinal round Eastern traveled to Tennessee State, a hostile environment for any opponent.

"When we pulled up in our bus some of the Tennessee State players came over and were talkin' big shit," Williams remembered. "Our white guys and even some of the brothers were shaken. It was no different than an all-black team going down to play in Dixie to play the University of Mississippi years ago. This was a lily-white team with a few brothers sprinkled in. I've never seen a bus that quiet."

Not one to sit back, Williams took control of the situation.

"I lit into them," he said.

Eastern battled Tennessee State all afternoon. Trailing 20-19 late in the game, Williams vowed to Wright that the defense would get the ball back and give Eastern one more shot of offense.

"We held them and got it back," he said. "Jeff Christensen and the offense moved the ball into field-goal range, but we missed it."

After the season, eight Eastern defensive players made the all-conference team.

"But I didn't," Williams noted.

However, the defensive back earned first-team Kodak All-American laurels.

Eastern's playoff loss not only ended a magnificent season, it also marked the end of an era. Darrell Mudra left the Panthers to become the head coach at Northern Iowa. Al Molde was then hired at Eastern.

"The coaching change was tough," Williams said. "I was used to Mudra. Moo didn't have a problem with me. He was a holistic coach, the best players played and the best coaches coached. Moo gave us a lot of respect."

Mudra was known for running a loose ship.

"He let the players have so much autonomy," Williams said. "Molde didn't want that."

Williams' senior season was bittersweet.

"It was turbulent, but the team was great," Williams said.

He took solace in the defensive coaches who were holdovers from Mudra's program.

According to Williams, he and some of his teammates were dismissed by Molde during the preseason.

"(Fellow defensive back) Gary Bridges got the team together and they rebelled," Williams said. "That got us back on the team, but it wasn't good for me."

Next came an incident that grabbed national headlines. Angered when a promise to fly to an away game by Mudra was turned into a bus trip, the players staged a walkout.

"I got blamed for that," Williams said. "Jerry (Wright), (running back) Roy Ellis and I weren't even in town. We were in Chicago. Jerry would drive me and Roy home after every game. I went home to see my mother."

When the trio returned to Charleston Sunday, they found a nearly empty locker room.

"We were busting our butts to get back and not be late," Williams recalled. "We walked into the locker room at 2:58 and only one guy was there."

The other players had instead gathered at Marty's, a bar just off campus and a short walk from the football stadium.

"I went down there and was livid," Williams said. "I told them, 'A *bar*? Why would you go to a *bar*?!'"

Williams then said he got the players to leave the establishment.

As one of the team leaders, he was involved in talks with the coaches and administrative staff.

"I wasn't even there when it happened, but I argued for my team," he said. "I was backing my team."

Williams added that there were rumors he had orchestrated the revolt and then left town.

"I heard that years later from Coach (Tony) Dungy when I was with the Steelers," he said.

Despite all the turmoil, the '83 Panthers qualified for the I-AA tournament field. Williams led the team with seven interceptions, the second-highest total in Eastern history. But Eastern lost its first-round game, 16-13, in double overtime at Indiana State.

After the season, Williams repeated as All-American. He and Pete Catan are the only Eastern players to have earned first-team All-American status twice. His Panther teams posted a combined 26-9-1 record with two playoff trips.

Yet, Williams didn't rest on his laurels. Just days before school was about to break for the holidays, a group of students were gathered in a room in Douglas Hall. They were crowded around student Bryan Sibert's color TV, one of the few in the dorm, watching *Rudolph the Red-Nosed Reindeer*.

Meanwhile, Williams was making his way down the hall.

"He was working out and preparing for NFL scouts (during that time)," said Jeff Westerhold, another Douglas Hall resident.

"We were all yelling, 'Come on, Robert, join us, it'll be a great time,'" said Sibert. "Aren't you going to watch Rudolph?"

Williams paused, smiled and said, "Hey, Rudy don't pay the rent next year!"

With that, Williams was gone in a flash, headed to the weight room.

A year later the same group gathered in Sibert's room again, only this time they were watching Williams play in the AFC Championship Game.

While Williams' pro career didn't last, his legacy at Eastern did. In 2007, he was inducted into Eastern's Hall of Fame. While he felt honored by the achievement, Williams wonders why more players from his era aren't there as well.

"The only way I got in was that I was Jerry Wright's presenter when he went in," Williams said. "The books didn't change. Look at our record. How is it that more of us aren't in there? If you look at this program, guys like us were used to build it. (Receiver) Roy Banks followed Jerry. Sean Payton followed Jeff Christensen. Tony Romo came because of Sean Payton.

"We were used to recruit. I've seen the programs and materials that we sent out to recruits. It's got our faces on it. I love Eastern now, I've got to admit, but how is that?"

Perhaps, like the fate that ended his playing career, fortune will intervene and more of his former teammates will join Robert Williams in the Panther Hall of Fame.

FOUR-DOWN TERRITORY

Favorite Football Movie: I took my youth football team to see *Rudy*. I enjoyed it because it reminded me of when I was a walk-on.

First Car: A 1974 Maverick. It was yellow with a blue hood and two mag tires. My high school sweetheart's brother sold it to me for $125 my sophomore year.

Worst Summer Job: I worked down on 39th and Cottage Grove. It was a job I got through the Urban League. It was run by some guy who was a civil rights activist. It was a bunch of paperwork. It was up on the second floor and all he had to drink was hot tea. I still don't know what we did.

Favorite Subjects in School: Talking. No, seriously, it was gym class in elementary. By high school it was whatever social studies class, especially sociology, which became my college major. When I finished with that, it was psychology.

EASTERN AIRLINES ERA

(1983–1986)

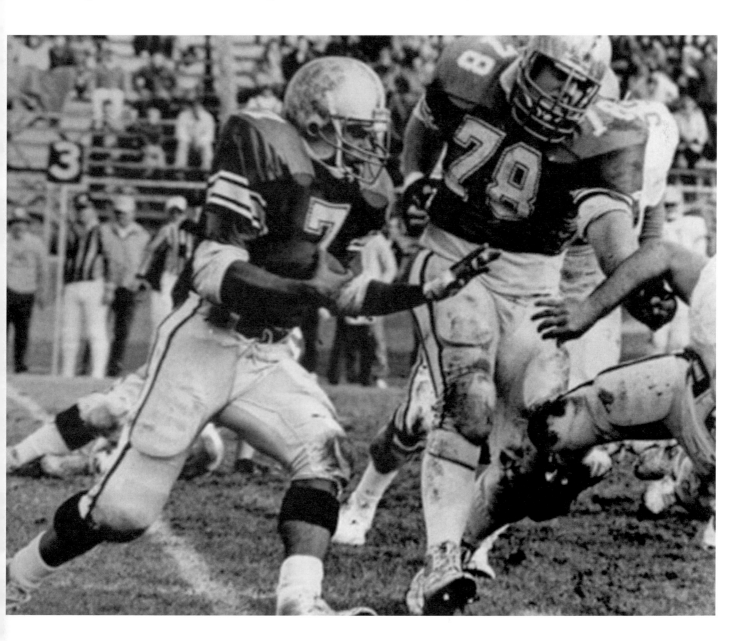

AL MOLDE

History and football fans have not always been kind to coaches who follow legends. Yet, Al Molde did not suffer such a fate.

Molde followed the highly successful Darrell Mudra when Dr. Victory left Eastern to become the head coach at Northern Iowa. Mudra had won the 1978 NCAA Division II national championship, finished runner-up in 1980 and turned the fortunes of Eastern football.

"As I recall, I received a phone call from R.C. Johnson, athletic director at EIU, near the end of the 1982 football season," Molde said in an e-mail. "I was then the head football coach and athletic director at Central Missouri State University. R.C. invited me to apply for their vacant football coaching position. Soon after doing so I was invited to Charleston for an interview and, subsequently, offered the position. I took over the head football coaching position at Eastern in mid-December of 1982."

What may have seemed like a wonderful Christmas present soon evolved into the harsh realities of following Mudra.

"The 1983 season was a roller coaster ride. It had its highs and lows," said Molde.

The highs came in the form of a 9-3 season that saw the Panthers win the Mid-Continent Conference and qualify for the I-AA playoffs.

The lows made what Molde termed "one of the most difficult of my 26-year coaching career."

First, Molde faced the task of blending the coaches he brought with him from Central Missouri State with the defensive coaches who were holdovers from the Mudra regime.

Mix in the factor of many returning players who felt abandoned by Mudra and it equaled a volatile situation. Things came to a head when the players staged a strike that grabbed national headlines.

"The player strike that occurred late in the season resulted primarily from a promise made by Coach Mudra that he would fly the team to the last game of the season at Western Kentucky," Molde recalled.

Amid "No Plane, No Game" protests, Molde and the Eastern administration eventually got things settled and the strike ended.

The next two seasons saw Molde and his staff put their program firmly into place, and Eastern took on a new look. While growing up in Montevideo, Minnesota, Molde probably never dreamed of running an airline. Yet, that's what his teams resembled.

"Our offensive philosophy centered around a strong passing game. We brought that with us," Molde said. "We were blessed to find outstanding quarterbacks: Sean Payton and John Rafferty who were on hand when our staff arrived at Eastern in the spring of 1983."

While Rafferty started for most of the '83 season, Payton replaced him during Eastern's game against Indiana State in the opening round of the playoffs. Payton rallied the Panthers from a deficit to force overtime. Though the Sycamores prevailed, 16-13 in double overtime, a new era was born.

The athletic department dubbed Molde's offense "Eastern Airlines." The combination of Payton and receivers the likes of Jerry Wright, Roy Banks and Calvin Pierce soon sent the Panthers into flight. The Panther record book was about to be rewritten.

Although the 1984 and '85 seasons produced identical 6-5 records, the stage was set.

In Eastern's 1986 media guide, Molde noted that virtually the entire offensive unit was returning.

"We have the capabilities to put points on the board anytime . . . anywhere," Molde was quoted.

The Panthers opened the season with a narrow 23-20 Gateway Conference loss at Illinois State. Critics wondered if the glory days of Eastern football had left with Mudra.

"We carried that opening loss with us all season. It was always hanging over us," Molde said afterward.

A sluggish showing in a 24-21 win at Northern Michigan the next weekend didn't give Panther fans or critics much confidence.

Then it happened: The game that changed the season and the team. Playing at home for the first time that fall, Eastern faced Southern Illinois, a team the Panthers had not beaten since 1982—Mudra's last year.

Molde decided to open the game with an onside kick. Eastern recovered the kick and then flattened Southern Illinois, 52-7, in what was billed as "a game of respect."

Molde said afterward, "Looking back on it, that's the game that really turned things around for us. That's when we realized our potential."

After an open week and a victory over Rev. Jerry Falwell's Liberty University, Eastern faced Mudra and his preseason conference favorite Northern Iowa Panthers. The game fell on Homecoming, and its theme that year was "It's Classic."

A Hollywood scriptwriter couldn't have done any better. After a scoreless first half, both teams' offenses shifted into high gear.

The fourth quarter turned out to be especially wild. Northern Iowa rallied from a late 28-16 deficit. With only 26 seconds remaining, UNI scored a touchdown to grab a 30-28 lead.

With the UNI sidelines celebrating, Mudra, coaching from the press box, tried in vain to communicate with his coaches on the field.

"We were screaming for them to go for the two (-point conversion)," Mudra said afterward waving his hands in anger.

The reason for Mudra's anger? Payton and Eastern moved into position for a last chance at victory—a 58-yard field goal attempt by junior college transfer Rich Ehmke from El Cajon, California.

"How can anyone connected with Eastern football ever forget the kick?" Molde said. "I remember the fourth down on the Northern Iowa 41-yard line. Payton had done a great job of moving the ball to that point with only seconds remaining in the game.

"The choice was whether to throw the ball into the end zone and hope for a catch or kick the field goal. I called Rich over and asked him, 'Can you make this kick?' I looked him straight in the eye to read his reaction. His look and response convinced me that he could."

Not only could he, Ehmke did.

The 58-yard game-winner is the longest in Eastern and Gateway history. With Mudra heard shouting obscenities, a good portion of the 11,052 hysterical fans stormed the field. Molde leaped onto a pile of elated Panther players.

"It turned out to be the right decision," Molde said 23 years later.

The kick transformed Ehmke from a virtual unknown on campus into an overnight celebrity.

After the game, an exuberant Molde said the game might have been the most exciting in Eastern history.

When Mudra was informed of the remark by an Iowa newspaper reporter, the former Eastern head coach retorted, "Does he know we won the bleepin' national championship?!"

Nevertheless, Eastern followed with conference wins over Western Illinois (37-3) and Southwest Missouri State (34-20). After routing Winona State, 64-0, in a game that saw Payton become only the seventh quarterback in NCAA history to throw for 10,000 yards, Eastern stood on the brink of the Gateway title.

That's when fate decided to play a cruel trick on Molde. His beloved mother Irene passed away.

"My mother's passing took me away from the team during a crucial week of the season. We were scheduled to play Indiana State on the day my mother was buried," Molde recalled. "I missed the entire week of practice and the game. It was very difficult. However, I was blessed to have an outstanding assistant head coach in Larry Edlund, my partner in coaching for 25 years."

The Panthers brought home the Gateway championship with a 31-14 victory over the Sycamores.

Al Molde's wide-open, pass-oriented offense brought school records and a Gateway Conference title in 1986.

Molde said, "I trusted him (Edlund) implicitly, and will never forget the call I received following the game on that Saturday in November. He just said, 'We won!' I don't remember much after that. I was so happy because it had been a very difficult day for me."

A week later Molde was back and Eastern closed its regular season with a 35-18 nonconference win over Western Kentucky. It was the Panthers' 10th straight victory and sent them into the I-AA playoffs ranked No. 4 in the country.

Eastern played both its playoff games at O'Brien Stadium. Both opponents came from the Ohio Valley, a conference Eastern would join 10 years later.

First up was Murray State. After falling behind 14-0, Eastern rallied to post a 28-21 victory that sent the Panthers into the quarterfinal round.

This time around, Molde's Panthers hosted Eastern Kentucky. Early mistakes put Eastern Illinois in a hole. Entering the fourth quarter, EKU led 24-10.

Payton and Banks brought the Panthers back. First, they combined on a 24-yard touchdown pass. However, Ehmke, the Homecoming hero, missed the extra point. The miscue would prove fatal for the Panthers.

Eastern Illinois drove 68 yards on 12 plays on the final drive of the Payton-Banks era. Payton completed eight of nine passes on that drive. Banks capped it with a diving nine-yard TD reception with only 27 seconds left.

Forced to go for the two-point conversion, Payton was flushed from the pocket by a heavy rush. His final pass sailed over the head of running back DuWayne Pitts in the right corner of the end zone. Officials waved off a pass interference penalty because the referees ruled the ball uncatchable.

"I will always remember the final game of the '86 season," said Molde. "It was a tough way to end the season for such a great group of winners among our seniors. We just couldn't get a break that day it seemed."

Molde was named Gateway Coach of the Year. Success brought interest from bigger programs, and the 42-year-old coach left Eastern to become the head man at Western Michigan of the Mid-American Conference.

The *ESPN College Football Encyclopedia* named Molde as the best coach in Western Michigan history. Inheriting a team that won just three games the previous season, Molde won five games at WMU in 1987.

The following year, Molde and the Broncos won the MAC title and earned a berth in the California Bowl. He was named MAC Coach of the Year.

Molde posted a 62-47-2 record in 10 seasons at Western Michigan, tying him with William Spaulding for the most victories in school history.

In 2008, Molde was inducted into the Western Michigan Hall of Fame.

"It was very exciting, and a great honor," he said. "Many of the members of our 1988 MAC championship team were on hand. That year was very special. We had an outstanding quarterback named Tony Kimbrough and some great wide receivers, just like we did at Eastern."

When his coaching career ended at the conclusion of the 1996 season, Molde returned to his alma mater, Gustavus Adolphus College, as athletic director. He stayed there until his retirement in 2012.

"I really miss game days . . . the coaching part," Molde said. "I don't miss all the travel during recruiting. I miss the relationship with the players, too. Those were my favorite things about coaching."

Molde's name still carries weight in the coaching ranks. He wrote a chapter called "Passing to Set Up the Run" in a book called *Offensive Football Strategies* that came out in 2000.

"I was asked to write an article about our successful passing offense," Molde said. "We were operating a ball control passing game utilizing the short passing game. In this way, we were able to control the clock, much as you would with a ball control ground game.

"When the defense loosened up in an effort to stop our short and medium passes, we would blend in the draw and screen games. Largely, this was our running game. It was very effective, especially with quarterbacks like Sean Payton."

As retirement neared, Molde again strategized.

"We are making plans to move to our lake home in northern Minnesota. From there we hope to travel a lot," he said. "We have four sons (Michael, Brian, Matthew and Evan), all of whom are married with children. We have seven lovely grandchildren whom we love to visit.

"My wife Ingrid grew up living in many foreign countries. It is a goal of ours to travel to some of those places and reconnect."

Molde and his wife did just that. In 2013, he coached the Saarland Hurricanes of the German Football League.

"At first I thought no, I'd just retired," Molde told Brian Nielsen of *Journal Gazette-Times Courier*. "But when I talked to my wife, we decided the experience of living in Germany would be worth the work of coaching."

Moreover, Molde talked his longtime friend Edlund into joining him as the team's defensive coordinator.

While he enjoyed it, Molde sees the German coaching experience as a one-time thing. Molde and his wife plan on living their retirement days back in Minnesota.

"(Coaching) eliminates time with the grandkids. We live right on a lake in Minnesota. It's tough being away in the summer," Molde told Nielsen.

FOUR-DOWN TERRITORY

Favorite Football Movie: *Rudy* . . . some of our players were in it, and I love the story line.

First Car: A 1966 Corvette convertible. Silver with a black rag top. Still love that car and wish I had it back.

Worst Summer Job: A couple of summers between my college years I worked on an extra gang on the railroad. We lived in a box car during the week out on the railroad. I was the spike mauler, which meant it was my job to nail in the spikes once the ties were replaced. This also meant that I worked alone all day, well behind the crew who were replacing the ties. I drove spikes all day and fell in bed exhausted every night. I couldn't wait to get back to college. One day near the end of summer in my second year of doing this, the foreman came by and asked me if I would like to stay. He thought I showed potential, and that I might be able to have a successful career on the railroad. I quickly, and politely, said, "No thanks, I'm going to be a football coach."

Favorite Subject in School: Biology. I majored in it in college, too.

SEAN PAYTON

Prior to raising the Lombardi Trophy for the Super Bowl–winning New Orleans Saints, Sean Payton earned his wings as the pilot of "Eastern Airlines."

Payton, who became an NFL head coach at age 42, was recruited out of Naperville Central High School in 1982.

"I was recruited by Eastern, Southern Illinois, Southwest Missouri State and Northern Illinois," said Payton during a bye week in the 2009 NFL season.

Bill Mallory was the Northern head coach at the time.

"We looked at Sean, but when Tim Tyrrell committed to us, we didn't pursue Sean," Mallory said.

Payton added, "In those days you could offer half scholarships, and that's what Northern offered me."

Thus, the door was opened for Darrell Mudra and his staff at Eastern.

"At that time there weren't any parents along on recruiting visits," recalled Payton. "It's a hard decision to make at such a young age when you look back on it."

Payton roomed with Calvin Pierce from Oak Lawn Richards on his recruiting trip to Eastern. Pierce was destined to become one of Payton's main targets in the passing game.

Mudra wasn't heavily involved in Payton's recruitment.

"Darrell pretty much let his assistants handle it," said Payton. "It was mainly Coach (Rick) Venturi and Chuck Dickerson, the offensive coordinator."

In the end, Payton signed with the Panthers.

"It was a good fit," Payton said. "There was a pretty good tradition there."

However, Mudra left Eastern after a 1982 season that saw the Panthers reach the NCAA I-AA quarterfinals. Enter Al Molde as Eastern head coach.

"Al Molde was very studious," Payton said. "He was a very calming influence, which was very different from Darrell Mudra."

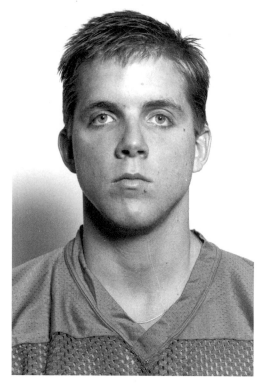

Sean Payton threw for 10,655 yards in his Panther career.

"The program needed Al Molde. I don't think people understand how important he was to the program."

Yet, Payton didn't start Molde's first season at the Panther helm. Instead, John Rafferty of downstate Mt. Carmel was the No. 1 quarterback.

"It was always challenging because John and I were roommates during that time," Payton said. "It worked because we had a separate friendship away from football."

Rafferty led Eastern to a I-AA playoff berth during that 1983 season. However, Payton was forced into action in the final regular season game at Western Kentucky when Rafferty was injured.

The following week, Eastern faced highly ranked Indiana State in Terre Haute. Payton came off the bench to force the game into overtime. However, the Sycamores prevailed, 16-13, in double overtime.

"I threw an interception that sealed the game," said Payton. "I can still picture that game to this day."

Molde and his staff took a long hard look at both Payton and Rafferty during spring practice and summer camp of 1984. In fact, there were even rumors that a dark horse candidate

named Gary Scott might emerge as the starter.

In the end, Payton got the nod when Eastern opened its season against Grand Valley State.

"There was no one moment," recalled Payton. "The staff was comfortable with two viable candidates. Raf had experience, which is pretty important."

With Payton in place, Molde and his staff launched their new offense, dubbed "Eastern Airlines."

It proved to be a high-flying success as the Panthers' offense took flight.

Payton threw for 3,843 yards and 28 touchdowns in 1984. That included a 461-yard, five-TD performance against Western Kentucky.

A year later, the Panthers were charter members in the newly formed Gateway Conference. Payton's 1985 statistics included 3,146 yards and 22 touchdowns. Eastern led the Gateway in passing offense, a mark that still tops the conference record book. He also set the school single-game record with 509 yards in a victory over Saginaw Valley.

Despite the big passing numbers, Eastern finished with consecutive 6-5 seasons during Payton's sophomore and junior years. However, the summer between Payton's junior and senior seasons forced a change.

"We had lost a key running back (Bernard Holland) to a car accident (in June)," Payton said. "The coaches decided to go with a one-back offense. So, we ran out of a spread set."

That spread meant DuWayne Pitts would be the single back. All-American Roy Banks and senior Willie Cain would be split wide. Pierce, a converted running back, took the slot.

When Pitts was sidelined with an injury, freshman James Marable took his place. Protected by a veteran line that included future New York Giant Dave Popp, Payton flourished.

"Sean is an intense competitor, an infectious leader and one of the most confident players I had the pleasure of working with in my career," said Molde in an e-mail. "He was a player who loved watching film and preparing for the next game.

"Certainly one of the keys to the team's winning was Sean's preparation for each game. He was able to make the checks during the games to get us in the right plays in order to be successful. So many times I saw him check a play at the line, drop back and throw a strike to

Banks or Pierce for big gains and touchdowns."

Molde also saw Payton's leadership skills off the field.

"He was our top recruiter," Molde said. "(He) was always able to land the prized recruits that we brought to campus. He took pride in winning at everything he was involved in."

Those wins also took shape on the field in 1986. After a 23-20 opening-game loss at Illinois State, Eastern ran the regular-season table.

"We were a close team," Payton said. "We fought back from that first game."

The Panthers' 10 straight wins included an electrifying 31-30 Homecoming victory over Northern Iowa.

"That game went back and forth all day," Payton recalled. "In the end, Rich Ehmke kicked a 58-yarder in the mud to win it."

Pete Rodriquez, the former Western Illinois head coach, was Northern Iowa's defensive coordinator that season.

"Sean was never going to be a pro quarterback because of his size," Rodriquez said. "But he was perfect for that division of football. He was smart and tough. He was a student of the game. He was a bright individual."

The electrifying Homecoming victory came against Mudra, the coach who had recruited Payton. However, the Eastern quarterback was more focused on the importance of the game.

"It was big because it meant the conference championship," Payton said.

Eastern wrapped up that Gateway Conference championship a month later against Indiana State in the very stadium where Payton had thrown the costly playoff interception three years earlier.

"It was an emotional day," Payton remembered. "Coach Molde was gone because of his mother's death. That game meant a lot on so many different levels."

It was also during that '86 season that Payton surpassed the 10,000-yard career mark. He ended his career trailing only Neil Lomax of Portland State (13,220) and Willie Totten of Mississippi Valley State (12,771) on the all-time list.

Eastern not only qualified for the I-AA playoffs, the Panthers entered the tournament field as the No. 3 seed.

"It's going to take someone playing really well to beat us," Payton said at the time.

When the playoffs opened, Eastern came from behind to defeat Murray State of the Ohio Valley Conference, 28-21, at O'Brien Stadium.

A week later, again playing on their home field, the Panthers fell to Eastern Kentucky, 24-22, in the quarterfinals. EIU staged a furious rally in the game's final minutes. Trailing 24-10 in the fourth quarter, Payton and Banks twice connected on touchdown passes.

However, a missed extra point forced Eastern to go for the two-point conversion after the second score. With the game on the line, Eastern Kentucky forced Payton from the pocket. Running to his right, Payton fired a pass intended for Pitts in the back of the end zone. A penalty flag flew as the ball sailed over the 5-foot-9 Pitts' head.

After a brief conference, the game officials waved off the pass interference call because the pass was deemed uncatchable.

"To overrule a call like that, it was a terrible way to go out," said Payton afterward. "I hate having a game taken from us like that. It's different if you go out, make the play and we don't get in or they make a play. But that was flagrant interference.

Payton led Eastern to the I-AA quarterfinals in 1986.

Payton threw for a school-record 509 yards in a 1985 game.

"It's a terrible way to go out like that. Eastern Kentucky, I have nothing against them. They had a great plan, they did a good job on us today, but I'm sure they would feel the same way if they were in a situation like that."

The loss ended Eastern's run and Payton's career. In the years that have followed, the Panthers have only twice advanced into the playoff quarterfinals.

"My favorite team was 1986," said former *Charleston Times-Courier* sports editor Carl Walworth. "Looking back, the offense of Al Molde–Sean Payton was ahead of its time."

With his collegiate career over, Payton began a brief professional one. He signed with Ottawa of the Canadian Football League. He spent the 1987 inaugural Arena Football League season with the Chicago Bruisers.

When the NFL players went out on strike in the fall of '87, Payton signed with the Chicago Bears. He appeared in three games, one which was ironically against New Orleans.

In 1988, Payton was the starting quarterback for the Leicester Panthers of the British League. Leicester advanced to the league quarterfinals.

With his playing career at an end, Payton moved to the coaching ranks. He began as an offensive assistant at San Diego State in 1988. After a stop at former Gateway Conference rival Indiana State, he returned to San Diego State as running backs coach. There, Payton worked with a young running back named Marshall Faulk. Later a star with the St. Louis Rams, Faulk finished as the runner-up in the Heisman Trophy balloting and was inducted into the Pro Football Hall of Fame in 2011.

Payton became the Aztecs' quarterbacks coach in 1993 and then moved to Miami (Ohio).

"I helped Sean land a job as quarterbacks coach at Miami of Ohio, but he has climbed the ladder primarily on his own talent as a coach," said Molde.

Payton spent two years at Miami, including being promoted to co-offensive coordinator. From there, he spent the 1996 season as quarterbacks coach at Illinois.

It was at that point that Payton's career path took a turn. He entered the National Football League with the Philadelphia Eagles.

Asked if he had planned on being a coach in pro football rather than college, Payton answered, "I don't think so. Coming from where I grew up, the Big Ten was the pinnacle. Being at Illinois was huge. But, the pro game just finds you."

Payton's collegiate days were over.

He soon made a name for himself in both Philadelphia and New York. Payton became the Giants' offensive coordinator under Jim Fassel.

"I knew he was smart, and I told him, 'Coach Payton, when you become a head coach, don't forget about me,'" said former Northern Illinois star running back LeShon Johnson, who played for the Giants.

According to his biography on the Saints' website, Payton solidified his reputation as one of the game's brightest offensive minds in 2000. In his first season as coordinator, the Giants captured the NFC title and went to Super Bowl XXXV. New York scored 328 points—the club's highest total since 1990—and finished 13th in the NFL in total offense.

Payton's next stop was Dallas, where he worked as assistant head coach under Bill Parcells. He also talked the Cowboys into signing a free agent out of Eastern named Tony Romo.

"Sean taught me a lot about the NFL game when I first got here," Romo told Bob Costas on NBC's *Sunday Night in America* in 2010. "Stuff I hadn't really heard too much about. I was able to really learn the Xs and Os from him."

Though he nearly became the head coach of the Oakland Raiders in 2004, Payton changed his mind and remained with the Cowboys. Payton worked in Dallas from 2003 to 2005.

Then, on Jan. 18, 2006, Payton was hired as the 14th head coach in New Orleans Saints' history.

His first season was a smashing success. The Saints got off to their best start in franchise history and rolled to the NFC South title. New Orleans then won its way to the NFC Championship against the team he once played for, the Bears.

Though the Saints lost the NFC Championship game, Payton earned Coach of the Year honors from numerous organizations.

As his career has progressed, Payton has gained the respect of colleagues, fans and the media.

In the 2009 *Sports Illustrated Football Preview* issue, writer Peter King named Payton as the league's "Best Quarterback Teacher."

King pointed out that Payton is credited with Romo's development in Dallas.

Saints' quarterback Drew Brees said, "If you're a quarterback, you couldn't have a guy who teaches it any better."

Brees should know. The former Purdue star thrived since arriving in New Orleans. In 2008, Brees became only the second passer in NFL history to throw for more than 5,000 yards in a season.

Since 2000, every passer under Payton's guidance has thrown for over 3,000 yards.

"I'm not surprised," Molde said. "He has all the tools with which to be extremely successful."

That success reached its summit when the Saints won it all.

"In four years he has turned America's lovable losers into Super Bowl champions," wrote King in *Sports Illustrated*.

Eastern alum and former NFL Pro Bowl punter Jeff Gossett lives in the Dallas area. He saw Payton up close when the former Panther quarterback was a Cowboys' assistant.

"You could see that Sean Payton was one of those guys who was just special," Gossett said.

"I was hoping that somehow he'd wind up as the head coach here."

Former Denver Broncos' head coach and Western Illinois Hall of Fame member Red Miller said, "He's a great coach. You can see his command of the football situation on the field as it happens. He's developed a bond with Drew Brees that is unique."

The success also didn't surprise North Carolina A&T head coach Alonzo Lee.

"When I started my coaching career (at Eastern), Sean Payton was my JV quarterback," said the former middle linebacker on the Panthers' 1978 national champions. "He always was such a sharp young man. He came in as a student of the game.

"When I was at Hampton we were playing at the Meadowlands. Sean was the New York Giants' offensive coordinator then. We got to talk briefly. As he rose through the ranks, it was just a matter of time before things really took off."

Things have taken off indeed—just like any successful pilot would.

FOUR-DOWN TERRITORY

Favorite Football Movie: *Brian's Song.*

First Car: A Chevy Cavalier.

Worst Summer Job: Painting condos.

Favorite Subject in School: Mass media.

ROY BANKS

Perhaps uniform No. 2 wasn't the right choice for Roy Banks. After all, when his collegiate playing days ended, his name was attached to virtually every season and career mark for receiving in Eastern history.

"Roy Banks was an All-American wide receiver," said former Eastern head coach Al Molde. "One of the best in the country when he played."

And play Banks did. The Detroit native left Eastern as the career leader in receiving yards (3,177), receptions (184) and touchdown receptions (38). Banks also held the single-season records for yards (1,269) and touchdown catches (17).

Yet, mere numbers don't tell the entire story of Roy Banks' collegiate career.

"The emergence of Roy Banks as a receiver was just as big as Sean Payton at quarterback," said fellow Eastern Hall of Famer Jerry Wright. "It marked a change in Eastern football."

Molde said, "Roy was on the receiving end of many of (Sean) Payton's passes, particularly the deep passes against man-to-man defenses."

Moreover, Banks seemed to excel when the Panthers needed it most. He caught a pair of touchdowns in Eastern's heart-stopping 31-30 victory against Northern Iowa in 1986. He hauled in a 57-yard touchdown as the Panthers clinched the Gateway Conference title at Indiana State that same year.

Eastern reached No. 3 in the national polls that season. In the I-AA quarterfinals, Banks caught two key touchdowns in the final 10 minutes as the Panthers rallied against Eastern Kentucky. Banks' final score came on an acrobatic nine-yard reception in the end zone with

Roy Banks ranks among the all-time leading receivers in Eastern history.

only 27 seconds remaining. However, Eastern's two-point conversion failed and Eastern Kentucky left with a 24-22 win.

"Roy was a guy you could always count on when you needed to make a play," said Payton years later.

Banks was a consensus First Team All-American in his senior season of '86. Banks caught 53 passes for 1,014 yards that fall. That followed two years that he was an honorable mention pick.

"He is one of the few players to (have) earned some type of All-American honors for three straight years," reads his Eastern Hall of Fame biography.

At the time his career ended, Banks was one of only five I-AA players to have surpassed the 3,000-yard mark as a receiver.

How good did Molde think his top receiver was back in '86?

"I think Roy Banks could step out of this room right now and put on a (St. Louis) Cardinals' uniform," Molde told J. Michael Flanagan of the *Decatur Herald & Review*. "He would not feel out of place with their receivers. He will have no trouble making the transition from college to the pros."

Banks didn't wind up a Cardinal. Instead, the Indianapolis Colts selected him as their fifth-round pick in the 1987 NFL Draft.

Banks lasted two seasons with the Colts. He went to training camp with the Buffalo Bills in 1990.

"He had pretty good hands," said former Colts' defensive back Mike Prior. "I don't remember him dropping many passes."

Banks was inducted into the Eastern Hall of Fame in 2002.

EVAN ARAPOSTATHIS

Evan Arapostathis vividly remembers sitting and looking at the statue of the old leather-helmeted football player that is part of the McAfee Gym architecture.

"I'd stare at that statue and dream of playing in the NFL," said Arapostathis.

Playing in the National Football League had been Arapostathis' dream since childhood.

"My father (Plato) would often have my brother and I just stop and look at something," Arapostathis said. "Usually it was something in nature. He wanted us to realize that each day was special and that each moment should be enjoyed." Plato Arapostathis was a man who saw the big picture.

"He was a teacher and a coach," Evan Arapostathis said. "If you mention his name today in the San Diego area, people still know of him and speak highly of my dad."

Plato Arapostathis passed away when Evan was nine years old. He died after contracting dermatomyositis, a rare connective-tissue disease related to polymyositis, which is characterized by inflammation of the muscles and the skin. The cause is unknown, but it is believed to result from either a viral infection or an autoimmune reaction. In the case of Plato Arapostathis, it was a systemic autoimmune disease.

"When it started, my dad just thought he had a case of the flu," Evan Arapostathis said. "It all happened so quickly. He told me, 'I don't want you to cry. You're the man of the house now.' And for a long time, I didn't cry."

According to his son, the disease was so rare that Plato Arapostathis was "something like the 13th or 14th person ever (known) to have

Evan Arapostathis punted for the St. Louis Cardinals after leaving Eastern (Photo courtesy of Evan Arapostathis).

died from it. It's the same disease that killed (former USC running back) Ricky Bell and (noted actor Sir) Laurence Olivier."

Ironically, however, when Evan Arapostathis attended Eastern in the mid-1980s, he discovered that one of his Panther teammate's mothers also had lost a battle with dermatomyositis.

"His mom was something like the 400th known person to have died from it," Arapostathis said. "What are the odds of that?"

Left to raise her son alone, Elaine Arapostathis firmly adhered to her late husband's wishes that Evan and his brother not play football until high school.

"I tried every trick I could think of but my mom wouldn't give in," Arapostathis said.

However, once at football-crazed Helix High School in La Mesa, California, Evan Arapostathis made a talent-laden team.

"We had guys like (future NFL player) Chuck Cecil, (future college coaches) Danny Hammerschmidt and Karl Dorrell on the team," Arapostathis said. "As a sophomore, I was a backup quarterback."

Arapostathis' dream of playing in the pros took a severe hit when he wound up in a body cast for eight weeks with what he described as "a broken back." Arapostathis theorized that an awkward baseball slide, the pounding of being a pole vaulter and a bout with mononucleosis caused his injury. "I had two cracked vertebrae in my back," Arapostathis recalled. "But the minute the doctors put me in the body cast, I felt instant relief. I was told there would be no more contact sports in my future."

However, Arapostathis was determined to keep his dream alive. When he returned to the football field the following year, he was again placed on the junior varsity.

"Being a junior, that was difficult," Arapostathis said. "But the team soon needed someone to punt. I became both a punter and kicker."

Arapostathis performed well at Helix, the school that later produced the likes of NFL players Reggie Bush and Alex Smith.

After high school graduation he set about landing a scholarship in search of his dream to play in the NFL.

"Another of my dreams was to go to the Air Force Academy and learn to fly A-10s," Arapostathis said. "I didn't get accepted and came home with my tail between my legs. My mom was there for me. She said, 'Evan, wherever you are, just be happy you are there.'"

Arapostathis enrolled at Grossmont Junior College. While the team struggled with only three wins in his two years there, Arapostathis honed his craft.

"I went to kicking camp and worked feverishly on getting better," he said.

The Grossmont coaching staff put together film and sent off letters in an effort to get the attention of four-year schools on his behalf. Yet, many just plain weren't interested in Arapostathis.

"Ted Tollner was at USC at the time and he wasn't interested," Arapostathis said. "Gary Zahn was the special teams coordinator at San Diego State. He told me, 'You'll never play.'"

Cal State-Fullerton offered a partial scholarship. That's when Joel Swisher, an Eastern assistant coach under Al Molde, entered the picture.

"He had seen some film from me kicking at camp," Arapostathis said. "I didn't even know where Eastern Illinois was. I was looking for it on the East Coast. I had no idea what the Midwest was."

Illinois State also expressed interest in Arapostathis, but following a visit to Charleston he signed with Eastern.

The California native soon received a geography lesson firsthand.

"I had this little windbreaker when the cold weather arrived," Arapostathis recalled. "I soon learned what windchill factor was. One time my ears got so cold I thought they were going to fall off (from frostbite). I remember thinking that I would give anything for a sunny day back home."

Yet, Arapostathis was moving closer to his dream. He remembers jotting down "I will be an NFL punter" on a 3-by-5 index card.

"Other players would be off at Marty's having a good time, and I would be in the fieldhouse kicking into a net for hours," he said.

His breakout game came against nationally ranked Indiana State. Arapostathis said he put three punts out on the one-yard line and hit all of his field-goal attempts.

"You know how athletes talk about being in the zone? Well, I was in the zone that day. I wound up on *The Al Molde Show* that week," he said.

On the flip side, Arapostathis remembers a terrible day against Illinois State. Facing 40-mile-per-hour wind gusts along with rain and hail, he missed "four or five field goals."

Scott Sanderson, his regular holder, had quit the team earlier in the week.

"I got on the phone in the locker room at halftime and called him at halftime. I begged him to come back," Arapostathis said.

He also recalled getting two personal foul penalties against Western Kentucky.

"I had a temper," he said. "They were taking cheap shots at me so I said the heck with this and retaliated. I grabbed one guy and threw him down."

Arapostathis' temper got him into a number of scrapes. Sometimes it was minor like the times he would hang out with St. Louis Cardinal fans and cheer for his hometown San Diego Padres in the 1984 National League Championship Series against the Chicago Cubs.

Sometimes it was major, like when he grabbed a steak knife and held it against the throat of an Eastern defensive lineman who had taunted him and thrown an apple at Arapostathis during training table.

"He came after me once and (Panther wide receivers) Jerry Wright and Roy Banks jumped him on my behalf," Arapostathis said. "It's stupid little stuff I remember."

Much like his scrapes, Arapostathis remained an enigma to his teammates.

"I was the kid from California and a kicker," he said. "That was two strikes against me."

Yet, Arapostathis was loved by many. He once put on a suit and tie and carried a briefcase into a meeting with a dean to speak on behalf of a teammate. He left many teammates in tears of laughter for his Johnny Carson–inspired Great Karnak routine at a team barbecue.

Arapostathis also helped to bring other Grossmont players to Eastern, including kicker Rich Ehmke, punter Steve Tillotson and defensive lineman Scott Pilkerton, who all had a hand in the Panthers' 1986 Gateway Conference championship team.

Following graduation, Arapostathis achieved his lifelong dream. Ironically, it wasn't far from the spot where he had often sat staring at a stone statue and fantasizing about playing in the NFL. Arapostathis was invited into the training camp of the St. Louis Cardinals—which in those days was held on Eastern's campus.

"I was on the seventh floor of Stevenson (Tower)," he said. "There were 157 guys in camp."

Arapostathis found himself competing for kicking duties against the likes of Bryan Wagner, Rohn Stark, Sean Landeta, Raul Allegre and St. Louis second-round draft pick Jon Lee from UCLA.

Arapostathis recalled the team's initial meeting with St. Louis head coach Gene Stallings, a man who played for and coached with the legendary Paul "Bear" Bryant.

"He began by saying, 'My family would soon be in town and that if I ever catch one of you with my daughter, I'll blow your head off.'"

Arapostathis' fear, meanwhile, came from being cut. Thus, he never unpacked his bags. Arapostathis managed to hang around until the 60-man roster was announced.

"My hope was to stay long enough so that some other team might sign me after I got let go," he explained. "I was the kickoff guy. I kicked off 10 yards farther than anyone else," Arapostathis said.

However, as is often the case in the NFL, Arapostathis was re-signed later by the very team that released him.

"They cut (former Pro Bowl punter) Carl Birdsong, which surprised me," he said.

Arapostathis averaged 38 yards per punt through five games of the 1986 season. It was then that he discovered how fickle the NFL can be.

"I got hurt in the fifth game," Arapostathis said. "I had two cracked ribs. They didn't care and released me."

Ironically, Birdsong returned as the St. Louis punter for the rest of the season. Arapostathis, meanwhile, had tryouts in Cincinnati and Dallas. A year later, he signed with Denver during the infamous player strike season.

"I wanted to play, so I crossed the picket line," Arapostathis said.

After he had been on the inactive list for two years, Denver head coach Dan Reeves and assistant Mike Nolan helped Arapostathis land a coaching job at San Diego State.

"I overlapped (former Eastern teammate) Sean (Payton) there," Arapostathis said. "I had a chance at a tryout with the San Diego Chargers in 1990, but my heart just wasn't in it anymore."

It also wasn't in a fulltime coaching position. Instead, Arapostathis began operating a summer kicking camp that lasted for 12 years.

"I worked with 30 kids who eventually made it into the NFL and around 200 who earned scholarships as kickers. Four were Parade All-Americans and two were Lou Groza Award winners," he pointed out.

Among those who benefited from Arapostathis' expertise were John Carney, Olindo Mare, Mike Saxon, Steve Weatherford and the son of a famous TV broadcaster.

"I worked with Dick Enberg's kid," he said.

When not working at his kicking camp, Arapostathis has worked in a variety of jobs.

"I've done everything," he said. "I've been the CEO of two companies that I started. I worked with the International Olympic Committee in Greece. Today, I'm a human resources

director. I don't know what I want to be when I grow up."

While that may be true today, once upon a time Evan Arapostathis knew full well what he wanted to accomplish in life. And for five Sundays in the fall of 1986, Evan Arapostathis lived his dream.

FOUR-DOWN TERRITORY

Favorite Football Movie: *The Best of Times*. I really identified with the Robin Williams character in that one.

First Car: It was a green 1969 semiautomatic Volkswagen Bug. I bought it for $900.

Worst Summer Job: I don't think I ever had a bad one. I learned something from every single one I had.

Favorite Subject in School: Psychology. It was easy for me; it came naturally. I majored in it. I've worked in human resources, which I know nothing about, but I know people and I can relate well.

JOHN JURKOVIC

John Jurkovic can be heard daily on Chicago sports talk radio. Most who knew him back in his days as an All-American defensive lineman at Eastern aren't surprised.

"(John was a) crafty player (with a) great entertaining personality," said Randy Melvin, who coached Jurkovic in his junior and senior seasons.

Today, Mike Fitzgerald is the assistant prosecuting attorney for Will County. Back in the late 1980s, Fitzgerald covered Panther football for *The Daily Eastern News*.

"All I can tell you about Jurko is that whenever I went to the locker room following a game or a practice and I needed a quote for a story or notebook material, Jurko was the man," said Fitzgerald. "He would usually say something off-color at first that you couldn't print, but then he would settle into something that was very insightful."

Off-color or insightful, Jurkovic could play.

He first caught the attention of the Eastern staff as a prep star at Thornton Fractional Township North High School in Calumet City.

"Coach (Joel) Swisher recruited him," said Larry Edlund, Jurkovic's first defensive coordinator at Eastern. "His dad spoke very little English. John interpreted for him."

The Jurkovic family had already been through one recruiting process. John's older brother Mirko was an offensive lineman at Notre Dame during Lou Holtz's tenure as the coach of the Fighting Irish.

His recruiting trip to Eastern made little impression on Jurkovic initially.

"I was hoping to go to a Big Ten school," Jurkovic said from his home in northwest Indiana. "Purdue expressed some interest. Ball State (of the Mid-American Conference) was another Division I school."

Jurkovic and TF North teammate Pat Munda made a joint visit to Eastern.

"It was like a Monday or Tuesday night," Jurkovic recalled. "It was the only time we could go down there. Those (Eastern) coaches were no dummies. They brought us over there at night. We parked right up close to O'Brien (Stadium). There was only that one single light bulb outside the elevator.

"We asked how much the stadium held. Coach Edlund told us about 14,000 and the seats wrap all the way around the end zone. I looked at the media guide a little while later and saw their biggest crowds were during the playoffs and just over 11,000."

Jurkovic and Munda ended the night at Wrangler Roast Beef, a local restaurant where the employees' uniforms matched the curtains.

"I told myself afterward that there was no way I was going to Eastern Illinois if somebody else offers me a scholarship," he said.

However, when no other offer came, Jurkovic made his decision.

"I called up Coach Swisher and told him I was ready," Jurkovic said. "He asked me if I wanted a big to-do. No, I said, just come up here and I'll sign (the letter of intent) at my kitchen table in my house with my mom and dad."

Thus, Jurkovic committed to playing for head coach Al Molde's Panthers.

"I was only 17 when I went down (to Eastern)," he said. "They had two guys—Bill Cochrane and Dan Polewski—who were already 24. I remember saying 'Sweet mother of God! These guys are grown men!'"

Edlund, now an athletic director at a Michigan high school, was quickly won over.

"John had a real air of confidence without being arrogant," Edlund said. "The other players really respected him. John was a blue collar kind of player."

Yet, Edlund was quick to point out, it wasn't just brute force that made Jurkovic an All-American.

"He and (fellow defensive lineman) Carl Parker watched so much film, they were calling out the opponents' plays. John was a very, very smart football player. It's amazing. He could tell what the linebackers and secondary had going.

"He controlled the inside game. You saw this when he was in the pros."

Jurkovic made an impact right away.

"From the get-go, I was competitive," Jurkovic said. "They planned on redshirting me my first year."

However, when injuries created depth issues, Eastern's coaches called him for a meeting.

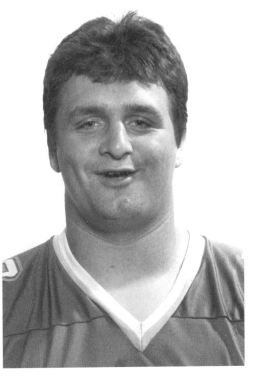

John Jurkovic won consecutive Gateway Conference Defender of the Year Awards in 1988 and '89.

Jurkovic, who later played successfully in the NFL, became the first Panther to participate in postseason all-star competition by playing in the 1990 Blue-Gray Game.

"They said, 'If we do (go ahead and not red-shirt you), you'll play a lot."

Thus, Jurkovic found himself squaring off against the Kansas Jayhawks of the Big Eight Conference in October 1985.

"The first play was a fake punt," he recalled. "I was the up back. I had to block Willie Pless. Bobby Bronaugh carried the ball and we ended up getting the first down."

On his first defensive play, Jurkovic forced a fumble. He recorded a sack later in the game.

Perhaps Jurkovic's greatest game came during the 1986 season when he tied fellow Hall of Famer Pete Catan's school record with six sacks against Southwest Missouri State.

"I don't know why they credited me with six sacks," Jurkovic said. "(Southwest Missouri head coach) Jesse Branch ran the option. It was more like four tackle for losses and two sacks, but who am I to argue with six sacks?"

Unfortunately for the Panthers, Jurkovic was injured in the final regular season game of the '86 season. While Eastern won the Gateway Conference championship, its playoff run ended with a narrow two-point loss in the quarterfinals to Eastern Kentucky at O'Brien Stadium.

"There's no doubt we missed having John in the lineup that day," said Edlund.

When Molde and his staff left Eastern to take over the Division I-A program at Western Michigan University, Jurkovic and his teammates had to adjust to a new coaching staff.

Eastern hired longtime Purdue assistant Bob Spoo as the 21st head coach in its history. Spoo and his staff faced adversity almost immediately when Jurkovic was felled by a torn anterior cruciate ligament injury during spring practice.

"I was going up against (future New York Giant offensive lineman) Dave Popp," Jurkovic said. "It was a Saturday morning. They had put a bunch of sand on top of the (practice) fields. I put a pass rush move on Popp. I never even touched him. I slipped and went to the ground and tore my knee to shreds."

"That's an injury that you don't just bounce back from easily," said John Smith, Eastern's then-defensive coordinator.

In fact, many a career has been derailed by a torn ACL.

After surgery, Jurkovic fought his way back to All-American status. He was twice named the Gateway Conference Defensive Player of the Year. His Eastern Hall of Fame biography calls him "one of the most dominating defensive players for Eastern Illinois during its NCAA I-AA football era earning several All-American honors from 1985 to 1989."

As a defensive coordinator, Smith loved having Jurkovic at his disposal.

"Opponents wanted to know where Jurko was," Smith said. "I moved him around. He created tremendous havoc. He's in the top three of the toughest players I ever coached. He played with pain."

Like Edlund, his predecessor, Smith was in awe of Jurkovic's football intelligence.

"He was such a smart player," Smith said. "He got great leverage against the offensive linemen he went against."

In his final season, 1989, the Panthers returned to the playoffs. Eastern, ranked No. 15, traveled to fourth-rated Idaho and stunned the Vandals, 38-21. Idaho was led by future San Diego Charger quarterback John Friez.

"We scored on the opening play of the game on a (74-yard) pass to Jason Cook, a fast little receiver we had," Jurkovic said. "We only ran that play a few times all year. It seemed like every time we used it, we scored. But we only used it about every fifth week or so. Since we had to do four weeks of tape exchange (with our opponents), that allowed the tapes to clear. I think we shocked them early and they didn't recover."

In the quarterfinals, Eastern fell to perennial I-AA power Montana, 25-19.

"That was a tough place to play," Jurkovic said. "It was cold and frigid. It was an icy field. They claimed they had a tarp down before the game. They didn't have any tarp down. The footing was so bad that you couldn't get a push."

Jurkovic earned All-American honors three times. He was selected as the Gateway Conference Defensive Player of the Year twice. He also became the first Panther to participate in postseason all-star competition by playing in the 1990 Blue-Gray Game.

"It was Christmas time," Jurkovic said. "The place and the stands were empty, but it was on TV. I enjoyed it (but) what it did was let people know for sure that I had a knee injury. They'd look at the brace on my (left) knee and say 'Oh my.'"

The injury certainly scared off NFL teams on the weekend of the draft. After not being taken, Jurkovic signed as a free agent with the Miami Dolphins.

"I got a $6,000 bonus and a $60,000 base salary," he said. "I just wanted to make the practice team. Then (the NFL) decided there wasn't going to be a practice team. So, then it became a matter of making the team."

However, a sprained ankle in the third game of the preseason ended those thoughts.

"About three weeks into the (regular) season, they decided to institute a five-man practice squad," Jurkovic said. "Coaches were tired of seeing guys get hurt and having nowhere to turn."

Jurkovic spent a year on the Dolphins' practice squad.

"The year before they only paid you $1,000 a week," Jurkovic said. "That's what Dave Popp got the year before with the Giants. It's pretty tough to live in New York on that. Anyway, they bumped the pay up from $1,000 a week to $3,000, which helped."

A year later, he spent time on the Green Bay practice squad before finally being activated. Jurkovic spent nine seasons as a defensive tackle in the NFL. His first five seasons were with Green Bay.

"It was a college atmosphere. You're the only show in town," he said.

The Packers were evolving into a Super Bowl contender.

"I had one big year in '93 when they let me rush the passer," Jurkovic said. "I got a few sacks (5.5 according to official NFL statistics)."

Green Bay's playoff road was, however, perpetually blocked by the Dallas Cowboys.

"They just had our number," Jurkovic said.

The rivalry was heated. In one game against the Cowboys, Jurkovic was cut down on a crackback block by lineman Eric Williams. He left the game with a knee injury.

"He went down hard," said former Packers teammate and Illinois State standout Mike Prior. "That's one of the plays that I still can picture all these years later. Jurko wasn't really happy afterwards."

Jurkovic said, "The funny thing about that play was that Williams didn't get off with the

snap count. Everybody else was in motion. Emmitt Smith was getting ready to cut back so (Williams) dove at me. You always wonder how the game might have been different (if I hadn't gotten hurt). Maybe it wouldn't have been any different. It's one of those things you just have to let go."

When the Packers finally got over the playoff hump and qualified for the Super Bowl, Jurkovic was no longer with the team. After earning All-NFL second-team honors in 1996, he signed as a free agent with Jacksonville for the '97 season.

"I made the playoffs three years in Green Bay and three years in Jacksonville," Jurkovic said. "I played in two (conference) championship games. Some guys never make the playoffs. (Former Tampa Bay offensive lineman) Paul Gruber played his whole career and never went to the playoffs."

Just as he had done in college, Jurkovic developed a kinship with his pro teammates.

Former Packer and Western Illinois offensive lineman Frank Winters became a good friend.

"Jurko, like me, was never the most gifted athlete. But he figured out what it took to be successful. He knew how to survive. Jurko was very smart. He was a student of the game."

Prior, the former Indianapolis Colt who joined Green Bay as a safety, had similar thoughts.

"Oh my God, talk about a character," Prior said. "He was fun. To look at John Jurkovic, you never thought he could play football, but he was a tough cookie.

"He wouldn't get pushed around inside. Jurko was always around the ball."

Jurkovic was inducted into the Eastern Hall of Fame in 1997.

"I like to tell people I'm a Hall of Famer," he said. "They say, 'Wow, I didn't know you were in the Pro Football Hall of Fame!' Then I say, 'No, the Eastern Illinois Hall of Fame.'"

Jurkovic was inducted on an NFL bye week. After returning to NFL action the next weekend, he broke his leg.

Jurkovic was also named to the Gateway/Missouri Valley Conference Silver Anniversary Team in 2009.

"It's nice because I don't think of it any-more," he said. "I feel like a football orphan. Eastern plays in the Ohio Valley (Conference) now. But, the honor is nice."

Jurkovic began his radio and TV career while still playing for the Packers. He has also dabbled in investments ranging from auto racing to minor-league hockey.

No matter his pursuits, Jurkovic still keeps up with Eastern.

"(Former Panther SID) Dave Kidwell sends me things," Jurkovic said. "I'm happy for Sean Payton's success. I'm happy for Tony Romo. I'm glad that Mike Shanahan is back coaching. Mike Heimerdinger, the offensive coordinator, had success."

Dallas tight end Jason Witten was a guest on Jurkovic's *Afternoon Saloon* radio show one year.

"He was busting me saying 'You Eastern guys, you got eight guys in the league and you know every one of them.' I'm happy whenever any Eastern guy makes it."

Jurkovic would know; he tasted success in both college and pro ball.

"Jurko always played better than he looked in Green Bay," said respected Packers beat writer Bob McGinn in an e-mail. "He had what scouts call a 'bad body' but he was stubborn at the point of attack and had a knack for finding the football. Plus, he was an all-time character. I mean, the man is laugh-out-loud funny."

No wonder he's such a hit on the airwaves.

FOUR-DOWN TERRITORY

Favorite Football Movie: *The Longest Yard* (the original). It was one of the first football movies I'd ever seen. It's the story of a bunch of guys taken advantage of who get together to win against the greater power.

First Car: It was an Econoline 150 conversion van. It was probably about an '86. I bought it off my parents for $7,500. It was probably worth about $5,000. My parents had used it to come down and see me play (at Eastern). I took it to Miami. They loved it in Green Bay. It was three different shades of blue.

Worst Summer Job: Roofing. I did it for 21 days. I got paid $100 a day cash. You didn't get paid until the project was done. It was a rock roof in Palatine. You had to clear off roof a section at a time. My job was to carry five-gallon buckets of hot tar. These Croatian guys would yell, "Hot, Johnny, hot!" I'd be running across the entire length of the roof with two buckets that were probably about 40 pounds each. "Hot, Johnny, hot! We need more!" they'd yell. Meanwhile, my brother and his buddies were sitting in the shade drinking beer.

Favorite Subject in School: Math, I loved math. I took calculus and interval calculus at Eastern. I loved numbers.

SEC/BOX D   ROW 6   SEAT 2
WEST SIDE

ADMIT ONE THIS DATE

PANTHERS VS.

1:30 PM
SEPTEMBER 25 2010
SATURDAY
HALL OF FAME

O'BRIEN FIELD

PRICE
NO REFUNDS   NO EXCHANGES

$15.00 ADULT
$5.00 YOUTH

SEC/BOX   ROW   SEAT
D   6   WEST SIDE   2

BOB SPOO ERA

(1987–2011)

Bob Spoo followed Pro Football Hall of Famer Len Dawson as the Purdue starting quarterback (Photo courtesy of Purdue University Athletics).

BOB SPOO

Dateline 1987: Bon Jovi's "Livin' On a Prayer" is the year's biggest chart topper. Former Eastern quarterback Sean Payton is a Chicago Bears' replacement player. EIU hires Bob Spoo as its 21st head football coach.

Dateline 2010: Bon Jovi's "Livin' On a Prayer" is a Guitar Hero favorite of kids not even born when it debuted. New Orleans head coach Sean Payton leads the Saints to a Super Bowl title. Bob Spoo announces the 2011 season will be his final year on the Panther sideline. In fact, he will retire as the school's winningest football coach.

Yet, Spoo isn't a man comfortable talking about himself. That's why it's often best to hear from others.

"Bob Spoo is a great man," said Randy Melvin, who began his collegiate coaching career back in the late 1980s under Spoo at Eastern.

"Look at his coaching tree; there are a number of coaches all over the place who were with him," said Melvin, who has since gone on to coach in both the National Football League as well as with Division I college programs. "He stands for the right things. His core values don't change."

Eastern assistant athletic director John Smith served as Spoo's defensive coordinator from 1987 to 1997.

"Bob Spoo has more integrity than any man I've ever coached with," Smith said.

To illustrate his point, Smith related a story he has told many times.

"One day we somehow ended up getting extra game films for a team we were about to play," Smith recalled. "Well, I'm all excited about it. I was about to sit down and start watching the films when Coach Spoo got wind of it."

The Panthers' head coach ordered Smith to repack the extra films and ship them back.

Spoo also had a simple philosophy on recruiting.

"He used to say it's okay to make a mistake on someone's ability, but don't make a mistake on his character," said Smith.

Two of the players Spoo coached whose characters wouldn't be regarded as mistakes are running back Willie High and linebacker Tim Carver. Each spoke highly of their former coach.

"Coach Spoo is a man of such great principles," said High, who later served in Iraq as a Marine Corps officer. "Eastern is fortunate to have had him all these years."

"He's a rock," said Carver, today an assistant principal in his home state of Iowa. "He's committed to the things he believes in. He wants you to be a good student and community leader. He's a high character guy. He's involved in all aspects of the game, but above all, Coach Spoo would say, 'You're going to class.'"

Carver felt so strongly about Spoo that he drove from his home in Iowa to Charleston to speak at the press conference when Spoo announced that he was retiring.

"He was a father-like figure to so many of us over the years," Carver said.

John Jurkovic started his Eastern career under head coach Al Molde, but twice earned Gateway Conference Defensive Player of the Year honors under Spoo.

"Spoo is a stickler for detail," Jurkovic said. "He had his hands in every aspect of the game, especially special teams. We worked on *everything*. We worked on extra points. We worked on punt blocks. He let his coaches coach, but if he saw something he didn't like, then he stepped in. He used a stopwatch. If things weren't done in the designated amount of time, you did it again. You did it over and over again until it was done right."

Illinois State head coach Brock Spack first met Spoo when Spack was a player at Purdue. He began his coaching career as a Boilermaker graduate assistant before becoming the defensive coordinator on Spoo's first Eastern staff.

"He's a very cerebral man and a family-oriented man," Spack said. "I owe him a lot."

Bill Legg has coached for more than 25 years at seven schools including Marshall, Purdue, West Virginia and Florida International. Before that, he was a four-year starter at center under Hall of Fame head coach Don Nehlen at West Virginia. Legg coached five seasons under Spoo at Eastern (1989–1993)

"Bob is an outstanding coach," Legg said. "I learned an unbelievable amount of football from Bob Spoo. The fundamentals I learned under him are still with me today. Everything I do is tied to Bob Spoo.

Spoo and his Panther team celebrate with the Mid-America Classic trophy in 2011.

"He enjoys developing people, not just players, but coaches as well. I came to him as a 26-year-old coach. When I left him, I was prepared to go anywhere to coach. Bob Spoo can't be measured in wins and losses. Look at how many coaches have come out of Eastern Illinois. There are coaches all over the country at every level from the NFL to major college football to I-AA down to the high schools. Bob Spoo is the reason why."

But, testimonials didn't just come from men who coached with or played for Spoo. They also came from men who were his rivals.

"Bob Spoo isn't just a great coach, he's a great person," said Bill Mallory, the former Northern Illinois head coach who competed against Spoo at Indiana University.

Former Illinois State head coach Todd Berry is another.

"He was great," said Berry. "We'd run into each other out on the recruiting trail. Bob was always above board. His teams always over-achieved, which to me is the mark of a good coach. They played hard and were quality teams."

University of Minnesota head coach Jerry Kill coached against Spoo while at Southern Illinois for seven years (2001–2007).

"A legend," Kill said. "People talk about Bobby Bowden and Joe Paterno? You look at what Coach Spoo has been through. He loves the institution, and they love him. You'll never see it again."

Spoo grew up on the southwest side of Chicago.

"It was called the Marquette Park district," Spoo said.

Spoo followed his older brother to St. Rita High School where he played quarterback. He also was the catcher on the baseball team. After graduation he was set to take an appointment at West Point.

"But, I was desperately homesick," he said.

In what he termed "a last-ditch effort," Spoo instead enrolled at Purdue University, where he roomed with future Kansas City Chiefs Hall of Fame quarterback Len Dawson.

"What a great individual Lenny was," he said.

Spoo became a three-year letterman and took over the reins from the graduated Dawson as the Boilermakers' starting quarterback. In 1957 and '58, Spoo guided Purdue to a combined record of 11-5. He cocaptained the 1958 Blue team in the Blue-Gray All-Star Game.

"That came about because Jack Mollenkopf, my coach at Purdue, was designated the Blue coach," he said.

When Spoo graduated in 1960, he was drafted by the Boston Patriots of the American Football League. However, Spoo had to fulfill a six-month ROTC commitment to the Army.

Spoo later played quarterback for the minor league Chicago Hornets of the Tri-State League. Spoo was named to the league's all-star team in 1960.

According to minor league football historian Bob Gill, Spoo led the Tri-State League in every important passing category the following season.

"In both years he was the only passer in the league to have more TDs than interceptions, and in the second year (1961) he completed almost 60% of his passes, which was very high for a minor-league passer at that time," Gill wrote in an e-mail.

Meanwhile, Spoo worked briefly for the Chicago Park District until he received a phone call from John Jardine.

"The Jardine name was big," Spoo said. "The father had been the water commissioner back in the 1950s. John and Len were his sons."

Jardine invited Spoo to become his backfield coach at Fenwick High School for the 1961 season. The next year he coached at St. Laurence High School.

In 1963, it was Len Jardine's turn to come calling. Spoo joined him at Loyola Academy in Wilmette. He remained there until 1972, taking over as the head coach in '67. Spoo was one of the most successful prep coaches in Illinois.

"I knew him when he coached at Loyola," said legendary Illinois prep writer Taylor Bell. "His 1969 team upset Mendel in the Prep Bowl. In fact, they beat them twice. Mendel had won it in 1968 and everybody assumed they'd repeat in '69, but Loyola knocked them off.

"And he did it with players who for the most part went on to Ivy League schools. Mendel had players who wound up in the Big Ten. Certainly, Spoo had a different kind of player."

Bell was impressed that Spoo recognized the value of teamwork.

"He had a great group of coaches with him. He was a great organizer. He knew how to delegate. He surrounded himself with great people at all positions."

Spoo finished his prep career with a remarkable 51-9-2 record. He was the 1969 Illinois Coach of the Year, 1970 National High School Athletic Coaches Association Football Coach of the Year and the 1972 Chicago Coach of the Year.

"Those were the best years of my coaching career," he said. "We were successful. I met my wife (Susan) during those years. I didn't have to worry about recruiting. It was just a special time.

"We had a reunion last June (2009). In 11 games, we only allowed 44 points. We had six shutouts including the Prep Bowl against Lane Tech."

Meanwhile, John Jardine had taken over as the University of Wisconsin football head coach in 1970.

"He called me back in 1969 to join his staff, but at that time I didn't feel I was ready," Spoo said.

By '72, Spoo was ready and became an assistant for the Badgers. He remained there until Jardine was fired after the 1977 season.

Purdue, his alma mater, then called. Spoo accepted. During the next nine seasons, working with the likes of Mark Hermann, Scott Campbell and Jim Everett, Spoo solidified his resume for developing quarterbacks.

When Al Molde left Eastern for the head coaching job at Western Michigan, Spoo was hired as the next Panthers' football coach.

"It was January 6, 1987, if I remember correctly," Spoo said.

The rest, as they say, is history.

Spoo has more victories than any coach in Eastern history. He was named the Ohio Valley Conference Coach of the Year three times (2001, 2005 and 2009). When Eastern played in the Gateway Conference, Spoo won that league's top coaching honor in 1995. In 2000, he was the runner-up for the Eddie Robinson Coach of the Year Award. In 1995, he was named *The Football Gazette* I-AA Coach of the Year.

Spoo has coached numerous all-conference picks, including seven OVC Offensive or Defensive Players of the Year since the 2000 season. Tony Romo blossomed into the 2002 Walter Payton Award winner under Spoo's tutelage. The Payton Award is the I-AA/FCS version of the Heisman Trophy.

"I've been very fortunate at Eastern," said Spoo.

Mike Fitzgerald, the assistant prosecuting attorney for Will County, covered Spoo's Panthers for *The Daily Eastern News* during the 1988 season.

"Everything everyone said about him was true. He is as honest as the day is long," said Fitzgerald. "He would answer every question I asked him, some of which he probably thought were stupid, but he knew that I was a student journalist and he took that into account. His players always played hard for him, no matter what, and he probably has forgotten more about football than a lot of people will ever know. I can remember asking him about why he, or his coordinator, would call certain plays in certain situations, and his answers provided tremendous insight into the game. I'm surprised he stayed at Eastern as long as he did only because a man with his knowledge, character and coaching acumen could have made it to a higher level. EIU should be thankful for Bob Spoo's tenure there."

Yet, it hasn't all been good times. After a string of four straight seasons with losing records (a combined 17-26-1 record), the pressure was on. In fact, the Panthers were coming off of a 3-7-1 season in 1993.

"I received a letter from John Craft, the former Olympian who was our interim athletic director, stating that I had to have a winning season to keep my job," Spoo recounted.

Eastern stumbled to a 2-5 start. With the vultures circling, the Panthers rallied to finish at 6-5.

"We knew what was at stake," said Carver, the team's middle linebacker.

A year later, Eastern posted a 10-2 record, won a share of the conference title and qualified for the playoffs. In the 15 years since the letter was delivered, Spoo's Panthers had only four losing records.

The other difficult time came in 2006, when Spoo did not coach because of a serious illness.

"Coach Spoo was more ill than most people even know," said a source close to the program.

Given a clean bill of health, Spoo returned in 2007 and led the Panthers into the playoffs once again.

"(Missing that whole year) put football in a different perspective for me," Spoo said. "It still means a lot to me, but it means a lot in a different way now."

When asked his coaching philosophy, Spoo told Bell, "Bring good people with you. Hire coaches you want your players to be around, who can influence the kids in the right way. Have a sense of values, graduate your kids, have them come out better than they come in. Try to be detailed. Leave no stone unturned.

You still have to keep a tight rein on your kids. Explain what you are about and hope they buy into it."

Those who have been touched by Spoo's legacy will no doubt look back fondly on his era at Eastern.

"I will always take a great deal of pride from working here because it means something in our profession to be a part of Bob Spoo's program. It means a great deal," said assistant coach Roy Wittke in a feature story on Spoo by Brian Nielsen in the Ohio Valley Conference Football 2009 Preview.

Hit songs come and go, team rosters change, but character never goes out of style. Bob Spoo is proof of that.

FOUR-DOWN TERRITORY

Favorite Football Movie: I enjoyed *Remember the Titans*. It was quite inspirational. It was true and showed the struggles of racial issues so well. It was a powerful movie.

First Car: It was a Chevy convertible. Other than that, I don't remember it much.

Worst Summer Job: I was hired by a construction company. I was tarring some roofs. That sun was just beating down on the back of your neck. I also had to haul bricks around in a wheel barrow. It was hard work that just wore you out.

Favorite Subject in School: Gym class, I guess. I was just lucky to get out.

TIM LANCE

Tim Lance isn't one to sit around and watch the world go by. He never has been and probably never will.

"When I was in (Chicago) Bears' camp, (former Eastern teammate John) Jurkovic told me not to let them lull you to sleep. Play every single down like it's your last play," Lance said. "That's what I did. I played every single play like it was my last."

It's that trait that made him one of the most decorated players in Eastern history.

"Tim Lance is the best pure football player I've ever coached," said former Eastern defensive coordinator John Smith, who also coached at Western Illinois. "He was so smart."

Smith cited Lance's instincts and remarkable peripheral vision.

"We were playing Indiana State and one of their wide receivers moved before the snap. Tim caught it out of the corner of his eye from his middle linebacker spot before the officials even had time to blow their whistles or throw their flags."

Smith enjoyed having Lance as the keystone to his defensive scheme.

"I loved moving him around, disguising what we were doing," Smith said.

Moreover, Smith enjoyed seeing Lance make plays.

"He could rock you with the way he hit," Smith said.

Though they never played together, fellow Hall of Famer Tim Carver was awed by Lance.

"I've seen him on film. That guy could play!" said Carver.

Let Lance's record speak for itself: Gateway Conference Defensive Player of the Year and Consensus First Team I-AA All-American honors in 1990, first-team selection by the Associated Press, Walter Camp Foundation and Sports Network. Moreover, he finished third in the balloting for the coveted Walter Payton Award as the best player in I-AA football. Lance also was chosen to play in the Blue-Gray All-Star Classic. He was inducted into the Eastern Hall of Fame in 2000 and named to the Gateway/Missouri Valley Conference Silver Anniversary team in 2009.

In his junior season of 1989, Lance earned third-team AP All-American status for a Panther team that made the playoffs.

Though he wasn't drafted, Lance found his way into Bears camp as a free agent.

"Tim played in the wrong era," said Smith. "He was like Doug Plank or Richie Pettibone. He was a true strong safety who would have excelled in the right system, and that being said, he didn't miss making it by all that much."

Lance came to Eastern out of Cuba, Illinois (population 1,648). Though he did get looks from the likes of Illinois State, Western Illinois and the University of Illinois, no one offered Lance a scholarship.

Tim Lance won the 1990 Gateway Conference Defender of the Year Award.

"(WIU head coach) Bruce Craddock thought I was too small," said the 6-foot-1, 220-pound Lance. "He recommended I go the junior college route."

However, Scott Noble, a former WIU defensive back who became an Eastern graduate assistant, recruited Lance for Smith, who had moved from Western to Eastern as defensive coordinator.

"I took a visit to Eastern and then Coach (Bob) Spoo came to my house," Lance said. "I asked him years later why he offered me a scholarship. Bob told me that he looked around my house and saw all these boxing trophies. I had boxed since I was six. Bob said he figured anybody who was willing to get into the ring was worth going after. He also took a look at my dad, who was a lumberjack of a man, and figured I'd grow."

When Lance reported to Eastern camp as a freshman he weighed around 155 pounds.

"I remember Coach Smith showing us game film when I was a freshman," Lance said. "He'd run a clip of me getting laid out or pushed aside. Coach Smith said things like, 'Men, this is why we have to hit the weight room!'"

And that's exactly what Lance did. As a result, he flourished in Smith's system.

"We had such a solid defense my junior year (1989)," Lance said. "We had guys like Jurkovic and defensive back Daryl Holcombe. Coach Smith came up with some great defenses. It kind of almost seemed like he built some of those defenses with me in mind."

In a game against Illinois State, for example, Smith lined Lance up seven yards deep between the linebackers.

"He told me that everywhere (ISU's) Toby Davis went, I was to go," Lance said.

Lance made his reputation as a hitter. By his junior season, the Panthers fielded one of their strongest teams. Eastern qualified for the I-AA playoffs and advanced into the quarterfinal round.

"That was a special year because we won so much. Our defense was just so balanced. We beat (future NFL quarterback John) Friesz and his Idaho team in the first round," Lance said.

Unfortunately, Lance also broke his ankle in the final moments of the 38-21 victory over the fourth-ranked Vandals.

"I picked off Friesz around the goal line and started back upfield on my return," Lance said. "One of their fast receivers caught me and then their big tight end piled on top of me."

The injury kept Lance from playing the next weekend against No. 6 Montana.

"I taped it up and tried to play," he said. "What killed me is that the ground was frozen. It was pretty cold. Had the ground not been frozen, I think I could have played."

Unfortunately for Eastern, Lance didn't and Montana prevailed, 25-19.

"I might remember that game more than any other because I didn't play," Lance said. "I ran into (former teammate) Brent Fisher the other day and he said, 'If you had played, we would have won.'"

The injury required surgery and Lance missed spring practice. Though he was named to nearly every All-American team as a senior, Lance felt his junior year was his best.

"That ('89) defense was just so good," he said. "The next year, teams were audibling away from my side of the field. I remember one game there were only a few plays run to my side. I got kind of bored out there."

Lance was also featured in a 1990 *Sports Illustrated* article by Austin Murphy that highlighted star players from small schools.

"That was neat. I have that framed in my basement," Lance said. "The funny thing is that I didn't get *Sports Illustrated* when I was in college. Somebody told me about it so I went over to Booth Library to read it. I picked up the issue but somebody had already ripped the article out of the magazine. I didn't see it until my mom showed it to me and had it framed."

Lance went undrafted by the NFL. Before signing with the Bears as a free agent, Lance also had interest from the Los Angeles Raiders.

"In hindsight I should have gone with Los Angeles because the Raiders had a position open at the time and the Bears didn't," he said. "When you're coming in as a free agent you have to be better (than the returning players). You can't be equal in your performance because teams will stick with what they already have. Teams know what they're getting with those returning veterans."

Sticking to Jurkovic's advice, Lance played every down in Bears camp as if it were his last.

"(My hitting), that's why I got as far as I did," Lance said. "I remember reading in one of the Chicago papers that I won yet another decision (in a fight) in Platteville (site of the Bears' training camp). It seems like every day I was in a fight. Most of the time it was with (Bears' receiver) Glen Kozlowski. He had to be sick of me by the end of camp."

Perhaps Lance's biggest play came in a preseason game against the Phoenix Cardinals at Soldier Field. Lance's hit caused receiver Derek Hill to fumble. The Bears recovered the ball for one of five turnovers Chicago forced in the game.

Lance said he went through a difficult time when the Bears released him.

"I felt like I let everybody down," Lance said. "I felt like I failed everybody who was behind me. For the first time in my life, I didn't succeed. It took me a while to get over. In the long run, it made me stronger, but it wasn't an easy time in my life."

After being released by Chicago, Lance's agent had some contact from other teams.

"(Mike) Ditka called Denver for me," said Lance. "Cincinnati or Cleveland, I can't even remember which, also expressed some interest."

However, no other NFL team materialized. Thus, Lance gave the World League of American Football a shot. The WLAF was used and partially funded by the NFL as a spring developmental league. It originally featured six teams from the United States, three in Europe and one in Canada. By the mid-'90s, the league had evolved into the six-team NFL Europe.

"It would have been better had I gone to Frankfurt," Lance said. "Frankfurt played a five defensive back scheme like the one we played at Eastern. It was basically a zone on one side and man on the other."

Instead, Lance went to camp with the Barcelona Dragons, coached by former Boston College head man Jack Bicknell.

"He brought in his defensive backs from Boston College," Lance said. "I only lasted about a week."

With football no longer part of his life, Lance put his Eastern degree to use.

"That's one thing about Coach Spoo's program, you're going to get your degree if you follow what he has set up," Lance said.

Lance has carried that message with him.

"I have been asked a few times to speak at area schools. I always stressed education to those groups. You can't rely on professional sports," Lance said. "First of all, you may never get there. Secondly, even if you make it, your career only lasts a few years. When it's over, you've got to do something else with your life so you've got to be prepared."

Lance was prepared. Today, he co-owns Digital Copy Systems, which he operates in the Peoria area. He also is the owner/operator of Lance Motorsports.

"My great-grandfather raced, my grandfather raced, my father and brother raced, so it's something that's been in my family," he said. "I run in what they call the super late model class."

The races, which often take him to southern states such as Georgia and Florida, provide Lance with something to fill the void of football.

"I started around 1993 or so," he said. "I got kind of addicted to it. You get an adrenaline rush like football, but it doesn't take the toll on your body like football does."

As one of the most decorated players in Eastern football history, Lance was asked if he has a favorite.

"A lot of those awards and honors are given because the word got out about me," Lance explained. "(Former EIU sports information director) Dave Kidwell did a great job with that. He got my name out there, and I have him to thank for that.

"I really enjoyed getting the blue shirt as the defensive player of the week for the team (from the coaches)."

Yet, when pressed further, Lance mentioned being named to the Gateway Conference/Missouri Valley Silver Anniversary Team.

"I did see (former Western Illinois and NFL star) Bryan Cox at that event," Lance said. "He brought up that I was named Defender of the Year for the conference in 1990. 'That's the only thing that bothered me . . . that I didn't win that,' Cox said. It feels pretty good to know that I won it that year."

Through it all, Tim Lance has kept his perspective on life. Along with the 1990 *Sports Illustrated* and his framed No. 48 jersey in his basement, Lance also posted his final check from the Bears.

"After all the fines and crap they took out, it was for $1.23," Lance laughed. "There it is, $1.23 with Michael McCaskey's signature."

FOUR-DOWN TERRITORY

Favorite Football Movie: I'd have to say *Rudy*. I didn't see it until after I was done playing. He's just a kid who kept trying and persevered. It made me think about all those guys on the scout team. It made me realize what they were thinking and why they kept doing it. They never got the chance to take the field, but they made us better. I really thought about those scout team guys.

First Car: A 1974 Chevy pickup I bought for about $300. It was rusted out. I tore it all up and redid it. I drove that in high school. When I was in Bears' camp, I drove a little Fiero I bought for about $600. All these other Bears were driving Mercedes and these other sports cars. Jurkovic told me to hang on to my money because it would go quick. Mark Carrier came up to me and asked what I drove. I told him a Fiero. He said that he was thinking about getting one because they were about to open a dealership in Lake Forest. I told him, "No, Mark, I said a *Fiero*, not a *Ferrari*." He said, "Oh, that's your little black piece of crap in the parking lot."

Worst Summer Job: This one taught me to get an education. I was 16 or 17, and I worked as a welder. Nothing against those guys who do it, but it was too damn hot. It was 100 degrees and you're wearing this helmet and heavy clothes. You can't run a fan because it will blow the gas away. I couldn't wait to get back out and detassel corn.

Favorite Subject in School: Math in high school. I just like numbers. In college, it was economics. Most of economics is theory. I liked that. Every president has a theory about how to help the economy. It's interesting to me to take a look at those different theories.

BRAD FICHTEL

Though he lives in football-crazed Texas, Brad Fichtel remains an Eastern Illinois Panther.

"I'm always braggin' on Eastern Illinois," Fichtel said from his home in a Dallas suburb. "I'm always telling people about (Tony) Romo, about Coach (Bob) Spoo being around for more than 20 years and our three NFL head coaches. The people of Texas think they are the capital of football. Well, Eastern has some pretty strong things to say."

Fichtel grew up in Minnesota and later moved to the Lone Star State when his father's job was transferred.

"I played two years of Texas high school football," Fichtel said. "It was a pretty neat experience."

However, Fichtel's family moved yet again going into his junior year of high school. This time they landed in Oswego, Illinois. Fichtel's transition was made easier when he starred for Karl Hoinkes' football team and Dave Elko's baseball team at Oswego High School.

"Both of those guys took a real liking to me," Fichtel said. "They are friends of mine to this day."

Like many Illinois high school football players, Fichtel dreamed of playing for a Big Ten university such as Illinois or Northwestern. Though he received recruiting letters from both schools as well as Northern Illinois, Eastern made Fichtel his one and only scholarship offer.

"I moved in late (to Illinois)," Fichtel explained. "I was an unknown. Coaches were asking, 'Who is this kid?'"

Veteran offensive line coach Bill Legg was at Eastern when Fichtel arrived.

"Coming out of high school, he was an undersized kid," Legg said. "He was in the 225–230-pound range. We thought he could get bigger, maybe somewhere around 265–270 pounds. We never envisioned him to get as big as he did (285)."

Fichtel flourished under Legg.

"My sophomore year Coach Legg told me I had a chance (to play pro ball)," Fichtel said. "That's all I needed to hear. He dangled that carrot out in front of me."

Legg said that Fichtel was the ideal player to coach.

"He was really strong and explosive," Legg said. "Brad was a relentless worker in the weight room. He was a very driven guy. Brad was a good kid off the field. He was going to go to class and do his homework. He wasn't a guy who was going to get into trouble that he shouldn't. You never had to worry about Brad away from the offices."

Though Fichtel played through some lean years at Eastern in terms of wins and losses, he wouldn't go back and change a thing.

"I was blessed to have played at Eastern," he said. "It's a great place. There's great tradition at Eastern. Coach Spoo had been there forever so that the guys (who played for him) have stayed close."

Fichtel can readily reel off the names of dozens of former Panther teammates and coaches.

"Looking back, it was such a special time," he said. "All of those guys I mentioned are still friends of mine."

The highlight of Fichtel's Eastern career was a 21-15 upset of rival Northern Iowa in 1992.

"They were ranked No. 1 in the nation," he said. "Coach Spoo was under the gun a bit (from the administration for not winning enough). Maybe that helped keep him going."

In addition to the coaching staff, Fichtel's good friend and Eastern teammate John Jurkovic provided inspiration.

"Jurko had made it (in the NFL)," Fichtel said. "I had great coaches. We all fed off each other."

Brad Fichtel (68) is flanked by Mirko (77) and John (64) Jurkovic (Photo courtesy of Brad Fichtel).

As his collegiate career unfolded, Fichtel developed into one of the best offensive linemen ever to wear an Eastern uniform.

"The most important thing about playing in the offensive line is the camaraderie," he said. "You take pride in your running back gaining 100 yards. You take pride in your quarterback not getting touched."

Fichtel's stellar play landed him on all-conference and All-American teams.

"Being from a small school I didn't get to play in any of the all-star games like the Blue-Gray Game or Senior Bowl," Fichtel said.

That left the NFL Combine, the annual weeklong showcase in which collegiate players perform physical and mental tests in front of pro coaches, general managers and scouts.

"That was my job interview," Fichtel said. "I went in and I kicked ass. I finished in the top three for centers in all the categories."

Listed at 6-foot-2 and 285 pounds, Fichtel drew the most attention from the Los Angeles Rams.

"They had me as the No. 2 center on their (draft) board," he said.

The 1993 NFL Draft began on Sunday and finished on Monday. Fichtel was preparing for a noon psychology class when the Rams called.

"It was about 11 o'clock and they said they had just taken me (in the seventh round)," Fichtel recalled. "I said that was great and then I went off to class. I still had to think about graduation after all."

Thus, Fichtel became the 10th player in Eastern history to be drafted by an NFL team.

"For a (Division) I-AA player to be drafted says a lot," said Legg. "I've coached 450–500 guys in my career. Brad is one of 17 or 18 that has been drafted. That speaks for itself."

Fichtel spent two years with the Rams.

"It was the Rams' last two years in L.A.," he noted. "It was weird. The Raiders played in the Coliseum and we played in the Big A in Anaheim. There were two teams in L.A. at the time. Then the Raiders went back to Oakland, and the Rams moved to St. Louis. Two teams in L.A. became no teams in L.A."

For someone who grew up in the Midwest, living in Los Angeles turned out to be quite an experience.

"It was fun and exciting," Fichtel said. "When I was there it was the O.J. (Simpson) trial with Kato Kaelin, the riots, wildfires and the Northridge earthquake."

When his time with the Rams was over, Fichtel went to camp with the Washington Redskins. After being cut, he attempted to play for the Scottish Claymores in NFL Europe. However, he never got across the Atlantic.

"I broke my ankle in training camp in Atlanta and that was that," he said.

With his football career over, Fichtel moved back to Texas and began a teaching and coaching career.

"I met a girl from Texas and married her," he said. "We have three boys. They're all big. I'm not pushing them, but they'll turn out to be linemen."

And should the Fichtel boys find success in football, their father knows where he'd like them to play.

"I joke with Coach Spoo that he needs to stick around and keep coaching until they can play for him," he said.

In fact, Fichtel has a picture of Spoo and his three sons prominently hanging in his Texas home.

"I cherish that photo," he said.

TIM CARVER

It may seem hard to believe, but Eastern's career leader in tackles couldn't get near contact as a high school senior.

"There was not much attention or interest (from schools recruiting me)," said Tim Carver, who holds nearly every school record for tackles that's kept.

Carver earned 1992 Elite All-State honors his senior season at Urbandale High School in Iowa. The Elite team also included future NFL player Ross Verba and major league baseball player Casey Blake.

Despite his accolades, Carver's small stature drew little interest from college football recruiters.

"I played linebacker at around 5-foot-11 and about 185 pounds," Carver said.

Yet, his desire was to continue playing. Thus, Carver sent tapes to a number of schools including Iowa and Notre Dame.

"My goal became to play at Northern Iowa," Carver said. "It's a great school for football and for training to become a teacher."

With his parents' help along the way, Carver attended Northern Iowa's final home game in 1991.

"It just so happened that they were playing Eastern Illinois," Carver recalled. "Jeff Thorne was the Eastern quarterback, and it turned out to be (running back) Jamie Jones' last game."

In the battle of the Panthers, heavily favored UNI slipped past Eastern, 18-17, on a last-second field goal. Still, an impression was made on Carver.

He wound up sending a tape to head coach Bob Spoo in Charleston. The move quickly paid dividends.

"Coach Spoo came into a meeting with the tape and said, 'This is my guy,'" said Eastern defensive coordinator John Smith. "Mike Mallory was our linebackers coach at the time. He said, 'What are we going to do with someone his size?'"

Spoo remembers getting both the tape and a letter from Carver.

"It was a beautifully composed letter with proper grammar," Spoo recalled. "As far as the film went, it didn't take a rocket scientist to figure he made plays."

While Spoo saw beyond what Carver lacked in size, other coaches didn't have the same reaction.

"(Northern Iowa head coach) Terry Allen told me I was a Chevy Celebrity and they were looking for Corvettes," Carver remembered.

Mankato State, a Division II school in Minnesota, offered to let Carver "try out" for its team.

"Tim was so little and so slow, people just couldn't believe what he could do. But, he just made plays," said Eastern radio play-by-play man Mike Bradd.

"Coach Spoo called right away," Carver said. "The fit was good from the beginning. Eastern had a good football tradition and was a good school for training teachers, which is what I wanted to be."

Carver quickly rose up the depth chart when other players went down with injuries. By the middle of his freshman season, Carver was playing regularly. Then, there was a little matter with Northern Iowa.

"They came in with an 8-0 record and we ended up beating them," Carver said. "We knocked them out of the No. 1 seed in the country."

Still, Carver's Iowa roots kept him grounded.

"The next year they had a guy named Kurt Warner at quarterback and they beat us," he said. "In fact, that win in 1992 was the last time we beat Northern Iowa when I was at Eastern."

UNI's recruiting loss proved to be Eastern's gain.

Tim Carver was the 1995 Gateway Conference Defender of the Year, marking the fourth time a Panther won the honor.

Carver only got better as time moved forward. He earned Associated Press All-American honors in 1994 and '95. In addition, he was named to the All-Academic team both years.

Carver capped his career by being named the Gateway Conference Defensive Player of the Year in 1995.

"He was the best linebacker in the conference," said teammate Willie High. "I went against him every day in practice. Once you hit the game, it was a step down (in competition)."

When asked to name the highlights of his collegiate career, Carver didn't single himself out. Of his school-record 31-tackle game against Texas-El Paso in 1994, Carver said simply, "Frankly, we should have won that game."

Eastern lost at UTEP, 22-20.

"They made us come back on the field with no time left to allow them to kick a field goal right before half," Carver remembered.

Instead Carver picked the end of the 1994 season and the carryover effect into 1995 as his highlights.

"My junior year (1994), it was pretty well known that the AD, a guy named Rich McBee,

Carver ranks as Eastern's all-time leading tackler with 565 stops. He also holds the school single-game record with 31 against UTEP in 1994.

told Coach Spoo that if we didn't have a winning season, the entire staff was going to be fired," Carver said. "In fact, it may have even been in writing somewhere."

The coaching staff looked like goners as the Panthers were 2-5 heading into their final four games.

"It had gotten to the point that Pete Mauch, our starting quarterback, had been benched for a freshman," Carver said. "In fact, Pete was returning punts for us."

On Homecoming, Eastern quickly fell behind Indiana State, 14-0, in the first quarter.

"Coach Spoo tells Pete to go back in at quarterback," Carver said. "We wound up winning the game. Then, we wound up winning out.

"That season, 1994, was the one that really showed our fortitude. The chips were down, and collectively we came through."

With a 6-5 record, Spoo and his staff kept their jobs. The next year brought a conference championship.

"My other highlight is winning the conference title our last year in the Gateway," Carver said. "We finished 10-1 and tied Northern Iowa for the title. That got us in the playoffs."

Though Eastern lost its playoff opener at Stephen F. Austin, Carver finished his career as a champion.

"To go out a winner, on top of the conference was a tremendous experience," Carver said. "It set the tone for all the current success. I feel a direct connection to guys like Tony Romo."

Today, Spoo still sings the praises of Carver.

"He's my favorite," the longtime Eastern coach stated simply.

With his size against him, Carver's pro football opportunities were quite limited.

"Chris Hicks, a former teammate of mine, played in Berlin, Germany, for a team," he said. "That was my best shot at continuing to play. I tossed that idea around for a little bit. Ultimately, I realized that I was fortunate to not have anything really substantial happen to me in terms of injuries, so I decided to move on."

Thus, Carver began his teaching career. He student-taught at Mount Zion High School with Tim Nolen, a former Eastern assistant.

"I made the right decision," Carver said. "I met my future wife shortly after that."

Carver returned to Iowa. After substituting for a short period, he landed jobs at Winterset and then at his alma mater, Urbandale. Ironically, Carver coached future Eastern place-kicker Austin Signor.

"I coached him in basketball as a freshman," Carver said. "We're really proud of him. Austin has a tremendous leg."

After earning advanced degrees from Iowa State and Drake, Carver became an administrator at Urbandale.

In the fall of 2005, Carver was inducted into the Eastern Hall of Fame. In addition, he was a nominee for the Missouri Valley Conference Silver Anniversary Team (the Gateway officially changed its name to the MVC in 2009).

Still, Carver continues to deflect any praise that comes his way.

"I played behind awesome defensive lines," Carver said. "They funneled the ball carriers to me. Those guys deserve so much of the credit."

While that may be true, it was still Carver's job to make contact and finish off the job. No doubt that also is something recruiters who passed on him wished they'd have done years ago.

FOUR-DOWN TERRITORY

Favorite Football Movie: *Rudy*. My brother and sister were at Notre Dame when they were making the movie there.

First Car: A 1985 Plymouth Horizon hatchback. It was blue with a white interior.

Worst Summer Job: Detasseling corn.

Favorite Subject in School: Speech and English. I majored in speech and minored in English at Eastern. I coached debate for awhile.

WILLIE HIGH

"One day you'll be an All-American."

Even today, Willie High remembers the words of his seventh grade physical education teacher.

"His name was Mr. Jarvis, he has since passed," recalled High. "But when it actually happened, his words were one of the first things that came into my head."

Mr. Jarvis's prediction became a reality in 1995 when *The Football Gazette* put High on its first team.

"It was an honor sure, but I'd had a better statistical season the year before," High said. "But, when your team is winning like we did that season, you get more recognition."

High gained plenty of recognition growing up in Mattoon. He was a multisport star in high school. High held the Mattoon career scoring record in basketball and earned *The Decatur Herald's* Player of the Year award in football.

Most observers had High pegged to sign with the University of Illinois.

"That's what everybody thought, but they didn't offer me a scholarship," High said.

Other Big Ten schools showed little to no interest.

"When the word got out, Wisconsin and Indiana told my high school coach (Larry Kane) that they had no more scholarships left," High said. "They both said that if something fell through and one came open, then I was welcome."

That opened the door for the Eastern coaching staff.

"He was right here in our backyard," said Eastern head coach Bob Spoo. "We were really fortunate to get him."

"I remember Coach Spoo and a few other coaches coming to one of my basketball games," High said. "Of course, I knew who he was from seeing his picture in the paper. They sat right behind our bench."

What the Panther staff saw on the court and in the football game film was more than enough for a scholarship offer. High never looked back.

"It was one of the best things that happened to me," he said. "The coaching staff was a great fit for me. I enjoyed the experience completely."

Success came early for High on the collegiate gridiron. In just his sophomore year, he garnered first-team Gateway Conference honors.

"When I had that early success, people asked me about transferring to a bigger school," High said. "That thought never crept into my head."

Remaining a Panther brought more success. By the end of his college career, High was a three-time first-team All-Gateway selection at tailback. His 4,231 career rushing yards stood second only to Chris "Poke" Cobb's on the all-time Eastern list. In addition, High became the

Willie High, a Mattoon High School graduate, held Gateway Conference career rushing record for a decade.

Gateway's career rushing leader, a mark that would stand for a decade.

High's single-season rushing totals for 1993 (1,487) and 1994 (1,458) ranked in the top five in school history. He ran for a career-best 240 yards against Northwestern (Louisiana) State. High surpassed the 200-yard mark on four different occasions. He scored 37 touchdowns, fourth best in Eastern history.

One of High's records may stand the test of time. He rushed 48 times in a 1993 game against conference rival Northern Iowa.

"That one is still in the record book," High said. "Kurt Warner was their quarterback so the game plan was to keep the ball as much as we could. I actually carried it over 50 times because some of the attempts didn't count because of penalties. The next day I couldn't move."

Offensive coordinator Roy Wittke described High as "an absolute workhorse."

"He was probably stronger in the fourth quarter than he was in the first quarter," Wittke said. "He was the strong, silent type. He was powerful and deceptively fast."

What does High remember most from his fabulous career?

"A couple of things," he said. "I got to play against my brother (Robert, a defensive back at Indiana State) twice. That was the first time that we went against each other.

"Winning the conference title (in 1995) stands out. The coaching staff was on the hot seat the season before. Coach Spoo admitted to that publicly at the end of the (1994) season. But the players knew it already. We saw what went on inside the locker room."

High noted that from the adversity of '94, the seeds of the '95 championship season were planted.

"We gained experience and our confidence level went up," he said. "There was a commitment level that developed into winning."

Former *Charleston Times-Courier/Mattoon Journal Gazette* sportswriter Al Lagattolla remembers the entire High family from his days covering prep sports.

"I will say that every time I've talked to Willie, he's been wonderful," Lagattolla wrote in an e-mail. "I know his brother and father were solid people, too. Willie was awesome at EIU, and it was great having a Mattoon guy do so well there.

"It was a pretty big deal there, but Willie was humble. That wasn't an act. It was just a matter-of-fact thing. It was his job to find the holes and run, and that's what he did. Willie, and Robert, too, for that matter, never thought the job as the running back was any more important or glamorous than the linemen or anybody else. Willie was an inspiring guy, and he was respected by his teammates. I think they appreciated his work ethic. He was a strong guy, and he never seemed to get tired. When his brother broke his records at Mattoon, Willie thought it was just a great time to celebrate."

High and his teammates usually gather together once a year to celebrate and relive those memories as they take in a game at O'Brien Field.

"Eastern has performed at a high level since our turnaround," High said. "We take pride in that."

High also took pride in his degree in industrial technology. Professional football didn't pan out for him.

"I had a few looks, the (New York) Giants showed the most interest," High said. "Sometimes it's a numbers game, but it didn't quite work out."

High did spend one year playing Arena football in Green Bay.

With the game behind him, High set out on fulfilling another dream. He enlisted in the Marines in October 1998.

"I always wanted to do it since I was a little kid," he said. "It was everything I thought and more."

High spent five years in the Marines and served in Iraq.

His memories of the events of September 11, 2001, like those of most Americans, are vivid.

"I had just finished an antiterrorist course at Fort Bragg in August," he said. "We had talked about that exact possible scenario, using aircraft as weapons. That's how you have to think in the military. You have to think like the bad guys and be ready for countermeasures."

High concluded his active duty in 2003. Today, he remains in the reserves.

"Athletics laid the foundation for me, (but my time in the military was) the most enhancing experience of my life," he said.

High uses the leadership skills honed in the military in his current job as a production manager.

Still, High is remembered for his athletic prowess in an Eastern uniform. When the Gateway officially changed its name to the Missouri Valley Conference in 2009, the league unveiled its Silver Anniversary team. High was honored as one of the running backs.

"I found out from (former Panther teammate) Tim (Carver)," High said. "He heard about it before me. It's a good feeling. To think that after a quarter century of conference football you've been selected is pretty flattering."

Carver was thrilled for his friend.

"Willie had a great career," said Eastern's all-time leader in tackles. "Then you look at what Willie has done since Eastern, it's remarkable."

All-American indeed.

FOUR-DOWN TERRITORY

Favorite Football Movies: *Remember the Titans* and *Any Given Sunday* are two, but I actually kind of like them all.

First Car: A beat-up Plymouth Horizon. I bought it off my uncle for $500, and I had to make payments.

Worst Summer Job: My brother and I worked for Imperior Bond Wear making paper products. We worked from seven in the morning until seven in the evening. Then I'd go over to Eastern and work out, go home, get up and do it all over again. The paper cuts on my fingers were unbelievable.

Favorite Subject in School: Science. I really liked chemistry class both in high school and college.

RAY McELROY

A number of athletes talk about their relationships with God, but Ray McElroy has turned his devotion into a profession.

"I'm the chaplain for the Chicago Bears," said McElroy in a telephone interview.

Moreover, the former Eastern and National Football League defensive back has worked for Sportsworld Ministry Incorporated since 2003. McElroy speaks to school groups about the dangers of drugs, alcohol and teenage sex.

"You'll never meet a nicer guy than Ray," said former Eastern teammate Willie High.

McElroy was a standout in both football and track at Proviso West High School. Yet, his prep football team was so bad that recruiters overlooked his talent.

"I think we only won one game in my two years on the varsity," he said. "I had no Division

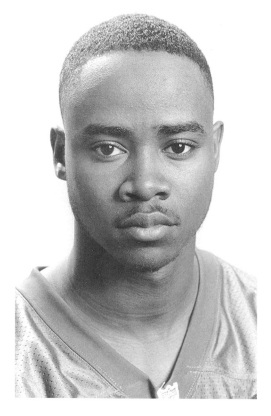

The Indianapolis Colts selected Ray McElroy in the 1995 NFL Draft.

McElroy was a starting cornerback.

"I called him in at the end of his first year and had a heart-to-heart talk with him," said former Eastern defensive coordinator John Smith. "I told him he could make the NFL because of his ability. But I also told him that it took more than ability. It also takes a whole lot of heart."

McElroy took those words very seriously. By his sophomore year, he was earning the first of three consecutive appearances on the All-Gateway Conference team.

"Ray was fast," said Smith. "In fact, he probably was faster than he was quick. Ray was a great hitter on defense. He was a great bump-and-run cover man. He made a lot of plays."

He also made headlines on the track team. McElroy earned all-conference honors as a member of the 1991 league champion 400-meter relay team.

"I enjoyed playing two sports," McElroy said. "Track and football really complemented each other."

One of the highlights of his track career came at a dual meet against Notre Dame in South Bend, Indiana.

"My father had driven over to see me compete," he said. "In dual meets you often compete in events that you aren't normally in because you want to get points for your team."

Thus, McElroy found himself in the 100-meter dash.

"I think I ended up fourth or fifth and got us some points," he said. "But that also meant that I had to go right into the 400-meter hurdles, which was my best event."

Still trying to recover from running in the sprint, McElroy quickly found himself behind in the hurdles.

"I was spent, running on fumes," he said. "But the night before I had challenged our team to come out and perform. I had to back up my own words."

McElroy then shifted into a higher gear.

"I walked down the Notre Dame hurdler and just nipped him at the tape," he said. "It was a big moment for me."

Another big moment came when he competed in the Drake Relays.

"I got to be on the same track as Carl Lewis,"

I offers, that's both I-A and I-AA. I had a couple of Division II offers and a few from D-III."

While his dream had been to "play football at a big-time school" McElroy settled for a track scholarship offer from Eastern.

"It was a partial scholarship," he said. "Neil Moore was the Eastern track coach back in those days."

McElroy accepted the offer on the condition that he could walk on to the football team.

"I wanted to play football more than I wanted to run track," he said simply.

After lettering in track for the indoor season, McElroy entered Panther football with a chip on his shoulder.

"I was the only freshman in the locker room with a letterman's jacket," he said.

While that was true, the football staff still had to be convinced.

"All I had was a helmet and a blue shirt," McElroy said. "I didn't even have a number. I told people I was No. 104 because that's the locker number I was given."

However, it didn't take long for the coaches to recognize his talents and issue him a real number. By the end of his freshman season, he said. "My good friend, (Eastern sprinter) Obadi Cooper, was leading Carl for the first 90 (meters) of the 100. But, Carl had that great kick. He just reeled him in and won. What a spectacle it was."

Meanwhile, there were spectacles on the football field as well. The first time McElroy touched the ball on a kickoff, he returned it for a touchdown.

Yet, McElroy listed two games as his personal favorites.

"Beating No. 1 Northern Iowa my sophomore year at home was a big deal," he said. "The other came when there was a threat to fire Coach Spoo. We rallied late that season (1994) to get a winning record and keep him there."

Like his teammates Carver and Willie High, McElroy sees that turnaround season as a precursor to future Panther success.

"The next year they won 10 games and a conference championship," McElroy said. "We got things going in the right direction. I take pride in that."

According to his 2002 Eastern Hall of Fame induction biography, McElroy led the Panthers in interceptions in 1994, but opposing offenses avoided his side of the field during his career.

McElroy credited Smith with his development.

"We grew together as player and coach," he said. "When you spend that much time together, it's special."

A third-team Associated Press All-American, McElroy played in the '94 Blue-Gray Classic all-star game.

"That was a pretty special moment for me," he said.

It also may have gotten him invited to the NFL combine.

"That was a meat market, just like it is now," he said. "I remember looking around and seeing Tyrone Wheatley, Ty Law, Kordell Stewart. I was nervous."

According to McElroy, everyone seemed to be running slow times in the 40-yard dash, the traditional timing distance used by NFL teams.

"Mentally I got pysched out," he said. "I remember thinking if other guys were running slow times, then what was I going to do?"

McElroy, normally a legitimate 4.4 in the 40, ran just 4.58 at the combine.

"The next week an Oakland Raiders' scout came to Eastern to work me out," McElroy recalled. "I felt more relaxed and comfortable. I was ready to knock off that (experience of the bad time at the combine)."

As McElroy was preparing to run the 40 for the scout, he was listening to the rap group NWA in an attempt to fire himself up to peak performance. What happened next became a defining moment in McElroy's life.

"I was a new Christian during that time," he said. "I remember God speaking to me saying, 'You need NWA to get you worked up when you have me?'"

The Oakland scout had McElroy run the 40 three times.

"That usually never happens," McElroy said. "Usually you just run two."

However, the scout had McElroy keep running because he doubted the times on his stopwatch.

"Finally, after the third one, which I stumbled on at the end, I asked him what was going on," he said. "He showed me the times: 4.33, 4.31 and 4.39.

"God blessed me that day. He was clearly sending me a message."

The Indianapolis Colts took McElroy in the 1995 NFL Draft. His rookie season brought one of his biggest thrills in pro football.

"We came within a Hail Mary pass, which we didn't complete, of going to the Super Bowl," he said.

McElroy played four seasons with the Colts. He spent the 2000 season with the Bears before playing his final year with the Detroit Lions.

McElroy took over as the Bears' chaplain in 2008. His duties run the gamut.

"I do in-season preached word from the Bible," he said. "I lead the team in prayer before and after every game you see. We have a couples (Bible) study. We have study for players; we have one for coaches. My wife (Michelle) conducts one with the players' wives, girlfriends and fiancées. There's premarital counseling. We do conflict resolution."

McElroy also provides counseling to players on a wide range of issues.

"Sometimes it's just to that point in the

season where a player is struggling, is having problems at home and he needs some help," McElroy said. "The counseling comes in many different forms."

McElroy speaks not only to church and school groups, but also at camps and corporate events.

No matter what path his travels take him on, McElroy always has a special place in his heart for his alma mater.

"Eastern Illinois is a very special university," he said. "It has given me an awful lot. No one else really reached out to me like they did. The classes and instructors, for the most part, really wanted to be there with the students and help your development. There was an academic foundation for me.

"I met my wife at Eastern. It's the place where I rededicated my life to Christ. Eastern birthed, molded and shaped me into who I am today."

FOUR-DOWN TERRITORY

Favorite Football Movies: There are several. *Remember the Titans* is one. *Any Given Sunday* had a lot of little sayings in there that I like. The "What is a team?" speech especially. I liked *The Longest Yard*; I'm a little partial to the Burt Reynolds version. I also liked *The Gridiron Gang*.

First Car: A 1985 Chevy Celebrity. My father gave it to me.

Worst Summer Job: It was at a factory in Mattoon. I was the widget guy. I put widgets together for eight hours on my feet on second shift. It really motivated me to get my (economics) degree.

Favorite Subjects in School: English and history.

CHRIS ANDERSON

Conventional wisdom makes assumptions about offensive linemen.

Just look at any number of the football movies produced over the years. Look how nearly all portray offensive linemen. The stereotype is big, dumb and socially ill-mannered.

Yet, there are those who know differently about the large men who open running lanes and protect the quarterback.

"You can't be dumb and play offensive line," said veteran coach Bill Legg, an Eastern assistant from 1989 to 1993. "If you play upfront you have to process information at a rapid rate and make fast decisions. You have to constantly make adjustments. You can't be the old adage of the big dumb guy upfront, and do that."

In his foreword to *The Ultimate Super Bowl Book*, Michael MacCambridge credits writer Bob McGinn with gaining his football insight "by asking smart questions of people who know the most: scouts, assistant coaches, team captains and offensive linemen."

Chris Anderson is one such offensive lineman.

Anderson was as accomplished as a student as he was as an Eastern offensive lineman in the 1990s. Anderson was a recipient of the Dr. Jerry Heath Scholarship, which is given to a varsity athlete in premedical studies. Moreover, Anderson capped his Eastern football career as an Academic All-American in 1995.

Then again, on the field, Anderson was no slouch. He anchored the Panthers' offensive line as a third-team All-American center his senior season.

Anderson grew up in Kaukauna, Wisconsin, which is "about 25 miles south of Green Bay."

Though he played basketball and competed in track, Anderson was like most of his fellow athletes.

"Football was the big draw," he said. "Kaukauna is an old blue-collar mill town. People in the community really get involved with their football."

Though a number of college football recruiters were interested in Anderson, he only took two official visits. One was to Northern Michigan, a Division II school. Eastern was the other.

"My uncle is a football coach," he said. "He and Roy Wittke had worked together. My uncle called down to Eastern. Coach Wittke became my recruiting coach. I'll be honest, I had never really heard of I-AA football. In Wisconsin, there's I-A football and then there are a lot of Division II schools from Minnesota that come over to look for players."

Anderson chose Eastern but insists that the higher level of football wasn't the only factor.

"On the way back from Charleston, I knew that I wanted to go to Eastern," he said. "There was a sign in the football office that said, 'Eastern Illinois, the difference is people.' That statement is so true. You don't have to have the best locker room door to be successful. It really is all about the people."

For Anderson, those people included not only Wittke and head coach Bob Spoo, but also assistants Randy Melvin and Clancy Barone.

Anderson began his career as a defensive lineman.

"I loved Coach Melvin," he said. "I didn't always love him when he was busting my butt in workouts or at practice. Coach Melvin was the hardest, most intense guy I've ever been around."

Anderson lettered his redshirt freshman season as a backup. It was at that point, however, that the coaching staff decided to switch him to the offensive line.

"I wasn't really too happy about it," he said. "When you go through something like that you don't always have a sense for why things get done. In the end, everything turned out great, but at the time I was pretty down."

Anderson knew little about offensive line play. In addition, players aren't shuttled in and out on the offensive line the way they are with their defensive counterparts.

"I wasn't playing as much," he said. "That was hard to take after being basically on the second team the year before."

Anderson struggled with the adjustment.

"I didn't really understand offensive line play," he said. "It was like trying to learn a whole foreign language and then being expected to speak it fluently."

Yet, the thought of giving up football never entered his mind.

"I never thought about quitting," he said, "I have an ability to deal with adversity that has helped me throughout my life."

Anderson began the transition as a 6-foot-5, 250-pounder who first saw action at guard. The transition was made easier when Barone replaced Legg as the team's offensive line coach.

"Coach Legg had me for one year," he said.

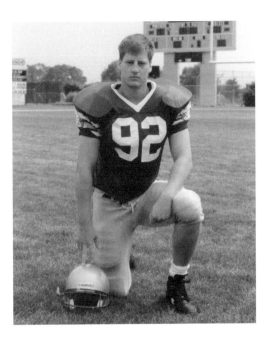

Chris Anderson, an Academic All-American, is an orthopedic surgeon.

"Coach Legg was a good coach. He was successful with a lot of linemen in the past, but Coach Barone had a different coaching style that was more suited to me. I was undersized and had a lot of technique to learn. Coach Barone was fundamentally sound. He suited my style."

Barone was recognized by the National Football Coaches Assocation as the Offensive Coach of the Year by his peers in 2002. Since leaving the collegiate ranks, Barone has coached with the NFL's Atlanta Falcons, San Diego Chargers and Denver Broncos.

Time in the weight room bulked Anderson up to 285 pounds. The coaching staff moved him from guard to center, a position he played for two seasons.

"The other (offensive line) positions require a little more size," he said. "A center has to be prepared to go either way (to block). You may have to pull. It's a little harder because you have to snap the ball before you engage the player across the line. You're responsible for snapping the ball. You look awful when it goes over the quarterback's head. You're also making calls for the offensive line if the defense switches or moves."

Like many of his teammates from the era, Anderson takes pride in the Panthers' 1995 season. Eastern shared the Gateway Conference championship with rival Northern Iowa. The Panthers also qualified for the I-AA playoffs.

Anderson earned first-team all-conference honors.

"On a personal level, that playoff game was the culmination of five years of effort," Anderson said. "There were some pretty low times in the program along the way. We had to fight through all that. That personal achievement was the cherry on top."

Anderson also cited a 1992 game in which Eastern upset No. 1–ranked Northern Iowa, 21-15, in a November showdown.

"We played in sloppy weather," he said. "It was a huge game for us."

Perhaps it was no bigger than a victory over Indiana State the following year. Eastern entered the game with a 2-5 record. Rumors swirled that head coach Bob Spoo would be fired.

"We came back and won that game," Anderson said. "We didn't know it at the time, but that game was very pivotal for the program. The whole history of Eastern football might be different now if we didn't win that game then."

After the victory over the Sycamores, Eastern won three more games to finish the season 6-5. Spoo and his staff returned to win the Gateway the following year.

Anderson also took great pride in blocking for Willie High, the Eastern Hall of Fame running back who held the career Gateway Conference rushing record for a decade.

"Willie was a hard, hard runner," Anderson said. "He wasn't going to back down from anything or anyone. To be a part of Willie's success meant a great deal. He was always very gracious toward his offensive linemen no matter how they performed."

When Anderson's career came to an end in 1995, he became that unique player to be honored for both on the field and in the classroom.

"Both were nice awards recognizing me as a student and as a football player," he said. "Back then I probably thought the all-conference award was a little more special. But, in retrospect, the academic award is a bigger deal now. To go to school and to play football is a delicate balance. The academic honor is all the Division I schools, that includes the I-A schools too. You don't have to be a starter either. So that's 400–500 guys out there who could win

the award. That means something to me."

Anderson graduated from Eastern in May 1996 as a zoology major and a chemistry minor. He applied for medical school, but wasn't accepted on his first attempt.

Anderson spent a year working as a graduate assistant on Spoo's staff and earned his master's degree in biological sciences. He reapplied to medical school and was accepted at the University of Wisconsin.

After four years, he completed his medical degree and then served his residency in Dayton, Ohio.

Today, Anderson, his wife Josie (also an Eastern graduate) and their three sons reside in Spokane, Washington, where he works as an orthopedic surgeon.

Despite the distance between his current residence and Charleston, Anderson continues to follow Eastern football.

"I always check the scores," he said. "Believe it or not, a couple of games are on TV out here. I keep tabs on where the coaches are. It's not just the team I follow, but all the people."

Anderson also keeps in regular contact with some of his former teammates.

"Like I said before, Eastern is a special place," Anderson said. "Coach (John) Smith is still there in the athletic department. (Former sports information director) Dave Kidwell is still there. It's a warm place for you. It's comforting that somebody will know your name."

Anderson experienced a perfect illustration of that a few years ago at a Panther Club golf outing.

"My father-in-law and I showed up there," he recalled. "It had been 15 years since I had played. I had on sunglasses and a hat. I had dropped my weight down to around 225 pounds. I looked a whole lot different from my days at Eastern. I was walking up there and Coach Spoo looked over and said, 'Hey, Chris Anderson. How are you doing?' He came over and shook my hand. It made my hair stand up."

Spoo's recognition of his former center notwithstanding, most people don't appreciate offensive linemen.

"We're the people nobody knows," Anderson said. "Even with good teams, most people don't know who the starting guards are. They know the quarterbacks and running backs. As an offensive lineman, you're rarely in the spotlight unless something goes wrong. It's hard to follow offensive line play as a spectator. I even have trouble with it, and I played."

Chris Anderson not only played; he excelled on the field and in the classroom.

"I wanted to be a doctor long before I wanted to play college football," he said. "Realistically, not many people play in the NFL. If you are lucky enough to make it, your career lasts just a few years. I can be a doctor for 30 years."

Conventional wisdom would agree with that assumption—even if it were made by an offensive lineman.

FOUR-DOWN TERRITORY

Favorite Football Movie: *The Program*. It came out in that time of my life when I was playing. In many ways it was accurate in what goes on all year long in football. Even though the movie was highly stylized, it showed things as they happen and not just the bad stuff. Players deal with their girlfriends. Their parents die. You're between the ages of 18 and 23, and the pressure is on to perform.

First Car: A 1982 Toyota Corolla. It was free from my aunt and uncle. It had a cracked drive train. I got that fixed. It was full of rust from sitting out in a field. It had a coat hanger for an antenna, but it got me through two years of high school.

Worst Summer Job: I worked at a pallet repair factory. It was a tin building in the middle of summer. It was hotter than hell, and I worked long hours.

Favorite Subject: Biology.

RYAN PACE

Ryan Pace grew up in the real Friday Night Lights culture. It took him to a college scholarship at Eastern and into the National Football League as the director of pro scouting for a Super Bowl champion.

Pace excelled at both football and track at Flower Mound Marcus High School in his native state of Texas, where football is akin to a religion.

"I was recruited by smaller schools in Texas, but my dad lived in Chicago and wanted me closer to him," Pace said in an e-mail. "We put together a highlight tape and sent it to most of the I-AA schools in Illinois."

Pace added that he was most aggressively recruited by Eastern and Western Illinois.

"What impressed me the most about Eastern was their coaching staff," he said.

That staff was led by head coach Bob Spoo.

"Bob Spoo has a huge impact on me," Pace said. "His ethics, leadership style and consistency all made lasting impressions on me."

Tim Carver, Eastern's all-time leading tackler, also made a lasting impression on Pace.

"Tim Carver was a senior when I was a freshman," Pace said. "Our lockers were side by side. I thought he was an outstanding football player. He was also an excellent leader with a very strong work ethic. The impression he made on me early in my college football career made a big impact."

Pace was a three-year starter on Eastern's defensive line. Two games stand out most in his memory.

"(My) junior season we played at Hawaii,"

Ryan Pace was the director of pro scouting for the Super Bowl champion New Orleans Saints.

he said. "We ended up losing the game, but it was close and we had an early lead. My family and my girlfriend, who's now my wife, were all there."

The other game was another road contest against Central Florida.

"One of the first plays of the game, I sacked Daunte Culpepper," Pace said.

Though he never made an all-conference team or set any Eastern records, Pace learned much from his time as a Panther football player.

"I think my work ethic grew stronger at EIU," Pace said. "I wasn't a naturally talented player and I felt like I had to outwork my competition in order to be successful. I always felt like I couldn't control what God-given ability I had, but I could maximize my abilities with hard work."

Pace added that he learned to multitask by balancing school, football and his social life.

"(It) forced me to be organized," he said.

After graduation, Pace sought to turn his interest in sports into a career. A trip into EIU Sports Information Director Dave Kidwell's office helped send Pace on his way. Kidwell advised Pace to be aggressive and somehow get a foot in the door of a professional sports franchise.

Pace did just that.

"In 2001 I sent resumes to every single professional sports organization," Pace said. "I only got responses from a couple. The Saints were having a job fair that you had to pay to interview for different jobs.

"I drove down from Charleston and waited in a line that went out the door and into the parking lot. I had no illusions about walking into a well-paid job. I told them I would come down and work for free in whatever position they had."

Two weeks later, Pace got a phone call offering an internship that paid $500 a month.

"It was the business side of the organization, which I thought was good because my degree was in marketing," he said. "After about five months, I found myself really missing football, so at night I would volunteer with the scouting department. Things kind of progressed from there."

Pace's career hasn't slowed down since the internship. Like anyone associated with an NFL team, he logs long hours.

"Seven days a week most of the year and during the season we will work to 11 p.m. frequently," Pace said. "Also, all of the traveling. During the season I'm on the road every weekend to scout our upcoming opponents."

Yet, the allure of the game and his job keep pulling at him.

"I love the competitiveness of it," Pace said. "Every single day we are competing with the other 31 teams. We are constantly trying to find the best players, whether it's a high-priced free agent or a player we are putting on our practice squad."

The hard work all came to a climax when the Saints won Super Bowl XXXXIV in February 2010.

"It was huge," Pace said. "I understand that a lot of people in the NFL go their entire careers and never achieve that goal. So I definitely appreciate it and respect it. It makes all the hard work and sacrifices worth it. If we can maintain success as an organization, I think professionally it will benefit everyone I work with. As far as personally, it will always be something I cherish and remember for the rest of my life."

Pace was able to enjoy the Super Bowl victory with head coach Sean Payton and assistant coach Greg McMahon, two fellow Eastern graduates.

"We never knew each other until we started working together in 2006," Pace said. "It's great to share that background with two coaches that I truly respect. We joke every now and then about restaurants we used to eat at or bars we used to go to."

Payton credited Pace with the Saints' success in his book *Home Team: Coaching the Saints and New Orleans Back to Life* (co-written with Ellis Henican).

"(Ryan) and his staff keep an up-to-date, go-to list for every position on the field," wrote Payton. "Ryan knows the free agents. He knows who is about to go on waivers from the other teams. He knows who's doing anything in the Canadian Football League and elsewhere."

Thus, if a Saint gets injured, Pace is there with a list of possible replacements for Payton and general manager Mickey Loomis.

"Ryan finds players like Jon Vilma, David Thomas, Garrett Hartley, Mike Bell, Jeff Charleston, Darren Sharper and many other great finds," wrote Payton. "It's his job to bring them to Mickey and me."

With success at the NFL level, Pace has definite goals for the future.

"Becoming a GM one day would be the ultimate goal in my profession," he said. "But more immediate goals are to help in any way I can to assist in the Saints having continued success. We are very proud of how far the organization has come since 2006 and our goal is to maintain some consistency."

Like any professional, Pace must also juggle his personal life with his responsibilities at work.

"We just had our first child in March (2010) and a new goal for me (is) to be able to continue to work as hard as I always have at my job, but to find time to enjoy my wife and daughter more often," he said.

Yet with his name being tossed about as a rising star among NFL executives, Pace still fondly remembers his days at Eastern.

"I'm very proud that I graduated and played at EIU," Pace said. "I received an excellent education that has prepared me for many of the challenges I encounter today. Playing football reinforced my beliefs in hard work and perseverance; these principles have remained a foundation in my duties with the Saints. As people associated with EIU have success, like Payton, Mike Shanahan, Brad Childress and Tony Romo, it puts Eastern more in the national spotlight and makes me proud to have graduated from there."

FOUR-DOWN TERRITORY

Favorite Football Movie: *Brian's Song* I know it's a "tear jerker" but I like the way it shows the value of friendship and how close your teammates can become.

First Car: F150 pickup truck. It was reliable. I had it in high school in Texas and when I went to Eastern it helped remind me of home.

Worst Summer Job: I worked at a ranch in Texas. Businesses would have company functions there to watch rodeos and barbecue. I was responsible for picking up all the trash.

Favorite Subject in School: History.

CHRIS WATSON

"Chris Watson . . . he's not a punt returner, he's a punt catcher and that's basically what we have to live with."—Wade Phillips, former Denver Broncos head coach

"Chris Watson is possibly my least favorite Bill. Ever."—posting on a Buffalo Bills fan website

Chris Watson may have been the highest National Football League draft pick in Eastern football history at one time, but that doesn't mean everyone was high on him.

Watson was one of the most talented athletes ever to don a Panther uniform. He starred on both the football and track teams. Yet, he left Eastern as one of the most perplexing athletes as well.

When ballots were sent out for this book to determine Eastern's All-Time I-AA/FCS Team, Watson received just one vote at defensive back. Moreover, Watson got no votes as either a kickoff or punt return man.

Watson arrived in Charleston after leading Chicago Leo to the 1995 Illinois High School Association Class AA boys' track championship. Watson won the 100- and 200-meter dashes and helped relay teams to first place in the 4x100 and second in the 4x200.

Yet, upon arriving at Eastern, Watson began to realize there was more to success than simply pure raw talent.

"It's much harder," Watson told Brian Nielsen of the *Charleston Times-Courier* in 1996. "The workouts you have to do are much harder, more intense."

As Nielsen pointed out, "Even this burner ran into speed bumps and defeats as a freshman."

Eastern track coach Tom Akers added, "Coming off of football, it became a pretty long year for him. I think he adjusted well. I think he was sort of surprised about college track and field, about what it entailed, how hard we worked.

"He faced some good runners early and had freshmanitis, I guess. But as the season went on he got stronger and had some good meets despite the weather we had to train in. By the end of the year he was surprised at how good of shape he was in."

Chris Watson was a third-round draft choice of the Denver Broncos.

As Nielsen noted, "Watson got into good enough shape to run farther than he was accustomed, helping Eastern's 4x400 relay."

"I don't like the open 400, I like the mile relay better," Watson told Nielsen. Watson ran a 47.1 split in the 4x400. "It's fun because it's the last race of the day, everyone is pumped up and pushing you."

Watson helped Eastern win the 4x400 relay in the Mid-Continent Conference, and also won the 100 and 200 dashes as an individual and was on the winning 4x100 team.

Watson grabbed Mid-Continent Outdoor Track Athlete of the Year honors for his performance.

Watson's track success came on the heels of a fall in which he was a backup cornerback for Eastern's team that went 10-2, reaching the playoffs.

"Chris was a true freshman my senior year," said all-time leading tackler Tim Carver. "He started right off the bat and played very well for us. In fact, in our last time to play in the UNI-Dome, he took the opening kickoff (100 yards) for a touchdown. He was a stud of an athlete!"

By the end of his career, Watson stood out as one of the greatest cornerbacks to wear a Panther uniform. A three-time All-Ohio Valley Conference performer, Watson was a first-team All-OVC selection as a junior. His senior season was curtailed by injury, yet Watson still landed on the all-conference second team.

In track, Watson won the Mid-Continent and OVC 100-dash titles. He was named OVC Outdoor Track Athlete of the Year as a sophomore. However, he did not participate in track as a senior, opting instead to prepare for the NFL draft.

"He more or less quit on the football team and then again on (the) track team. If he had a hangnail, he couldn't play because he was saving himself for the NFL," said an Eastern insider.

Watson's speed was his biggest asset. One draft preview lauded the 6-foot, 190-pound Watson for his "great size, speed (4.34 in the 40) and instincts." However, the same draft preview noted that Watson "has been injury prone" and "his attitude and determination will need to be adjusted before he makes the NFL."

Those concerns came from his reputation as an athlete more interested in playing at the next level rather than helping his college team win. Those concerns were reflected on draft day. After the Denver Broncos selected Watson in the third round with the 67th overall pick, making him the highest choice in EIU history, head coach Bob Spoo weighed in.

"I'm very happy for him personally and for his mother," Spoo told Nielsen. "I think it's a great opportunity for a young man. I hope that he will take seriously the obligation to make it. Being drafted is just one thing. He still has to make the team. He does have the abilities and the Broncos saw that.

"It was something that I would hope he would have in his future to have greater resolve. It's his job now. He's playing for the world champions. If that can't give you motivation, I don't know what will. He has the ability and I hope he has the resolve now to carry it through to the end."

According to Nielsen's article, the Eastern coaching staff was not thrilled when Watson chose to skip spring drills before his senior season and didn't run track because of what he said were some nagging injuries.

Aware of his reputation, Watson told Nielsen, "That was the past. I've just got to do well in the future. I can't worry about what happened at Eastern. That's behind me now. Things I didn't do right, I have to improve on."

Watson tasted some success in the NFL. He returned punts and kickoffs for Denver his rookie year in addition to playing as a reserve defensive back. Watson ran back one punt for a touchdown.

However, the Denver staff—headed by former Eastern player and coach Mike Shanahan—soured on Watson. The Broncos traded him to the Buffalo Bills.

Watson spent three seasons with the Bills, appearing in 44 games and making 13 starts. He had two career interceptions, both with Buffalo. Though he got one last chance when he signed as a free agent with Green Bay, Watson failed to make the Packers.

By 2004, Watson was out of the NFL.

FRANK CUTOLO

If Tony Romo was looking for an Eastern receiver downfield, chances are it was Frank Cutolo.

"We have this special bond," Romo told Kristin Rojek of *The Daily Eastern News* in 2001. "We seem to understand each other's game. We have some adjustments at first, but then we see each other and know what to do. He's a great player. He's the best receiver I've ever thrown to."

High praise indeed. Higher still when one reads it a decade later.

Cutolo set the Panthers' single-game record with 239 receiving yards in a 2001 game against Tennessee State. His 2,182 yards rank seventh on the Eastern career receiving list.

"My speed was definitely my best asset," Cutolo said from his home in Florida. "I had pretty good hands. I don't think I dropped a ball at all my senior year. My route running was pretty good, too."

Cutolo refined those routes during night workouts with Romo on parking lots.

"We needed somewhere that had lights, and that worked for us," he said. "You won't find too many people willing to do what we did (to get better).

"I was a year older than Tony was. He was willing to put in the work (to get better). I was really dedicated. Tony was right there with me."

Cutolo most enjoyed running post corner routes.

"I loved the double move," he said. "I would sell the post and then break it to the corner."

Cutolo grew up in Boca Raton, Florida. While he played baseball as a youth, Cutolo didn't play organized football until his sophomore year at Olympic Heights Community High School.

"That's the first time I ever put on pads," he said. "I gave up baseball. In Florida, football is year-round whether it's Pee Wee, high school or college. It never ends."

Cutolo also ran track. In fact, as a senior, he won three individual titles at a district meet. Cutolo won the 200- and 400-meter dashes and tied for first in the 100.

"Yes, I could run," Cutolo said. "The way you're timed is so different at each level. I was timed at 4.4 (in the 40-yard dash) in high school, but everybody runs that in high school."

On the football field, Cutolo played quarterback, wide receiver and defensive back on a team that won 26 regular-season games in a row from 1992 to 1994. He impressed recruiters enough to earn a full scholarship to the University of Mississippi under head coach Tommy Tuberville.

"(He) could be a corner or safety for us," Tuberville said of Cutolo on signing day.

As things turned out, Cutolo played neither. He spent just one year at Ole Miss.

"My son was born from a previous relationship," Cutolo said. "I came home in order to be with him."

A year later, Cutolo "got the itch to play again."

With just a few weeks left before the signing deadline, Cutolo's high school coach helped him field offers.

"There were two, one from Colorado State and one from Eastern Illinois," he said.

Signing with Colorado State meant sitting out a season as a Division I-A transfer. As a result, Cutolo chose Eastern.

"Coach Brian Jenkins and (Roy) Wittke

Frank Cutolo once held the Eastern record for the most receiving yards in a single game.

handled most of my coming to Eastern," he said.

Thus, the Florida native found his way to Charleston.

"I hated the weather," Cutolo said. "Being told not to go outside with your skin exposed. Scraping ice from your car. I hated it."

Yet, Cutolo loved the people.

"Here (in Florida) people walk by you and won't acknowledge you. The Midwest was different," he said.

Cutolo quickly became a success at Eastern. As a sophomore, he earned honorable mention all-conference honors.

Cutolo led the Panthers in receptions and receiving yards his junior and senior seasons. He landed on the All-Ohio Valley Conference team both years. He also returned punts and an occasional kickoff. Cutolo returned a punt 77 yards for a touchdown in 2001.

"I put in a hell of a lot of work," he said.

Cutolo credits much of his improvement to time spent at former NFL receiver Cris Carter's training facility in Florida.

"I was there every year, every Christmas break, every spring break, every off-season," he said.

The hard work paid off as the tandem helped lead Eastern to the 2001 OVC championship. The ninth-ranked Panthers also qualified for the I-AA playoffs, hosting a first-round game with rival Northern Iowa.

Cutolo proved to be a prime-time playoff performer by catching 11 passes for 217 yards and three touchdowns. Eastern, however, fell 49-43 in the shootout that saw Romo throw five TD passes.

Romo's final touchdown pass came on a three-yard toss to Brandon Robinson with 3:27 remaining. Trailing by six points, the Eastern defense appeared to have stopped Northern Iowa.

"There was a play that went for just a short gain and (Eastern defensive tackle) Gonzalo Segovia hit the Northern Iowa runner out of bounds. The flag got thrown and it was 15 yards (and a first down).

"Sure, we still would have had to score, but that play killed us."

It's plausible that Eastern may have scored given a final possession. The Panthers racked up 525 yards in total offense that day. Cutolo scored on receptions of 15, 39 and 71 yards.

Instead, given new life with the penalty-induced first down, Northern Iowa ran out the clock and moved to the next round of the playoffs.

Cutolo had dreams of playing in the NFL. However, as with any dream, there were obstacles.

"Our pro day (when NFL coaches and scouts come in to look at college players) was the same day as the University of Illinois, which makes total sense (given the close proximity of the two schools)," Cutolo said. "Eastern's defensive backs coach was in charge of it. Then, without even telling us, he just canceled it because he was going to be out of town. I got screwed."

Scouts from the Chicago Bears and New Orleans Saints later visited Charleston to look at Cutolo and other Panthers.

"I ran a 4.37 for the Saints," he said.

Yet, the NFL wasn't in the cards for Cutolo. The Canadian Football League, however, was in his future. Bob O'Billovich, the general manager of the BC Lions, called Cutolo to inform him that his team held his draft rights.

"To me, it was a chance to play, maybe a chance to earn my way into the NFL," Cutolo said. "I loved the game. I loved to compete."

Cutolo did more than just compete.

"The (CFL) season started and I took off with a bang," he said. "I was something like No. 2 in the league in total yards early on. I touched the ball more than any other player. I caught passes. I returned punts and kickoffs."

Cutolo finished the 2003 season with 64 catches for 908 yards and eight touchdowns. He was selected as the CFL Most Outstanding Rookie.

Cutolo followed with a 47-catch, 9-touchdown season in 2004. Among the season's highlights was a 102-yard touchdown.

With former TCU quarterback and CFL Most Outstanding Player Award winner Casey Printers leading the way, the Lions made it all the way to the Grey Cup Final.

"I was Frank's roommate while in Canada, and we had a magical chemistry. He wanted the ball, and I wanted him to have it," said Printers.

However, an undisclosed injury to Cutolo surfaced the following season. As he played with the Ottawa Renegades, the injury got progressively worse.

"There's a more scientific name for it, but basically I had a pain in my pelvis," he said. "It got to the point where I could barely run. If I was able to run, I couldn't stop."

Team doctors were puzzled.

"I wasn't getting better, so I finally went back to Florida," he said. "I went to see the (Miami) Dolphins' team doctor. He diagnosed it right away. I got a shot, and it took care of it right away. I had wasted six months in Canada because they couldn't figure it out.

"By then, it was almost a year that I was out of football. I took a job with Fed Ex and got used to living the family life. In retrospect, I wish I would have tried to play again, but that's easy to say now."

Since his pro football career ended, Cutolo has worked a series of jobs and coached youth teams. He completed his Eastern degree through online classes.

"I'd like to try a career in law enforcement or maybe training athletes," he said. "I really like coaching kids."

Cutolo also keeps in touch with his former Panther teammates.

"I keep in touch with Scotty Gilkey and Kourtney Young. Kenny Alsop lives in the Orlando area," he said. "I speak to Tony every so often."

All these years later, Cutolo and Romo are still making connections.

FOUR-DOWN TERRITORY

Favorite Football Movie: I really can't think of one. I'm not that into it all.

First Car: It was a black Hyundai Tiburon. I had it my first year in college.

Worst Summer Job: I never had a summer job. I was always training.

Favorite Subject in School: Human physiology.

TONY ROMO

Long before becoming *People* magazine fodder, being lampooned by Eminem and appearing in Starter ads, Tony Romo was about as far away from the limelight as you can be.

After starring at Burlington High School in Wisconsin in football and basketball (as well as stints with golf and tennis), Romo had only one school offer him a scholarship—Eastern.

Yet, it took the salesmanship of Panther assistant coach Roy Wittke to head coach Bob Spoo to bring Romo to the Charleston campus.

"I first learned about Tony from some newspaper clippings my parents sent me," said Wittke, a native of Racine, Wisconsin. "I followed up by watching him on film and then went up to see him play basketball."

What Wittke saw wasn't just Romo dribbling, passing, shooting and rebounding.

"He had great vision and great anticipation," Wittke said. "I saw his quick release of the ball. You could see that he was a playmaker, a guy who showed athletic skills and leadership ability.

"There was also something about the way he carried himself that made him a little bit different than the other players. He was special."

Wittke relayed his findings back to Spoo.

"We hadn't even bothered to watch him play football, but Roy had seen him play for the Burlington basketball team," Spoo recalled.

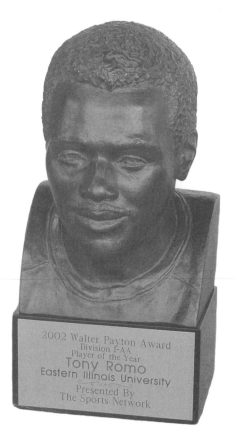

Tony Romo won the 2002 Walter Payton Award as the top player in I-AA football.

"He convinced me that Tony had great leadership qualities and the ability to make plays. In any sport, that's what you look for, a leader and a playmaker."

Yet, the road to success was just beginning. Romo struggled in his first season at Eastern.

Eastern associate athletic director John Smith said, "It was always tough to sell a quarterback to Bob Spoo. In fact, he considered moving Tony to tight end."

Thoughts of quitting the team entered Tony's head. Yet, the desire to excel carried him through.

"There are a thousand Tony Romos out there, players with high-level potential," said Wittke. "But he did something about his."

Romo set his sights on improving his game. He took time to work on his weaknesses.

"It didn't start out that way," Wittke said. "He had been virtually the best in anything he did at Burlington. But, he came here and was redshirted. Then, he was a backup. But to Tony's credit, he realized what he had to do. He's very intelligent. He does a lot of reading. Tony took that and picked up the thought process needed to get better."

As a result, the Panther staff saw that thought process kick into high gear.

"He was a gym rat," Spoo said. "He would stay afterwards and practice throws he wasn't happy with. He's not afraid to work."

After taking the starting reins of the Panther offense his sophomore season, Romo ranked second in Division I-AA passing efficiency. That year, Romo completed 164 of 278 passes (59%) for 2,583 yards and 27 touchdowns. Those numbers helped earn him an All-American honorable mention and Ohio Valley Conference Player of the Year.

"He just burst onto the scene," said Eastern play-by-play announcer Mike Bradd. "It wasn't clear he would be the starter early on. They had a guy named Julius Davis, who was an athletic option-type quarterback. As the year went on, it became pretty clear Tony was going to be something. He was magical right from the start."

As a junior, Romo led the nation in passing efficiency, completing 138 of 207 passes for 2,068 yards and 21 touchdowns. He was selected to the Associated Press All-America third team, All-Ohio Valley Conference first team and the OVC Player of the Year.

Romo's senior year didn't disappoint. In fact, he became the first player in both Eastern and OVC history to win the coveted Walter Payton Award, given annually to the top player at the I-AA/FCS level.

Romo passed for 2,950 yards and 33 touchdowns while completing 237 of 363 throws (65.3%). Those numbers were compiled against two Division I-A opponents (Hawaii and Kansas State) and no sub-I-AA foes on the 2002 Eastern schedule.

Romo finished his collegiate career with 84 touchdowns, shattering the previous Eastern record of 75 set by Sean Payton.

"Walter Payton exemplified what dedication and commitment can accomplish," Spoo said after the season. "Tony is a classic example of what can be achieved by following Payton's qualities. Tony earned the respect of his teammates by his work ethic. No matter how much individual success he achieved, he still was one of the hardest-working players right up to his final collegiate game. That work ethic and leadership resulted in his teammates expecting to succeed. Tony is a quality young man who led his team to victories."

Spoo's words were echoed in the Panthers' 8-3 season that was capped with a second straight OVC title and a third consecutive I-AA playoff appearance.

Romo also became the first player to win the OVC Offensive Player of the Year Award three straight seasons.

"We really got spoiled," said Bradd. "Tony was really consistent for all three years."

Bradd was asked to compare Romo with his predecessor Payton.

"Sean played in a less balanced offense," Bradd said. "It was a system ahead of its time. Tony always had a better-balanced team behind him.

"Sean threw the ball more. He also threw more short passes. Tony was very accurate with deep balls. Tony's receivers were more of an average set whereas Sean had receivers like Jerry Wright, Roy Banks, Calvin Pierce, (DuWayne) Pitts out of the backfield."

When asked to choose between Romo and Payton for the quarterback on Eastern's All-

Time I-AA/FCS Team, Brian Nielsen of the *Journal Gazette-Times-Courier* wrote in an e-mail response, "It's got to be Romo. I hate to go into being negative against Payton because there was little negative about him, but Eastern has never had anything like Romo in any sport. Even if you take away the NFL stuff, where Tony obviously has separated himself, Tony was just a winner. Eastern had a more balanced offense when he played than when Sean put up good numbers in (Al) Molde's system. But Romo took EIU to the playoffs three straight times, at that time a first. He set TD pass records and when needed he ran for the game-winning touchdown of the final play in

During his brilliant career, Tony Romo broke numerous Eastern records.

Romo had his No. 17 retired by Eastern in 2009.

the regular season's biggest game against Eastern Kentucky. To not recgonize him by himself, I think, would be a major mistake."

Meanwhile, Wittke has no doubts about the secret behind Romo's success.

"In the 30-some years I've been a part of this game, Tony Romo is the best practice player I've ever been around," Wittke said. "He truly enjoyed the process and the challenge of getting better on a daily basis. He got better each and every year. He didn't level out."

It was that exact process that would help Romo to further develop as a pro. Despite drawing some interest at the NFL Combine, Romo was passed over in the 2003 NFL Draft. However, he was pursued by a pair of Eastern graduates: Payton, an assistant under Bill Parcells with the Cowboys, and Mike Shanahan, head coach of the Broncos. Romo signed as a free agent with Dallas.

In his book *Quarterback Abstract*, writer John Maxymuk noted, "Tony did not get to take even one snap in 2003, 2004, or 2005, but he slowly developed as a series of more highly touted quarterbacks came and went in each Cowboy training camp. He outlasted and outplayed the competition of Quincy Carter, Chad Hutchinson, Drew Henson, Vinny Testaverde and Drew Bledsoe and maintained his

smile in the face of Bill Parcells' pointed barbs."

Maxymuk noted that Romo took over the starting job from Bledsoe in the seventh game of the 2006 season.

"Romo was ready and provided an immediate spark that drove the team to the playoffs where they lost a heartbreaker when Tony fumbled the snap to botch the game-winning field goal attempt."

Playing his first full season as the Dallas starter in 2007, Romo led the Cowboys to a 13-3 record. Romo threw for 36 touchdowns and averaged over eight yards per throw en route to Pro Bowl status.

"Tony has a good arm and throws long and short with accuracy and touch," wrote Maxymuk. "Much like Brett Favre, Romo, a Wisconsin native, is very creative in extending plays by slipping away from trouble and throwing on the run. He is adept at avoiding sacks, but sometimes makes risky choices under pressure and forces passes into coverage. . . . Through it all, Tony has proven himself a worthy heir to Don Meredith and Roger Staubach as the gambling, scrambling quarterback with the star on his helmet."

Bradd said it's ironic that Romo is often credited for his mobility.

"(When he was at Eastern) Tony always

made fun of his running ability," Bradd said.

As the quarterback of "America's Team," Romo was high on everybody's radar screen. Criticism and praise came from all angles.

"He was an egotistical jerk when he started, but now he's grown up. He's finally getting smart with himself, that's my opinion," said Western Illinois graduate and former Denver Broncos' head coach Red Miller.

"Tony Romo threw for 351 with no turnovers and took only one sack . . . without Terrell Owens and Roy Williams. He threw for Miles Austin, Patrick Crayton and Sam Hurd 25 times and netted 304 passing yards from those throws. What's that say to you? Says it's a blue-collar game to me," wrote Peter King of *Sports Illustrated* in 2009.

"I like him. When I played against him I thought he was very smart. He has the ability to make dynamic plays. He has good vision and can be a top-quality quarterback. He has to remain consistent," said former Western Illinois star and Pro Bowl defensive back Rodney Harrison in a 2009 article in the *Dallas Morning News*.

"I thought Tony could play in the NFL," said Bradd. "A lot (of attention), of course, is based on where he's at. If he were the quarterback of the Kansas City Chiefs, it wouldn't be the same."

Instead, as the quarterback of the Dallas Cowboys, Romo constantly is making news. Here is a sampling:

- His high school sold replicas of his prep jersey as a fund-raiser. "We've been having all kinds of interest in it," said Eric Burling, the high school's vice principal and athletic director. "We've probably been going through three to five a day recently."

- A 2008 Randy Galloway column profiled the tale of a Dallas-area couple who Romo stopped to help with a flat tire on his way home from a road game in which it took several stitches to close a gash to his chin. "Didn't surprise me one bit. That's Tony," said former Eastern sports information director Dave Kidwell.

- In the fall of 2009, Romo returned to Charleston as Eastern inducted him into its Hall of Fame and retired his number, the first in Panther football history. "It holds a special place in your heart," Romo said that day.

For Eastern fans, the feeling is mutual.

MICAH RUCKER

At 6-foot-6, Micah Rucker was huge in the red zone as Eastern's prime target during the 2006 and 2007 seasons. However, the two-time All-Ohio Valley Conference selection has never stood taller than when he set up a chapter of Mothers Against Drunk Drivers.

"We're trying to do whatever we can to stop another family from having to go through what we did," Rucker said in 2007. "I want to be able to help kids and spread the word of what happens when people drink and drive."

Those words followed the tragic death of Rucker's girlfriend, Rebecca Fissehatsion Yacob, who died in an accident involving a drunk driver on January 28, 2007.

"I got a call early that Sunday morning, probably around six a.m. or so," said Rucker from his native Florida in April 2010. "I was running track then so I didn't wake up until around 11. Her brother left me a voicemail. There was also one from her sister."

When the news of Rebecca's death reached him, Rucker remembers "being in shock."

"I called my mom and she broke down. That's when it hit me," he said. "I went to the funeral that Wednesday. I just tried to regroup and be positive. I just keep asking, 'What can I do?'"

What Rucker did was to establish the campus-based organization at Eastern to honor Rebecca's memory. The organization became known as Respect for Youth.

"That name came from Rebecca's initials," said Eastern receivers coach Mike Lynch. "Micah was really at the forefront. He would talk at the meetings. He organized the T-shirts."

Those RFY T-shirts were worn on the first day of the academic school year as well as on

Micah Rucker (80) proved to be a winner on and off the field.

game days. RFY members included not only Panther football players but Eastern students as well.

"Rebecca always preached to me to help, give back and do whatever I can," said Rucker. "Everything I'm doing is something she would have been doing if she was alive."

In conjunction with RFY, Rucker also helped establish an Eastern chapter of UMADD, a campus-based organization with ties to Mothers Against Drunk Driving that focuses on preventing underage drinking, high-risk drinking and impaired driving.

Rucker's off-the-field work drew attention that transcended football.

"Micah has taken on this challenge head on," said Panther head coach Bob Spoo at the time. "He has shown he is a man both on and off the field, a player whom others can emulate. Micah has also shown to people that there are other things in life other than football. If we had a team of players who had his character and drive, we would be one heck of a football team."

Rucker tasted success from an early age while growing up in Florida. He was a three-time all-conference, all-area and all-state football selection at Estero (Florida) High School. In his senior season, Rucker hauled in 55 catches for 900 yards and 9 touchdowns. In

addition, Rucker was an all-district basketball player and an honor roll student.

After his high school graduation, the heavily recruited Rucker landed at the University of Minnesota. Though he sat out his freshman season as a redshirt, Rucker was selected as a scholar-athlete award winner.

However, after appearing in six games for head coach Glen Mason's Golden Gophers, Rucker decided to transfer to a school where he would get more playing time. With NCAA rules allowing Division I-A players to transfer to I-AA schools without losing a year, Rucker wound up at Eastern.

"It was pretty much a slam dunk," said Lynch. "It was a quick deal."

Panther quarterback Cole Stinson played a key role. Stinson, a transfer from Ball State, helped recruit Rucker to Eastern.

"Cole and I went to high school together," Rucker said. "He was a year younger than me. Cole talked to (Eastern assistant coach) Jorge Munoz about me. Cole pretty much pulled me along. We were sort of a package deal."

Lynch added, "There was a comfort level with Cole being here."

Rebecca Yacob also had a hand in Rucker's decision.

"Part of the whole reason for me going to Eastern was her," Rucker said. "She knew that

I was thinking about transferring. She encouraged me to go somewhere else."

That somewhere else was Eastern. After having only caught four passes as a sophomore for Minnesota in 2005, Rucker became the main target for the Panthers, particularly in the red zone.

"We put a lot of play action (passes) into our offense," said Lynch. "Micah would go attack the football. He didn't wait for it to come down. Inside the 20, if the defense showed one-on-one coverage, we'd throw a fade."

With his 42-inch vertical leap, Rucker proved to be a big-play receiver for the Panthers. Rucker caught 49 passes and averaged nearly 20 yards a catch as a junior. In addition, he found the end zone 11 times.

"Sure, Micah had natural ability," said Lynch. "But he was also a hard worker. He caught over 500 balls a day (for practice). We caught all kinds of passes at different angles. He did this year round, every day."

Lynch added that Rucker went through a routine in which he caught tennis balls and even bricks to improve his hands and concentration.

"I picked that up from Jerry Rice," Rucker said. "It strengthens your hands so that the defensive back doesn't rip the ball away from you."

Eastern often designed plays to take advantage of its big-play receiver.

"For one of our plays, we'd have two backs and two tight ends with one wide receiver (Rucker)," said Lynch. "He'd run a streak (pattern). It would most always result in a catch or pass interference penalty for a first down."

Rucker's success brought added attention from opponents.

"I saw a lot more one-on-one coverage that first season (at Eastern)," Rucker said. "There was more double coverage after that."

The added attention benefited the Panther offense.

"He made running the ball easy because he was double-teamed," said Lynch.

However, Rucker still managed to reel in a career-high 55 receptions his senior year. Though his yards-per-catch (14.1) and touchdowns (seven) dipped from his junior year, Rucker earned All-Ohio Valley Conference First-Team honors for the second straight season.

Rucker signed as an undrafted free agent with the Pittsburgh Steelers. After being cut, he spent time with the Kansas City Chiefs and the New York Giants.

"I had a strained hamstring," Rucker said. "It just wouldn't heal for me. I sat out minicamp. (The injury) lingered and lingered. I couldn't perform at a high level."

While Rucker never got back into the NFL, he spent part of the 2011 season with the Chicago Rush of the Arena Football League. Rucker prepared for time after football.

"I have a communications degree from Eastern," he said. "I did some work in radio when I was there."

In addition, a friend and Rucker set up a sports performance business that trains aspiring high school athletes in search of scholarships.

"It's a chance to help young people get to where they want to be," he said.

Rucker is always ready to help others. After all, he will always remember one who helped him.

"Rebecca taught me so many things," Rucker said. "She taught me how to treat a woman and how to be a man."

On the field or off, Micah Rucker is still standing tall.

FOUR-DOWN TERRITORY

Favorite Football Movie: *Any Given Sunday* first comes to mind. *Varsity Blues* is another one I love too. *The Express* was pretty good.

First Car: A Pontiac Grand Am. It was a maroon two-door. I paid $1,700 for it. It was around a 1989 (model) or so.

Worst Summer Job: It was when I was at Eastern. There weren't really too many jobs in the area. I worked at a factory. I stacked boxes and manila folders. It was repetitious; eight hours straight of stacking boxes and manila folders.

Favorite Subject in School: English. I was a pretty good speller and writer.

OTIS HUDSON

After spending his first two years of high school on Chicago's West Side, Otis Hudson knew he had to get out.

"I was born and raised in Chicago," Hudson said from Cincinnati Bengals' training camp. "I went to John Marshall High School. The gangs were always trying to recruit me because of my physical size. I had to fight or run pretty much every day. I knew that the city wasn't the place for me and my future."

Thus, Hudson approached his parents with the idea of moving and transferring to a suburban school.

"I had some buddies I knew through AAU basketball," he said. "I knew about Barrington (High School). I knew it was a good school academically and athletically."

Hudson and his family made the move to the northwest Chicago suburb before his junior year. He played both sides of the line on Barrington's Class 8A quarterfinalist that season.

"Explosive, that's what Otis is," Barrington offensive line coach Steve Galovich told Bill McLean of the *Barrington Courier-Review*. "And he's so athletic for someone his size. But what he did after coming here was incredible. It took a lot of work and patience from him— in the classroom, in sports, dealing with an entirely different social atmosphere. But he did it, and he found people who wanted to help him along the way."

For Hudson, the move was a life-altering experience.

"It worked out great," he said. "I met different types of people. I grew as an athlete and a student."

Hudson also competed in basketball and track as a prep athlete. Both sports assisted in his growth as a football player.

"Basketball really helped with my feet," Hudson said. "Track gave me speed and endurance."

Scholarship offers came from the University of Minnesota, the University of Illinois, Northern Illinois University and Eastern.

"I had always wanted to play in the Big Ten," Hudson said.

That, combined with the prospect of play-ing with two future National Football League running backs, led Hudson to pick Minnesota.

"At that time they had two great backs in Laurence Maroney and Marion Barber," Hudson said. "I was excited about the running game with those two guys."

Initially, Hudson saw playing time as a defensive tackle for the Golden Gophers. However, the Minnesota coaching staff moved him to the offensive side of the ball. Thus, Hudson became a right guard.

Though he had reached his dream of playing Big Ten football, Hudson wasn't destined to remain at Minnesota. A coaching change at Minnesota brought uncertainty to Hudson's career.

Therefore, just as he had done as a high school athlete, Hudson made a move for his final two years of eligibility. Hudson transferred to Eastern for the 2008 season, where he joined former Golden Gopher teammates Micah Rucker and Chris Campbell.

"I went on Chris's recommendation," Hudson said. "He had left Minnesota to go to Eastern. He said he was happy being at Eastern."

Though he was 6-foot-5 and 320 pounds, Hudson wasn't immediately handed a starting job for the Panthers.

"I'm a blue-collar guy. I just wanted to play," Hudson said. "I had to earn my job. Nothing was given to me."

Hudson started 24 of his 26 games for the Panthers at right tackle. He capped his career with an Ohio Valley Conference championship and a playoff berth in 2009.

"We came together and did very well as a group," Hudson said of the Eastern line that included Campbell.

Eastern's season came to an abrupt end with a loss at Southern Illinois in the first round of the playoffs. Football became an afterthought when Hudson and his teammates received word that offensive line coach Jeff Hoover had been killed in an automobile accident on his way home from Carbondale.

"It was late at night," Hudson recalled. "I was getting ready for bed when I got a text message. It said that Coach Hoover had been in an accident. Later I got another message that said Coach Hoover had passed."

With his collegiate career over, Hudson next

focused on training for the NFL Draft.

"I came home and trained and then went to California to continue my preparation," Hudson said. "Leading up to the draft, I just continued to work."

As the April draft approached, Hudson had strong indications that either Cincinnati or Philadelphia would most likely take him.

When the draft unfolded, Hudson grew weary of sitting around.

"I was on my way to the mall," he said. "I got tired of watching the draft (on TV). Then my phone rang. It was the Bengals. I was told, 'We just put your name up.' That's how I found out."

Just like that, Cincinnati selected Hudson in the fifth round as the 152nd overall pick. Hudson was the first OVC player taken in the 2010 draft. Moreover, he was the first Eastern player to be chosen since Denver took cornerback Chris Watson in 1999.

Cincinnati line coach Paul Alexander said of Hudson, "Otis is a big, explosive man with NFL talent. In camp, you'll see that physically he's a good-looking prospect. He's a guy who has more ability than polished technique at this point, but in the fifth round, you want a guy with ability rather than just another lineman who might not be good enough. Otis is a player I can work with and develop."

Hudson's first game action as a Bengal came in the annual Hall of Fame exhibition game in Canton, Ohio. Yet, the former Panther wasn't concerned with the likes of Emmitt Smith and Jerry Rice, who were being enshrined that weekend.

"I was just focused on beating the Dallas Cowboys," he said.

Did he find irony that Dallas' starting quarterback Tony Romo was also from Eastern?

"No, I didn't," Hudson said. "Maybe I would have if I were playing defense and chasing after him. My goal was only on doing my job as an offensive lineman and beating the Dallas Cowboys in the game."

Though he remained on the Cincinnati practice squad, Hudson never player in a regular season game with the Bengals.

In the spring of 2014, Hudson signed as a free agent with the Kansas City Chiefs.

"I'm all about hard work," said Hudson.

FOUR-DOWN TERRITORY

Favorite Football Movie: To tell you the truth, I don't really have one. You can't really put football into a movie. You can't make it like it really is.

First Car: A Ford Taurus. It was a 2000 (model). I bought it from a guy who was getting a new car for himself.

Worst Summer Job: I never really had one. I was always busy with sports.

Favorite Subject in School: English. I was pretty good at it and enjoyed it.

Otis Hudson (63) was a fifth-round selection by the Cincinnati Bengals in the 2010 NFL Draft.

DINO BABERS

(2012–2013)

	1	2	3	4	T	TO
PANTHERS	7	12	7	14	40	2
AZTECS	13	3	3	0	19	0

2ND DOWN   10 TO GO   BALL ON 47   QTR 4

0:00 SYCUAN

UnionBank

TOYOTA

NO CAROLINA   10   F
SO CAROLINA   27

UNLV   23   F
MINNESOTA   51

UTAH STATE   26   F
UTAH   30

RUTGERS   51   F
FRESNO STATE 52

BOLT VISION

NEXT HOME GAME
AZTECS VS.
OREGON STATE
SEPT. 21
4:30 PM

Dino Babers succeeded Bob Spoo as Eastern head coach in 2012.

DINO BABERS

Many coaches have been around the block, but Dino Babers has been around the country—and that was even before he started his coaching career.

Born in Hawaii as the son of a navy officer, Babers later spent time on both the Atlantic and Pacific coasts. He also made stops at other U.S. locations. All of the packing and unpacking ultimately paid dividends for his coaching career.

"I knew I wanted to be a coach from the age of five or six," said Babers, the man hired to follow Bob Spoo as Eastern's head coach. "I knew I wanted to be a coach before I ever played football. I wanted to be a football coach before I was any good. I used to watch games all the time: Michigan and Ohio State, Texas-Texas A&M. I would watch every football game I could watch on an old black-and-white TV and listen to the announcers talk about strategies and this and that. It's something that I've always wanted to be."

Before he started a coaching career, Babers was a three-sport star at Samuel F.B. Morse High School in San Diego.

"I loved basketball, good sport to keep you in shape. I love track. If I weren't a football coach I would be a track coach, I love it that much," he said.

On the football field, Babers played quarterback, running back and safety. College recruiters flocked to see the 6-foot, 200-pound Babers.

"I had an opportunity to get an appointment to the Naval Academy, a chance to go to Cornell University, an opportunity to go to the University of Washington," he said.

Yet, Babers instead decided to accept a scholarship offer from the University of Hawaii.

"A, I was born there and had moved away when I was very young and had an opportunity to experience that and B, I had a recruiter at the University of Washington who, basically, didn't tell me the truth. Based off my interactions with him, I felt that if he couldn't be truthful with me before I signed, what kind of person would he be after I signed? I signed with the people I thought were the most truth-ful and honest with me during the recruitment process, and that was the University of Hawaii."

That experience has remained with Babers and shaped his philosophy as a coach.

"The hardest thing about coaches is that they try to please a lot of people because there are so many different people they have to interact with. The biggest thing is that you need to please your Maker and yourself. I want to be as honest as I can be," he said.

How honest?

"If I'm in a situation where I may hurt you or hurt your feelings, then most likely, I'm not going to say anything, but if you put enough direct questions at me, with my military background and the way I was raised, if you ask me a direct question, you're going to get a direct answer. So you need to be careful what you ask me.

"I treat people the way I want to be treated, and I try to live my life by the rules of that book, and hopefully that's enough."

Not only did Babers' recruiting experience influence him, so did his time on the field. Babers played outside linebacker, strong safety and free safety on defense for the Rainbow Warriors. In addition, Babers started at tailback and served as Hawaii's backup quarterback his senior year. He led the Warriors in rushing, while also serving as the team's special teams captain.

"I played all those positions in college because I always knew I wanted to be a coach," said the 1984 graduate, who also earned All-Western Athletic Conference Academic honors.

Babers spent one year in the Canadian Football League before an injury ended his playing career. He returned to Hawaii to begin his coaching career as a graduate assistant. Babers spent the next two seasons in a similar position at Arizona State, where he earned his master's degree in education administration and supervision.

When Spoo announced his first Eastern staff in 1987, Babers was the running backs coach.

"Coach Spoo actually hired me sight unseen," Babers recalled. "The offensive coordinator, Kit Cartwright, actually hired me at the (NCAA coaching) convention. I talked to Coach Spoo on the phone and he brought me out."

The first time Babers entered Eastern's football offices, he ran into a name familiar to Panther fans.

"The first player that I met was Sean Payton. Sean had just finished his last season here and was working out. He was walking through the football offices, and he came in and wanted to say 'hi' to the new coaches. I hadn't met any of the players who were on the team, but the first person I met was Sean Payton. He was the first player I shook hands with here at Eastern Illinois," Babers said.

Though he spent just one season as an Eastern assistant before moving on to UNLV, Babers had no trouble imagining returning to Charleston as the Panthers' head coach one day.

"Absolutely," he said in 2012. "This was always a special place for me. My dad was in the military. We moved around quite a bit, so I'd been in large cities. I'd been in small towns. I think I'm easily adaptable. I've always loved this town, it's so . . . I don't want to use the term 'perfect,' but it almost seems perfect. It's a great community, a great educational base. I love the location of it. When you come here, you're really kind of here. It's not like you can go to school here and run off somewhere else and come back. No, you're going to Charleston, Illinois. You're going there to go to school, and you're going to have a great experience. I love everything about this town, from Lincoln Avenue all the way over to Mattoon."

Another factor was Spoo, a man Babers doesn't view as only Eastern's all-time winningest coach.

"Bob and I have always been in contact," Babers said. "I started a little tradition when I would go the convention. We used to have a Bob Spoo (coaching) tree. We'd meet and have dinner at night. During that dinner I would get my cell phone, and we would call Bob and pass the phone around at dinner. Bob doesn't go to a lot of conventions. It was a way to tell Bob how much we love him, how much we appreciate him. It was a way to remind him of all those stories and how he has impacted all these people in coaching.

"When you look at the Bob Spoo tree, that tree is as impressive as Miami of Ohio, 'the Cradle of Coaches . . . Eastern Illinois' tree is just as impressive. For me to come here is a blessing. He's like a father figure to me. He's a guy I've always idolized. All those things being said, I can also sit down and we can talk football. We can talk about things we need to do to get this program going so that it's a consistent winner all the time. There is a great deal of mutual respect between both of us."

Before he had even coached his first game, Babers had made history as not only the first African-American head football coach in school history, but also as the first at an Illinois state institution.

Babers was asked if the landmark meant anything to him, or whether our society should be at a point in our history where we should be discussing other matters.

"A, we should be at a point in history where it shouldn't be a big deal. B, it means something to me, but I can't let that define me. I've always been an African-American coach," he chuckled. "But outside of that, I would like to think that I am good at my job. Others feel that I do my job well. I would just like to go out and represent Eastern in the best way that I can and try to follow a man that I admire, Bob Spoo and the job he has done here for 25 years, and if along the way I happen to represent the African-American community in a positive fashion, that would be fantastic."

Babers arrived at Eastern following a four-year stint at Baylor University, a highly successful program that produced Heisman Trophy winner Robert Griffin III. Much of Baylor's success came from its no-huddle spread offense. Babers immediately installed the offense at Eastern.

According to Babers, the team would run 150 plays in a 90-minute practice.

"Whew! Wore me out watching it . . . it wasn't quite Oregon speed, but it was no huddle, fast-paced. They kept shuttling different lines in and out, and the guys were gassed every time they came off the field. It's going to be interesting to see if this practice can be transferred to game day pace, but I was impressed by the 30 minutes I watched," said one veteran EIU observer following the opening days of spring practice.

Yet, Babers realizes that football isn't just an offensive game.

"Our defense will be the most physical, most aggressive, best you've ever seen," he declared at his introductory press conference.

While at Baylor, Babers coached special teams as well as receivers, thus the third aspect of the game shouldn't be overlooked under his leadership.

Yet, Babers' plan to make Eastern a consistent contender for the OVC crown and a regular playoff participant was focused elsewhere.

"We have to get a rallying cry. We have to get the community back involved. When Sean Payton was here, they filled up those stands and they were feeling it. Those stands were noisy. Home field advantage was an advantage. When Tony Romo was here (the same thing was true). We've got to get the community to buy back in. We've got to put a product out on that field that people want to spend their entertainment dollars on. That being said, we need to get stronger, we need to get tougher, we need to get faster. The bottom line is that those things will come if you put a product on the field that people want to see."

Babers' Panthers certainly accomplished that and more. Under his guidance, Eastern took the Ohio Valley Conference by storm. The Panthers won consecutive OVC championships, qualified for the FCS playoffs and rewrote the record books along the way. In addition, Babers won consecutive OVC Coach of the Year trophies. In 2013 he finished as the runnerup for the Eddie Robinson Award as the top FCS coach.

Baylor head coach Art Briles said, "Dino is a man that I would love for my son to play for. He combines passion with compassion. He's motivated with inspiration. He's in it for the right reasons, to help young people to succeed."

In October 2013, Josh Buchanan of *Phil Steele Football Magazine* said, "The way Babers is going he will be in the BCS, if he wants to, within two years."

It didn't take that long. Just days after Eastern lost in the FCS quarterfinals, Babers was hired as the head coach at Bowling Green State University of the Mid-American Conference. He was reportedly inked to a five-year contract worth $400,000 per season.

FOUR-DOWN TERRITORY

Favorite Football Movie: *Remember the Titans* because at the exact same time that that football team was in high school I was starting school in Norfolk, Virginia, in kindergarten. I was in the military, and we lived in a duplex home. My mom got me and my next-door neighbor, who happened to be white. Her daughter was the same age as me and we walked to school together the first day. We go into kindergarten and they tell the kids they can sit down wherever they want. She's the only one I know and we sit down next to each other. The teacher comes over and asks us if we're sure we want to sit together. She asks me and she asks the girl, and we both say, 'Yes.' Then she says, 'Well, why don't you guys change seats?' We said we didn't want to change seats. Then she forced us to change seats and then she got an African-American girl, who I did not know, to sit next to me and a Caucasian boy, who my neighbor did not know, to sit next to her. So here we are in this class where we could not sit next to each other where everybody got to sit where they wanted. Everyday we walked to school together and everyday we walked home together, but we couldn't sit next to each other in the classroom even though we played together with each other all the time. The exact same date (as "Remember the Titans") so that's why it's my favorite movie.

First Car: The first cool car I ever bought was in Charleston from Ken Diepolz, a 1985 Cutlass Supreme, a two-door hardtop with spoke rims. It looked like a gangster car. I went there to buy it. He was trying to sell it to me, and I walked away. I came back the next day and he was trying to sell it to me, and I said, "Hey, look, nobody else in this town is going to buy this car from you, so if you don't give me a good price. . . ." That wasn't my first car, but that is a true story. My first car was a four-door Buick Apollo that I bought in Hawaii off of an older lady for $450, drove it for three years and sold it to another guy on the team for $450.

Worst Summer Job: I had a summer job in Hawaii that changed me, it put me on the honor roll. After this job I was never off the honor roll. At this job, you're in a factory making cardboard boxes. You get the boxes and you push them through. The gold little staples go into the brown box. One staple went into my hand and that was just awful. But that wasn't the worst job . . . I worked in a tuna factory in San Diego. I was making more money than my dad. It was like $7.15 an hour. You got time and a half . . . double time. I was bringing in more money than my father, who had just retired from the service and getting a check from that and working as a security guard at the junior college. You got up and grabbed tuna and you put them in these trays and put them in this giant oven, cooked it and then had to debone it. I never knew tuna was that big. I was on the line where you were getting the tuna with the saws and cutting them in half and you're trying to keep up with the conveyor belt. I was trying to grab underneath the dorsal fin and cut all the way through (my hand). It was all infected. That job was bad, but the *worst* job was at the C&H sugar cane factory in Hawaii as a security guard. You had to walk around with a time card that you had to punch so they knew you were there. They didn't want you going there and going to sleep. The sugar was just out there, and people could come up and just take the sugar if you weren't there on guard. The time clocks were all around this walk. You had to punch in every so many minutes. Let's say you punched in at eight o'clock. You then had to punch in at 8:07, but you couldn't punch in until that exact time. You could walk at 8:02 and try to punch in, but it wouldn't take it until 8:07. The job was you had to figure out how to sleep and rest for exactly five minutes. You were there in the middle of night trying to figure all this out. It was stupid. It was a game I played every night. All those jobs were awful, but they all made me want to get my degree.

Favorite Subjects in School: I have two. Math because I always thought math was like football. There are rules, and if you follow the rules you can come out with a judgment that will be fair. If you know the rules you're going to come up with an answer, so I've always looked at football like that. People always say life isn't fair, well I always looked at football as fair. The game can be tilted one way or another, but in the giant scheme of things, unless they're try-ing to pull off a Titan thing like in the movie, I think that officials are fair and, in the end, it all comes out in the wash. My second thing is history. I love history. I gobble up history. When The History Channel came out, I almost ruined my marriage. I couldn't stop watching it. I like history because it's true. I like it because it's knowledge, and I like it because with that knowledge it can help you lead a better life, make better decisions, not make the same mistake twice. The Aesop fable type of thing because it can teach you things that can help you down the road.

ERIK LORA

One national preview magazine dubbed Erik Lora "The Astronaut" because "he's great in space."

"That actually came from (Eastern offensive coordinator) Coach (Sterlin) Gilbert. He made that up and it's been going around throughout the team," said Lora in the summer of 2013.

Regardless of the source, quarterback Jimmy Garopollo likes the moniker.

"I haven't seen too many people, if any, who can run the routes he runs. He gets the defensive back thinking he's going left and all of the sudden he goes right and then back left. It's hard for the DBs to react," he said. "His nickname, The Astronaut, really does fit him well because he does work so well in space."

In 2012, Lora found enough space to catch an FCS record 136 passes for 1,664 yards (both Eastern records) and 12 touchdowns.

"He had 13 catches on opening night against Southern Illinois, which at the time seemed like a huge number, but turned out to be routine," said Eastern broadcaster Mike Bradd.

FCS contributor Josh Buchanan of *Phil Steele's Football Magazine* said, "It's one of the best seasons I have seen. He's a sure-handed guy who just makes plays."

Lora came to Eastern from Miami Columbus High School. Lora followed in the footsteps of recruits Kenny Whitaker and Carlos Reyna from Miami to Charleston.

"(Eastern assistant) Roc Bellantoni recruited me," Lora said. "When I got here it felt like home, kind of family-like. The coaches were

Receiver Erik Lora rewrote the Eastern Illinois, Ohio Valley Conference and NCAA record book.

good to me. As for the school and the community, I had never been around such a small town. It was definitely a different scene from Miami. That definitely caught my eye."

Lora's potential also caught Panther followers' eyes as well.

"Erik showed a lot of promise as a freshman and sophomore and his absence due to injury in 2011 certainly hurt that team's chances of having a better year," Bradd said.

The injury forced Lora to take a medical redshirt and also tested him mentally as well as physically.

"A lot of stuff goes through your head when you have been playing football for 11 or 12 years straight and all of the sudden you can't play anymore," Lora said. "It was very depressing for awhile. I wasn't sure if I was going to be able to play again or be back to where I was."

Lora credits the hard work ethic his parents Raul and Elia—both Cuban immigrants—had instilled in him as a key to his comeback. The time away from the game also put things in perspective.

"You take football for granted, but having to sit there in the stands or stand along the sideline and not be able to play just gave me the desire to get back even more," he said. "I told myself I would never let this happen again."

When Lora did return, new head coach Dino Babers and his wide-open offense was waiting.

"There is definitely pressure on the receivers in that offense but all of the receivers, including me, embraced it," he said.

Bradd noted, "It was obvious right from the start in 2012 that Erik was a great fit in the system and was going to have a big year."

For Lora, the season's most vivid memory came at home against Murray State. Lora caught a conference-record 21 passes for 269 yards and three touchdowns. He capped it off by throwing the game-winning two-point conversion in overtime.

"That whole game is just a blur of excitement and enjoyment," he said.

Lora and his teammates won the OVC title and qualified for the playoffs.

"That was really the cherry on top after a couple of really rough seasons," he said.

Lora's jaw-dropping, record-setting junior season brought numerous accolades his way. He earned consensus First Team All-American honors and the OVC Offensive Player of the Year Award. Lora was also the league's Male Athlete of the Year, an honor that includes all OVC sports. He finished fourth in the Walter Payton Award voting.

While some may question Lora's numbers, don't count those close to the program among them.

"Erik is a high-effort guy who catches a lot of short passes and turns them into big gains, more through determination than anything else," said Bradd. "Statistically he obviously benefits from the system, but he's not catching shovel passes. Those catches last year were almost all legitimate passes and many times he took a pretty good pounding by making the catch underneath and having multiple tacklers come up to hit him. Throughout 2012 I kept thinking that Erik's numbers would drop off as defenses adjusted, but they never were able to shut him down. He has a knack for getting open, Jimmy knows how to find him, and Erik is hard to bring down after the catch."

Head coach Dino Babers told reporter Mike McGraw, "Eric Lora is a throwback, old-fashioned player. He is a guy that comes to practice every day with a smile on his face and just works his tail off. He loves the game. He works extremely hard at every single technique, every fundamental."

Lora said his best attributes as a receiver are his hand-eye coordination and his flexibility.

"Not flexible as in stretchwise, but flexible as in being able to go the right ways. I have little tricks of getting open and running after the catch. That comes from the experience of playing for so long," said the 5-11, 190-pounder.

Buchanan called Lora and Garoppolo "among the best in FCS at their positions."

Despite sitting out the final week of the 2013 regular season, Lora again earned First Team All-OVC accolades and placed seventh in voting for the Payton Award.

In the Panthers' FCS quarterfinals loss, Lora caught 18 passes for 129 yards and a touchdown.

He finished the season with 123 catches for 1,544 yards. His 19 touchdowns set the OVC single-season record as did his 33 career TD receptions. Lora set the OVC career record with 4,006 receiving yards. Lora's name tops nearly every major receiving record at Eastern. He became the first Eastern player to earn First Team All-American honors two years in a row. Lora also joined Garoppolo in the East-West Shrine All-Star Game.

Neal Bradley, winner of the 2011 OVC Media Award, said, "Lora was one of those guys who I knew was good but at the end of the game I would look up and he had eye-popping stats. Plus, there may never be a better big-play receiver than Lora."

Does Lora like being called "The Astronaut"?

"I've embraced it. I'm kind of a science/philosophy/nerdy kid so it fits my style," he said.

Lora signed an NFL contract with the Minnesota Vikings in 2014.

FOUR-DOWN TERRITORY

Favorite Football Movie: As I was growing up, *Friday Night Lights* was definitely my favorite. As I've gotten older, some of the older movies like *Any Given Sunday* have to be added.

First Car: A 2006 Mazda-6. It no longer exists; it's crushed metal. I crashed it, nothing too serious, but it's gone.

Worst Summer Job: I've never worked a real job. I never really had time to work a job between school and football and track.

Favorite Subject in School: My best subject would be math but the one I like the most is science. I'm a big fan of the unknown. I'm a big fan of space and the oceans along with archeology and geography and stuff like that.

JIMMY GAROPPOLO

Jimmy Garoppolo easily recalls his reaction to the hiring of Dino Babers.

"Baylor was playing in a bowl game a couple of weeks after Coach Babers was hired. We were sitting at home watching with RGIII going out there doing his thing, throwing it and running it. It really is a quarterback's dream offense. There are so many aspects of your game. You can throw the deep ball, the short ball, run it a little bit. It's just a great offense. I was thrilled to have it here," said Garoppolo in the summer of 2013.

That reaction came from a player who took over the Panthers' starting quarterback job just four games into his true freshman year. In fact, the opportunity to play as a true freshman was among the reasons he signed with Eastern out of Rolling Meadows High School.

"In the whole recruiting process there is a lot of deception that goes on with schools and coaches telling you one thing or another and you don't know who to believe, but Coach (Roy) Wittke and Coach (Mike) Lynch were really honest with me from the get-go. I appreciated it. It was refreshing.

"There were other quarterbacks here, but I felt I could beat them out," he said.

That wasn't the case initially as veteran transfer Brandon Large was the starter. However, Large struggled with turnovers and some poor decisions early in the season. Thus, the coaching staff began to discuss inserting Garoppolo into the backfield.

"Coach Wittke told me there was a chance it could happen at some point," Garoppolo recalled. "Coach Wittke and Coach (Bob) Spoo told me (that I would start). I was excited and a little nervous and it just went from there."

Like Large, Garoppolo would be playing behind a struggling offensive line with little support from the running game. His approach was what many would guess for a freshman thrust into such a role.

"I didn't want a loss to be my fault. I didn't want to do anything crazy. I wanted to go out there and play my game of football. I wanted to do what I normally could do. I was an 18-year-old kid going against Jacksonville State, which was ranked at the time. Naturally I was a little nervous, but I went out and held my own. It worked out well.

Jimmy Garoppolo took over as starting quarterback as a freshman and developed into one of the all-time Panther greats.

"The speed was so much faster than high school, there's no comparison. One game after another you get accustomed to it. Eventually things slow down for you and you can move forward."

Garoppolo not only moved forward, he began to see success. By season's end, he had landed on the OVC All Newcomer Team. In the freshman's final four games, he completed 68 of 109 passes for 1,052 yards. Better yet, he tossed 12 touchdowns compared to just three interceptions.

"Jimmy had some ups and downs as a freshman, but Bob Spoo deserves a great deal of credit for sticking with him and letting him mature," said Eastern broadcaster Mike Bradd. "Bob could have switched back to Brandon Large, a junior who had started the first three games, but Bob stuck with Jimmy and it was clear by the end of the year that was the right choice."

That choice only looked better as the years passed. He continued to improve as a sophomore and then had his coming out party as a junior in 2012, the season that Babers took over as Eastern head coach.

"When Dino arrived, I wasn't certain how Jimmy would fit in because I think Dino would prefer a quarterback who runs a little better

than Jimmy does. So Dino deserves credit for taking some of the running out of the system and tailoring it to suit Jimmy's strength, which is throwing the football from the pocket," said Bradd.

In 2012, Garoppolo amassed a school-record 3,823 yards of total offense. He set Eastern records for attempts (540) and completions (331). Furthermore, Garoppolo came within 20 yards of equaling Sean Payton's 3,843 passing yardage set in 1984 and fell just three touchdown passes shy of Tony Romo's 34 TDs in 2002.

"As a freshman, he was thrown into the fire real quick and he had to learn on the fly," said receiver Erik Lora, who caught 136 passes in 2012. "But he worked hard and got better every year. He's really progressed."

Garoppolo's breakout season corresponded with the change of his uniform number.

"They gave me (No.) 15 when I got here and the starting quarterback (Large) was No. 10, so I didn't really have a choice there," he said. "I had been 10 pretty much my whole life growing up, whether it was baseball, basketball or football. I wanted to get back to my roots, I guess, to lucky No. 10."

Lucky or not, Garoppolo and the Panthers won the OVC title and earned a berth in the FCS playoffs. Garoppolo set the conference single season record with 3,823 yards. He finished 10th in the Walter Payton Award balloting while also earning Second Team All-OVC accolades.

Garoppolo credited former Eastern star Jeff Christensen with his development as a quarterback. According to a *Chicago Tribune* article by David Haugh, Christensen rebuilt Garoppolo's delivery by focusing on his shoulder and fingers more than his arm.

"I used to throw like a baseball player," Garoppolo told Haugh. "He also fixed my feet."

Meanwhile, Garoppolo also began an assault on the Eastern record book, where nearly every passing category was topped by Sean Payton and Tony Romo.

"It's an honor to be mentioned in the same sentence with those two. They are two of Eastern's legends so if I'm being compared to those two then I must be doing something right," he said.

When asked to compare Garoppolo with Payton and Romo, color analyst Jack Ashmore responded, "I would be hard pressed to pick one over the other. Tony played in a more traditional offense with a strong running back, J.R. Taylor, carrying the ball. Payton and Jimmy each played in offenses that threw the ball all over the field."

Garoppolo continued his record-setting ways as a senior in 2013. He shattered nearly every Eastern record in the book. Garoppolo became the OVC's all-time leader in total offense. Moreover, he attracted national attention and looks from all 32 NFL teams, including in-person looks from three general managers. Ohio State head coach Urban Meyer called him "one of the best quarterbacks I've ever seen" after noticing Garoppolo on film while preparing for San Diego State, a team Eastern had upset in its season opener. Garoppolo was featured on ESPN's *Game Day* as well as in publications ranging from Chicagoland daily newspapers to a wide variety of Internet sites.

Garoppolo also caught the attention of rivals. Fellow First Team All-American defensive end Colton Underwood of Illinois State said, "He's unbelievable. He's so cool and calm at quarterback. There were times I would be in his face, tackling him, bringing him down and he's still completing a 60-yard bomb or a 15-yard pass for first down.

"I remember a couple of times before plays he would look over at me and wink as if to let me know it's going to be a pass play. It's confidence like that that makes him special."

Ryan Pace, former EIU lineman turned Director of Pro Scouting for the New Orleans Saints, said, "We've had multiple looks at Garoppolo. Good player. Very productive."

Longtime NFL personnel executive Gil Brandt ranked Garoppolo No. 40 in his Hot 100 Seniors rankings.

"Garoppolo has a real strong arm and is athletic (he has a 40 time of 4.8 seconds). He hails from the same school that produced Dallas Cowboys quarterback Tony Romo. Garoppolo will be a project in the NFL, but some team is going to end up with a good player after several years of work," wrote Brandt in his online column.

Meanwhile, *Chicago Tribune* columnist David Haugh wrote that Garoppolo blossomed "into the state's best-NFL caliber quarterback not named (Jay) Cutler."

Babers told Haugh, "I've been around RGIII, but Jimmy has the fastest release I've ever seen."

Bradd said, "I can't really choose between Romo and Garoppolo. Jimmy's numbers are better, but some of that is due to the system. My opinion of Jimmy has grown a lot since the season started. I think he has been tremendous all year and has improved his accuracy and decision making a lot over his junior year. It appears Jimmy will be drafted, where Tony wasn't. I'm still not ready to say Jimmy is better than Tony, but it's probably pretty close to a tie. I feel very fortunate to have been the broadcaster for their games in both cases."

Garoppolo joined Romo by winning the Walter Payton Award.

"I know it's an individual award but I couldn't have won it without all of my teammates," said Garoppolo, who also won the OVC Offensive Player of the Year Award.

Garoppolo finished the 2013 season with FCS passing highs of 374 completions (a national single-season record), 5.050 yards and 53 touchdowns while being intercepted just nine times.

Neal Bradley, who has broadcast Murray State football for 22 years, compared Garoppolo to Casey Brockman, the Racers' own record-setting quarterback.

"The thing that set Garoppolo apart was his quick release and decision making. At times, he was so good, he was more like a video game QB. Amazing skill and no weakness. A pleasure to watch. It may be because he was the most recent, but I rate him above Tony Romo, and I saw both."

FOUR-DOWN TERRITORY

Favorite Football Movie: I'd have to go with *Friday Night Lights*. It's a classic. When it first came out, I was in middle school. My team and I went and saw it in the theater. It's a very inspiring story even though they lose at the end. It's always been one of my favorites.

First Car: I couldn't even tell you the name of it. It was a small, black sports car that was nothing fancy. Actually when I came to college my parents sold it and got my little brother a new car. I'm carless right now.

Worst Summer Job: I've never had a job in general. I've never gotten a paycheck. Sports and school have occupied my time.

Favorite Subject in School: I've always liked history, whether it's U.S. history or whatever history there is. I've always been interested in the past. I think it's very true that you can't know where you're going unless you know where you've been. I've always been interested in history. The History Channel is my favorite to watch.

2013 PANTHERS RISE AS RECORDS FALL

The 2013 Eastern Illinois Panthers definitely weren't your father's football team.

Under second-year head coach Dino Babers, the Panthers reached unprecedented heights that seemingly rewrote record books week after week.

Eastern opened the season with a rousing 40-19 road victory over San Diego State, the defending Mountain West Conference champion and a Eastern opened the season with a rousing 40-19 road victory over San Diego State, the defending Mountain West Conference champion and a team bowl-bound by season's end." by season's end. After wins over instate rivals Southern Illinois and Illinois State of the Missouri Valley Football Conference, the Panthers suffered their lone loss of the regular season to Northern Illinois, a Mid-American Conference team that climbed as high as No. 14 in the BCS rankings. The Panthers lost to the Huskies by just four points (43-39) in DeKalb.

Once conference play began, Eastern rolled through the OVC by winning all eight games. Moreover, the Panthers won in dominating fashion, outscoring OVC foes 409-137. That worked out to an average score of 51-17.

Jack Ashmore has followed Eastern football since the 1970s. He has been doing color commentary since the Tony Romo years.

"This (2013) is the most exciting Eastern team I've seen," Ashmore said. "The offense is incredible and the defense gets overlooked. They (defense) are out on the field a lot given how quickly the offense scores, but they're not giving up points. The special teams play has been spotty. But, against a tough schedule, this team has been dominant."

Brian Nielsen has covered Eastern football on a regular basis since the late 1980s. He was a student during the glory years of the late 1970s and early '80s. What is his take?

"This (2013) is the best team in EIU history combining offense and defense. The defense is really good. The style of play inflates the stats not only for the offense but for the defense in a negative way. The offense is better than the 1978 and '80 teams and the defense is better than the Romo teams."

Tim Carver, Eastern's all-time leading tackler and a mainstay in the 1995 Panthers' defense, was asked what makes the 2013 so difficult to defend.

"As I look at the 2013 team in person and on TV, they appear to be much bigger and faster and athletic as a team than the 1995 team," Carver said. "The 2013 has so many quick and explosive weapons to defend that it makes them a tough team to stop for 60 minutes. Plus, they have a tremendous talent and leader in Jimmy G, who is able to get the ball wherever he wants it in the blink of an eye. We never faced anyone as good as him nor did we have to cover the entire field like the 2013 EIU offense makes you do."

Karl Park served as sports information director at Eastern Kentucky University 1970–2004. Since 2008, he has served as the executive director of the EKU Hall of Fame and coordinator of the Colonels' football boosters. According to Park, he has witnessed 511 EKU games since 1969 and seen more than his share of OVC football.

"This year's EIU team is the *most* potent offensive machine that I can remember among OVC teams that I have seen play. I believe their margin of victory in the conference games this season would bear this fact out. . . . Modern West Coast football has led to high scores and very proficient quarterbacks that can throw the ball all over the lot.

"The OVC has had some really good quarterbacks through the years. From our school, Jim Guice and John Sacca come to mind. Of course, Phil Simms of Morehead State, Kelly Holcomb of Middle Tennessee and Tony Romo of Eastern Illinois also rank very high in my 'OVC Hall of Fame Quarterback List.' Jimmy Garoppolo, to me, has accomplished the most because of his surrounding cast and his unmatched talent of getting the ball to the open man. He is at the top of the list along with Romo, who was a winner all the way and had the 'it' factor to the nth degree. Lora also ranks high among all-time OVC receivers and with his stats deserves to be considered among the best in conference history."

Writer Brandon Lawrence of *The Sports Network* was asked to rank the Eastern offense among the best in FCS history.

"It's hard to judge this offense against others in history because it's a slightly different system. The competition this team faced throughout the season provided constant challenges for which the Panthers had to adapt and conquer, and they did week after week.

"I will say this, the fewest points the Panthers scored in a single game this season was 34 against one of the top defenses in the country (Tennessee State), if that gives you any indication of the strength of this offense," Lawrence said.

Following a first-round bye, the Panthers racked up even more points on that very same TSU defense in a 51-10 second round playoff rout. However, Eastern's season ended against Towson State in the FSC quarterfinals. The Tigers rode a playoff record 354-yard, five-touchdown performance by running back (and Walter Payton Award finalist) Terrance West as Towson State outscored the Panthers 49-39. The game, played on a snowy Friday night in December at O'Brien Field, was broadcast nationally on ESPN2.

"I've been the head coach here since December of 2011 and this is the first time I've had to talk to the team after losing at home," Babers said afterward. "It's the first time we haven't sung the school song. It's pretty emotional down there. Just really hurting now in front of the cameras."

Despite the loss, Eastern finished with a 12-2 record. Meanwhile, Towson won the next week at Eastern Washington and advanced to the FCS championship game against top-ranked and two-time defending champion North Dakota State.

Babers won his second consecutive OVC Coach of the Year Award. In two seasons, Babers' Panthers went 14-1 in league games. Eastern won 11 regular season games and earned the No. 2 seed in the FCS playoffs. Babers left EIU to become the head coach at Bowling Green State University.

Quarterback Jimmy Garoppolo put together one of the best seasons ever by an OVC quarterback. He holds nearly every major season and career conference passing record. His name tops almost every Eastern record as well. Garoppolo won the OVC Offensive Player of the Year Award.

Eastern landed nine players of the OVC All-Conference First Team. Six of those selections came on offense: Garoppolo at quarterback, Shepard Little at running back, Erik Lora at wide receiver, Jeff LePak at tight end, Collin Siebert at guard and Dominic Pagliara at tackle. Meanwhile, three Panthers made All-OVC on defense: Pat Wertz at defensive lineman and Jourdan Wickliffe and Nick Beard as defensive backs.

Five Panthers earned All-OVC Second Team honors. They were running back Taylor Duncan, wide receiver Adam Drake, center Nick Borre, defensive lineman Dino Fanti and linebacker Robert Haynes.

Three Eastern players made the OVC All-Newcomer team. They were Little, LePak and offensive lineman Jimmy Lowery. Little also earned Second Team honors on the all conference specialists list as a returner.

"In terms of statistics Eastern Illinois put together arguably the greatest season in OVC history. Not only did they rank first nationally in total offense and scoring offense, but they broke nearly every offense record as a team and numerous individual records," said Kyle Schwartz, OVC Assistant Commissioner for Media Relations.

Neal Bradley, Murray State play-by-play broadcaster since 1991, said, "Offensively, the EIU team is the best I have ever seen in the OVC. The team speed, dominance and efficiency was unparalleled. Offensively, they were truly a team for the ages."

Garoppolo won the Walter Payton Award as the best FCS player while Lora finished seventh in the voting. Both players were named to numerous All-American teams, including first team spots on the prestigious Walter Camp All-America list. Garoppolo and Lora were also selected to play in the annual East-West Shrine Game, the longest running college all-star game in the country.

Siebert joined Garoppolo and Lora as first team members as Sports Network All-Americans. Drake and LePak were third team selections. The Associated Press lauded Garoppolo and Lora on its first team while Pagliara and Siebert made the third team. Sterlin Gilbert was named FootballScoop FCS Coordinator of the Year.

KIM DAMERON

On January 11, 2014, Kim Dameron was introduced as the 24th head coach in Panther history (and the fifth in the NCAA Divison I era).

Dameron had ties to Eastern, having served as Bob Spoo's defensive coordinator for the 2000 Ohio Valley Conference champion Panthers. Dameron returned to Charleston with 13 years of experience as a collegiate defensive coordinator. Moreover, he had served as the defensive coordinator at OVC member Murray State from 1993 to 1995.

Dameron began his coaching career as a graduate assistant for Lou Holtz at Arkansas in 1983. Dameron's coaching stops include Missouri State, UNLV, Murray State, Cincinnati, Stephen F. Austin, Louisiana Monroe, Ole Miss, Cornell and Louisiana Tech. He also coached a year in the Canadian Football League. His coaching experience includes four trips to the I-AA/FCS playoffs and three bowl games.

Dameron played collegiately at Arkansas as a wide receiver and defensive back from 1979 to 1982. He participated in four bowl games, including the 1979 Sugar Bowl.

Dameron married his wife Debbie shortly before leaving Charleston.

"The wedding party was the EIU coaching staff, the preacher and our families and then we went and had barbecue back at our place," he said.

The Damerons have one daughter, Krystle, who now resides in Omaha, Nebraska with her husband Mike.

Dameron acknowledged Spoo and former Missouri State head coach Jesse Branch as key figures in his coaching career. However, Dameron had no trouble naming his greatest influence.

"I was raised by a coach . . . I'm not the original Coach Dameron. It's my father, and there's no question about it, hands down," he said.

When asked about following Babers' success of consecutive OVC championships, Dameron didn't back down.

"My answer was absolutely I want to follow a coach that won like that," he said. "It means it's not broke. I have taken some jobs in my career as an assistant where it was broke and let me tell you it is tough when you start from ground zero. Let me tell you this is not ground zero. This is taking over a program that was first class and at a high level under Coach Spoo and then Coach Babers here the last two years. I'm very thankful for where they left the program and standards they set. I can't wait to get started."

EXTRA POINTS

Former Illinois governor Jim Edgar remains a big Panther fan. Here he is pictured with entertainer Bob Hope at Parents' Weekend in 1986.

JIM EDGAR

During Jim Edgar's long tenure in Illinois government, the Land of Lincoln's sports fans had plenty to celebrate. The Bears shuffled their way to a Super Bowl title. The University of Illinois men's basketball team flew into the Final Four. Northwestern played in the Rose Bowl. The Bulls won six NBA championships.

Yet, for Edgar, all of those paled in comparison to his alma mater's NCAA Division II national championship in 1978.

"Nothing was more thrilling for me than being there when they won it," said the former Illinois secretary of state and governor. "I grew up going to Eastern football games and they nearly always lost. People just couldn't believe after all those losing years that they had won. That game marked a sea of change for Eastern football."

Edgar was born in Oklahoma in 1946. However, his family moved to Charleston when he was young. Edgar attended Charleston High School where he played football and basketball. He participated in student council and served as class president. Edgar graduated from CHS in 1964.

Former Eastern quarterback Merv Baker was his football coach.

"He was kind of the god," Edgar said. "At the time I went to school you either played sports or you didn't. Those of us who played worshipped him."

Baker, an Eastern Hall of Fame inductee, was a powerful figure.

"At football practice he used to say that we would run one more play (and practice would be over)," Edgar said. "We knew that meant we still had two hours to go."

Edgar played end for Baker's Trojans. He recalled a bonfire speech that Baker gave on the eve of Homecoming.

"Coach Baker would introduce each of the players at the bonfire," Edgar said. "He called me up and said, 'Edgar, you don't have much ability, but you sure have a lot of desire.' That was probably true, but it's not exactly what I wanted to hear at the time. I was too slow to play in the backfield and not big enough to be in the line."

Upon graduation from Charleston High School, Edgar enrolled at Wabash College in Crawfordsville, Indiana.

"I left Wabash for two reasons," he said. "One was that it was very expensive. The other was that Wabash was all boys, and that's a terrible way to get an education."

Thus, after one year at Wabash, Edgar transferred to Eastern.

"I started in the summer and worked at Cavins and Bayles, which was a clothing store," he said. "It was ideal because it got me in the middle of everything. Eastern was a well-dressed school at that time. We wore blazers to class. The store was kind of a social center at Eastern."

Working in the store put Edgar in touch with a number of Eastern students.

"It was a big help when I ran for student body president," he noted.

He also met his wife Brenda there.

"She came in to buy a Father's Day present for her dad," Edgar said. "We later saw each other walking to class. Then we started dating that fall."

Edgar was elected and served as Eastern's student body president. He graduated with a bachelor's degree in history in 1968.

"Back then Eastern probably had an enrollment of 7,000 or 8,000 students," he said. "President (Quincy) Doudna ran the university. He was the dictator. That was back in the days when the university president ran things. There weren't really any faculty councils and so forth."

According to Edgar, Doudna purposely slowed Eastern's growth. At the same time, the other state schools were dramatically increasing their enrollments.

Edgar spent much of his leisure time at Eastern going to Panther athletic events.

"I used to go to all the football games and a lot of the basketball games," he said. "I knew a lot of the football players. Some were from Charleston."

Edgar's political career really got off the ground when he was elected to the Illinois House of Representatives in 1976. He was reelected two years later, the same year that Eastern captured its football national championship.

"That was such an exciting season," Edgar

said. "The year before, you thought they might have a decent team but things didn't work out."

Prior to the 1978 season, Eastern athletic director Mike Mullally hired Darrell Mudra as the Panthers' head coach. Things took off from there.

"The ('78) team was fun to watch," said Edgar. "They could pass the ball more than in other years. They could come from behind. It was really a thrill."

When Eastern qualified for the NCAA Division II playoffs, the Panthers opened the doors to a whole new world.

"Everyone was stunned they had made the playoffs after all those years of losing," Edgar said. "The day of the home playoff game was miserable with rain and cold, yet you couldn't find a seat. All those years you had seen teams like Youngstown State have success, and now here you were playing against them in a big game."

Eastern avenged an early season loss to Youngstown State in the national semifinals and earned a berth in the national championship game against the University of Delaware. Edgar was among those who traveled to Longview, Texas, for the title game.

"There were two or three chartered jet planes that flew down (to Texas for the game)," he recalled.

When Eastern pulled off the improbable 10-9 upset victory and raised the championship plaque, Edgar was among those captivated by the sheer joy of the moment.

"I just couldn't believe it," he said. "As the game played out, you just thought something would go wrong and they wouldn't win."

Yet, the Panthers pulled out the victory.

Edgar, however, didn't get to partake in the celebrations that had already broken out back in Charleston.

"There was something wrong with one of the planes," he said. "They sent the team back first. By the time we got back (to Charleston) everybody was exhausted. It was very dark by the time we got home."

The Panthers traveled to Springfield for an honorary dinner with Jim Thompson at the governor's mansion.

"He promised he would come to a game the next season," Edgar said.

With Edgar helping with the arrangements, Thompson followed through with his promise the following fall.

"I remember that Eastern fell behind something like 21-0 early in the game," Edgar said. "Governor Thompson gave me this look like, 'What are you doing to me here?' But Eastern came back and won the game."

After the national championship, both Eastern and Edgar enjoyed future success. While the Panthers played in the Division-II championship game again in 1980, Edgar was appointed secretary of state in Illinois in 1981.

Edgar would hold that position for a decade. During that time, he often attended Eastern home games at O'Brien Field. It became customary for Eastern students to hold up their drivers' licenses when he was introduced to the crowd.

"They paid more attention to the secretary of state than to the governor because the secretary of state was in charge of the licenses. That meant more to them," he said.

Edgar recalled meeting entertainer Bob Hope, the headliner for Eastern's Parents' Weekend in 1986. The Panthers' football opponent was Winona State.

"Bob Hope joked that he thought he once dated a woman by the name of Winona," Edgar remembered.

During his years as secretary of state, Edgar's mother worked for Eastern athletic director R.C. Johnson.

"We had season tickets right in front of the press box," he said. "I always preferred to sit outside rather than being in the press box. I never liked domes."

Edgar became the 38th governor of Illinois in 1991.

"My mother worked at Eastern right up until about that time," he said.

Edgar was reelected as governor, winning all but one of the state's 102 counties. His tenure as governor lasted until 1999.

"I didn't get to very many (Eastern) games once I became governor and lived in Springfield," he said. "I watch the Bears every weekend if I can. I grew up with them. I remember Red Grange doing their games back in the '50s."

In addition, Edgar's former lieutenant governor Bob Kustra is the president of Boise State University.

"I've become a Boise State fan," Edgar said. "We've gone to their bowl games."

In fact, Edgar was in attendance when Boise State used a Statue of Liberty play to shock Oklahoma, 43-42, in overtime in the 2007 Fiesta Bowl.

"That's the most exciting ball game I've ever seen," he said.

Yet, Edgar still takes pride in his hometown university and its success.

"People always talk about Eastern's football program being so good," Edgar said. "I just chuckle because when I was growing up, they never had winning seasons. When I grew up, all the winning talk centered on the years when Burl Ives played. They talked about the 'Uncrossed Goal Line' team (of 1930)."

Favorite Subject in School: History, by far. Everything else was a chore.

NICKNAME, COLORS & MASCOTS

Eastern Illinois University hasn't always gone by the nickname Panthers, worn blue and gray nor had a mascot named "Billy Panther."

According to Eastern's official athletics website, the Panther nickname "was developed after the start of intercollegiate athletics at that school. At EIU the name Panthers has not always been around, but it does date back to the 1930s."

In fact, for many years the school colors, blue and gray, were used to describe Eastern's sports teams. This was a common practice during the

Billy Panther is the official mascot of Eastern athletics.

FOUR-DOWN TERRITORY

Favorite Football Movie: *Rudy* was good, but I really liked *The Longest Yard*. It's not usually the kind of movie I like, but it stands out. The good guys won. They overcame the obstacles. When I go to the movies, I want the good guys to win.

First Car: It was my mother's car, a 1951 Chevy Fastback. It was the first year they made an automatic. When I went to Wabash, I won a car in a raffle from a clothing store. It was a 1954 Packard convertible. This was in 1965 so the car had seen better days. It had stickers all over it from different clothing manufacturers like Jockey underwear. I drove it back to Charleston. I could have gotten into trouble because I didn't register it. I sold it off because I had all kinds of problems with it.

Worst Summer Job: When I was a kid, my Little League manager was a Phi Sig. He had me clean the fraternity house for 35 cents an hour. Later they cut my pay to 30 cents an hour. I didn't know a thing about mopping the floor. There was water all over the place. I didn't realize you had to wring out the mop until they showed me. It wasn't that bad of a job, but that's what comes to mind.

early part of the 20th century for most U.S. colleges and universities. Another common practice was referring to teams by their coach's surname. Thus, the term "Lantzmen" was sometimes used to refer to Eastern's athletic teams.

Eastern's athletic website notes, "The circumstances and exact date of the derivation of Panthers can be pinpointed, although the reason why that particular 'tag' was chosen is still uncertain."

In 1930, the *Teacher College News*, forerunner of today's *Daily Eastern News*, set in motion the move toward an official nickname.

Thus, in conjunction with the Fox Lincoln Theatre, a nickname contest was held. The winner received $5 worth of tickets to the theatre.

Football coach and athletic director Charles "Pop" Lantz, football captain Gene Kintz and *TCN* sports editor Irvin Singler served as the contest judges. The October 16, 1930, edition of the student newspaper announced the Panther nickname. Three individuals—Harland Baird, Paul Birthisel and Thelma Brock—all submitted the winning nickname and split the prize.

Several other nicknames were considered. Many had Native American Indian backgrounds (Kickapoos, Ellini and Indians). Other possibilities were Blue Racers, Blue Boys, Blue Battlers and Greyhounds.

Meanwhile, the athletic website states, "The current name for EIU's mascot is Billy Panther, a nickname of the former Panther mascot in the early 1980s and 1990s that was never officially adopted by the university. The current Billy Panther made his debut on Sept. 13, 2008 prior to the Eastern Illinois football game versus Indiana State."

RIVALS

Which school was Eastern's biggest rival? It depends on whom you ask and when he played for the Panthers. However, some familiar schools crop up no matter the era.

For Lou Stivers and his teammates back in the post–World War II period, that rival was "probably Western Illinois."

"They had a quarterback named Francis McIllerney that I had been in the service with," recalled Stivers in 2010. "We got along really well while we were in the military. We used to joke about Eastern and Western and someday playing against each other. Well, we played them and I didn't have any idea that he was their quarterback. But, there he was across the line from me. On defense, I was the middle linebacker and broke through the line and tackled him. He said to me, 'I knew you were coming sometime, I just didn't know when it would be.'"

In the early 1960s, two-way star Rod Butler picked the Illinois State Redbirds.

"Personally for me, it was Illinois State because I knew more about ISU than any other school," Butler said. "That and the fact that I nearly went to school there."

Butler played in the final decade of the Interstate Intercollegiate Athletic Conference. So did Eastern quarterback Roger Haberer. Like Butler, Haberer favored ISU.

"I guess the biggest rival was Illinois State," Haberer wrote in an e-mail. "I don't have any specific memory, but we were always ready to play them. At the time Eastern wasn't a good football school/team. We struggled through almost every season.

"Indiana State and Western Illinois were two other schools that we fought but with little success, especially Western. They were always big and tough, and we were not able to beat them any of the four years I was at Eastern."

Jack Dean played on Northern Illinois' 1963 NCAA College Division national championship team. He earned IIAC Most Valuable Player honors in 1964. In the early 1970s, Dean became Eastern's head coach.

"The biggest rival I can remember was Illinois State because they were in the conference and close proximity. Another big rival was Indiana State because we were very close to Terre Haute," Dean said.

Ted Petersen played for the Panthers in the early '70s before becoming a Super Bowl champion with the Pittsburgh Steelers.

"Western Illinois was a big one, probably the biggest," Petersen wrote in an e-mail. "They were a good program, and we were a wannabe program. One of their defensive backs wore a red bandana out the back of his helmet, and the offensive line wanted to get downfield and crush him!"

Mike Mullally served as Eastern's athletic director from 1975 to 1979.

"At the time I was there it was Western (Illinois)," said Mullally. "Western was very successful. (Darrell) Mudra had been there. Illinois State was also another rival. They were closer to Charleston than Western was."

During Mullally's tenure, Mudra's Panthers won the 1978 Division-II national championship. James Warring, a Florida native, started at wide receiver for the title team.

"The year before, we only won one game (in 1977)," said Warring. "You don't really have rivals when you only win one time. During the championship season, we played Youngstown State twice, losing once and then beating them (in the national semifinals). If you want to call that a rivalry, then call that a rivalry."

Punter Jeff Gossett, a Charleston High School graduate, punted for the Panthers during Warring's era.

"Youngstown (State) was usually the team to beat, but Indiana State and Illinois State were closer rivals," Gossett said.

R.C. Johnson followed Mullally as Eastern athletic director. Johnson rated Western Illinois and Indiana State as the Panthers' top two rivals during his tenure. While WIU was a natural rival, the Sycamores' Terre Haute campus was just 52 miles from Charleston. In addition, Indiana State spent much of the early 1980s ranked among the nation's top teams.

During the same era, Mudra departed to accept the head coaching position at Northern Iowa while Eastern joined the newly established Gateway Conference in the mid-1980s. Rivalries thus took on a different look.

"During the 1980s and the early 1990s, Northern Iowa seemed to be a major rival," wrote Panther play-by-play broadcaster Mike Bradd in an e-mail. "In the '80s both schools regularly competed against each other at the top of the Gateway. Darrell Mudra left Eastern to become the head coach at Northern Iowa after the 1982 season, although I can't speak to how many bad feelings that caused. I wasn't close to the situation then."

Ironically, both schools' teams are named the Panthers.

Bradd added that Northern Iowa's home field, the UNI Dome, was "a house of horrors."

"I don't think EIU ever won there," Bradd said. "There was a 10-10 tie in Mudra's last year (1982) and after that Northern Iowa won eight straight in the Dome. EIU lost by one point there in 1985, two points in 1987, three points in 1989, one point in 1991 and four points in 1993."

Eastern fared much better against Northern Iowa at O'Brien Stadium. In one of the most memorable games in school history, Eastern slipped past UNI 31-30 on Rich Ehmke's 58-yard last-second field goal in 1986.

"That game was tied 0-0 at the half," noted Bradd.

Though the teams stopped playing each other after 1996 when Eastern moved to the Ohio Valley Conference, EIU and Northern Iowa faced each other twice in the I-AA playoffs, with UNI winning both.

"EIU lost a first-round playoff game in the Dome in 1996 when they couldn't score on first-and-goal from the four at the end of the game, down by a touchdown," Bradd said. "EIU was short-handed that night because several players got food poisoning at the hotel in Cedar Falls/Waterloo earlier in the day."

Eastern's other playoff loss to UNI came in a 2000 game in Charleston.

"They (UNI) won 49-43 in a game where (Tony) Romo passed for five touchdowns," said Bradd.

Though they no longer play in the same conference, Eastern and Southern Illinois continue to square off against one another on a regular basis.

John Jurkovic, the Gateway's 1989 Defensive Player of the Year, supported Bradd.

"Northern Iowa was our biggest rival and Western (Illinois) because they were good," said Jurkovic, an 11-year NFL veteran.

Tim Carver followed in Jurkovic's footsteps by winning the 1995 Gateway Defensive Player of the Year Award.

"There is no doubt who was our biggest, hated rival—Northern Iowa," wrote Carver in an e-mail. "Over the course of almost a decade, we traded hard-fought victories with them that were all decided by 10 points or less. As a high school senior, I watched UNI kick a last-second field goal in the dome to beat EIU 18-17. Little did I know I'd be playing in the game the next year when we knocked them out of the national #1 spot with a 21-15 victory.

"The next year, 1993, we blew our chance to beat the future NFL star QB (Kurt Warner) in the dome. We allowed Warner and (Dedric) Ward to drive 90 yards with one minute left to beat us 28-24. The sad part was that we had picked him twice in the fourth quarter previous to that last drive."

Carver added that Illinois State and "maybe" Western were also rivals.

During the last part of the first decade of the 2000s, Eastern and Eastern Kentucky regularly competed for the OVC title. In fact, from 2001 to 2009, Eastern Illinois and Eastern Kentucky combined to capture the OVC title seven times. This led to beat reporter Brian Nielsen comparing the OVC rivalry to that of Ohio State and Michigan in the Big Ten.

According to Bradd, Illinois State has emerged as Eastern's top rival in recent years.

"They play every year and it became a major point of frustration during the 2000s when ISU won five straight games. ISU won 8 of 9 over EIU from 1997 to 2007. During that stretch it seemed EIU would always find a way to let the game slip away. In 2000, EIU had a 10-point lead in the fourth quarter and ISU rallied to tie and win in overtime. In 2004, EIU had a 10-point lead in the fourth quarter, but ISU scored to get to within three and EIU fumbled the ensuing kickoff and ISU scored again to win. In 2007, EIU was driving for what looked like the winning touchdown in the final minute and fumbled the ball on a play where the

quarterback was trying to spike the ball to kill the clock. During that period, if you asked any EIU player who they were looking forward to playing the most, he would say Illinois State. We have finally broken through and won (in 2008, 2009, 2011 and 2013)," Bradd said.

On September 1, 2011, Eastern hosted ISU for the 100th meeting between the two schools. The game was broadcast on Comcast Chicago by Dan Roan, an ISU graduate, and John Jurkovic, an EIU alum. The Panthers came away with a 33-26 victory and claimed the newly established Mid-America Classic trophy.

HOMECOMING

Eastern first celebrated Homecoming in 1915 under university president Livingston Lord and head football coach Charles Lantz.

Eastern sent its alumni home happy with a rousing 52-6 victory over Shurtleff College of Alton, Illinois. The Panthers have held Homecoming activities—highlighted by their football game—every fall since with the exception of interruptions by the two world wars.

Eastern, in fact, won its first three Homecoming games. After a year with no festivities because of World War I (1918), Eastern suffered its first Homecoming loss at the hands of Illinois Intercollegiate Athletic Conference rival Millikin University in 1919.

Over the years, Homecoming has provided Eastern alumni a chance to return to campus, reacquaint with old friends and cheer on the Panthers.

Furthermore, Eastern has had more Homecoming victories than losses. Through 2013, the Panthers are 49-39-8 in Homecoming games. Since joining the OVC in 1996, Eastern is 13-5 in Homecoming contests. Since moving to the NCAA I-AA/FCS ranks in 1981, the Panthers are 24-8-1 on Homecoming.

Eastern has seen its share of key victories in championship seasons: a 19-0 shutout of Illinois State in 1928, a 15-6 triumph over Northern Illinois in 1948, a 42-7 win over ISU in 1978 and a 31-14 victory against the Redbirds in 1980. In 1982, Eastern racked up an 18-0 shutout of Akron.

Yet, the most stirring Homecoming victory

came in 1986 when head coach Al Molde's Panthers pulled out a miraculous 31-30 victory over former head coach Darrell Mudra's Northern Iowa team. Rich Ehmke's school-record 58-yard field goal on the game's final play sent a swarm of fans onto the playing field to tear down the goalposts.

The '86 victory stood as the largest EIU Homecoming crowd (11,052) until 11,549 turned out to see the Panthers throttle Southeast Missouri 55-33 in 2013. Quarterback Jimmy Garoppolo broke Sean Payton's school record for career passing yards in that game.

Eastern's longest losing streak in Homecoming games was five (1956–1960). Following a 20-20 tie with Northern Illinois in 1961, the Panthers lost four more in a row before tying Illinois State, 0-0, in 1966. A year later, Eastern snapped its winless string with a 12-7 victory over Western Illinois.

Eastern's longest Homecoming win string is 10 (2000–2009). Head coach Bob Spoo's streak began with a 33-10 win over Tennessee State and ended with a 38-28 loss to Murray State.

Spoo took over the Eastern program in 1987. His teams were a combined 17-6-1 in Homecoming games. The 17-17 tie with Illinois State in 1993 was the last tie in Panther history.

Yet for players, the game isn't always what stands out in their memory banks.

"There was a house on 7th Street, known as 'The Football House,'" said former Panther center Brad Fichtel. "Football players had been living in this house as long as I was there, and

Rich Ehmke's (6) school-record 58-yard field goal defeated rival Northern Iowa 31-30 in the Panthers' 1986 Homecoming game at O'Brien Field. Pat Carroll (11) was the holder while Calvin Pierce (21) and Derrick Wilhelms (40) provided blocking.

Quarterback Sean Payton speaks at the 1986 Homecoming pep rally while head coach Al Molde and receiver Roy Banks look on.

I had a chance to stay there a couple of years. The parade always came down 7th Street right in front of our house."

Eastern Hall of Fame linebacker Tim Carver recalled a Friday night pep rally leading up to the Homecoming game.

"One memory I do have from outside of the game was from our senior year," said Carver. "We were 6-1 at the time and the campus was pumped. The captains were invited to speak at the pep rally with Coach Spoo and give the Homecoming queen an autographed ball.

"So Coach Spoo speaks first then gets down from the stage. A couple of us are still up there on stage to share a few words then give the queen, Gina Zamboni (of the Zambonis that make hockey ice machines), the ball and congratulate her. She was a nice girl and also attractive. This is relevant because upon receiving the ball, Gina gives me and the other captains a kiss on the cheek to thank us. From out of nowhere, Coach Spoo leaps up what must have been at least three or so feet onto the stage and says into the mic with a big grin, 'Well I want a kiss, too.' Which she proceeds to give him on the cheek with a smile. Just hilarious!"

Carver has since returned to campus from his Iowa home as a fan.

"I've enjoyed experiencing the parade and general spirit on campus," Carver said. "I've also enjoyed connecting with old teammates and their wives. I've also enjoyed showing off our campus and town to my wife. It's also been impressive to see all of the new and improved buildings around campus."

O'BRIEN FIELD

The Eastern Illinois Panthers have played home football games at their present site since 1970 with several upgrades along the way.

According to Eastern's official athletic website, O'Brien Field "is a 10,000-seat stadium with Pro-Grass artificial turf that was installed in 2004."

The facility first opened as Lincoln Field, but was later named for the late Maynard "Pat" O'Brien, the Panthers' former football, track and cross-country coach and one of 10 charter members of EIU's Hall of Fame.

Mike Mullally, Eastern's athletic director from 1975 to 1979, fondly remembers the stadium.

"For a Division II program, which we were at the time, it was fine," Mullally said. "It was basic but it had all the things you needed. It was a good facility for the coaches and for the people who used it."

Eastern Hall of Fame wide receiver James Warring was one of those who enjoyed O'Brien.

"My freshman and sophomore year, it was okay," Warring said. "But when (head coach Darrell) Mudra and (offensive coordinator Mike) Shanahan and the rest of the new coaching staff came in, they redid the locker room. They made it more like a pro locker room with open lockers. It was like when you have a house and it doesn't look all that great but you throw a fresh coat of paint on it. You take pride in how it looks."

An extra press box was built atop the stadium during Mullally's tenure.

"It was a pretty casual atmosphere when I first came there to say the least," Mullally recalled. "People would walk back and forth through there and were bothering the coaches from both teams before we added on."

Mullally said the addition cost somewhere in the area of $100,000.

"That was paid for with money we raised," he said.

John Jurkovic, who played at Eastern in the 1980s and for over a decade in the NFL, often talks of his recruiting trip to Charleston.

"Those coaches weren't any dummies," Jurkovic said. "They took us there at night and tried to keep us from getting too close a look."

Yet, both Jurkovic and Warring agree that facilities are only a part of a successful football program.

"Our weight room wasn't all that big, but we made the best of what we had. Do fancy facilities make a winning program? I tell people all the time it's what's inside the people who use those facilities that really determines results," Warring said.

Perhaps one of the most compelling reasons for the continued upgrades of O'Brien was Eastern's acquisition of the Illinois High School Association's state track meets.

O'Brien Field has been the home to Eastern football since 1970.

"EIU got the girls' track meet in 1973 and the boys' in 1974," said longtime sports information director Dave Kidwell.

"The University of Illinois couldn't do it for some reason, and we got a hold of it," recalled Mullally. "It was a great thing for us."

Mullally immediately did virtually everything in his power to ensure the IHSA events would remain at Eastern on a permanent basis.

"We went above and beyond," Mullally said. "We repainted every hurdle. Can you believe that the words 'Eastern Illinois' weren't on any of them? It's been at Eastern ever since. It's one of the greatest things ever done for both the community of Charleston and for Eastern."

According to Eastern's athletic website, the meets feature nearly 5,000 competitors and 15,000 spectators each spring. In addition, a regional Special Olympics is also held each spring.

Thus, Eastern has continued to update and improve its facilities on a regular basis. Lights and another level to the press box were added in 1986 as part of the "Brighten O'Brien" project.

"('Brighten O'Brien' was) extremely important because it was the first major capital adventure we did with private funding. It began to make people believe," said former athletic director R.C. Johnson in an e-mail response.

The running surface includes a 400-meter track with nine lanes. The rest of the stadium has long jump pits, space for high jump and pole vault events and a throwing area for the shot put.

The annual track meets bring not only business to the Charleston and Mattoon areas, but also exposure and public relations for Eastern that is difficult to measure.

Johnson called the annual state track meet "huge."

"It brought potential students and student-athletes to campus that otherwise may not have known we existed," Johnson said. "I always felt it was a significant factor in our university enrollment."

Other upgrades also came during the six summers the St. Louis Cardinals used Eastern as their football training camp (1982–1987).

How important to the university and the community was it that Eastern hosted the Cardinals for those seven summers?

"(It meant) prestige, publicity, visitors coming to Charleston and some financial rewards," Johnson said.

In 1999, a $2 million "Reach for the 21th Century" renovation added new offices for coaches, meeting and video rooms, locker room, expanded weight room and athletic training facilities.

In 2004, Pro-Grass artificial turf was installed. In the summer of 2008, the team locker room was renovated.

A year later, Eastern debuted a state-of-the-art video scoreboard in the north end zone. Its estimated cost was in excess of $400,000.

Yet, Eastern football didn't always feature fancy graphics, video replays and theater-quality sound.

"We played where the library is today," said Lou Stivers, the captain of Eastern's 1948 Illinois Intercollegiate Athletic Conference team. "We had bleachers. It's nothing like they have now of course.

"During our conference championship season, they were deciding what to do with the field so we played some games over at Charleston High School. It's been a lot of years, but it seems like we played there at least twice."

"We came to the field dressed and ready to play. We went back to wherever we lived and showered after the games. That didn't bother us because most of us had been in the service for three or four years."

A decade and a half later, Roger Haberer starred at quarterback for the Panthers.

"(We played at) approximately the same location but a little closer to Grant Street to the north," Haberer said. "The field had a cinder track around it as did most in those days. The grass field was excellent, one of the best that we ever played on."

In Haberer's era, the field seated around 3,000 spectators.

"The wooden bleachers were the temporary type," Haberer said. "Some were taken down in the spring and moved to the baseball diamond. The press box was just that, a rectangular box on top of a pedestal, probably large enough to hold 8 to 10 people inside and a ladder to the top for the spotters to stand.

"Our locker room was located at the northeast corner of the field. The area is covered by a parking lot now. It consisted of two locker rooms and a storage area. Concrete floors and benches. Very Spartan, but back then we didn't know any difference. We just enjoyed playing college football."

When Eastern took to the road, Haberer noted, "most places we played had a larger seating capacity. However, we did play in a couple of high school fields in Milwaukee and one time in Michigan."

Some 30 years later, linebacker Tim Carver

relished O'Brien's "intimate" feel.

"I remember feeling like the fans were right on top of you when coming out from underneath the stands before kickoff," Carver said. "The field, being natural grass, provided us an advantage over turf teams, especially when the weather was bad."

Whatever the game's outcome, Carver maintains special memories of O'Brien.

"I have lots of memories, and pictures, from behind the stadium after games. Family, friends, and even an occasional autograph seeker, gathered to welcome us after wins and losses," Carver said.

RECRUITING

Recruiting is the lifeblood of any college football program. However, recruiting has changed just as much as any part of the game over the years.

"The biggest change (in recent years) is the pressure to commit before the senior year (of high school)," said Jerry Pettibone, who coached from 1966 to 1996 at six different universities, including Northern Illinois.

Today, Pettibone maintains a personal evaluation service for high school and junior college athletes. The main focus of the service includes determining each athlete's playing ability level and helping navigate him through the college recruiting process.

"The rules as far as contact are completely different today (than when I coached)," Pettibone said. "Now, coaches can only have contact once a week. They only get to see them play or practice a limited amount.

"There's not as much time in the player's living room. There's pressure to make an offer as soon as possible these days."

Former Eastern associate head coach and defensive coordinator Roc Bellantoni agrees.

"If you get a kid to talk for three minutes now, that's a long conversation," Bellantoni said. "In the past, it was 10 or 15 minutes."

Recruiting has become a high-speed game in which coaches are trying to nail down commitments before the opposition can do the same.

"It's so much faster," said Bellantoni. "It used

to be that we'd go down to Florida in December or January to the all-star games looking for players. Now, you go down there to show up and meet some other coaches more socially. For the most part, everything has been done by then."

Bellantoni noted that bigger programs such as the University of Illinois have already landed their commitments as far back as summer. That domino effect then steps things up for schools like Eastern.

"We're competing with Western Illinois, Southern Illinois, Illinois State, Northern (Illinois) to a degree and sometimes even with Northwestern and Illinois," Bellantoni said. "We have to get on kids early and make our offer so we get in there for our shot."

With so much competition for Illinois high school stars, Bellantoni has expanded Eastern's recruiting base.

Under Bellantoni's watch, Illinois and Florida were the core areas. When Dino Babers came in as Eastern's head coach, the focus shifted to states like Texas and Hawaii where Babers and his staff had connections.

Much of the added pressure comes from the growth of technology into the recruiting process.

"The Internet has changed it all," said Mike Sabock, who coached for 24 seasons at NIU and served as the Huskies' recruiting coordinator under head coach Joe Novak.

"There are no secrets out there," Sabock said. "Kids and parents now see who's getting offered scholarships. It's natural for them to say if so-and-so is getting an offer, what about me? I'm better than he is."

Prospective players are also now taking an active part in the process. Many of them make their own highlight DVDs or upload them onto You Tube for college coaches and recruiters to see their skills.

"It used to be that we'd send out 1,000 videotapes and you'd go out to recruit at a school and see your videos in a stack with all the other videos (sent out by universities)," Bellantoni said. "Everything is online now. The information overload is unbelievable."

Pettibone views that as a danger zone.

"A lot (of recruiting) is done over the Internet and on websites," he said. "The official (campus) visit used to be the most important part of the process. Now, it's an afterthought. The personal side of it has been removed."

Bellantoni agrees.

"You don't get to know the kid as well as you should," he said. "There are no personal relationships now compared to the past."

As a result, the odds of coaches making mistakes in their offers have increased. It also means that schools like Eastern are finding it harder and harder to get players who have slipped through the cracks.

"You don't really have those diamonds in the rough anymore," said Bellantoni.

One such example would be Pierre Walters, who came to Eastern as a 217-pound freshman who evolved into a 6-foot-5, 270-pound All-American. Walters later played with the Kansas City Chiefs.

"The chances of finding another Pierre Walters are extremely thin," Bellantoni said.

Thus, coaching staffs around the nation are spending much of their time focusing on high school players who are not only upperclassmen but rather sophomores. Some high-profile college coaches have even made offers to players still in junior high or middle school.

"That's just crazy to me," said Pettibone.

While coaches have always needed to establish bonds with prospective players, that process has also changed in the fast-paced, digital society of today.

"You have to think like an 18-year-old kid," said P.J. Fleck, the 32-year-old head coach at Western Michigan. "Texting, Facebook, Twitter, cell phones, that's how they communicate."

Bellantoni said he didn't have a cell phone until 2000 when he was the recruiting coordinator at Drake University.

"First, we were using cell phones to reach recruits," he said. "Then everybody was texting. It's illegal to text now (according to NCAA recruiting regulations)."

Thus, coaches often use any and all of these tools in their attempts to sign the next recruiting class.

Yet, coaches have to make sure their communication isn't too impersonal.

"You can't just mass-produce," Fleck said. "You have to be really careful."

Not only do coaches need to keep up with the latest technology, they also need to keep their facilities updated. In 2009, Eastern installed a $450,000 scoreboard complete with state-of-the-art audio and video capabilities. Southern Illinois opened the 2010 season in a brand-new stadium. Illinois State recently renovated Hancock Stadium and built an indoor practice facility.

"In today's economic climate it's a very tricky thing politically," ISU's Brock Spack, a former Eastern assisant, said. "It's hard for me, even as the head football coach, to see a $40 million to $50 million investment when the library needs an upgrade or the chemistry building's roof is leaking. If you're going to do it, do it right. Make it a one-time thing, not an erector set project that's going to need more later."

Bellantoni doesn't see the recruiting pace slowing down or changing.

"There's no turning back," he said.

Yet, not all see the modern recruiting game as being more difficult than that of yesteryear.

Brodie Westen, who served as both an assistant and head coach at WIU in the 1970s, recalled the days of no limits on recruiting.

"It was worse back then because it was less restrictive," Westen said. "You had coaches who were practically living at high schools. There weren't any dead periods (for recruiting) like there are now. You could be on the road for 12 months. It got way out of hand. There was a lot of babysitting that went on."

Tom Katsimpalis was a Hall of Fame basketball player at Eastern who later became the Panthers' director of athletics. He came to Eastern in 1948 from Gary, Indiana.

"Recruiting has changed so much," Katsimpalis said. "In my day, coaches packed a sack lunch, got in their cars and took off. They didn't stay in any nice hotels. They were on very strict budgets. Many of them probably spent money out of their own pockets (for their road expenses)."

No matter the era, no matter the school, no matter the financial picture, recruiting will always dominate a coaching staff's time and energy. It was true when players wore leather helmets; it remains true today.

DIVISION I-A TRANSFERS

A major shift has taken place on Football Championship Subdivision (previously known as I-AA) rosters in the past two decades. And its impact has sent shock waves throughout the game.

Starting in the late 1980s, the NCAA allowed players who met the requirements of a one-time transfer exception to go to FCS schools and play right away regardless of how many years of eligibility they had remaining.

One of the first high-profile players to take advantage of this rule was quarterback John Sacca who, having lost his starting job to Kerry Collins, left Penn State for Eastern Kentucky in 1994.

"(The rule) really changed the I-AA level dramatically," said former Eastern head coach Darrell Mudra.

After leaving Eastern following the 1982 season, Mudra spent the next five seasons at the University of Northern Iowa.

"I didn't have any transfers," Mudra said. "But, I know (former Mudra player and current UNI head coach Mark) Farley has several."

Furthermore, Mudra likes the rule.

"A lot of these players at the I-A level would just be sitting on the bench for four years," he said. "It's a nice opportunity for them to go and play right away without having to sit out. I'm all for giving kids a chance to play."

Wide receiver Frank Cutolo was one of those kids looking for a chance to play. After spending a year at the University of Mississippi, the Florida native transferred to Eastern. Though he had an offer from Colorado State, Cutolo chose to sign with the Panthers.

"I was just looking for a place to play," Cutolo said. "Sitting out a year (to transfer to a I-A school) wasn't something I wanted to do."

Former NIU head coach Bill Mallory was on the other side of the fence at I-A Indiana University.

"I had no hang-up with that at all," Mallory said. "If a player wasn't happy and thought an opportunity was better somewhere else, we wouldn't hold him up."

Perhaps Western Illinois cashed in the most quickly.

"We had our share," said John Smith, former WIU defensive coordinator.

The Leathernecks accepted the transfer of running back Aaron Stecker from Wisconsin in 1997. Stecker had seen his playing time diminish with the emergence of future Heisman Trophy winner Ron Dayne.

Stecker rushed for 2,293 yards en route to being named the Gateway Conference Player of the Year. Stecker, who later played more than a decade in the NFL, finished as WIU's career rushing leader with 3,799 yards in only two seasons in Macomb.

"Aaron Stecker proved to be a great recruiter for us," said former Western head coach Randy Ball. "People knew of his reputation and what he had done in the Big Ten. If he chose to come to Western, then it looked pretty good in their eyes."

Brandon Jacobs is another prime example of the power of the transfer. With one year of eligibility remaining, Jacobs was stuck behind future NFL first-round picks Carnell "Cadillac" Williams and Ronnie Brown at Auburn.

Thus, Jacobs transferred to Southern Illinois for the 2004 season. He rushed for 922 yards and 16 touchdowns for the Salukis. He also attracted the attention of NFL scouts and found himself being drafted by the New York Giants in the fourth round. Three years later, he was a Super Bowl champion.

However, the success of Jacobs and others like him spurred the NCAA to implement a little-known rule in 2006. The rule prohibits seniors-to-be in Football Bowl Subdivison programs (formerly I-A) from transferring to FCS schools and being able to play immediately.

The rule change occurred because the NCAA was concerned that such players were transferring for purely athletic reasons, and thus a market was being created for top-tier talent by FCS schools seeking one-year "hired guns."

As a result, a transfer must now have at least two years of eligibility left to be allowed to play right away, or, as in the case of Jake Christensen, must have already earned a degree from his first school.

Having lost his starting quarterback position to Ricky Stanzi at Iowa, Christensen transferred to Eastern, a school his father Jeff had starred for in the early 1980s. Ironically, the elder Christensen had transferred from Northwestern under the old rules.

Yet, it wasn't so easy for Jake Christensen. First, there was the matter of earning his degree from Iowa. According to his father in an August 2009 *Times Courier-Journal Gazette* story by Brian Nielsen, Jake Christensen did so by earning 42 credit hours after January 2 of that year.

Next, Christensen had to enroll in kinesiology and sports management graduate school programs that didn't exist in the University of Iowa's curriculum.

Finally, he had to be granted eligibility by the NCAA.

Christensen, the former *Champaign News Gazette* Illinois Player of the Year, led Eastern to the 2009 Ohio Valley Conference title and an automatic playoff berth. Joining him in the Panther backfield were fellow transfers Mon Williams and Chevon Walker (Florida) and Jimmy Potempa (Michigan).

Despite the transfer rule, most coaches would still prefer to have players from the time they are freshmen.

"I'd like to be able to develop a kid from year one but there are circumstances that don't always make that possible," said Eastern head coach Bob Spoo.

The long-time Panther coach has seen the positives and negatives of the transfer rule firsthand. While Christensen was a success, Walker and University of Illinois transfer D'Angelo McCray were ultimately kicked off Eastern's football team for rules violations. Interestingly, Walker wound up leading the University of Sioux Falls to the NAIA national championship game after being dismissed by Spoo.

Despite its risk, the transfer rule is not likely to disappear. Therefore, coaches must see its value.

"You've got to go after transfers these days (if you want to be successful)," said Smith, now an associate athletic director at Eastern.

Mudra agreed.

"That's true for all the top contending schools in I-AA," he said.

An example of this occurred in the 2010

FCS Championship game. Eastern Washington and Delaware met for the title. Each team was quarterbacked by an FBS transfer: Bo Levi Mitchell from SMU and Pat Devlin from Penn State, respectively.

Still, not everyone likes the transfer rule.

"I never liked it because there are some I-AAs that are basically upper level junior colleges," said Todd Berry, who coached Illinois State from 1996 to 1999.

"Schools that consistently took transfers were certainly within the rules and had the right to do so," Berry continued. "One school in our (Gateway) conference in particular seemed like that's all they did. They'd lose players and have a different team every year. It was easy to get rich every year."

Berry has seen the rule from both levels. After his success at ISU, Berry fulfilled a lifelong dream as the head coach of Army, the Division I school at West Point, New York.

"I always felt that you cheated players out of a bonding experience. I have nothing against giving kids a second chance. But too often, it's too easy of a way out," he said. "It's easy for the I-AA schools, but it's also the Division I-A schools not taking responsibility for the guys they recruited."

Berry was especially bothered by the schools that didn't offer scholarships for football.

"I-AA is a great brand of football when it's played by the all-encompassing group that fully funded their programs," Berry said. "But there are schools that are only around because of Division I-A basketball and want to get into the (NCAA) tournament. They should be playing at the Division III level (in football). They really dilute the (I-AA) level."

Illinois State head coach Brock Spack views accepting transfers as walking a fine line.

"You've got to be careful who you bring in," said Spack, the former Purdue defensive coordinator under Joe Tiller. "If you bring in the wrong guys, you can rot your program from the inside out. You have to look at the motivation for the player who is leaving. Was he having off-the-field issues? Was he struggling academically? Was he stuck behind really talented players?"

Jerry Kill, head coach at Northern Illinois and Minnesota, has seen the transfer rule from both sides.

"We didn't take a lot of them, maybe two or three," said Kill, who coached at Southern Illinois from 2001 to 2007. "You don't want to punish a kid, but then again, you don't want them to always have an easy way out. It's a fine line."

Kill added that the 2006 rule change was a step in the right direction.

"The way the rule stands now is probably the way it should be," he said.

Ultimately, no matter one's view of the transfer rule, it has become part of today's college football world. If you're an FCS coach these days who's after a conference and/or national championship, transfers have become yet another aspect of the crazy world of recruiting.

THE MONEY GAME

Having a Football Championship Series school like Eastern playing games against its big brothers of the Football Bowl Subdivision has become as much of a late summer occurrence as bees and fantasy football drafts.

Occasionally there are upsets such as defending FCS national champion Appalachian State shocking Michigan in Ann Arbor in 2007, or Ohio Valley Conference contender Jacksonville State rallying past Ole Miss in 2010.

However, usually teams like Eastern find themselves on the wrong side of lopsided scores. Case in point: the Panthers suffered double-digit defeats to the likes of Purdue, Illinois, Penn State, Iowa and Northwestern in recent years.

So, why in the world would these games be scheduled?

"Mostly for the paycheck," said Stewart Mandel of *Sports Illustrated* in an e-mail. "These (FCS) schools are operating on a small budget to begin with and the guarantees from those games ($300,000–$400,000) account for a good chunk of it. It's also considered a big thrill for the players to be able to play a brand-name team in their stadium."

That's *their* stadium as in the big boys from the FBS stadium. You won't see any of these games taking place on FCS fields.

So, what's in it for the BCS schools? Why

bring in a team like Eastern?

"Mostly, because they are cheap," Mandel said. "A guarantee to get even a low-level FBS team is running around $800,000 these days, with some getting $1 million. Supply and demand. The FCS schools come cheap."

For Eastern, this trend started in 1985. The Panthers played at the University of Kansas of the Big Eight Conference. Eastern came home with $200,000 and a 44-20 thumping.

"The game came about because of my friendship with the Kansas AD," wrote former Eastern athletic director R.C. Johnson in an e-mail. "It was a significant payday. The primary reason to play a game like that is for the financial boost. Secondary is the recruiting and stature of the program. However, the chances of winning are so slim you cannot do a steady diet of it. The additional revenue helps to balance the athletic department budget and therefore puts less of a strain on the university's budget."

Fast forward to 2009, when Eastern received a $400,000 payday when it traveled to play Joe Paterno's Penn State Nittany Lions. Similar paydays came against Purdue and Iowa. Moreover, these games also gave the Panthers the opportunity to play on television for outlets like the Big Ten Network.

Johnson later sat on the other side of the fence as the athletic director at the University of Memphis, an FBS member.

"The larger school gets a home game which they do not need to return. The revenue you generate far exceeds the guarantee," Johnson said.

However, not everyone shares in Johnson's sentiments.

"I have lots of thoughts about doing it," said former Eastern athletic director Mike Mullally, who presided over the Panthers' Division II program from 1975 to 1979. "You ruin a team. First off, you're telling (your) kids they are for sale. You may be somewhat close in talent against the (FBS) opponent with your starters, but once you get beyond the first 22 players on offense and defense, the depth takes over. They are better.

"It beats you down physically and emotionally. In fact, it's more of an emotional problem. It's going to take your team awhile to recover from it. It bothers the hell out of me, and I just wouldn't do it."

In addition to the schools listed earlier, Eastern has played the likes of BYU, Navy, Missouri, Kansas State and Hawaii. The Panthers have posted five victories over Division I-A/FBS schools. Interestingly, the first four are now members of the Mid-American Conference: Akron in 1989, Western Michigan in 1996, Northern Illinois in 1998 and Eastern Michigan in 2004.

However, the most significant victory came on August 31, 2013, when Dino Babers' Panthers routed San Diego State, the defending Mountain West Conference champion, 40-19, on the road.

Veteran Eastern broadcaster Mike Bradd said that "San Diego State is the most highly regarded opponent that Eastern has ever beaten."

Beat writer Brian Nielsen added, "I would agree with Mike that there is no question this has to be the best team EIU has ever beaten. On the other hand, no win in August can ever top a national championship regardless of the division. The likelihood of going from 1-10 and talk of dropping the program, to winning an NCAA Division II title, is still the most unlikely story.

"It is too bad a lot of people here probably don't recognize how good a Mountain West Conference champion San Diego State is. This is really a great one-night accomplishment."

That accomplishment looked even better when San Diego State finished second in the Mountain West standings and earned a berth in the Famous Idaho Potato Bowl.

Eastern has played in four NFL stadiums. The Panthers have played San Diego State at Qualcomm Stadium, home of the San Diego Chargers. They have also played at Joe Robbie Stadium, home of the Miami Dolphins, against Florida Atlantic in the early 2000s. Eastern played several games against Illinois-Chicago in the early 1970s at Soldier Field, home of the Chicago Bears. The Panthers regularly played Ohio Valley Conference foe Tennessee State at LP Field in Nashville, home of the Tennessee Titans.

If history is any indication, each fall big-time FBS schools will continue to take heat for scheduling teams like Eastern. Yet, while the national media and bigger schools' alumni may thumb their noses at these games, these road contests will continue to be played.

Mark it down on your calendar just like those reminders to buy bee repellent and fantasy football draft guides.

THE DEFENSE DOESN'T REST

While it's usually the offense that grabs the headlines and highlight reels, defense certainly plays a key role in producing winners.

That concept is no different when it comes to Eastern football. When one examines the recent success of Panther football, defense is right at the forefront.

"Look at just about any championship team or contender and defense is always a key," said John Teerlinck, the former Indianapolis Colts defensive line coach.

Teerlinck saw firsthand what a stout defense could do. After a standout career as a defensive lineman at Western Illinois University, Teerlinck served as the defensive coordinator for Darrell Mudra's 1978 NCAA Division II national champions.

"Teerlinck's defense deserves much of the credit for that championship," said head coach Darrell Mudra, a College Football Hall of Fame inductee.

That championship defense featured the likes of future Eastern Hall of Fame players

Pete Catan and Randy Melvin. Yet, there were also players such as Alonzo Lee, Tom Seward, Ray Jeske and Rich Brown.

"Rich Brown was big-time," said two-time All-American Robert Williams. "People forget just how good he was back there in the secondary."

Brown led the Panthers in 1978 and 1980 with seven interceptions. In fact, Brown ranks as Eastern's career leader with 17 interceptions. He and Kevin Gray (also with seven interceptions) anchored the '80 defensive backfield as Eastern spent most of the season ranked No. 1 in the national polls. Catan and Melvin were joined by Ira Jefferson in leading the Panthers' defense.

Two seasons later, Eastern qualified for the Division I-AA playoffs for the first time in school history. The Panthers turned in an unbeaten regular season and advanced to the quarterfinal round of the playoffs.

Defense again reigned supreme as the Panthers yielded just 8.8 points per game during the regular season. In fact, in its final four regular-season games that season, Eastern allowed only 21 total points.

While Williams ruled the defensive backfield, defensive ends Greg Duncan and Keith Wojnowski were bookends who collapsed the line of scrimmage.

"We dominated games that season," Williams said.

Following the "Eastern Airlines" offensive era of head coach Al Molde in the mid-1980s, defense again returned when Bob Spoo began his long tenure as head coach.

John Jurkovic, a holdover from the Molde era, won consecutive Gateway Conference Defender of the Year Awards in 1988 and 1989. Tim Lance captured the honor in 1990, making three straight years that a Panther won the award.

"That was quite a run we had for sure," said defensive coordinator John Smith.

Tim Carver became the Panthers' all-time leader in total tackles and solo tackles in the mid-1990s. Carver grabbed the Gateway's Defender of the Year hardware in 1995.

"His tackle totals were amazing," said Panther play-by-play broadcaster Mike Bradd.

The Panthers left the Gateway and joined

Defense has always been a part of Eastern football success. Tyrone Covington (33) once recorded 25 tackles in a single game.

the Ohio Valley Conference in 1996. While a new era of Eastern football began, much of its future success relied on defense. In 2002, Nick Ricks became the first Panther to win OVC Defender of the Year honors. Ricks was inducted into Eastern's Hall of Fame in 2011.

"Nick is one my favorites," said defensive co-ordinator Roc Bellantoni. "He was a great player. He was a little undersized, which stopped him from playing at the next level. Nick is the smartest player I ever coached. He could have played any position. He had great instincts."

Clint Sellers and Donald Thomas won the OVC Defender of the Year in back-to-back years (2005 and 2006).

"Clint just took over games," said Bellantoni. "Four or five plays can pop into my head that were significant in Clint's career. There was a game in 2005 against Jacksonville State that decided the conference title. Clint grabbed an interception and ran it back 30 yards.

"Clint was a Ray Lewis–like inspiration guy. He would make a play and the whole stadium knew about it. Clint Sellers had a little wild side to him. He lived on the edge. He walked the line. But in football terms, he was the best teammate you'd want. The other guys loved him and followed his lead."

Bellantoni called Thomas "the most talented

Donald Thomas (54) was the 2006 Ohio Valley Conference Defender of the Year.

and fastest" of the award winners.

"Donald didn't really have a good 2005 season," Bellantoni said. "He was the third wheel behind Sellers and Lucius Seymour."

However, Thomas underwent what his defensive coordinator termed "an amazing transformation" during the off-season.

"Nobody had more of a burning desire than Donald Thomas," Bellantoni said.

When Sellers got hurt on the first play of the 2006 season, Thomas became the rock

Pierre Walters (91) earned All-American honors before an NFL career with the Kansas City Chiefs.

that anchored the Panther defense. By season's end, he stood out as the top player in the OVC.

"He was probably the most satisfying to watch (win the award) because no one expected it," Bellantoni said. "All of the effort and time he put in paid huge dividends."

Thomas spent some time playing football in Europe. He also pursued a graduate degree toward a career in law enforcement.

Though he didn't win the OVC Defender of the Year, Pierre Walters enjoyed post-Panther football success. Walters played with the Kansas City Chiefs of the NFL.

"Pierre came to us at 217 pounds as a freshman," Bellantoni said. "He lived in the weight room. By his sophomore year he was 235. By his junior year he was 245."

Walters topped out at 6-foot-5 and 270 pounds. He earned Associated Press Second Team All-American status in 2008.

"Pierre didn't qualify (academically) as a freshman, but he got his degree and was a two-time captain of our team when it was all said and done," Bellantoni said. "He might have won the top defensive player in the OVC if not for the fact that we were 5-7 that year. Usually those awards go to guys on winning teams."

Bellantoni also felt the same was true for linebacker Nick Nasti, a first-team all-conference selection in 2010.

"Nick played the best linebacker technique than anybody we've had," Bellantoni said. "He was always in the right spot."

Nasti led the OVC in tackles, but Eastern won two games his senior year.

"We had him for 143 tackles but the conference had him for 114," Bellantoni said. "We have the advantage of looking at game tape in super slow motion. He had 26 tackles against Jacksonville State."

Yet, Bellantoni was quick to point out that Nasti also excelled off the field.

"He had over a 3.5 (GPA) as a finance major," Bellantoni said. "He's the kind of kid we want representing Eastern Illinois University."

The 2013 Panthers boasted three All-OVC First Team selections: defensive lineman Pat Wertz along with defensive backs Nick Beard and Jourdan Wickliffe. Beard was a repeat pick, having also been selected in 2012.

NORTH OF THE BORDER

The Canadian Football League has felt an Eastern influence over the years. To date, a dozen Panthers have played professionally in the CFL.

The migration to Canada began in 1951 when three-sport star Ed Soergel signed with the Toronto Argonauts. A quarterback in his college days, Soergel originally signed with the Cleveland Browns of the NFL but decided to play for the Argonauts.

Soergel, an All-Canada selection at defensive back his rookie year, made a key interception as Toronto captured the 1952 Grey Cup. Soergel, who passed away in 1975, was inducted posthumously into Eastern's Hall of Fame in 1984.

Eastern's 12 players in the CFL include 5,000-yard collegiate rusher Chris "Poke" Cobb, defensive lineman Pete Catan and wide receivers Scott McGhee and Frank Cutolo.

Cobb played one season in Canada. He rushed for 61 yards on 12 carries while playing for Hamilton in 1980.

Catan and McGhee, Cobb's teammates on Eastern's 1978 national championship team, enjoyed longer CFL careers.

Catan spent three seasons with the Winnipeg Blue Bombers and Hamilton Tiger-Cats before jumping to the United States Football League for the 1983 season.

"Pete was one of the best players in the league," said Ted Schmitz, who coached for 10 years in Canada. "He was a dominant player in the CFL. No one could handle him. You had to double-team him."

McGhee played two seasons with Toronto. In both of McGhee's years in the CFL, the Argonauts played for the Grey Cup. Like Catan, McGhee left the CFL to sign with the Houston Gamblers of the USFL.

Schmitz, meanwhile, had played at Eastern in the 1960s. He called the CFL "a true speed league."

"It's the speed and the wide field that really make the Canadian game different (from the NFL)," said Schmitz. "There are 12 players on a wide field. You only have three down-linemen (on defense). What's more is that those linemen have to start a yard off the ball on the snap."

Frank Cutolo won the 2003 CFL Most Outstanding Rookie Award (Photo courtesy of Frank Cutolo).

Schmitz said the CFL is comparable to today's college game.

"The types of spread offenses you see these days are what you see in the CFL," he said. "Coaching in Canada prepared me well (for later coaching and radio commentary assignments)."

Cutolo, who played at Eastern from 1998 to 2001, won the CFL Most Outstanding Rookie Award in 2003 while a member of the BC Lions.

"I enjoyed my time in the CFL," Cutolo said. "While the game is more wide open in Canada, I wouldn't say it benefited my game any more than had I played in the NFL. The hardest adjustment for me was getting used to the 12 guys on defense. All the motion was really different too. I didn't really like it. Fortunately for me, I didn't have to go in motion that often."

Casey Printers quarterbacked the Lions when Cutolo played.

"The guy (Cutolo) was a blazing receiver," Printers said. "He caught the longest touchdown pass of my career (105 yards). He was sure-handed and aggressive. He also was a pretty good punt return guy for our club. Frank Cutolo is one of the guys I will never forget."

Perhaps no Panther was more popular, however, than native Canadian Chris Szarka. Born in Vancouver, Szarka played fullback for two seasons at Eastern (1995–1996). After leading the team in receptions, Szarka was a second-round selection by Saskatchewan in the 1997 CFL draft.

Szarka was twice been named his team's most popular player. He played 14 years in the CFL.

"The fans have always loved the big fullback," said Murray McCormick of the *Regina Leader-Post*. "They all feel he's underutilized, which has led to his popularity. He's also a guy who just runs forward and runs over people. Kind of hard not to like that kind of a football player."

Meanwhile, Panther players aren't the only ones to find success north of the border. Head coach Kim Dameron spent the 1999 season as the secondary coach with the Toronto Argonauts.

Darrell Mudra, Eastern's head coach from 1978 to 1982, coached the Montreal Alouettes into the CFL playoffs in 1966.

"It was an experience that I enjoyed for the most part," Mudra said.

Like Mudra, George Bork is a member of the College Football Hall of Fame. The record-setting quarterback from Northern Illinois University played for Mudra in the CFL.

"He was a great motivator and he was very intense," Bork said of Mudra. "He really worked at the psychological part of the game.

"He's had success everywhere he's gone. There were times when I thought he was a genius, and there were times when I would just shake my head. But, if you look at his record, you lean toward genius."

USFL

While to some sports fans and historians the short-lived United States Football League may be a footnote, it was so much more to players and coaches from the era.

"There were a helluva lot of good players in that league when you look back on it," said John Teerlinck, who has coached defensive linemen in both the USFL and the NFL.

For the record, the USFL played three seasons (1983–1985). The league proved to be the NFL's strongest competitor since the American Football League of the 1960s. After a reported loss of more than $163 million, the USFL folded after its antitrust lawsuit appeals ended.

As Teerlinck noted, the USFL sent a number of players into the NFL. As of the publication of this book, six USFL alumni are enshrined in the Pro Football Hall of Fame: coaches Marv Levy and George Allen, along with players Jim Kelly, Steve Young, Reggie White and Gary Zimmerman. In addition, well-known stars such as Doug Flutie, Herschel Walker and Sean Landeta cut their teeth in the league.

Teerlinck also experienced his first taste of coaching pro football after six years in the college game. Teerlinck coached under Allen with the Chicago Blitz and Arizona Wranglers/Outlaws.

Renowned heart surgeon Dr. Ted Diethrich originally owned the Blitz. However, in one of the strangest transactions in history, Diethrich sold the Blitz to Milwaukee heart surgeon James Hoffman. The Diethrich group then bought the Arizona Wranglers from Jim Joseph. Diethrich and Hoffman then agreed to swap their assets—players, coaching staffs and all. The result was that, with few exceptions, the 1983 Blitz became the Wranglers, while the 1983 Wranglers became the Blitz.

"That was some deal," Teerlinck said. "He arranged to swap the two franchises. We made out pretty well because we got the better team by far."

Teerlinck, who played at Western Illinois and coached at Eastern, was reunited with two players from his past. Former Eastern rush end Pete Catan played for the Houston Gamblers. Dave Tipton, Teerlinck's former teammate at WIU, played for the Michigan Panthers when the franchise won the inaugural USFL championship game. Teerlinck later coached Tipton with Arizona.

Joining Teerlinck on Allen's staff was former WIU player and record-setting Illinois high school coach Don "Deek" Pollard.

"The best job I ever had in pro football was working for George Allen," said Pollard. "We'd go to camp in January or February, then open the season in the spring. Once the season ended, you'd have four or five months to live like a normal human being. There wasn't any combine. There wasn't any minicamp. Yes, you still worked, but it was out of the office and hours that were like 9-5. You had a life to do things other than football. There's no such thing like that in the NFL these days."

Pollard didn't start with Allen. Instead he began his USFL coaching career on Red Miller's Denver Gold staff for the 1983 season. Miller had coached Pollard as a WIU player in the late 1950s.

However, Miller's USFL stay was short-lived. He and Gold owner Ron Blanding clashed almost from the very beginning. Pollard's loyalties remained with Miller.

Pollard said, "(I remember) seeing Red Miller reach into his own pocket to pay for Larry Canada's signing bonus with Denver. I don't remember the amount, but I saw it firsthand."

"Red sold 42,000 seats that first season. People bought those tickets because of him. Red and the owner didn't see eye-to-eye. The owner was penny-pinching."

Though his tenure in the USFL lasted only into the middle of the '83 season, Miller saw enough of the league to believe in its concept.

"That league had a chance because it had a TV contract. That gave them a base to fight their way to be competitive," Miller said.

However, when owners such as Donald Trump of the New Jersey Generals began to overspend, the USFL began to struggle.

"The downfall was the signing of Herschel Walker. He made more money than my whole team," Miller said.

While owners like Trump tried to buy their way to a championship, others relied on territorial rights to collegiate players and former NFL and Canadian Football League veterans to fill out their rosters.

Thus, players like Tipton and former Eastern stars Catan, Scott McGhee and Jeff Gossett found themselves in the USFL.

"It's the same old story that every year there's so many good players that never get a chance," said Pollard. "They get left behind and never get to show their wares. Sometimes the best player is the ninth picked (in the draft)."

As with any upstart league, there are wild tales. Pollard remembered one from his days with the Gold.

"That first season several teams trained in Phoenix. Red worked it out that our ownership got each of the coaches a car to use. But, they were rent-a-cars and they were wrecks. Well, Charley Armey was driving to practice. It had rained hard that day. We got to the practice facility, which was only about two blocks away. Charley was doing wheelies on this open concrete area. We started stretching and heard these police sirens approaching. I told Charley he'd better hide behind a tree or something. When the police came, I was pointing at him, everybody was breaking up. But, it turned out, the police were there for something else."

Catan, meanwhile, brought his unique way of looking at life to the USFL.

"Pete was such a solid Christian, but there was a part of him that had that crazy streak," said former Houston Gambler teammate Joe Bock. "He was a practical joker."

Bock recalled a time when Catan shot Roman candles off his helmet one day during practice.

"He always had something going on," Bock said. "It was like the Fourth of July with him

Former Eastern standout Pete Catan (77) flushes Steve Young (8) from the pocket during USFL action (Photo courtesy Pete Catan).

every day. He never let up. The coaches would just shake their heads and walk away. 'That's just Pete being Pete,' they would say."

One of the most bizarre and entertaining stories from the USFL occurred on the campus of Northern Illinois University in DeKalb. When Bill Mallory left NIU after winning the Mid-American Conference championship and California Bowl in 1983, former Indiana head coach Lee Corso was hired to coach the Huskies.

Corso, who has since moved into a highly successful analyst position on ESPN, didn't even last a single season.

"There were rumors swirling about the USFL and the Orlando Renegades," said former NIU assistant Mike Sabock. "We were playing our ninth game of the season against Central Michigan. Lee always assigned us certain things to watch during warm-ups like if the other team was wearing the right shoes for our turf or whatever. Lee always slapped the table and off we went. So we (coaches) went back inside to meet. After we all gave our reports, Lee said, 'One more thing, staff meeting tomorrow at eight o'clock.' He slaps the table and leaves. We're all sitting there wondering the worst.

"Well, Lee lived in the stadium. His wife never moved to DeKalb. She was still back in Bloomington (Indiana). So, Lee lives in the stadium. Actually it was the room that later became my office. He slept on a couch, used the bathroom down the hall and showered in the locker room.

"So the next morning we pull up to see his car packed with all his belongings. There's only enough room for the driver. The car is parked facing the exit. He gathers us together, tells us that he's leaving to coach Orlando in the USFL, slaps the table and leaves."

Just like that, Corso was gone from DeKalb and into the USFL.

Pete Rodriquez, the former Western Illinois head coach, recalled his first USFL training camp as special teams coach with the Michigan Panthers.

"We had no goalposts," Rodriquez said. "We were practicing on baseball fields. You had to kick the ball between the scoreboard and a tree."

Rodriquez also remembers the Panthers' equipment manager being handed a bag full of quarters to get the team's laundry done.

While Rodriquez and the rest of the USFL debuted in the spring of 1983, Rick Johnson was preparing for his final year as Southern Illinois quarterback that fall. Johnson helped lead the Salukis to their only national championship.

As a pro, Johnson earned his way onto a USFL roster. Moreover, Johnson earned four starts over two seasons with the Oklahoma Outlaws.

"Jim Lampley was interviewing me one time before a start against Steve Young," Johnson said. "He was really working the low-budget, free-agent quarterback vs. the $40 million man angle. He asked me if I felt any pressure. I told him no that I didn't. He responded by saying. 'Really?' Sure, I said, because if I play half as well as Steve does, then I should get $20 million. He (Lampley) really liked that."

Despite success in the USFL, nearly all of the players harbored hopes of returning to the NFL.

Gossett, the former Eastern punter and baseball star, played for the Chicago Blitz and Portland Breakers.

"I always believed that playing in the USFL helped me get back to the NFL," he said.

While Gossett was able to get back to the NFL, many players saw their careers come to an end when the USFL ceased operations. The league shut down after its lawsuit yielded only $1 in damages.

With CNN emerging as a media leader with its 24-hour coverage, the network quickly broke into its schedule to report the legal decision. Among the first members of the general public interviewed was former Eastern backup quarterback Gary Scott.

Talk of the USFL moving to a fall schedule to compete with the NFL also proved to be a failure.

"I never could understand that (move to fall). They had a good thing going," Gossett said.

Yet, history has proven the USFL legacy to be rich.

"There were 166 (former USFL) players under NFL contracts at the end of the (next NFL) season," Pollard said. "Some of the good quarterbacks too."

In the fall of 2009, ESPN featured the USFL in one of its "30 for 30" documentaries.

"It was pretty good," Miller said. "It didn't tell the whole story, but that's hard to do with so much to cover."

While the league may seem to be only a footnote 30 years later, Rodriquez summed up his feeling for the USFL.

"I only wear one piece of jewelry from my time in pro ball," he said. "My 1983 championship ring from the Michigan Panthers."

THREE NFL HEAD COACHES

It has been well documented that Eastern has produced three NFL head coaches.

This remarkable feat first came to light when Sean Payton, class of 1987, was hired as the New Orleans Saints' head coach in 2006. Payton joined Mike Shanahan, class of 1974, and Brad Childress, class of 1988, as NFL head coaches.

A January 19, 2006, *Chicago Tribune* article by David Haugh noted that Payton had joined "an elite NFL fraternity that has only 32 members."

At the time of Payton's hiring by the Saints, the University of Southern California and San Diego State also had three NFL coaches. Eastern, however, was the lone Division I-AA institution with as many.

Though Shanahan was fired by the Denver Broncos after the 2008 season, he was hired by the Washington Redskins as head coach and executive vice president of football operations in January 2010. No other university—Division I-AA or otherwise—could make the claim of three NFL head coaches at the time of Shanahan's hiring.

A new round of feature stories and commentary on Eastern's churning out NFL head coaches emerged. Dallas Cowboys' quarterback Tony Romo, another Eastern alum, was asked about the former Panthers as NFL head coaches in an interview by Bob Costas for NBC's *Sunday Night in America* pregame show.

"They breed 'em out there," Romo said with a huge smile. "It's hard to keep those big football guys out at Eastern Illinois."

Payton was a focal point of a *New Orleans Times-Picayune* story by James Varney after Shanahan's hiring by Washington.

"There's been a number of people pass through that school (Eastern) and had success in football, either playing or coaching," Payton told Varney.

John Jurkovic—Payton's former Eastern teammate, fellow Panther Hall of Famer and Chicago radio talk-show host—took pride in the NFL trifecta.

"It's something you can certainly get chesty about if you're an alum," Jurkovic told Haugh.

Adding to Eastern's coaching legacy is the fact that Shanahan won two Super Bowl championships with Denver while Payton raised the Lombardi Trophy for New Orleans.

Franklin Park native Shanahan played quarterback at Eastern until a lacerated kidney ended his playing days and forced him into a coaching career that Haugh deemed "bound for the Pro Football Hall of Fame."

Childress never played for the Panthers. Instead, the Aurora native earned his diploma from Eastern after transferring from the University of Illinois.

After serving as the Philadelphia Eagles' offensive coordinator from 2003 to 2005, Childress became the head coach of the Minnesota Vikings in 2006. His tenure with the Vikings lasted until he was fired in late November 2010 during a disappointing season.

Payton was far and away the most successful as a collegiate player. Payton, who prepped at Naperville Central High School, held more than 10 Eastern passing records 25 years after he left the Panthers. His jersey No. 18 was retired by the school in 2010.

"I recruited Sean Payton to Eastern," said former Panther head coach Darrell Mudra, who left Charleston for the University of Northern Iowa. "I wasn't around for most of his success as a quarterback, but I still take pride in what he has accomplished with his coaching."

Al Molde was around for Payton's on-field success at Eastern.

"I knew from the get-go that he had an effervescent personality and was a special guy," Molde told Haugh. "Things are much more complex, but I've seen similarities in games (during Payton's days as both pro coordinator and head coach) to what we did in the three-step drops and blitz checks in the passing games. There's still a little bit of Eastern in him, and now in New Orleans."

Praise and commentary to a university roughly the size of 10,000 students hasn't just been limited to those with ties to Eastern or the Chicago media.

In 2010 *The Sporting News* ranked NFL head coaches from 1 to 32. Payton was rated No. 2 behind only multiple Super Bowl–winning head coach Bill Belichick. Shanahan, meanwhile, was rated No. 4, while Childress was ranked No. 14.

Larry Kindbom began his coaching career in 1974. After stops at Kalamazoo College, Western Michigan, Ohio State, Akron and Kenyon College, Kindbom has been the head coach at Washington University in St. Louis since 1989. His Washington teams have won or shared eight conference titles. In addition, Kindbom is considered by many to be a true historian of the game.

Just how does a university like Eastern place three head coaches in the NFL at the same time?

"This question leads to a greater one: Why do coaches seem to come from pockets of programs? Why are they not as equally dispersed across all universities like teachers and accountants are? Eastern Illinois is one of those 'pockets,' like Miami of Ohio (Cradle of Coaches), Chicago or Albany State in New York. I would have to guess that people get into coaching because they like their coach (or 'mentor'), and often see the value of emulating him because of the impact that he had on their lives. The other reason is winning. Championship programs have people that so thoroughly enjoy the high that comes with winning that they want to duplicate that again in their lives.

"Eastern Illinois had the elements of both, as did the other programs that I mentioned. Eastern Illinois won the national championship in 1978. That helped attract coaches that led to more achievement. Whether they were a product of the environment, or they created the environment, coaches wanted to be part of the success."

Len Ziehm covered sports for the *Chicago Sun-Times* for more than 40 years. He spent 11 years on the Northwestern Wildcats beat before spending 5 years covering the state schools.

"What Eastern has done is amazing," Ziehm said. "They are the lost cousin out there. What they've produced over the years down there in Charleston is really incredible."

Former NFL offensive lineman Michael Oriard is an associate dean in the College of Liberal Arts at Oregon State University. Oriard, an English professor, has published numerous selections, including *Bowled Over: Big-Time College Football from the Sixties to the BCS Era* and *Brand NFL: Making and Selling America's Favorite Sport.*

"In the 1950s and 1960s, Miami University became known as 'the cradle of coaches,' having produced graduates including Paul Brown, Red Blaik, Ara Parseghian, John Pont, Weeb Ewbank and several others," Oriard said. "With three graduates as head coaches in the National Football League, Eastern Illinois University is looking remarkably like a new 'cradle.'"

Further adding to Panther pride have been others who have tasted success at the NFL level. Indianapolis Colts defensive line coach John Teerlinck served as Mudra's defensive coordinator from 1978 to 1979. Teerlinck was part of Shanahan's Super Bowl staff. He also coached for the Colts in two more Super Bowls, including a victory over the Bears in 2007.

"He could have been a defensive coordinator had he chosen to do so," said former Eastern athletic director Mike Mullally.

Like Teerlinck, Mike Heimerdinger was part of Shanahan's staff in Denver and has the Super Bowl ring to prove it. Heimerdinger, who played both baseball and football for Eastern, was the offensive coordinator for the New York Jets and Tennessee Titans.

"Both Mikes (Shanahan and Heimerdinger) stayed on after their graduation time and served as assistant coaches on our EIU staff," said former Panther coach Jack Dean. "Mike Shanahan was an offensive backfield coach and Mike Heimerdinger coached the receivers. They did it for a few meals and the opportunity. They did all the grunt work of picking up film, breaking it down, etc., just to get an opportunity.

"I was very fortunate to have them around.

They also coached our freshman team, who played some games against some other schools. They lived in a house on campus with some other guys and spent most of their time at the stadium offices. They were willing to do anything and were very competent and helpful. There was no doubt in my mind then that both of them would go on to bigger and better things in coaching. They both had a passion to coach, paid their dues and the proof is in their successes. They are also great people."

Just prior to Thanksgiving 2010, Heimerdinger left the Tennessee Titans to undergo treatment for cancer. A few months later, he was fired by the Titans. Soon afterward, he passed away.

Randy Melvin has spent time as a defensive assistant in both the NFL and collegiate football ranks. He wears a Super Bowl ring from his time with the New England Patriots.

"I'm proud to be from Eastern," Melvin said.

In addition, Payton's New Orleans staff included Greg McMahon, a defensive back at Eastern from 1978 to 1981, and Ryan Pace, a defensive lineman in the 1990s.

THE VIOLENT SIDE OF THE GAME

In recent years, alarm bells have been raised concerning the dangers of concussions that result from football. Those bells have been sounding for years.

"Violence has always been there," said former Eastern defensive coordinator Roc Bellatoni. "You look back on that famous picture of Frank Gifford after he took that big hit (in 1960). The media and its coverage are bigger than ever now. We see these violent hits on a regular basis all the time."

Violence has long been a part of football, dating back to the game's primitive origins in the mid-1800s. According to *Rites of Autumn: The Story of College Football* by Richard Whittingham, football was banned at Harvard in 1860 for being too violent. Though the ban was lifted 11 years later, the violence and concerns did not go away.

By 1905, published reports directly attributed 18 deaths and 159 serious injuries to football. A nationwide furor spread. President Theodore Roosevelt, an avid sportsman himself, insisted measures be taken to reform the sport to make it less brutal and dangerous. By some accounts, Roosevelt went so far as to warn the game could be banned if changes were not made.

Eastern Illinois football did not go unscathed from the game's brutality. In 1915, Paul Root was injured on a hard tackle against Illinois State. Root played one more down, collapsed on the field and later died at the hospital of a broken neck.

Devasting injuries didn't go away with the passage of time. Perhaps the most devasting injury in NFL history occurred on August 12, 1978, when New England Patriots' wide receiver Darryl Stingley was severely injured from a hit by Oakland Raiders' defensive back Jack Tatum. Stingley spent the remainder of his life as a quadriplegic. He died in 2007.

Stingley's older brother, Wayne, played at Eastern during the 1960s. The elder Stingley was a multisport star. In fact, Stingley was the last Eastern athlete to letter in three sports. He lettered three times in football and was named Little All-American honorable mention in addition to all-conference in 1964 and 1965. Stingley also lettered four years in basketball and four years in track.

"Wayne Stingley was a heck of an athlete, great speed for that time," said former Panther teammate Ted Schmitz. "He would have been good today in a spread offense, playing in space as a receiver or running back."

Another example of extreme violence in football occurred in 2006. On the opening kickoff of the 2006 season, Eastern All-American linebacker Clint Sellers severely injured his shoulder against the University of Illinois.

According to a *Daily Eastern News* story by Joe Waltasti, Sellers' tackle on Illinois' E.B. Halsey separated the brachial plexus bundle in his right shoulder. Since the brachial plexus bundle connects nerves to the spinal cord, Sellers' arm was paralyzed.

In a 2007 *Journal Gazette-Times Courier* story Sellers told writer Rick Dawson, "When I hit him I was paralyzed from the neck down . . . I remember (EIU head athletics trainer) Mark Bonnstetter, (assistant trainer) Jenn

Clint Sellers, the 2005 Ohio Valley Conference Defender of the Year, saw his football career end on the opening kickoff of the 2006 season opener at Illinois.

(Tymkew) and the doctor standing over me. I was face down and couldn't move and couldn't feel anything. Then everything came back except my right arm."

Sellers, the 2005 Ohio Valley Conference Defender of the Year, underwent a nerve transplant surgery performed by Dr. Susan Mackinnon at Barnes-Jewish Hospital in St. Louis.

Mackinnon, who performed the first nerve transplant surgery in 1988, took nerves from Sellers' ribs to replace the destroyed nerves in his shoulder.

"It was nine-and-a-half hours of surgery," Sellers told Waltasti. "They cut me across my chest to my armpit and down to my elbow."

Despite the surgery, Sellers later lost his right arm from the resulting spinal damage.

Sellers' injury was one of the incidents that Brian Murphy of the *Idaho Statesman* focused on in a 2010 online column.

"If we're serious about improving safety and we should be, let's eliminate the kickoff. Simply give teams the ball at the 30-yard line," Murphy proposed.

Murphy quoted Boise State special teams coordinator Jeff Choate, who served Eastern in the same capacity in 2005.

"Basically, it's a 70-yard blitz," Choate said. "The guys that do that (cover kicks) for us, a lot of them miss games, whether it's a stinger or some other shoulder injury. Some things

need to be examined in that regard."

One of Choate's later quotes no doubt had Sellers in mind.

"While we want to play the game a certain way, the most important thing is these kids' health and safety. You got to examine what you're doing. Are we asking these guys to do something that's putting them in a bad spot?" Choate told Murphy.

"It was just terrible," said Bellantoni. "Clint was like a son to me when he was here. He was probably at my house as much as I was. My kids loved him."

Sellers' injury resulted in litigation. As a result, Bellantoni and his former player don't speak on a regular basis as they once did.

"That's something I really miss," Bellantoni said.

The violent nature of the game certainly isn't lost on the former player, coach and father of four boys.

"My biggest fear is serious injury," Bellantoni said. "I pray every Saturday that no one gets injured the way I've seen guys get injured."

Former Eastern defensive back Adrian Arrington made national headlines as one of the plantiffs in a concussion lawsuit against the NCAA. Arrington, who ended his Panther career in 2009, suffered five documented concussions in his collegiate career. Moreover, he still suffers seizures that have lasting impacts on his life.

Meanwhile, former Eastern center Brad Fichtel is one of several ex-NFL players who have committed themselves to a Boston University study on the impacts of concussions on the human brain.

"I've donated my brain for this study," said Fichtel, a 1993 seventh-round draft pick of the Los Angeles Rams. "When I die, they get it. It's a good cause. You look at all the issues with concussions and there's got to be something to all this."

MARCHING PANTHERS

In 1927 Charles Lindbergh took flight on his historic transcontinental solo flight. That same year, the air in Charleston was filled with the rhythmic sounds of the Eastern Illinois marching band.

According to its official website, "one of the primary goals of the marching Panthers had been to maintain and foster the SPIRIT of Eastern."

The marching Panthers made their debut on October 27, 1927. After playing at chapel, the band played at the football game against Evansville College. Dr. Ora L. Railsback, a physics instructor, is given credit for starting the band.

The inaugural band featured 28 members, four of whom were faculty members. Funding for the band came from a variety of sources, including donations and a gift from the diploma class of 1927. Later in the year the faculty also made contributions.

Thus, in 1928, the band was able to purchase instruments and uniforms. The first uniforms consisted of white sailor caps, blue coats and white trousers or skirts. In 1929, the familiar blue and gray uniforms debuted.

With the band in place, the university added a teacher of instrumental music other than piano to its faculty. Harlan L. Hassberg was hired to direct the band and orchestra. Railsback continued to play and serve as the business manager for the band. Railsback's wife also played with the band in its early years.

In 1936, the band performed as both a marching unit and a concert entity.

Through the 2013–14 academic year, Eastern has had 24 band directors. Dr. George S. Wescott held the longest tenure. Wescott served as the director from 1949 to 1972. J. Corey Francis is the current director, taking over duties in 2012.

In keeping with its goal to establish school spirit, the Panther marching band performs four traditional songs. These songs are "I'm So Glad," "Hot Time," "Alma Mater" and the "Eastern State March." The latter is better known as the fight song.

The marching band's website states, "They (the songs) will become part of you and your legacy at EIU—treat them with the respect similar to 'God Bless America' or the 'Star Spangled Banner.'"

On a typical football weekend, the marching band rehearses on Friday afternoon. On Saturday, the band warms up in front of Booth Library and Doudna Hall 90 minutes before kickoff. An hour before kickoff, it is inspected and then marches to O'Brien Field. Upon arriving at the stadium, the marching band performs at tailgates. Once inside the stadium, the marching band entertains and leads the spirit of the game-day crowd.

PINK PANTHERS

The Pink Panthers are listed under the "Traditions" banner on Eastern's official athletic website.

Eastern's marching band has been thrilling and entertaining Panther fans since 1927.

According to original dance team member Nancy Marlow, that tradition dates back to the 1964–65 academic year.

"I was a member of the first dance squad—then called simply the pom pon squad," Marlow wrote in an e-mail. "It was started by Barb Fritze, an EIU student, during the 1964–65 school year."

According to Marlow, the squad performed only during the halftime at basketball games for several years.

"Our performances were to recorded music," Marlow wrote. "I remember some of the early performances included dancing to "Going to Kansas City" and "Baby Elephant Walk." We also performed to the school's fight song."

The squad was then under the supervision of Dr. Glen Williams, the Dean of Student Academic Services. Williams later became a Vice President for Student Affairs and was later inducted into the Eastern Athletic Hall of Fame as a contributor.

"Our faculty advisor was Dr. Bill Cash of the speech department," Marlow wrote. "Our beginnings were rather simple. Our uniforms consisted of a short white skirt and a blue sweater. We made our own pom pons."

Marlow returned to Eastern as a marketing professor in 1986.

"A couple of years later I was asked to coach the Pink Panthers," Marlow wrote.

She held the position for 12 years. Marlow added that the squad's budget was $3,000 and she was "paid a little more than that for my time."

Marlow enjoyed her time in the position.

"The most gratifying thing about being the Pink Panthers coach was getting to know an outstanding group of young women, some of whom I'm still in touch with today. They really enriched my years at Eastern," Marlow wrote.

In Marlow's view, the Pink Panthers and the Eastern marching band serve as ambassadors for the university. In addition, they provide Eastern with another avenue for marketing.

"First and most important, is that they can attract well-qualified musicians and dancers to the university. Most experts in the areas of student recruitment, retention and success would agree that those students with a commitment to some aspect of student life have an edge over those who merely attend class. Having a top-notch marching band and dance team will attract top-notch individuals. In addition, the

The Pink Panthers trace their roots to the 1964-65 school year and have remained an Eastern tradition up through today.

band and dance team can also provide a positive image for the university. For example, Eastern's band, along with the Pink Panthers, have performed at the Chicago Bears opening home game," Marlow wrote.

When asked what is unique about the Pink Panthers, Marlow wrote, "How much they were able to accomplish with few resources. One of the years I was in charge, we submitted a tape for competition. These young women finished as one of the top 20 teams in the nation. That is no mean feat when you realize that most of the large schools who finished above us also have mega budgets."

Marlow added that schools like Illinois and Indiana actually have two dance teams—one for football and basketball and the other to compete.

"The Pink Panthers also participated in a lot of community service and occasionally performed at soccer games, baseball games, etc." Marlow wrote.

One of the unique Pink Panther traditions is entering the field to the "Pink Panther Theme."

"This has remained unchanged for decades (except for those years that uncooperative band directors did not want to play it!)," Marlow wrote.

While fans often recognize the dedication and sacrifices made by members of the football team, Pink Panthers likewise work hard to hone their craft.

"Probably the major thing that the average football fan may not realize is how hard the band members and the dance team members work to put on a halftime and pregame performance," Marlow wrote. "What the fan sees on the football field is the result of hours of practice. The Pink Panthers under my leadership practiced two hours per day, five days a week plus they had 2–3 hours of practice on game days. These students bring a lot of talent with them, but that talent alone is not sufficient to produce even a mediocre performance."

DID YOU KNOW?

* Eastern graduates are 3-0 as Super Bowl head coaches. **Mike Shanahan** (class of 1974) won back-to-back Super Bowls with the Denver Broncos in the late 1990s. **Sean Payton** (class of 1987) won a Super Bowl with the New Orleans Saints in 2010. If you factor in offensive lineman **Ted Petersen's** two Super Bowl victories with the Pittsburgh Steelers, teams with Eastern graduates as either head coaches or players are 5-0.

* Super Bowl XLIV featured distinct Eastern flavor. In addition to Payton, New Orleans' staff included **Greg McMahon** and **Ryan Pace** of Eastern. The Indianapolis Colts boasted head coach **Jim Caldwell,** who coached wide receivers at Southern Illinois University from 1978 to 1980. The Colts' defensive line coach **John Teerlinck** played at Western Illinois and was the defensive coordinator for Eastern's 1978 Division II national champions.

* Academy Award–winning actor and folk singer **Burl Ives** played on Eastern's undefeated 1928 Illinois Intercollegiate Athletic Conference champions. Ives also narrated *Three Cheers for the Redskins* for NFL Films in the 1960s.

* **Merv Baker** was voted as Eastern's Most Popular Athlete in 1938. Baker was a four-sport, 13-letter winner from 1936 to 1940. He later became one of the most successful prep coaches, with stops at Findlay, Bradley, Dupo and Charleston. He was named to the Illinois State High School Coaches Association Hall of Fame for football and basketball.

* After his days as the cocaptain of Eastern's 1940 football team, **Paul Henry** was a World War II paratrooper carrier pilot. Henry was honored with the Air Medal and Oak Leaf Cluster for duty with the Army Air Corps. Henry later flew for Eastern Airlines for 30 years as a captain and senior pilot.

* **Bill Glenn** was the first Panther ever drafted by the NFL. Glenn was the Chicago Bears' 19th-round pick in 1941 (159th overall). Glenn holds the Eastern record with five interceptions in a single game. He accomplished this feat against Northern Illinois in 1940.

* **John Stabler** and **Howard Barnes** shared the Illinois Intercollegiate Athletic Conference Most Valuable Player Award in 1945. Stabler played both offensive and defensive halfback. Barnes played on both the offensive and defensive lines. He also saw action as fullback.

* **Bob Babb** holds the Eastern single-game

records for longest punt (against Illinois State in 1946) and longest punt return (against Millikin in 1949). Both the punt and punt return went 100 yards.

* Though known more for his success as EIU tennis coach, **Rex Darling** was the Panthers' head football coach in 1951. Darling's team posted a 4-2-2 record. Following that season, Eastern would not sport a winning record for 10 years. Darling, a member of the Eastern and Illinois State Halls of Fame, coached five conference tennis champions and six conference runners-up at Eastern. His tenure as tennis coach covered 1946 to 1974.

* Former Eastern baseball and football standout **Jeff Gossett** was voted as the second-greatest punter in United States Football League history in a fan poll on a league memorial website. Only Sean Landeta was ranked higher.

* When Southern Methodist University received the NCAA's "death penalty" in the 1980s, the school's traditional football Homecoming game was replaced with a soccer match. SMU was coached by former Eastern player and coach **Schellas Hyndman**.

* Eastern has a history of referees in the National Football League. Former Panther baseball coach **J.W. Sanders** was a back judge in the NFL for many years. Meanwhile, **Ken Baker** served as a football referee for the Big Ten Conference (1984–1990), a referee for the NFL (1991–2001) and replay official for the NFL (2003 to the present). Baker, who received both his undergraduate and master's degrees from Eastern, also served as the Panthers' interim athletic director. The son of EIU Hall of Fame member Merv Baker, he has served as the replay official for the Super Bowl.

* In 1986, Eastern became the first school to have a quarterback with 10,000 career passing yards (**Sean Payton**) and a running back with 5,000 career rushing yards (**Chris "Poke" Cobb**).

* **Sean Payton** finished his career with 10,655 passing yards. Wide receivers **Roy Banks** (3,177) and **Calvin Pierce** (2,548) accounted for more than half of those yards. Offensive lineman **Mark Petersen** caught one Payton pass for minus two yards.

* Defensive back **Scott Johnson** blocked

three kicks in a single 1988 game—*twice*. Johnson accomplished the feat against Western Illinois and Western Kentucky.

* Former Eastern tight end **Dirk Androff** was inducted into the Illinois USSSA Hall of Fame (slow pitch softball) in 1999. Androff, who also played basketball for the Panthers in the early 1980s, had a career batting average of .733 with 1,814 home runs at the major level. Androff died of a heart attack in 1997 at age 35.

* All-Gateway Conference quarterback **Jeff Thorne** (1990–1993) was a four-year starter. Today, Thorne is the offensive coordinator at North Central College in Naperville.

* **Ken Wooddell** broadcast Eastern football games for 17 seasons (1983–1999). He also called some EIU games in the 1940s and '50s.

* **J.R. Taylor** is tops among Eastern running backs with a 5.83 yards-per-carry average for his career.

* **Tony Romo** threw the longest touchdown pass in school history with a 98-yard throw to **Will Bumphus** against Eastern Kentucky in 2000.

* Southern Illinois running back **Deji Karim** went the entire 2009 regular season and 205 carries without fumbling. Eastern forced Karim to fumble in the first quarter of the Panthers-Salukis playoff game that season.

* Eastern quarterbacks **Jeff** and **Jake Christensen** are father and son. Jeff played from 1980 to 1982 while Jake played the 2009 season for the Panthers. Both wore No. 11.

* To celebrate its 25th year, the Gateway/Missouri Valley Conference unveiled Silver Anniversary teams in 2009. Though it had not competed in the Gateway since 1995, Eastern landed four players on the team. Quarterback **Sean Payton** and running back **Willie High** were named to the offense while defensive lineman **John Jurkovic** and defensive back **Ray McElroy** were listed on the defense. Jurkovic and McElroy also were named to the conference's All-NFL Select Team.

* When **Tony Campana** made his major league baseball debut with the Chicago Cubs in 2011, his surname may have rung a bell with long-time Panther fans. Tony's father, **Mark Campana**, played on Eastern's 1978 national championship team. In fact, the senior

Campana returned a kickoff for a touchdown against Youngstown State in the national semi-finals at O'Brien Field.

* In 2012 wide receiver **Erik Lora** and quarterback **Jimmy Garoppolo** both finished in the top 10 among those getting votes for the Walter Payton Award. That marked the first time in Payton Award history that two players from the same team accomplished that feat in the same season. A year later, the dynamic duo were even better with Garoppolo (after being fourth in 2012) winning the award while Lora finished seventh in the balloting.

WHAT IF?

The world of sports often revolves around debate that takes place everywhere from the schoolyard to the water cooler to the tailgates of America.

It seems everywhere one turns there is a list or rankings of some sports-related topic. Who is the greatest player in school history? Who was the best quarterback? Which defense was the stingiest? Eastern Illinois football is no different.

Since football is a team game, let's examine the question of the greatest Panther team ever.

There are a number of candidates to wear the all-time champion crown. While the 1928 and 1948 Panthers won the Illinois Intercollegiate Athletic Conference titles, the brand of football they played was quite different from the game of the "modern era." So, both are dismissed from this discussion.

At the top of the list of candidates is the 1978 Eastern team led by Darrell Mudra, who took the Panthers from a 1-10 record in 1977 to a Division II national championship.

Two years later, in 1980, Mudra's Panthers spent much of the season ranked No. 1 nationally. Eastern again played for the national title, but this time around the Panthers lost in the national championship game.

Continuing the two-year pattern, Mudra's final Eastern team went unbeaten during the 1982 regular season. Perhaps making things more impressive, the Panthers had moved to the Division I-AA level the previous season. Eastern won its first-round playoff game be-fore suffering a one-point quarterfinal loss at Tennessee State, a Tiger win that was later vacated due to the use of an ineligible player. The '82 Panther defense surrendered only 8.8 points per game during the regular season. In addition, Eastern recorded three shutouts.

Though Eastern returned to the playoffs the following year under first-year head coach Al Molde, his 1986 Panthers get the nod as the next candidate.

In his final season at Eastern before leaving for Division I-A Western Michigan, Molde coached the Panthers to a No. 3 national ranking, a Gateway Conference crown and a berth in the I-AA quarterfinals. The "Eastern Airlines" offense averaged 37 points per game during the regular season.

After taking over for Molde in 1987, Bob Spoo began his remarkable tenure at Eastern. Spoo's 1989 Panthers put on a late-season surge to qualify for the I-AA playoffs. Once the postseason began, Eastern upset fourth-ranked Idaho. The following week, the Panthers fell, 25-19, against I-AA power Montana in the quarterfinals.

After nearly losing his job with a 2-5 start in 1994, Spoo rallied the troops in 1995. That year's Panther team posted a 10-1 regular season record and a share of the Gateway title. An Eastern rally fell short as the Panthers dropped their opening playoff game at Stephen F. Austin, 34-29.

Next on the list are the 2001 Panthers. Eastern lost only one regular-season game (at Division I-A San Diego State) en route to the Ohio Valley Conference title. Eastern dropped its opening-round playoff game, a 49-43 shootout with Northern Iowa.

Rounding out the list of great Panther teams is Dino Babers' 2013 edition. Eastern surprised defending Mountain West Conference champion San Diego State in the opener and narrowly lost to Mid-American Conference champion Northern Illinois on the road. The Panthers went 11-1 in the regular season, won the OVC title and ascended to No. 2 in the national polls.

The previously mentioned teams featured high-profile quarterbacks (Steve Turk, 1978; Jeff Christensen, 1980 and 1982; Sean Payton, 1986; Tony Romo, 2001; and Jimmy Garoppolo, 2013).

There were standout running backs (Chris "Poke" Cobb, 1978; Kevin Staple, 1980 and 1982; Jamie Jones, 1989; Willie High, 1995; J.R. Taylor, 2001; Shepard Little and Taylor Duncan, 2013) and big-play receivers (James Warring, 1978; Scott McGhee, 1978 and 1980; Jerry Wright, 1982; Roy Banks and Calvin Pierce, 1986; Frank Cutolo, 2001; and Erik Lora, Adam Drake and Keiondre Gober, 2013).

Each team also possessed rock-solid defenders in the front seven (Pete Catan, Randy Melvin, and Tom Seward, 1978; Ira Jefferson, 1980; John Jurkovic and Jeff Mills, 1986 and 1989; Tim Lance, 1989; Tim Carver, 1995; Nick Ricks, 2001; and Pat Wertz, Dino Fanti and Robert Haynes, 2013) and steady performers in the secondary (Rich Brown, 1978 and 1980; Kevin Gray, 1980; Randy McCue and Robert Williams, 1982; Ray McElroy, 1995; and Jourdan Wickliffe and Nick Beard, 2013).

The coaching was impressive. Mudra was inducted into the College Football Hall of Fame. Molde became the most successful coach in Western Michigan University history. Spoo stands as the winningest coach in Eastern history. Babers brought a high-octane offense that completely rewrote the school and OVC record book.

It's time for those in the know to weigh in with their thoughts about which team is the greatest in Eastern Illinois football history.

Prior to the 2013 season, longtime Eastern sports information director Dave Kidwell chose the 1978 national champions. However, his opinion was swayed in late November 2013.

"This (2013 team) is the best ever ... in a way it's difficult to say that over a team that won a national championship since that's the ultimate 'prize' but facts are facts," said Kidwell.

Kidwell's facts included that the 1978 Panthers were a Division II team, the 2013 team's strong schedule (especially when one considers the nonconference opponents) as well as the record-shattering offense.

"No question, this is the best ... this team is No. 1 in EIU history," said Kidwell, whose ties to EIU go back to his days as a student in the late 1960s.

Meanwhile, play-by-play broadcaster Mike Bradd said, "For anyone who's been around Eastern very long, the 1978 team will always have a special place. Coming off a 1-10 year, with no expectations and not much local enthusiasm for football, that team started fast, stumbled a bit in the middle, then finished strong. Then they made a Cinderella run through the playoffs and beat an established power to win the title. It's the most amazing turnaround I've ever seen firsthand in sports."

Yet, like Kidwell, as the 2013 regular season was nearing its end, Bradd said, "This year's team is the best I-AA/FCS team EIU has had. The offensive numbers speak for themselves, but the defense has been very good for the last two-thirds of the season. To me the combination puts them a little ahead of the mid-1980s Sean Payton team and the 2001-02 Romo teams that all reached the top 5 in the national polls.

"I hesitate to compare this team to the Division II championship game teams from 1978 and '80. That was a little before my time. I know some will dismiss those teams because that was Division II, but the list of schools in that division then is pretty similar to the current FCS list so my guess is the quality of play was pretty comparable to FCS today. My guess could be wrong."

Beat writer Brian Nielsen said, "If I had to pick an offense to go 80 yards for the winning score, it would be between the Romo team and the Garoppolo team. You could flip a coin. The difference to me is the defense. This (2013) team has no one standout defensive star, but they just take care of things every week."

Robert Williams was a two-time I-AA first-team All-American defensive back (1982 and '83) who later played two years with the Pittsburgh Steelers. Williams was a freshman on the 1980 team but did not travel to the championship game.

When asked to compare the '82 Panthers to the 1980 version, Williams didn't bat an eye.

"I believe we (the '82 team) would have whupped them," he said. "We had a more sound defense. I'm a football historian. I watched all the film back to 1972. Our defense was incredible that year."

Carl Walworth covered EIU football for the *Charleston Times-Courier* from 1984 to 1988. In addition, Walworth has "been around the area much longer than that."

"I was in high school in 1978 and didn't see the team play, but it's hard to argue against a national championship, particularly given their record the season before. So I would go with 1978," wrote Walworth in an e-mail.

Even former Illinois secretary of state and governor Jim Edgar weighed in with opinions.

"That (1980) was probably a better team (than '78)," said the 1968 Eastern graduate. "Those (later) teams moved up a division. They were really fun to watch with the way they could throw the ball. Those teams just might have been better than the earlier teams."

So where does this leave us? Is there a way to determine the greatest Eastern Illinois Panther football team ever?

While none of these debates will ever be completely resolved, technology does provide some interesting possibilities.

Game designer Dr. Wayne Poniewaz, in conjunction with programmer Richard Hanna, are the creators of Second and Ten Football, a highly acclaimed computer simulation lauded for its statistical accuracy. The game contains a ratings adjustment to allow for teams from different eras to compete against one another on an even footing.

"It adjusts each team's defensive ratings based on the average of the season averages of the two teams playing," explained Poniewaz, a PhD in experimental psychology.

Thus, SAT is the means by which the All-Time EIU Panthers will be crowned as the greatest team in school history.

So, it's time to tee up the ball with the click of a mouse and the stroke of a keyboard. . . .

The All-Time EIU Panther Tournament was played out in a round-robin format, with each team playing the other on a neutral field in ideal weather conditions. For the sake of statistical reliability, each "game" was simulated 500 times. The results are an average of those results and are presented as one game that represents the entire simulation.

FINAL STANDINGS

2013 Panthers 7-0
1980 Panthers 6-1
1982 Panthers 5-2
1978 Panthers 3-4*
1986 Panthers 3-4
2001 Panthers 2-5*
1995 Panthers 2-5
1989 Panthers 0-7
*head-to-head tiebreaker

In what turned out to be the game that determined the All-Time EIU Champion, Dino Babers' 2013 Panthers defeated Darrell Mudra's 1980 team in 70% of the simulations. The average score was 28-17.

In that average simulated matchup, quarterback Jimmy Garoppolo completed 22 of 38 passes for 229 yards and two touchdowns. Erik Lora led the receivers with eight catches for 78 yards and a touchdown. Shepard Little rushed 12 times for 83 yards and a touchdown while Taylor Duncan ran 11 times for 53 yards.

The 1980 Panthers' combination of Chuck Wright and Jeff Christensen passed for 186 yards but was intercepted twice. Kevin Staple carried the ball 11 times for 68 yards. Wilbur James led all tacklers with 11 stops.

In the game that determined second place, the '80 Panthers defeated the '82 Panthers by an average score of 24-21. The '80 Panthers won 64% of the simulations.

In a clash of record-setting quarterbacks, Sean Payton's 1986 team knocked off Tony Romo's 2001 Panthers in 52% of the matchups. The average score was 37-36. Payton completed 27-of-36 passes for 289 yards and two touchdowns. Romo went 17-for-26 with 274 yards and three touchdowns. J.R. Taylor rushed for 105 yards.

But in the end, according to the computer, the 2013 EIU Panthers emerge as the greatest team in school history. Head coach Dino Babers' team featured a record nine first team OVC performers, six on offense. Eastern had 18 total selections across the first-team, second-team and All-Newcomer OVC squads.

Thus, the 2013 Panthers wear the crown as EIU's best ever.

Let the debates begin (or continue) . . .

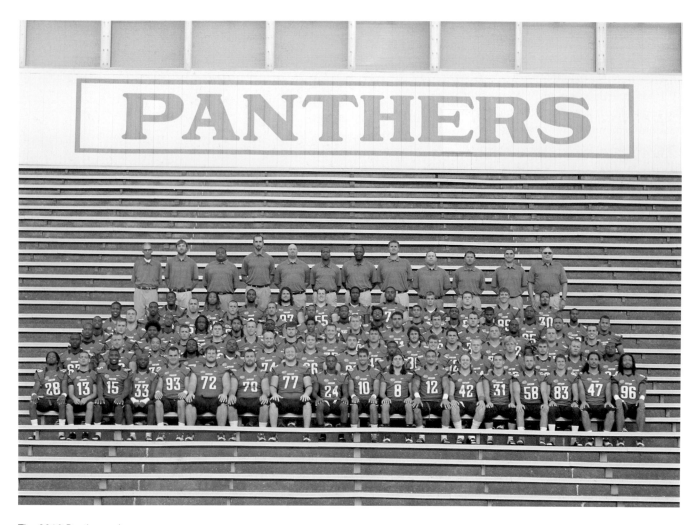

The 2013 Panthers reign as
the greatest Eastern football
team of all-time according to a
computer simulation.

APPENDIX

THE BEST EIU PANTHER EARLY-ERA TEAMS

1899–1929 ERA

George Sumner Anderson
Herman Cooper
Bruce Corzine
William James Creamer
Peter Fenolio
James Funkhouser
Joe Galbreath
Frank "Hoot" Gibson
Mack Gilbert
Forrest Greathouse
Ruel Hall
Lenny High
Burl Ives
Edwin Leamon
Clyde Leathers
Hank Osborn
Johnnie Powers
Andy Taylor
Everett Warner
Sumner Wilson

1930–1941 ERA

Merv Baker
Howard Ballard
Bill Glenn
Paul Henry
Okey Honefenger
Jim Hutton
Dave Kessinger
John Ritchie
Ray Suddarth
Myron "Jim" Tedrick
Lloyd Thudium
Joe Ward
Joe Zupsich

1942–1949 ERA

Howard Barnes
Earl Benoche

Tom Carlyle
Bill Crum
Donald Davisson
Russ Ghere
Bernie Hayton
Neal Hudson
Don Johnson
Lee Roy LaRose
John Lopinski
Frank Pitol
Bob Smith
Ed Soergel
John Stabler
Ross Stephenson
Lou Stivers
Andy Sullivan

1950–1959 ERA

Gary Anderson
Don Arnold
Darrell Brown
Bob Calvin
David Cohrs
Dave Fields
Ray Fisher
Paul Foreman
Arnold Franke
Bob Fulk
Bill Hardin
Don Henderson
John Keiser
Carl Magsamen
Joe Patridge
Mike Phillips
Dwayne "Moose" Roe
George Rykovich
Gene Scruggs
Art Thompson
Dick Vaughn
Roger West

1960–1971 ERA

Larry Angelo
Dennis Bundy
Rod Butler
Joe Davis
Ron Gustafson
Roger Haberer
Ken Heffley

Tad Heiminger
Bob Jensen
Mark O'Donnell
Dick Portee
Ray Schaljo
Ted Schmitz
Ed Stephens
Wayne Stingley
Lynn Strack
Gene Vidoni
Ben Ward
Ken Werner

THE BEST EIU PANTHER ALL-DIVISION-II TEAM (1972–1980)

Offense		Years	Hometown
WR	James Warring	1976–1979	Miami, FL
WR	Willie White	1970–1973	Gary, IN
TE	Rob Mehalic	1978–1981	Streator, IL
OL	Clinton Davenport	1977–1980	Washington, DC
OL	Jack Lafferty	1976–1979	Waukegan, IL
OL	Bob Norris	1978–1981	Pittsfield, IL
OL	Ted Petersen	1972–1975	Momence, IL
OL	Tom Pettigrew	1976–1979	Roanoke, VA
QB	Jeff Christensen	1980–1982	Gibson City, IL
RB	Nate Anderson	1970–1973	East St. Louis, IL
RB	Chris "Poke" Cobb	1976–1979	Clover, SC
PK	Dan DiMartino	1976–1979	Batavia, NY
All-Purpose	Chris "Poke" Cobb	1976–1979	Clover, SC
KO Returner	Marcus Potts	1975–1978	Chicago, IL

Defense		Years	Hometown
DL	Pete Catan	1976–1980	Penfield, NY
DL	Randy Melvin	1977–1980	Aurora, IL
DL	Steve Parker	1978–1979	Evanston, IL
DL	Keith Wojnowski	1979–1982	St. Anne, IL
LB	Ira Jefferson	1978–1981	Momence, IL
LB	Alonzo Lee	1978–1979	Washington, DC
LB	Bill Mines	1979–1982	Washington, DC
DB	Rich Brown	1977–1980	Akron, OH
DB	Kevin Gray	1979–1980	Chicago, IL
DB	Wilbert James	1978–1981	Chicago, IL
DB	Donald Pittman	1977–1980	Fort Mill, SC
P	Jeff Gossett	1976–1977, 1979	Charleston, IL
Punt Return	Scott McGhee	1977–1980	Tinley Park, IL

Best Panther Team of Division-II Era: 1978 (Coach Darrell Mudra) 12–2, National Champions

NOTE: The EIU Panther All Division-II Team was selected by the following voters: Mike Bradd, EIU play-by-play broadcaster; Dave Kidwell, EIU Athletic Department; Bill Lair, *Journal Gazette/Times-Courier*; Mike Mullally, former EIU Athletic Director; Brian Nielsen, *Journal Gazette/Times-Courier*; Carl Walworth, *Journal Gazette/Times-Courier*.

THE BEST EIU PANTHER ALL-I-AA/FCS TEAM (1981–2013)

Offense		*Years*	*Hometown*
WR	Roy Banks	1983–1986	Detroit, MI
WR	Erik Lora	2009–2013	Miami, FL
TE	Nick Eller	2000–2003	Hubbard, IA
OL	Chris Anderson	1992–1995	Kaukauna, WI
OL	Chris Campbell	2006–2009	Chicago, IL
OL	Brad Fichtel	1990–1992	Oswego, IL
OL	Chaz Millard	2006–2009	St. Charles, IL
OL	Bob Norris	1978–1981	Pittsfield, IL
OL	Dave Popp	1985–1988	Libertyville, IL
QB	Tony Romo	1999–2002	Burlington, WI
RB	Willie High	1992–1995	Mattoon, IL
RB	J.R. Taylor	1999–2002	Mt. Zion, IL
PK	Rich Ehmke	1986–1987	El Cajon, CA
All-Purpose	DuWayne Pitts	1984–1987	Detroit, IL
KO Returner	Daryl Holcombe	1986–1990	Ft. Lauderdale, FL

Defense		*Years*	*Hometown*
DL	John Jurkovic	1985–1989	Calumet City, IL
DL	Marcus Lorick	2001–2004	Terre Haute, IN
DL	Kory Lothe	2002–2005	Sun Prairie, WI
DL	Pierre Walters	2005–2008	Forest Park, IL
LB	Tim Carver	1992–1995	Urbandale, IA
LB	Nick Ricks	2000–2003	Deerfield Beach, FL
LB	Donald Thomas	2004–2007	St. Louis, MO
DB	Tim Lance	1987–1990	Cuba, IL
DB	Ray McElroy	1991–1994	Bellwood, IL
S	Tristan Burge	2003–2006	Romeoville, IL
S	Robert Williams	1980–1983	Chicago, IL
P	Kevin Cook	2007–2010	Libertyville, IL
Punt Return	Frank Cutolo	1998–2001	Boca Raton, FL

Best Panther Team of I-AA/FCS Era: 2013 (Coach Dino Babers) 12–2, Ohio Valley Conference champion, playoff quarterfinalist & No. 2 national ranking

The EIU Panther All I-AA/FCS Team was selected by the following voters: Mike Bradd, EIU play-by-play broadcaster; Dave Kidwell, EIU Athletic Department; Bill Lair, *Journal Gazette/Times-Courier*; Brian Nielsen, *Journal Gazette/Times-Courier*; John Smith, EIU Athletic Department; Carl Walworth, *Journal Gazette/Times-Courier*.

PANTHERS IN THE PROS

PANTHERS SELECTED IN THE NFL DRAFT (THROUGH 2014)

Player, Position	Team	Round	Year
Bill Glenn, QB	Chicago Bears	19th	1944
Rod Butler, RB	Chicago Bears	16th	1964
Roger Haberer, QB	Chicago Bears	19th	1966
Nate Anderson, RB	Washington Redskins	16th	1974
Ted Petersen, C	Pittsburgh Steelers	4th	1977
Tom Pettigrew, OT	Los Angeles Rams	8th	1980
Jeff Christensen, QB	Cincinnati Bengals	5th	1983
Roy Banks, WR	Indianapolis Colts	5th	1987
Dave Popp, OT	New York Giants	7th	1989
Brad Fichtel, C	Los Angeles Rams	7th	1993
Ray McElroy, CB	Indianapolis Colts	4th	1995
Chris Watson, CB	Denver Broncos	3rd	1999
Otis Hudson, G	Cincinnati Bengals	5th	2010
Jimmy Garoppolo, QB	New England Patriots	2nd	2014

PANTHERS SIGNED AS NFL FREE AGENTS (THROUGH 2014)

Player, Position	Team	Year
Lenny High, E	Decatur Staleys	1920
Ed Soergel, QB	Cleveland Browns	1951
Lou Stivers, C	Detroit Lions	1951
Ray Fisher, DT	Pittsburgh Steelers	1958
Steve Turk, QB	Green Bay Packers	1980
James Warring, WR	Oakland Raiders	1980
Jack Lafferty, C	Seattle Seahawks	1980
Jeff Gossett, P	Kansas City Chiefs	1981
Kevin Gray, S	New Orleans Saints	1982
Steve Paker, T	Baltimore Colts	1983
Dirk Androff, TE	New York Jets	1983
Robert Williams, DB	Pittsburgh Steelers	1984
Jerry Wright, WR	Tampa Bay Buccaneers	1985
Evan Araposthathis, P	St. Louis Cardinals	1986
Tom Moskal, DT	St. Louis Cardinals	1986
Melvin Black, LB	New England Patriots	1986
Sean Payton, QB	Chicago Bears	1987
Chris Geile, OL	Detroit Lions	1987
John Jurkovic, DT	Miami Dolphins	1990
Tim Lance, DB	Chicago Bears	1991
Duane Conway, OL	Indianapolis Colts	1995
John Moyer, DE	Indianapolis Colts	1997
Bob Rosenthiel, TE	Los Angeles Raiders	1997
Dave Thomas, DT	Arizona Cardinals	2000
Kourtney Young, DB	Detroit Lions	2002
Frank Cutolo, WR	New Orleans Saints	2002
Tony Romo, QB	Dallas Cowboys	2003

Pascal Matla, C	New Orleans Saints	2006
Kory Lothe, DE	St. Louis Rams	2006
Tristan Burge, S	Green Bay Packers	2007
Micah Rucker, WR	Pittsburgh Steelers	2008
Pierre Walters, LB	Kansas City Chiefs	2009
Chris Campbell, OL	Green Bay Packers	2010
Austin Signor, K	New York Giants	2010
Mike Garrity, OT	Chicago Bears	2012
Roosevelt Holliday, DT	New York Jets	2013
Erik Lora, WR	Minnesota Vikings	2014

PANTHERS SELECTED IN THE WFL DRAFT

Player, Position	Team	Round	Year
Nate Anderson, RB	Chicago Fire	18th	1974

PANTHERS IN THE USFL

Player, Position	Team	Year
Steve Turk, QB	Denver Gold	1983
Pete Catan, DE	Houston Gamblers	1983
Bob Norris, OG	Tampa Bay Bandits	1983
Scott McGhee, WR	Houston Gamblers	1984
Kevin Gray, FS	Jacksonville Bulls	1984
Jeff Gossett, P	Chicago Blitz	1984
Randy McCue, DB	Memphis Showboats	1984

Notes: Pete Catan earned All-USFL honors in 1984. John Teerlinck, the defensive coordinator for Eastern's 1978 national championship team, was a defensive coach for George Allen with the Chicago Blitz and Arizona Wranglers.

Source: *Eastern Illinois University Kickoff Game Day Magazine*

PANTHERS SELECTED IN THE USFL DRAFT

Player, Position	Team	Round	Year
Jeff Christensen, QB	New Jersey Generals	17	1983
Bob Norris, OG	Tampa Bay Bandits	19	1983
Gary Bridges, DB	Memphis Showboats	7	1984
Robert Williams, S	Birmingham Stallions	7	1984
Chris Nicholson, DT	Memphis Showboats	18	1984

PANTHERS IN THE ARENA FOOTBALL LEAGUE (THROUGH 2013)

Player, Position	Team	Year
Sean Payton, QB	Chicago Bruisers	1987
John Moyer, DT	Florida Bobcats	1999
Ethan Banning, DE	Grand Rapids Rampage	2000

Ryan Shuff, G	Houston Thunderbears		2000
Phil Taylor, WR	Toronto Phantoms		2001
Dave Thomas, LB	Detroit Fury	2001	
Anthony Buich, QB	Grand Rapids Rampage		2004
Nick Allison, DB	Orlando Predators		2008
Terrance Sanders, DB	Arizona Rattlers		2010
Micah Rucker, WR	Orlando Predators		2010
Pierre Walters, DL	Chicago Rush		2012
Mike Garrity, OL	Iowa Barnstormers		2013

Note: Lists the first team and year that the player appeared in Arena Football
Source: *Eastern Illinois University Kickoff Game Day Magazine*

PANTHERS IN THE XFL

Player, Position	*Team*	*Year*
Obadiah Cooper, WR	New York–New Jersey Hitmen	2000
Bob Rosentiel, TE	New York–New Jersey Hitmen	2000
Dave Thomas, IB	San Francisco Demons	2000

Source: XFL website

RETIRED PANTHERS JERSEYS

17	Tony Romo	2009
18	Sean Payton	2010

BIBLIOGRAPHY AND RESOURCES

BOOKS

Bell, Taylor. *Dusty, Deek, and Mr. Do-Right: High School Football in Illinois*. Urbana: University of Illinois Press, 2010.

Dunnavant, Keith. *The Missing Ring: How Bear Bryant and the 1966 Alabama Crimson Tide Were Denied College Football's Most Elusive Prize*. New York: St. Martin's Griffin, 2007.

Fleder, Rob, ed. *The Sports Illustrated College Football Book*. New York: Sports Illustrated Books, 2008.

Layden, Tim. *Blood, Sweat & Chalk: The Ultimate Football Playbook: How the Great Coaches Built Today's Game*. New York: Sports Illustrated Books, 2010.

MacCambridge, Michael. *America's Game: The Epic Story of How Pro Football Captured a Nation*. Anchor, 2004.

MacCambridge, Michael, ed. *ESPN College Football Encyclopedia*. ESPN Books, 2005.

Maxymuk, John. *Quarterback Abstract*. Chicago: Triumph Books, 2009.

Maxymuk, John. *Strong Arm Tactics: A History and Statistical Analysis of the Professional Quarterback*. Jefferson, NC: McFarland & Co., 2007.

McGinn, Bob. *The Ultimate Super Bowl Book: A Complete Reference to the Stats, Stars, and Stories Behind Football's Biggest Game—and Why the Best Team Won*. Minneapolis: MVP Books, 2009.

Payton, Sean, with Ellis Henican. *Home Team: Coaching the Saints and New Orleans Back to Life*. New York: New American Library, 2010.

Shanahan, Mike, with Adam Schefter. *Think Like A Champion: Building Success One Victory at a Time*. New York: Collins, 2000.

Whittingham, Richard. *Rites of Autumn: The Story of College Football*. New York: The Free Press, 2001.

NEWSPAPERS AND PERIODICALS

Clark, Brooks. "Small Colleges." *Sports Illustrated*, September 10, 1979, 83.

Claypool, Dave. "Panther Miracle Hopes Crushed." *The Daily Eastern News*, December 14, 1980, 1.

Corkran, Steve. "Raiders Set to Name Payton Head Coach." *Knight Ridder/Tribune News Service*, January 20, 2004.

Dawson, Rick. "Injured EIU Talent Remains Positive During Recovery." *Charleston Journal-Gazette and Times-Courier*, July 11, 2007.

"Delaware Football History." *2008 Delaware Blue Hens Football Media Guide*, 2008, 131.

Flanagan, J. Michael. "Banks Attends to Eastern First." *Decatur Herald & Review*, August 21, 1986.

Gerdovich, Carl, and Norm Lewis. "Miracle Panthers No. 1." *The Daily Eastern News*, December 10, 1978, 1.

Haugh, David. "Cutler Not the Only Important QB in the Area." *Chicago Tribune*, October 25, 2013.

Haugh, David. "EIU QB on Way to Bigger Things." *Chicago Tribune*, September 19, 2013.

Haugh, David. "Xs and Os U." *Chicago Tribune*, January 19, 2006.

"Illinois Intercollegiate Athletic Conference-IIAC-Little Nineteen." *NCAA News*, June 6, 1970.

King, Peter. "Hardest, Riskiest, Toughest, Greatest Job in Sports." *Sports Illustrated*, September 27, 2009, 69–83.

Kirschenbaum, Jerry. "Scorecard." *Sports Illustrated*, November 19, 1979, 31.

Lair, Bill. "EIU Shocked Football World in '78 Season." *Charleston Journal-Gazette Times-Courier*, November 10, 2003.

McLean, Bill. "Does It Get Any Better Than This? NFL Draft Pick Hudson Won't Forget His Days as Barrington Bronco." *Barrington Courier-Review*, April 10, 2010.

Meinheit, Mark. "Romo Arigato!" *The Daily Eastern News*, January 13, 2003, 11.

Merda, Chad. "Football Team of the Century: Simply the Best." *The Daily Eastern News*, August 31, 1999, 10–12.

Merda, Chad. "The One-Year Quick Fix." *The Daily Eastern News*, October 16, 1998, 12C.

Murphy, Austin. "Treasure Hunt." *Sports Illustrated*, September 3, 1990, 109.

Murphy, Brian. "Eliminate Kickoff, Make Sport Safer." October 27, 2010. <http://www.onlineathens.com/stories/102710/spo_726516018.shtml> (accessed November 7, 2010).

Nielsen, Brian. "Bob Spoo: A Man of Great Character." *Ohio Valley Conference Football 2009*, 2009, 28–33.

"Panthers Come Back, Take II Championship." *NCAA News*, January 1979.

"Titans Are Corn Bowl Champs." *The Illinois Wesleyan Argus*, December 1, 1948.

Verdun, Dan. "Glory Days Haven't Passed by Former Football Legends." *Verge*, October 11, 1985, 1.

WEBSITES

Brandt, Gil. "Northern Illinois' Jordan Lynch among Top Mid-Level QBs." October 21, 2013. <nfl.com> (accessed October 22, 2013).

Byrne, Kerry J. "Romo Shoots Down Doubters with Attack on Passing Efficiency Records." September 16, 2009. <cnnsi.com> (accessed September 17, 2009).

"Dallas Cowboys' Romo Still Big Man on Campus." October 18, 2009. <dallasnews.com (accessed October 20, 2009).

Dawon, Rick. "Injured EIU Talent Remains Positive During Recovery." July 11, 2007. <http://nl.newsbank.com/nl-search/we/Archives?p_action> (accessed October 10, 2009).

De Franco, Luca. "Kickboxers in the Ring." January 3, 2006. <thesweetscience.com> (accessed March 18, 2010).

Everson, Darren. "The Wall Street Journal Blogs." October 21, 2010. <http://blogs.wsj.com/dailyfix/2010/10/21/paterno-lose-face-masks-for-safety/> (accessed November 5, 2010).

Grant, Evan. "Tony Dungy: Cowboys Should Be Concerned." December 6, 2009. <dallasnews.com> (accessed January 4, 2010).

McGraw, Mike. "Former Meadows QB Has EIU Offense Rolling." September 18, 2013. <dailyherald.com> (accessed October 29, 2013).

Nielsen, Brian. "As Eastern Freshman, Chris Watson Builds on His Success." May 25, 1996. <http://jg-tc.com/> (accessed November 10, 2010).

Nielsen, Brian. "Eastern's Watson a Third-Round Draft Pick." April 15, 1999. <http://jg-tc.com/> (accessed November 10, 2010).

Nielsen, Brian. "EIU's Watson May Get Drafted." April 14, 1999. <http://jg-tc.com/> (accessed November 10, 2010).

Nielsen, Brian. "A Game to Make an Eastern Alum Proud." November 2, 2008. <http://jg-tc.

com/sports/article_dbe590d6-94a8-58e0-80b4-0fac79161769.html> (accessed November 2, 2010).

Nielsen, Brian. "Romo Learned Lessons on Way to Stardom." October 18, 2009. jg-tc online (accessed October 19, 2009).

Rojek, Kristin. "A Mutual Understanding: Relationship between Cutolo and His Quarterback Has Resulted in Success." October 31, 2001. <http://media.www.dennews.com/media/storage/paper309/news/2001/10/31/Sports/A.Mutual.Understanding-136291.shtml> (accessed January 7, 2011).

Townsend, Brad. "Favorite Son: Hometown Cheers Romo's Rise." October 29, 2006. <cowboysplus.com> (accessed February 27, 2010).

Waltasti, Joe. "Sellers Travels Road to Recovery." April 6, 2007. <http://media.www.den>news.com/media/storage/paper309/news/2007/04/06/Sports/Sellers.Travels.Road.To.Recovery-2826884.shtml> (accessed November 10, 2010).

"Warbler 1913." August 2010. <http://www.idaillinois.org/cdm4/document.php?CISOROOT=/eiu&CISOPTR=2841&REC=1> (accessed October 28, 2010).

"Warbler 1923." August 2010. <http://www.idaillinois.org/cdm4/document.php?CISOROOT=/eiu&CISOPTR=2847&REC=7> (accessed October 28, 2010).

Whitchurch, Collin. "Homecoming 2009: Romo Gracious, Humble in Honor." October 19, 2009. <dennews.com> (accessed October 19, 2009).

PERSONAL INTERVIEWS

Chris Anderson
Nate Anderson
Evan Arapostathis
Dino Babers
Randy Ball
Tom Beck
Taylor Bell
Roc Bellantoni
Todd Berry
Joe Bock
George Bork
Mike Bradd
Rod Butler
Tim Carver
Pete Catan
Jeff Christensen
John Craft
Frank Cutolo
Jack Dean
Jim Edgar
Booker Edgerson
Larry Edlund
Brad Fichtel
Ray Fisher
Mike Fitzgerald
P.J. Fleck
Jimmy Garoppolo

Jeff Gossett
Roger Haberer
Bob Heimerdinger
Mike Heimerdinger
Willie High
Otis Hudson
LeShon Johnson
John Jurkovic
Tom Katsimpalis
Dave Kidwell
Jerry Kill
Tim Lance
Alonzo Lee
Bill Legg
Erik Lora
Wayne Lunak
Mike Lynch
Bill Mallory
Stewart Mandel
Nancy Marlow
Ray McElroy
Scott McGhee
Randy Melvin
Red Miller
Al Molde
Darrell Mudra
Mike Mullally
Brian Nielsen
Anthony Nunez
Ryan Pace
Sean Payton
Ted Petersen
Jerry Pettibone
Jack Pheanis
Donald Pittman
Dick Portee
Casey Printers
Mike Prior
Pete Rodriquez
Micah Rucker
Mike Sabock
Ted Schmitz
Carver Shannon
John Smith
Brock Spack
Bob Spoo
Kevin Staple
Jeff Strohm
Terry Taylor
John Teerlinck
Gene Vidoni

Mike Wagner
James Warring
Brodie Westen
Willie White
Robert Williams
Frank Winters
Roy Wittke
Ken Wooddell
Jerry Wright

ABOUT THE AUTHOR

Dan Verdun grew up in Odell, Illinois, and attended Eastern Illinois University. He graduated with bachelor's degrees in journalism and history in 1988. While serving as the sports editor for the university's daily newspaper, Verdun won a number of awards for sportswriting, including placing in the William Randolph Hearst Collegiate Awards (the first in EIU history). Later, he worked in the sports information office. Verdun holds a master's degree in curriculum and instruction from Northern Illinois University. He has taught language arts and social studies for the past 26 years. Currently, he teaches in Naperville District 204, where he lives with his wife Nancy, son Tommy, and daughter Lauren. He previously wrote a book on Northern Illinois Huskies football.

FOUR-DOWN TERRITORY

Favorite Football Movie: As a kid it was *Gus*, the Disney movie about a field goal–kicking mule. I have used both *Brian's Song* and *Remember the Titans* in my classroom. Both are entertaining and enjoyable, with Billy Dee Williams, James Caan, and Denzel Washington stealing the show. As an educator there are so many themes to build upon—racism, friendship, team unity, adversity—the list goes on and on. Yet, I'm going with *Friday Night Lights*, the 2004 film based on the book by H.G. Bissinger. I love the book so much that I reread it every few years. And the truth be told, I loved the TV series more than the movie. In fact, I'm hopeful that another movie will be made with Kyle Chandler, Connie Britton, and company.

First Car: A 1981 Chevrolet Citation with the hatchback. I had that car my last two years of college until I bought my first new car in 1991.

Worst Summer Job: Feeding the phone book assembly line at R.R. Donnelly in Dwight, Illinois. I worked the overnight shift one summer. It really made me appreciate school and what I do now.

Favorite Subjects in School: History and English. This book is a tribute to my teachers.

Author Dan Verdun appears with his son Tommy (left) and Eastern linebacker Alex Helms (42) following the Panthers' Homecoming victory in 2013. Interestingly, Helms was a student in the author's language arts class when the player was in seventh grade. Yes, he grew over the years.